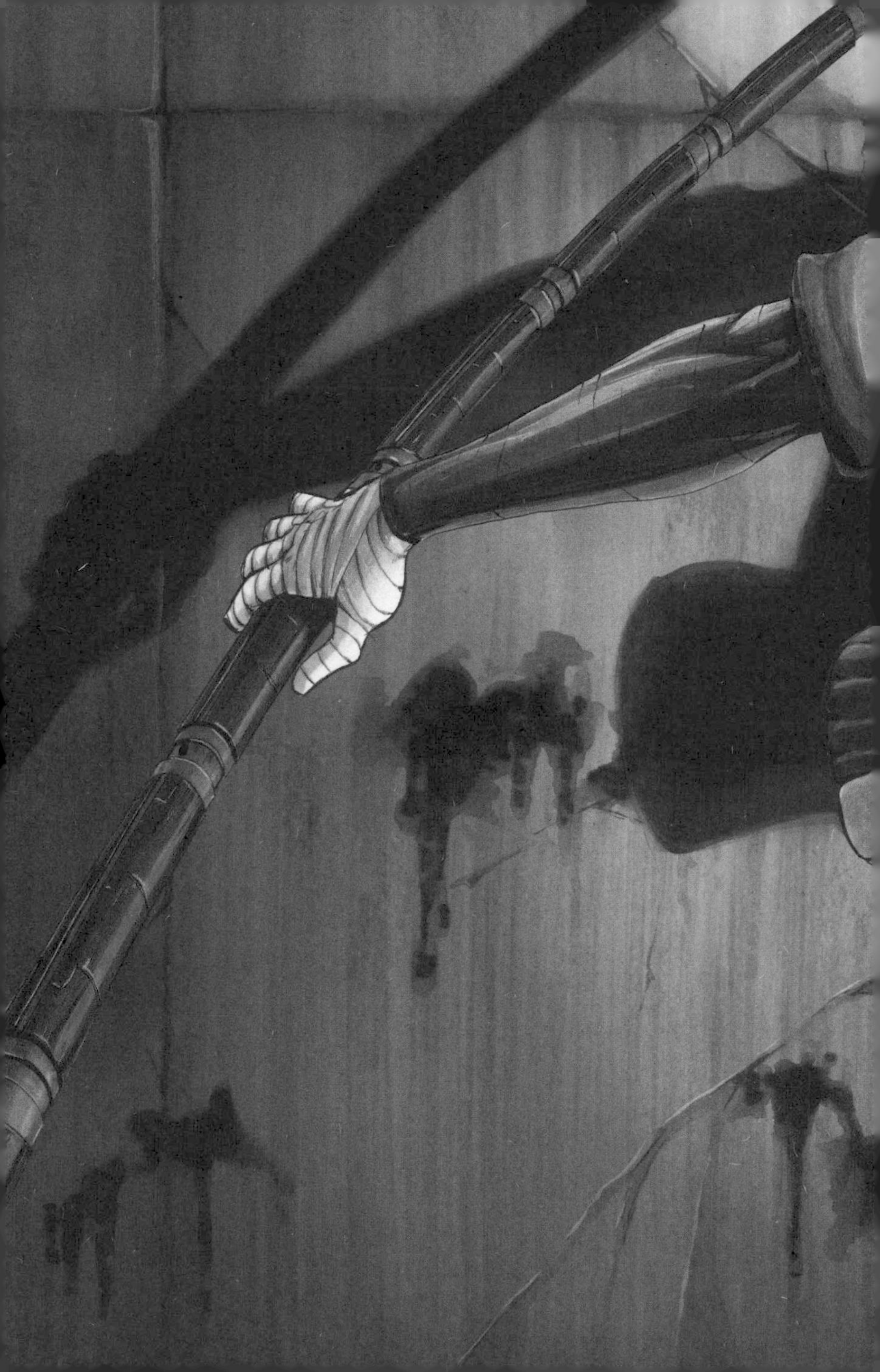

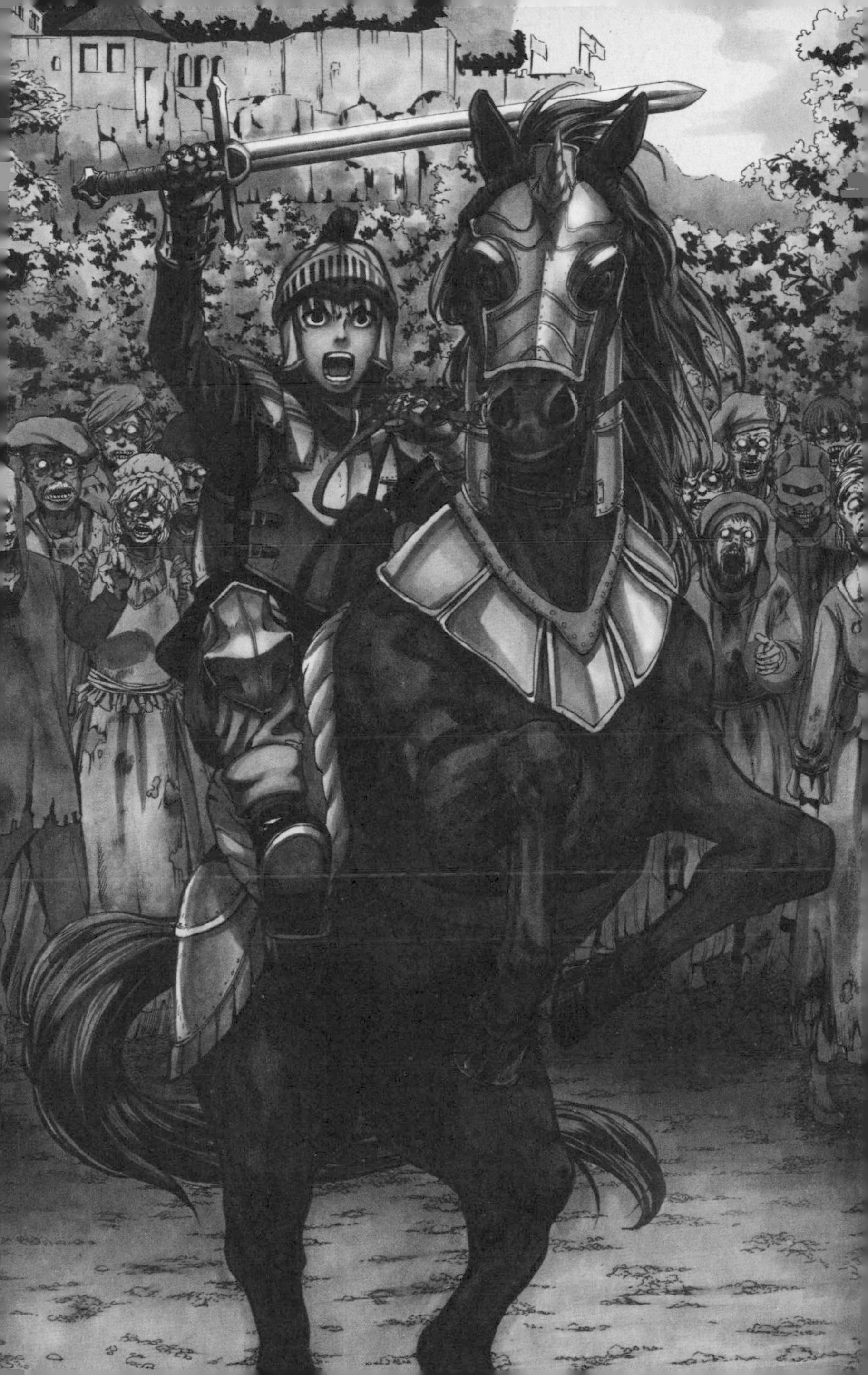

## Previously

Solothurn, Switzerland

Zombie fanatic Tim encounters the completely disfigured corpse of his neighbor. When he realizes the perpetrator is his own father, Alex, who has turned into one of the living dead after visiting the hospital, Tim's initial euphoria quickly fades. He then ties his father up and locks him in the basement, before joining forces with his best friend M-Kay to investigate the zombie infested hospital. There he discovers that his father apparently had an affair and he has a half-brother named Elian. Elian seems to have been born at the same time as the epidemic broke out in the hospital. But another has become aware of Elian's birth: Ritch, the mysterious savior from the viral YouTube videos who allegedly has to power to heal people and create miracles. Ritch kidnaps the newborn. Tim and M-Kay defend themselves against the undead and want to save Elian, but they are arrested by the military. However, Tim manages to escape and he returns home to warn his mother about his zombie father. But he is too late - his father has already killed his mother. Father and son fight against one another when suddenly Tim's dad shows a flash of human emotion and remembers Tim's name. At this very moment, Ritch's weapon pierces Alex's skull.

## Characters

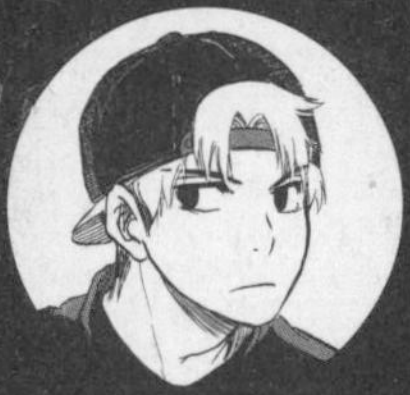

### Tim

The biggest zombie fan of all time, feels responsible for his half-brother Elian.

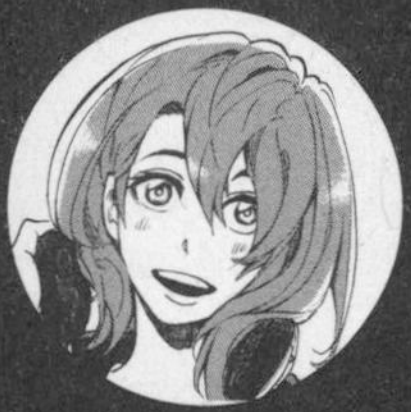

### M-Kay

Has been friends with tim since the 5th grade, grew up in an orphanage.

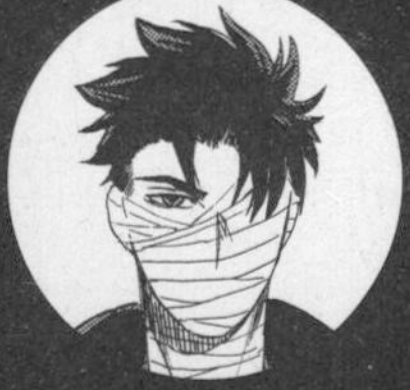

### Ritch

Praised as a "savior" by viewers on the internet, his true intentions are unknown.

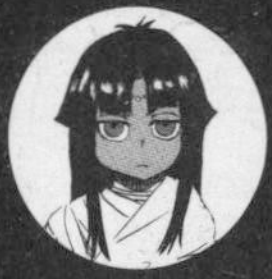

### Bêbe

Ritch's one-armed disciple.

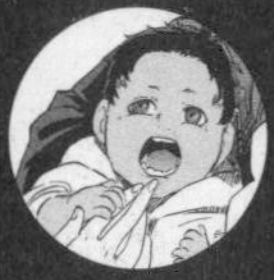

### Elian

Has red eyes and already has teeth.

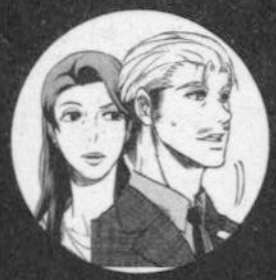

### Noémie And Alex

Tim's parents, deceased.

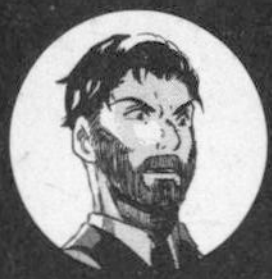

### Allen

Tim's Uncle, a Police Officer.

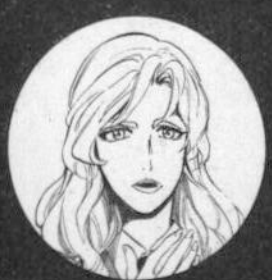

### Viktoria Forster

First lieutenant of the Swiss Army.

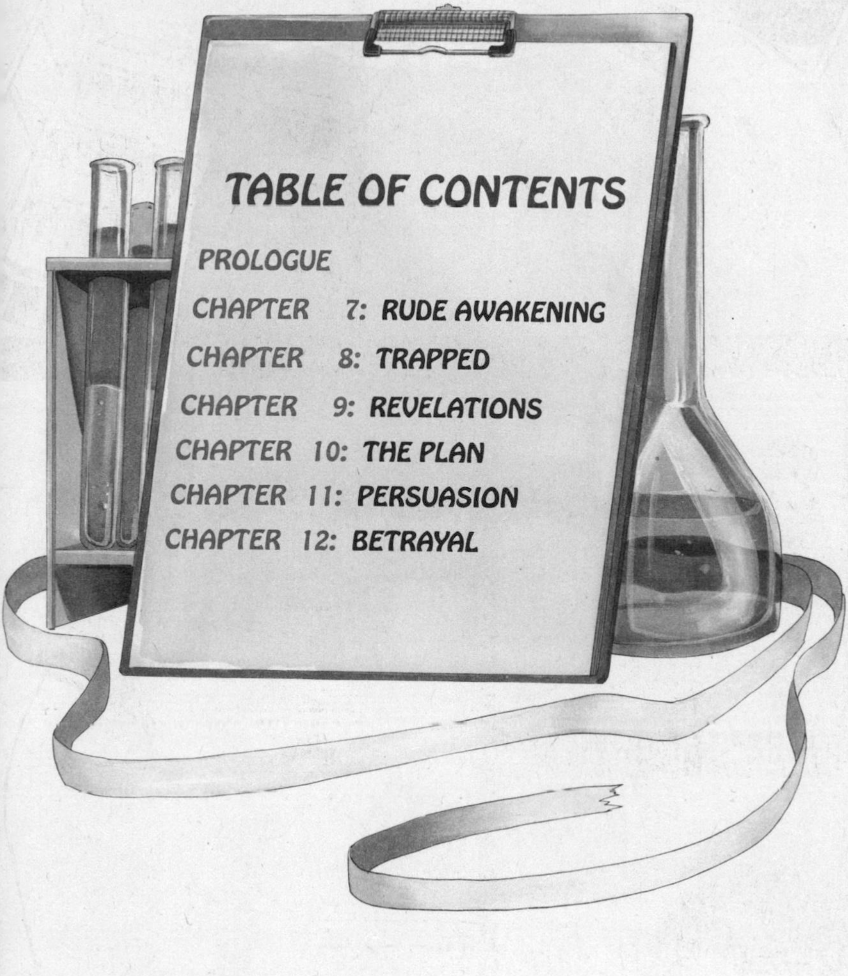
TABLE OF CONTENTS
PROLOGUE
CHAPTER 7: RUDE AWAKENING
CHAPTER 8: TRAPPED
CHAPTER 9: REVELATIONS
CHAPTER 10: THE PLAN
CHAPTER 11: PERSUASION
CHAPTER 12: BETRAYAL

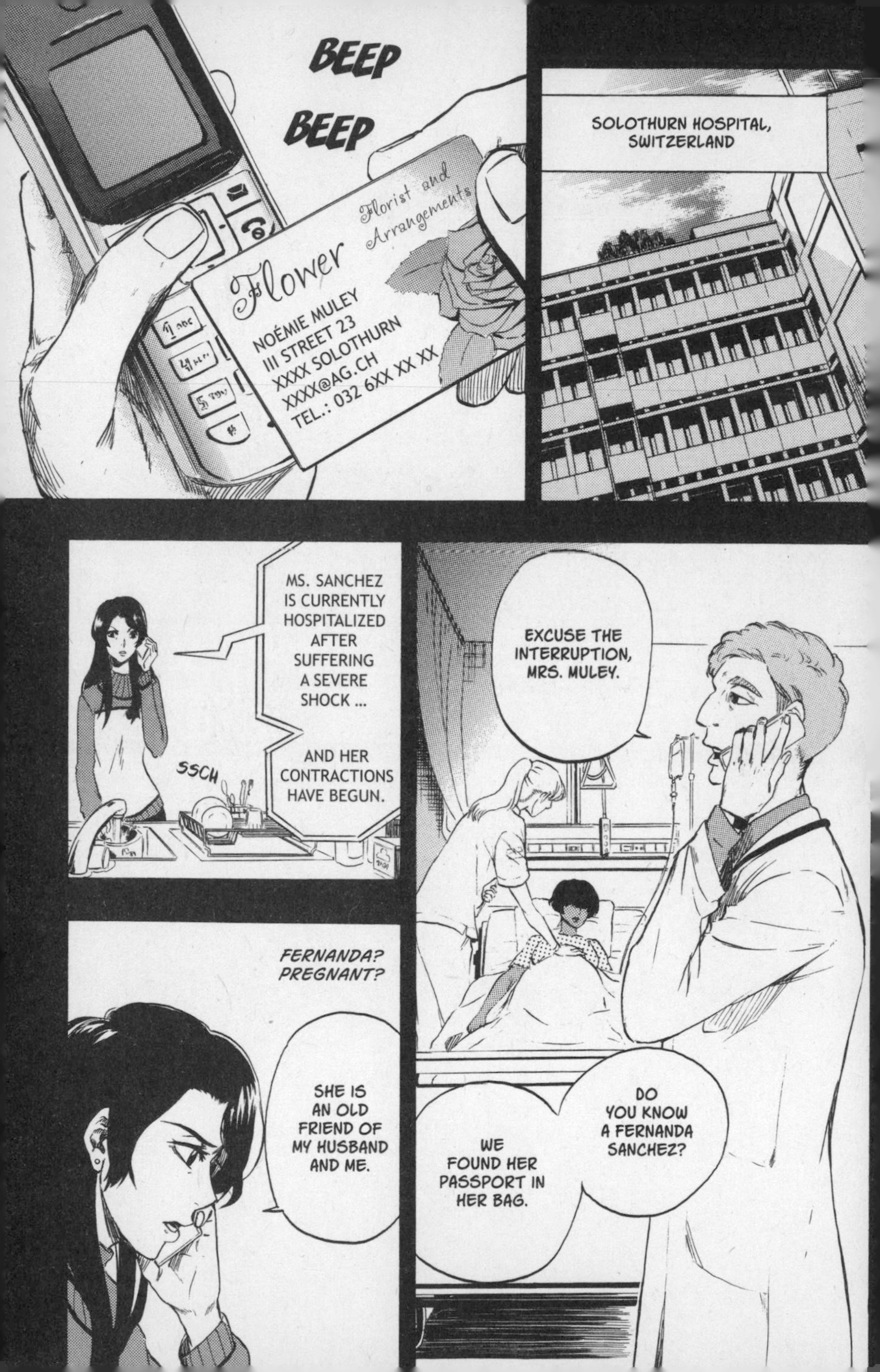
SOLOTHURN HOSPITAL, SWITZERLAND
BEEP
BEEP
Flower
Florist and Arrangements
NOÉMIE MULEY
III STREET 23
XXXX SOLOTHURN
XXXX@AG.CH
TEL.: 032 6XX XX XX
EXCUSE THE INTERRUPTION, MRS. MULEY.
DO YOU KNOW A FERNANDA SANCHEZ?
WE FOUND HER PASSPORT IN HER BAG.
MS. SANCHEZ IS CURRENTLY HOSPITALIZED AFTER SUFFERING A SEVERE SHOCK ...
AND HER CONTRACTIONS HAVE BEGUN.
SSCH
FERNANDA? PREGNANT?
SHE IS AN OLD FRIEND OF MY HUSBAND AND ME.

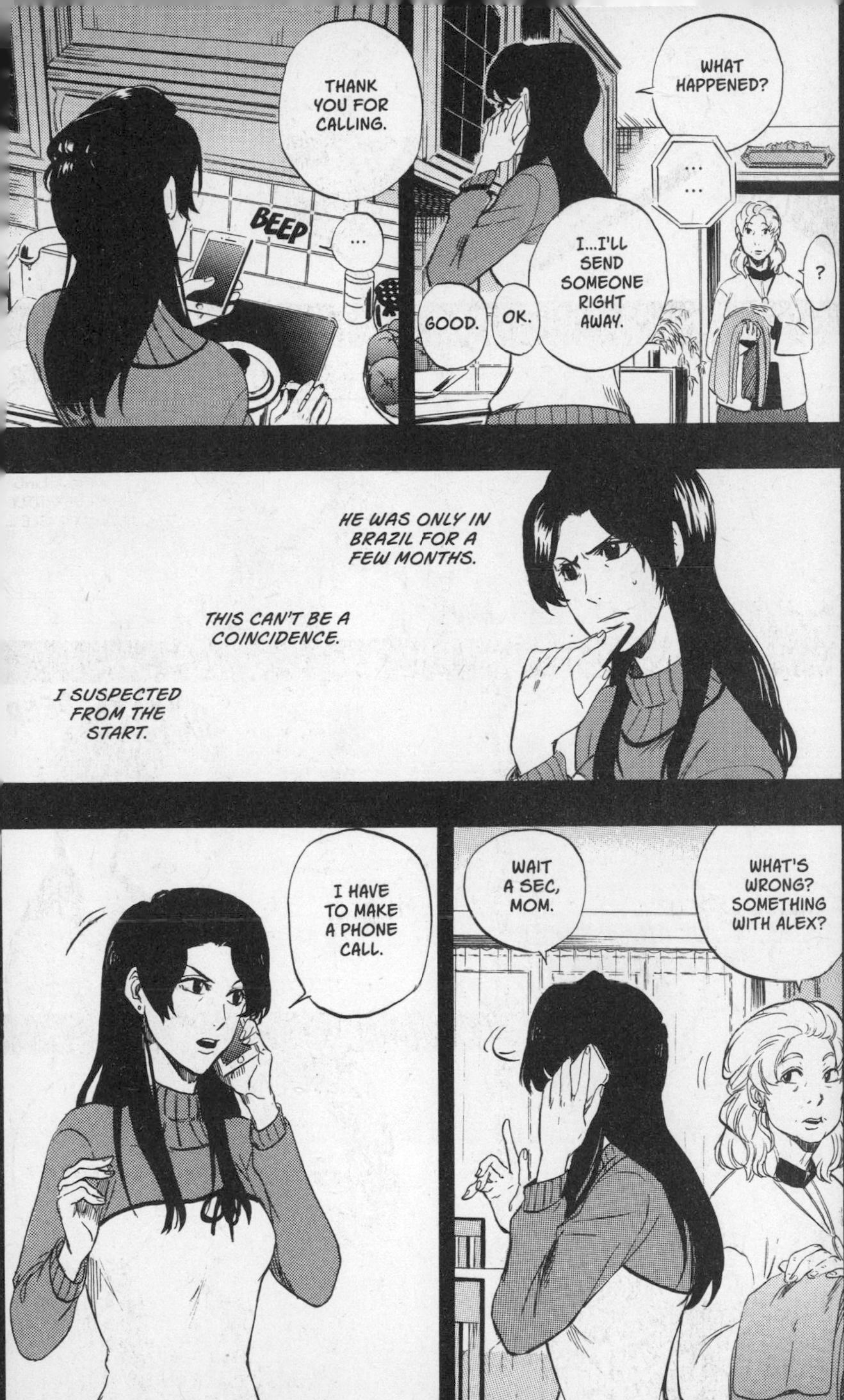
WHAT HAPPENED?
... ...
?
I...I'LL SEND SOMEONE RIGHT AWAY.
OK.
GOOD.
THANK YOU FOR CALLING.
BEEP
...
HE WAS ONLY IN BRAZIL FOR A FEW MONTHS.
THIS CAN'T BE A COINCIDENCE.
I SUSPECTED FROM THE START.
WHAT'S WRONG? SOMETHING WITH ALEX?
WAIT A SEC, MOM.
I HAVE TO MAKE A PHONE CALL.

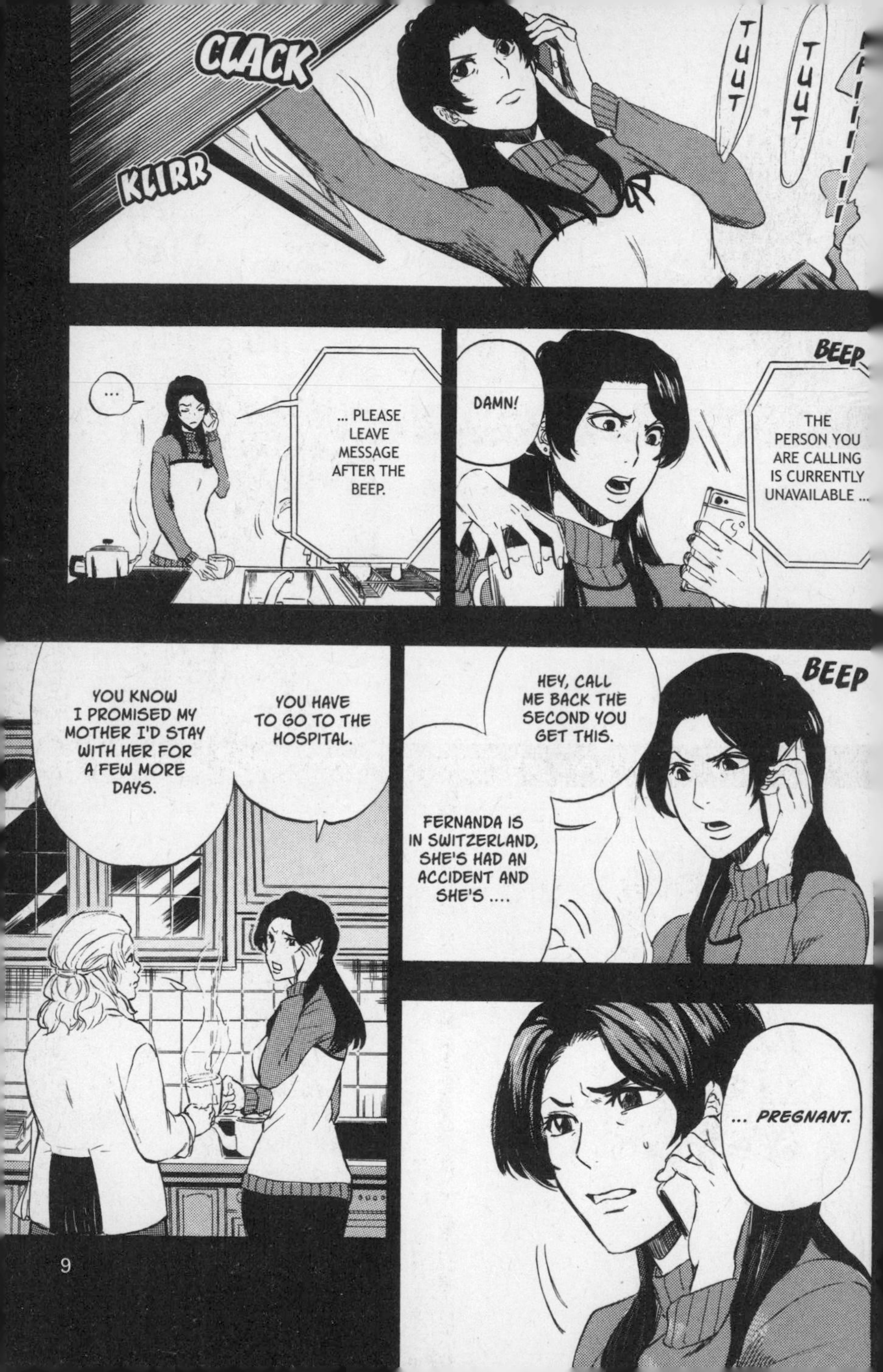
TUUT
TUUT
CLACK
KLIRR
BEEP
THE PERSON YOU ARE CALLING IS CURRENTLY UNAVAILABLE ...
DAMN!
... PLEASE LEAVE MESSAGE AFTER THE BEEP.
...
BEEP
HEY, CALL ME BACK THE SECOND YOU GET THIS.
FERNANDA IS IN SWITZERLAND, SHE'S HAD AN ACCIDENT AND SHE'S ....
... PREGNANT.
YOU HAVE TO GO TO THE HOSPITAL.
YOU KNOW I PROMISED MY MOTHER I'D STAY WITH HER FOR A FEW MORE DAYS.

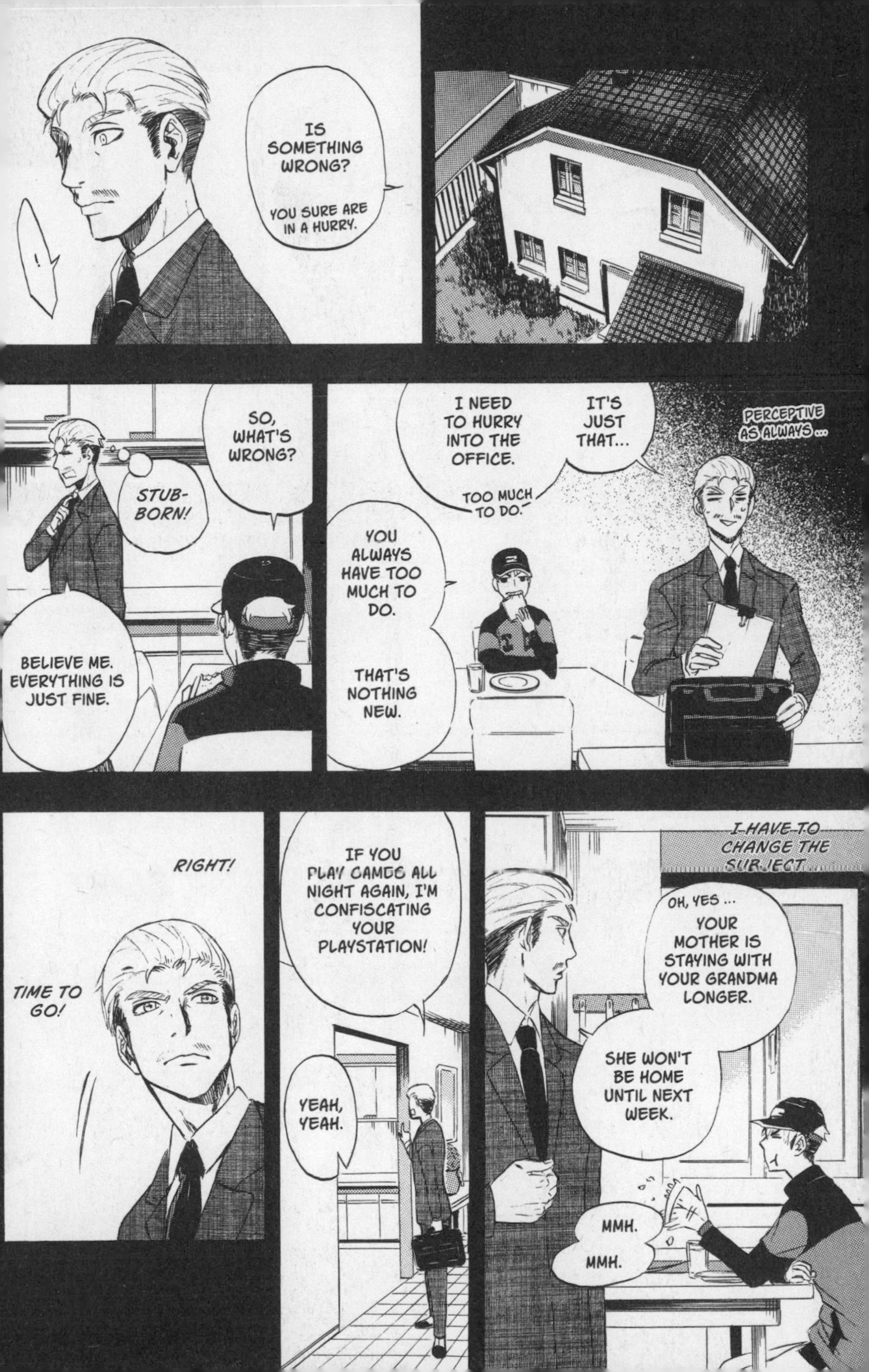
IS SOMETHING WRONG?
YOU SURE ARE IN A HURRY.
!
IT'S JUST THAT...
I NEED TO HURRY INTO THE OFFICE.
TOO MUCH TO DO.
PERCEPTIVE AS ALWAYS...
YOU ALWAYS HAVE TOO MUCH TO DO.
THAT'S NOTHING NEW.
SO, WHAT'S WRONG?
STUB-BORN!
BELIEVE ME. EVERYTHING IS JUST FINE.
I HAVE TO CHANGE THE SUBJECT...
OH, YES ... YOUR MOTHER IS STAYING WITH YOUR GRANDMA LONGER.
SHE WON'T BE HOME UNTIL NEXT WEEK.
MMH.
MMH.
IF YOU PLAY GAMES ALL NIGHT AGAIN, I'M CONFISCATING YOUR PLAYSTATION!
YEAH, YEAH.
RIGHT!
TIME TO GO!

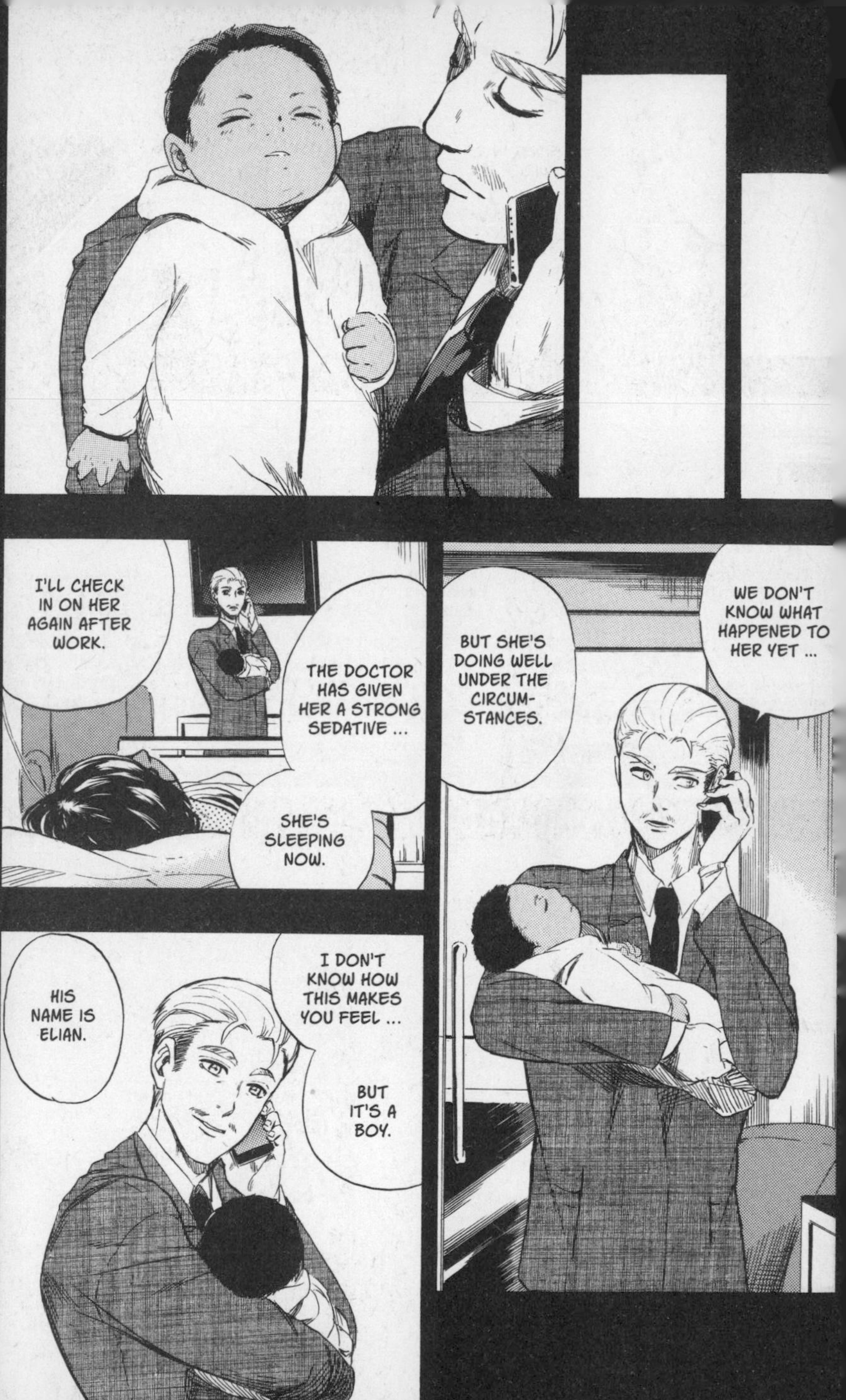
WE DON'T KNOW WHAT HAPPENED TO HER YET ...
BUT SHE'S DOING WELL UNDER THE CIRCUM-STANCES.
THE DOCTOR HAS GIVEN HER A STRONG SEDATIVE ...
SHE'S SLEEPING NOW.
I'LL CHECK IN ON HER AGAIN AFTER WORK.
I DON'T KNOW HOW THIS MAKES YOU FEEL ...
BUT IT'S A BOY.
HIS NAME IS ELIAN.

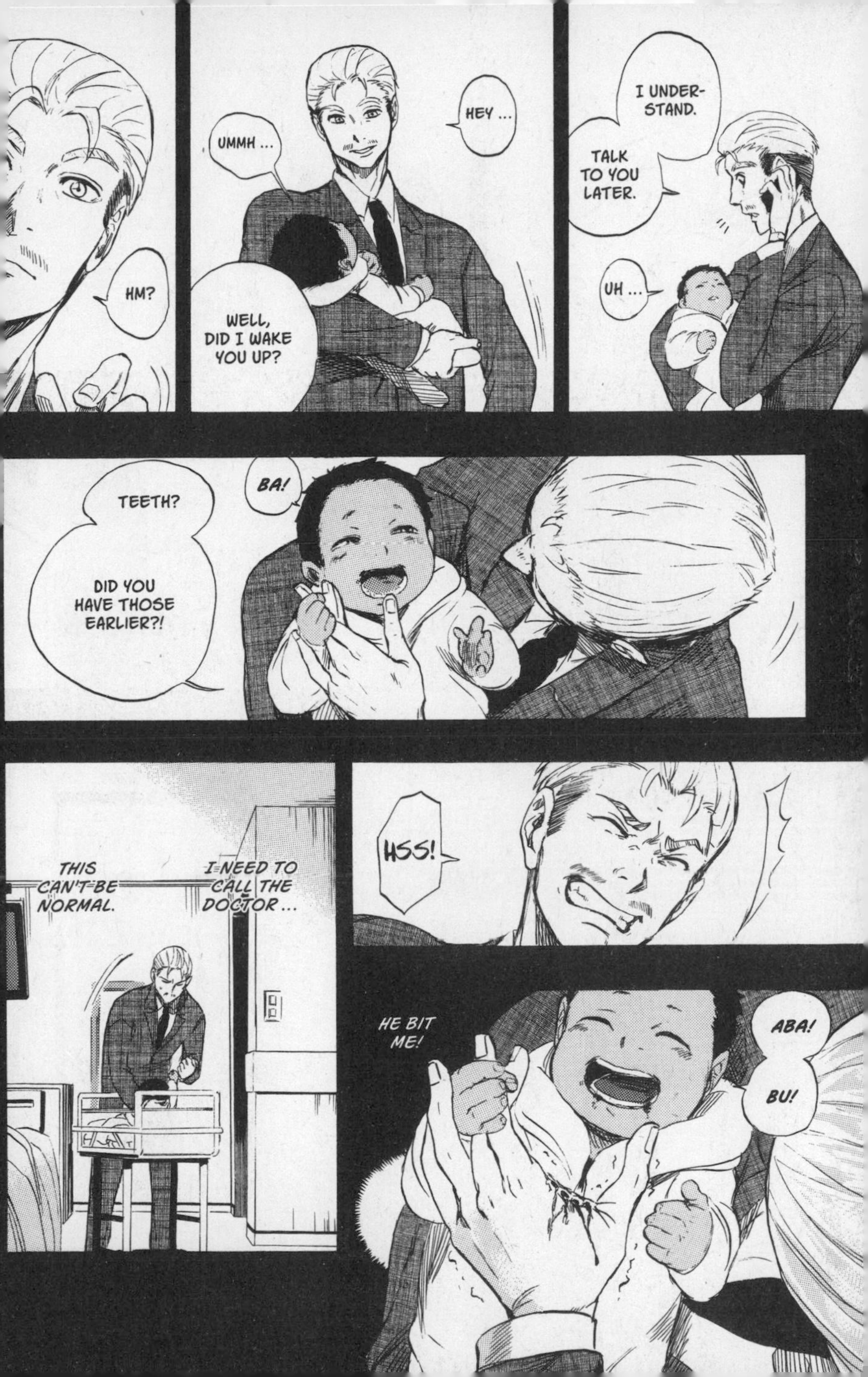
I UNDER-STAND.
TALK TO YOU LATER.
UH ...
HEY ...
UMMH ...
WELL, DID I WAKE YOU UP?
HM?
BA!
TEETH?
DID YOU HAVE THOSE EARLIER?!
HSS!
ABA!
BU!
HE BIT ME!
I NEED TO CALL THE DOCTOR ...
THIS CAN'T BE NORMAL.

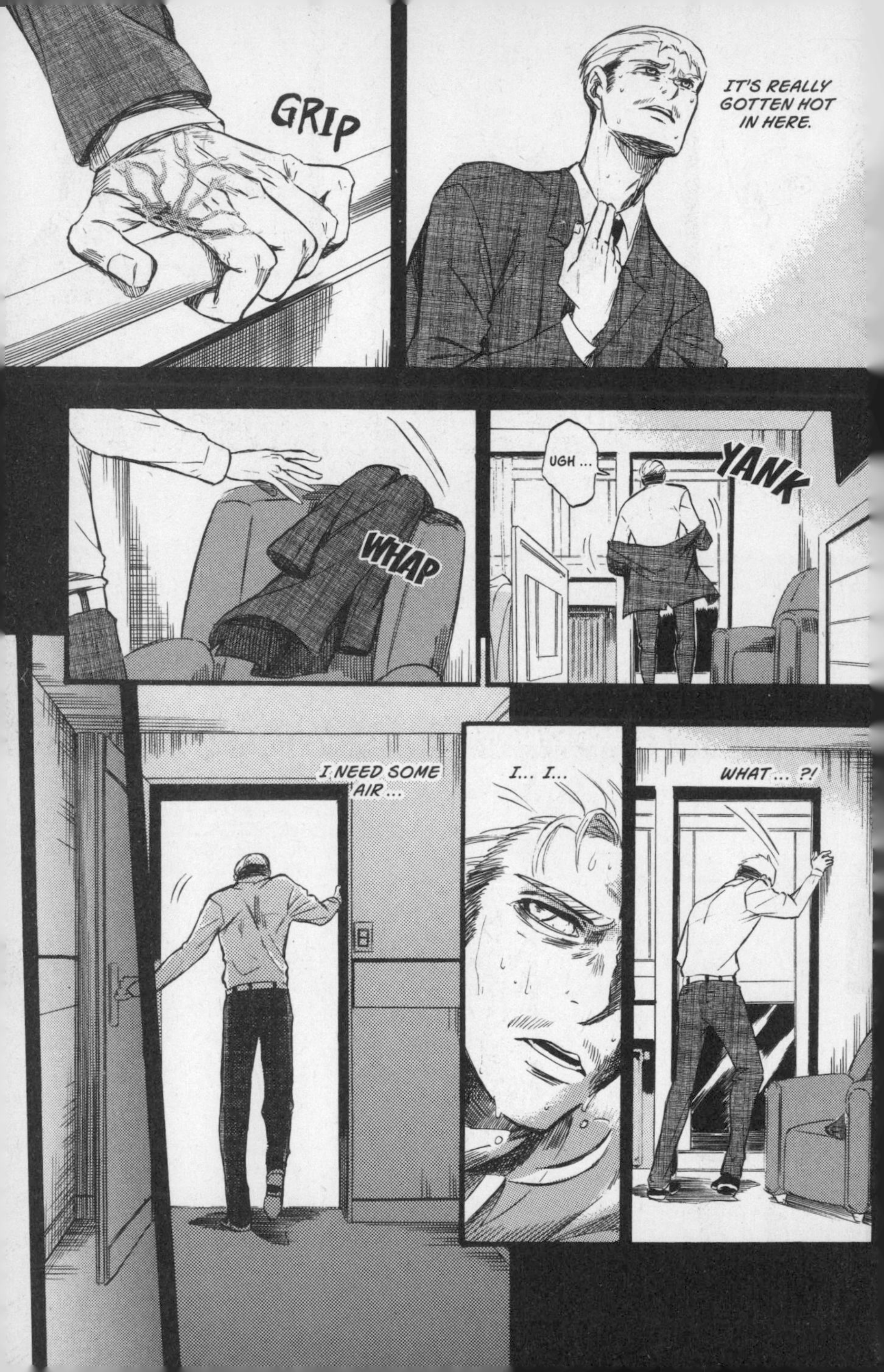
IT'S REALLY GOTTEN HOT IN HERE.
GRIP
UGH ...
YANK
WHAP
WHAT ... ?!
I... I...
I NEED SOME AIR ...

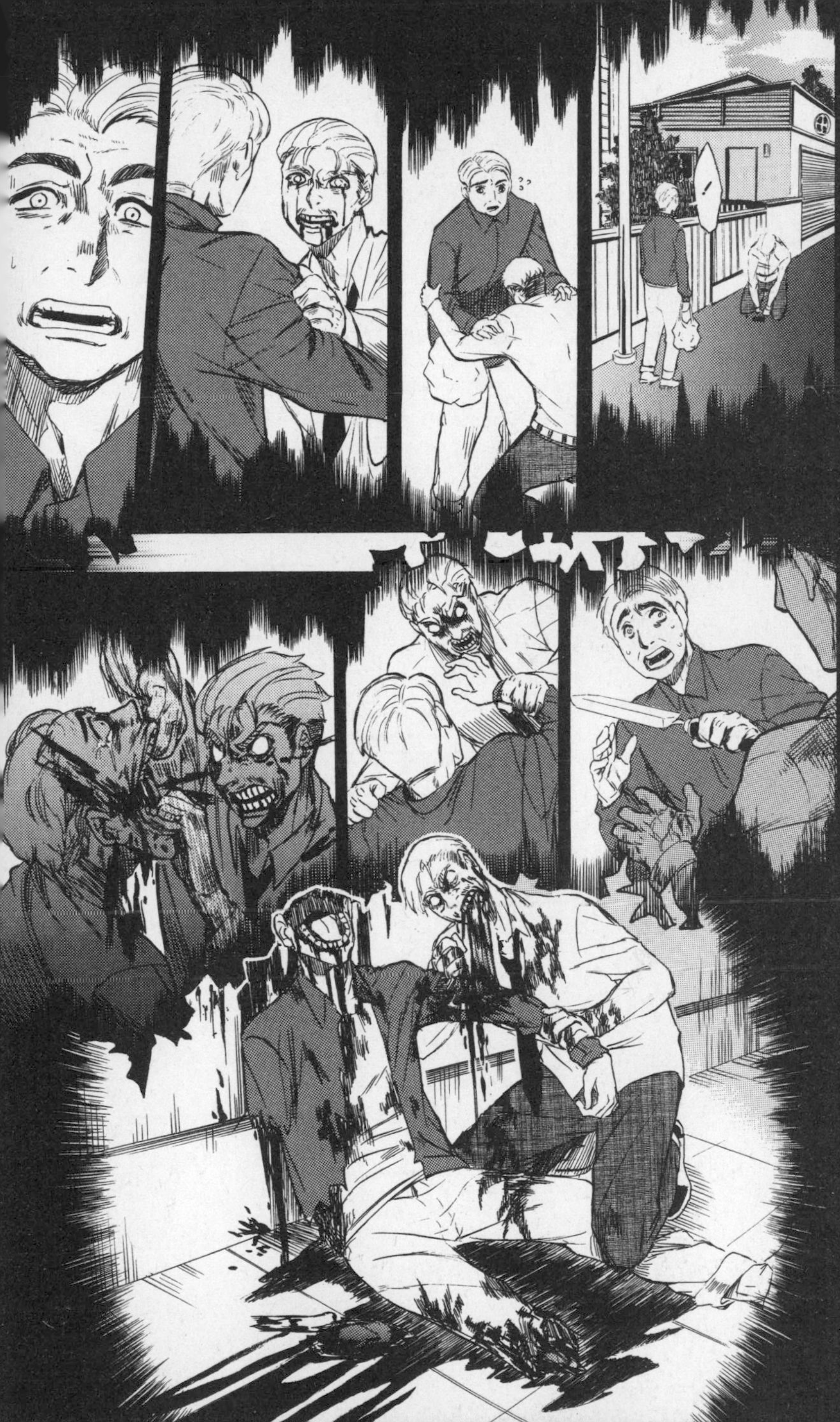

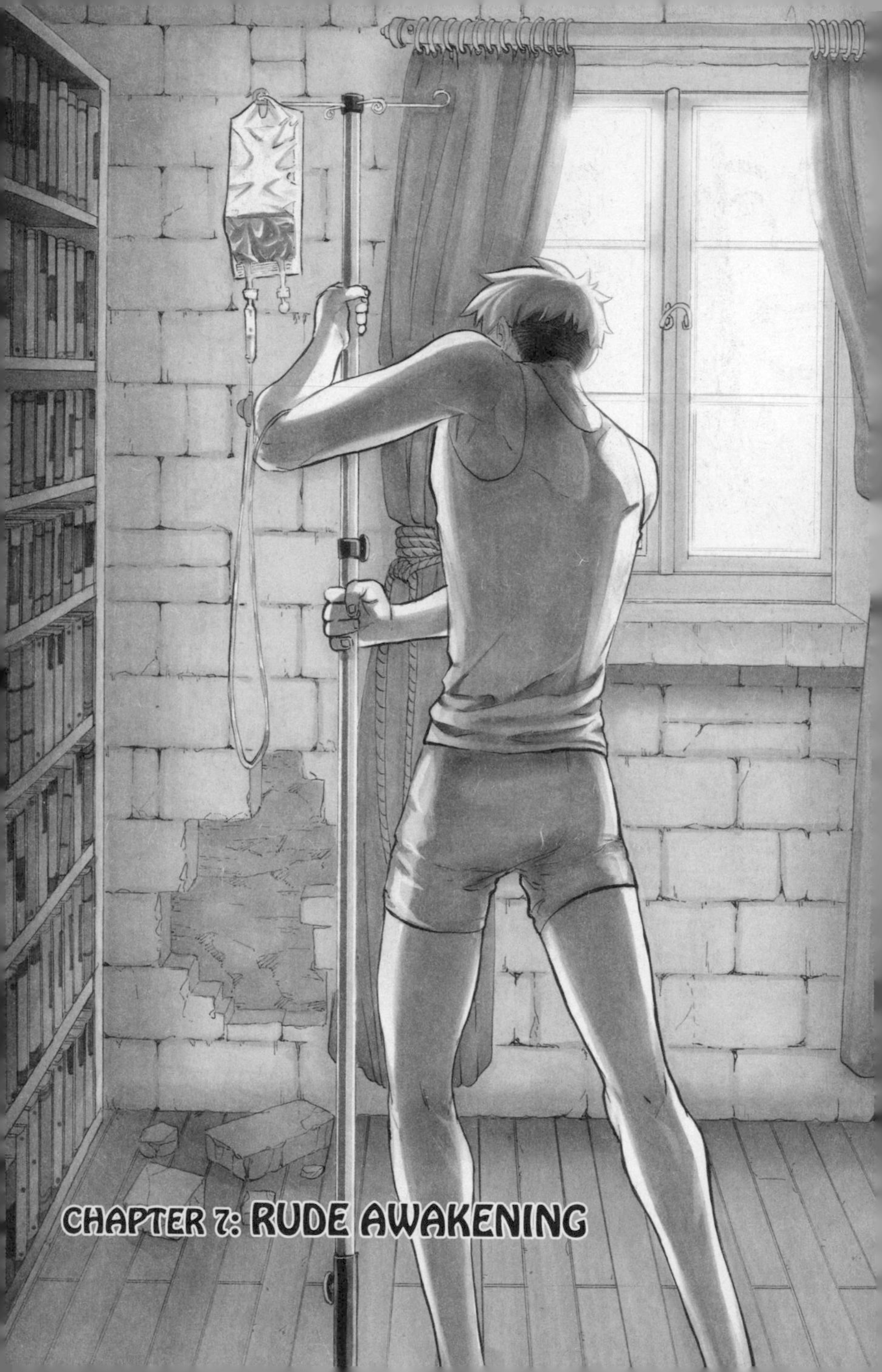
CHAPTER 7: RUDE AWAKENING

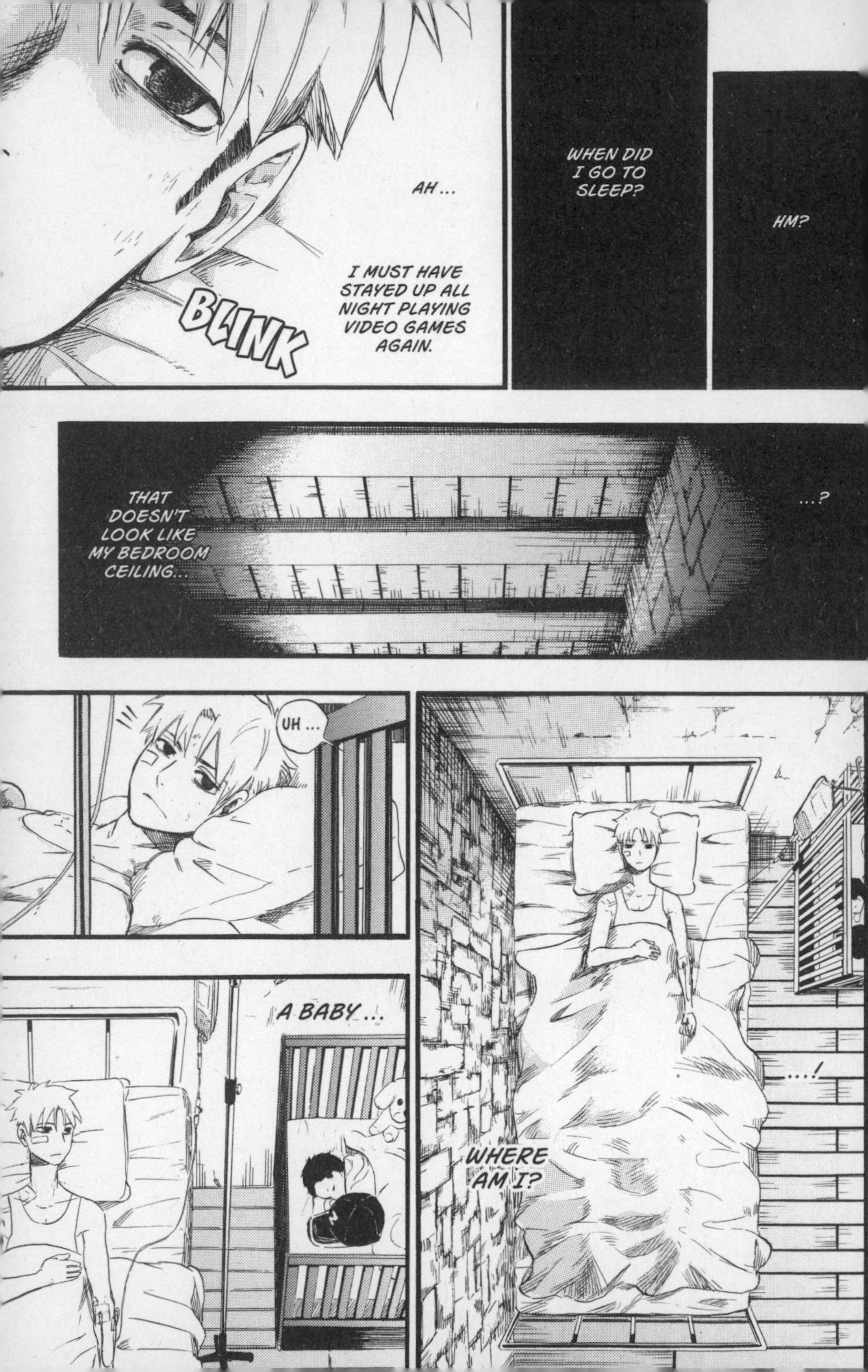
HM?
WHEN DID I GO TO SLEEP?
AH ...
I MUST HAVE STAYED UP ALL NIGHT PLAYING VIDEO GAMES AGAIN.
BLINK
...?
THAT DOESN'T LOOK LIKE MY BEDROOM CEILING...
...!
WHERE AM I?
UH ...
A BABY ...

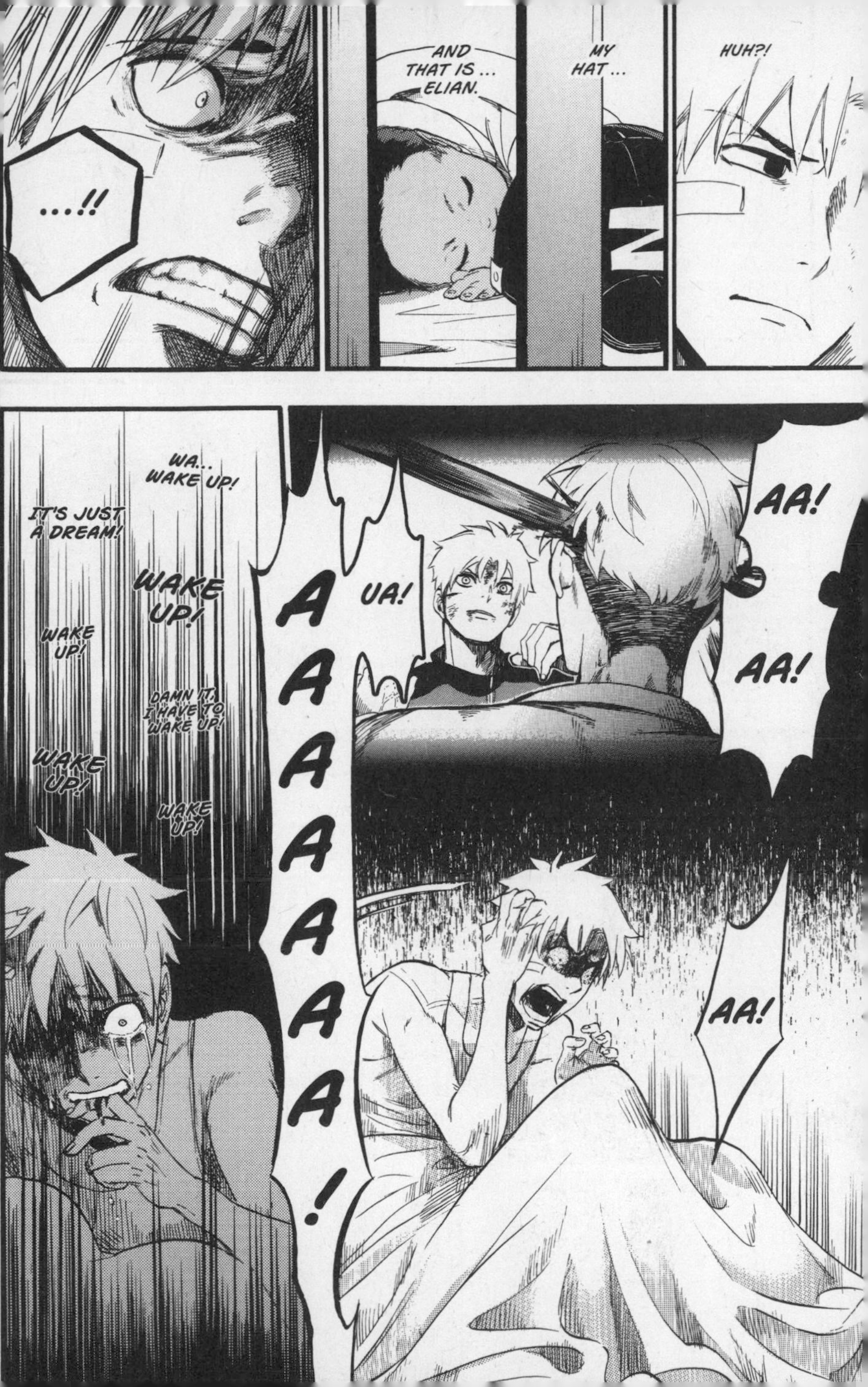

HUH?!
MY HAT ...
AND THAT IS ... ELIAN.
...!!
AA!
AA!
AA!
UA!
AAAAAAAA!
WA... WAKE UP!
IT'S JUST A DREAM!
WAKE UP!
WAKE UP!
DAMN IT, I HAVE TO WAKE UP!
WAKE UP!
WAKE UP!

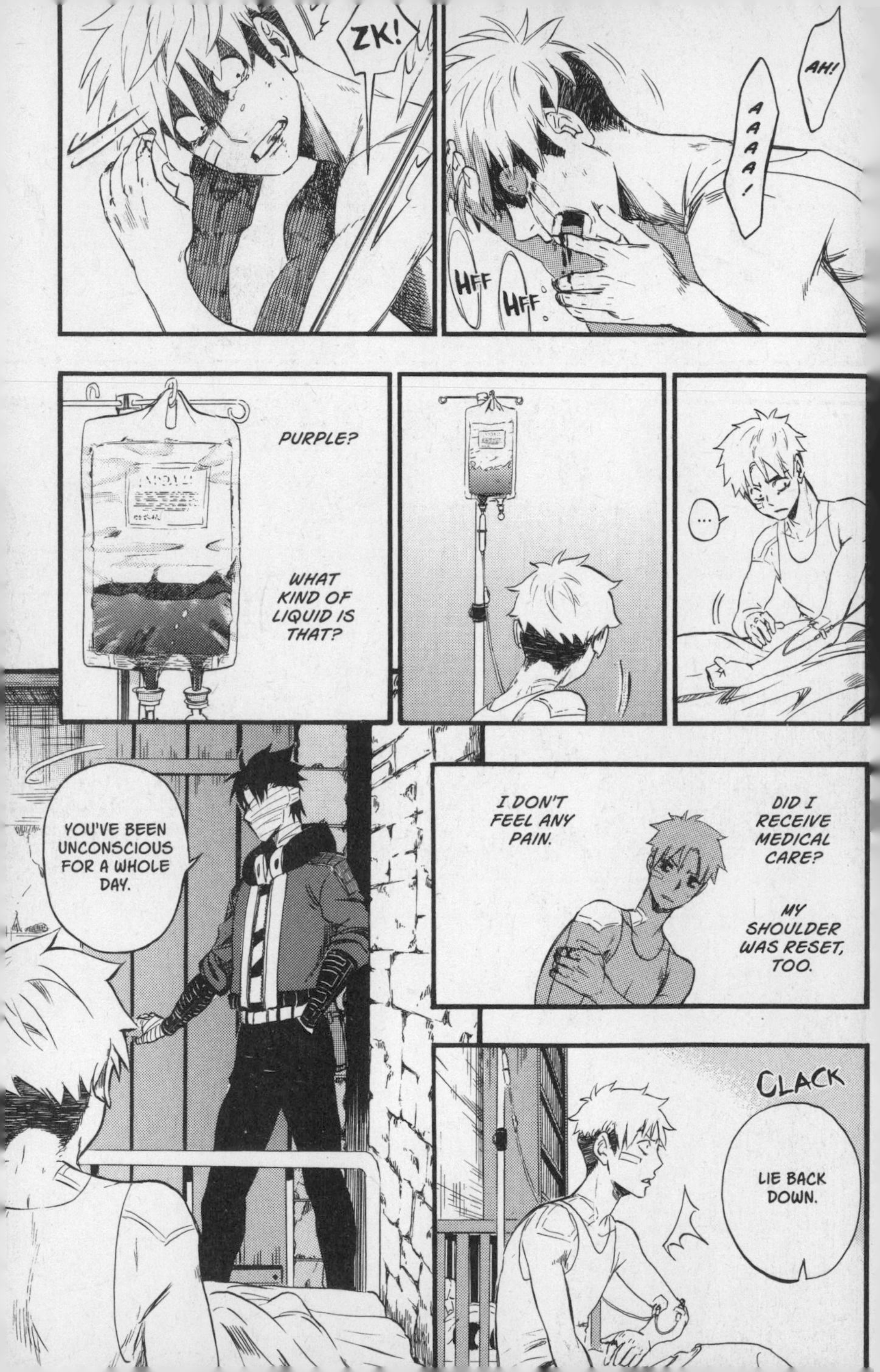
AH!
AAAA!
HFF
HFF
ZK!
...
PURPLE?
WHAT KIND OF LIQUID IS THAT?
DID I RECEIVE MEDICAL CARE?
MY SHOULDER WAS RESET, TOO.
I DON'T FEEL ANY PAIN.
CLACK
LIE BACK DOWN.
YOU'VE BEEN UNCONSCIOUS FOR A WHOLE DAY.

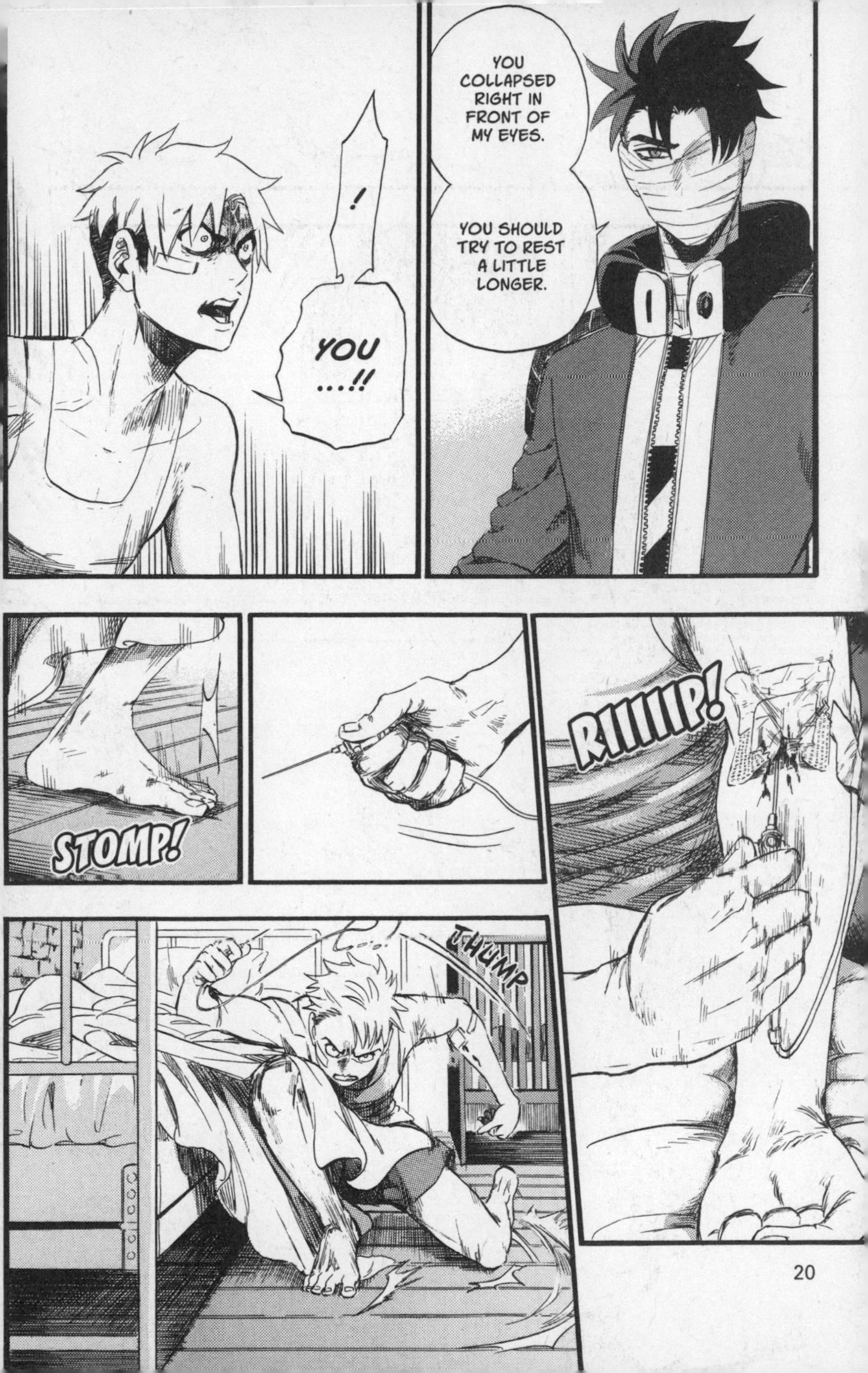
YOU COLLAPSED RIGHT IN FRONT OF MY EYES.
YOU SHOULD TRY TO REST A LITTLE LONGER.
!
YOU ...!!
RIIIIP!
STOMP!
THUMP

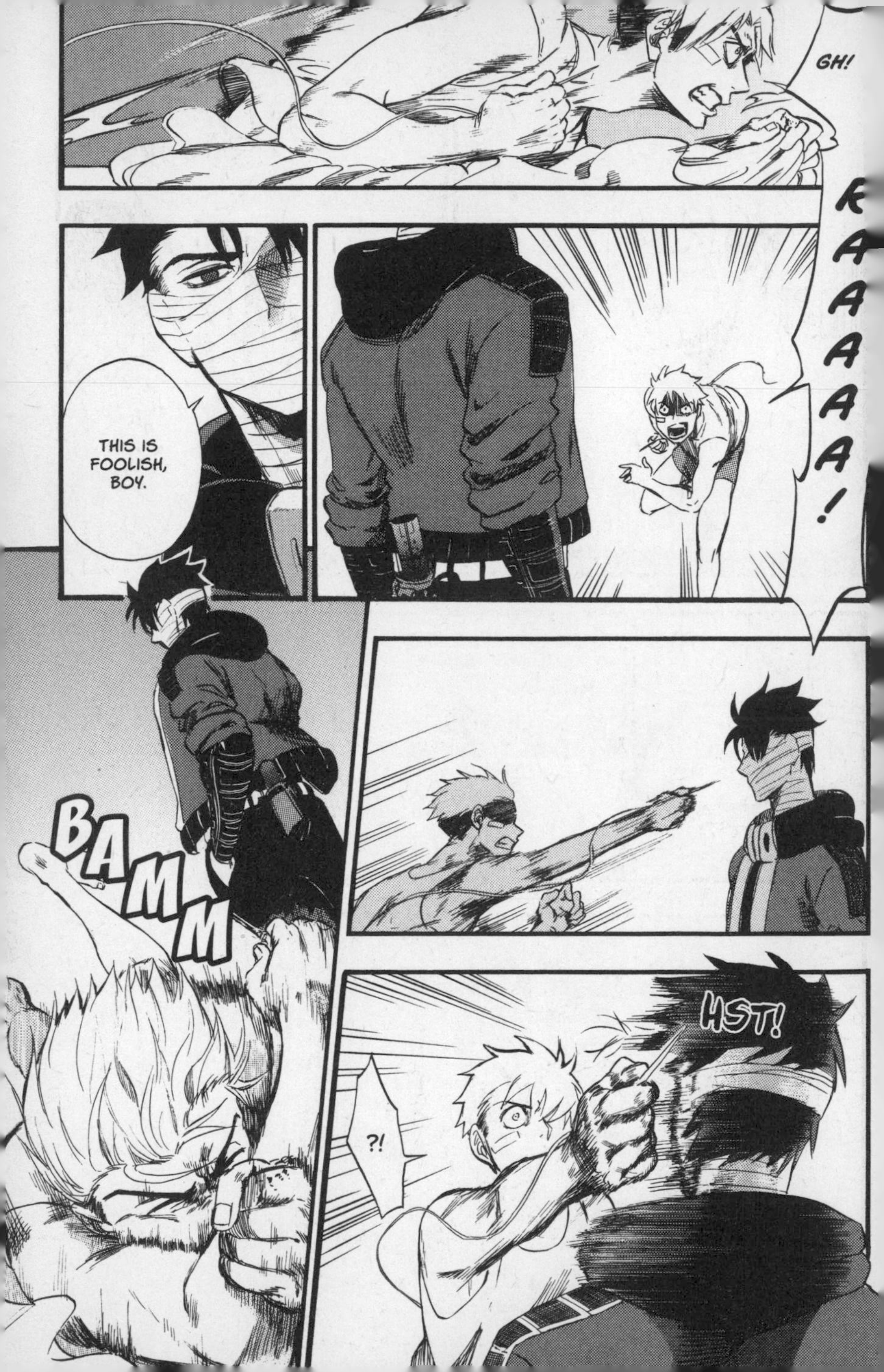
GH!
RAAAAAA!
THIS IS FOOLISH, BOY.
HST!
?!
BAMM

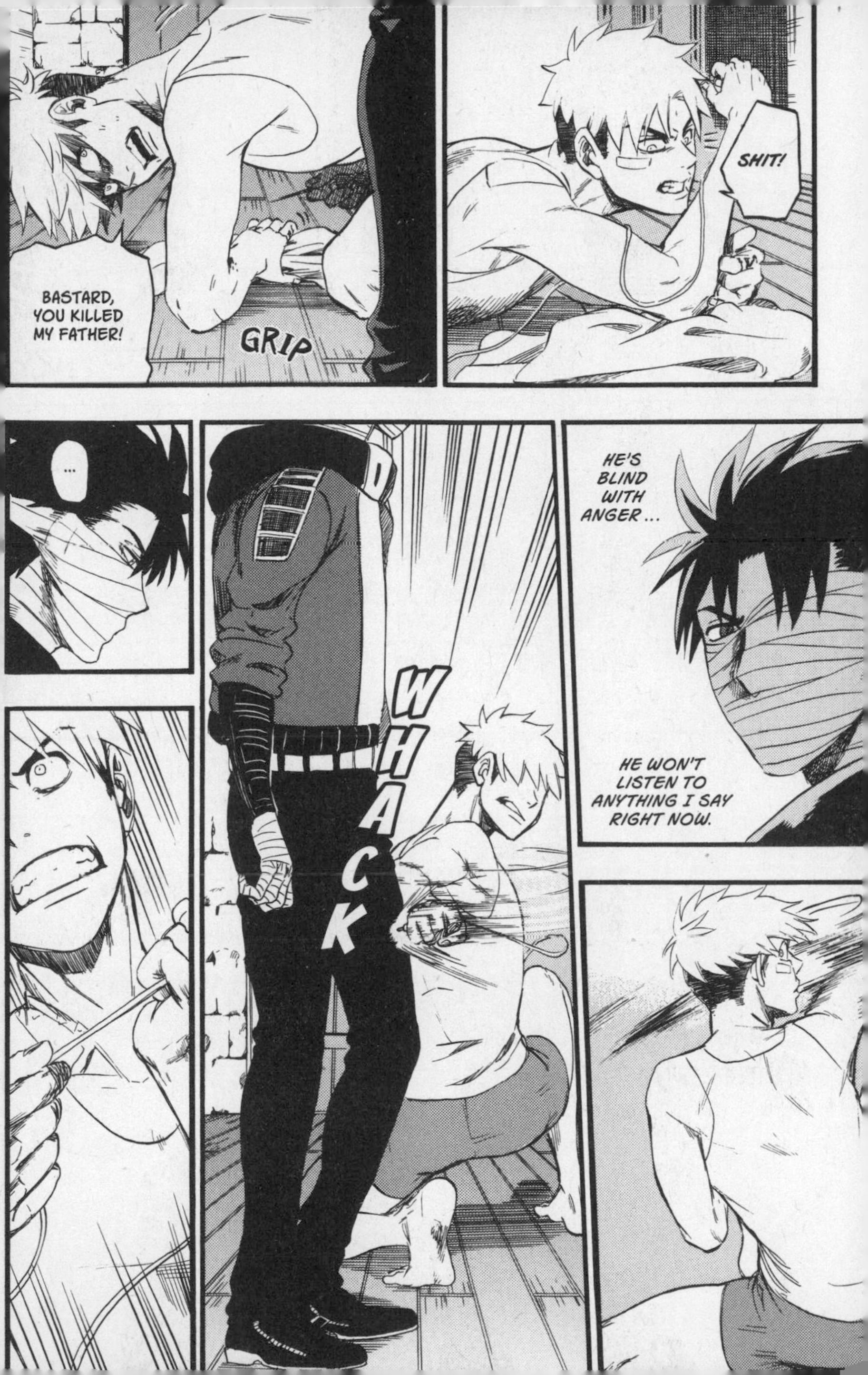
SHIT!
BASTARD, YOU KILLED MY FATHER!
GRIP
HE'S BLIND WITH ANGER...
HE WON'T LISTEN TO ANYTHING I SAY RIGHT NOW.
WHACK
...

HOW MANY TIMES DO I HAVE TO TELL YOU?

....!

SSR

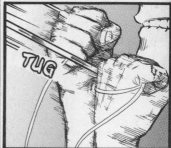

TUG

ZIP

HUH?

TRIP

YOU CANNOT KILL ME.

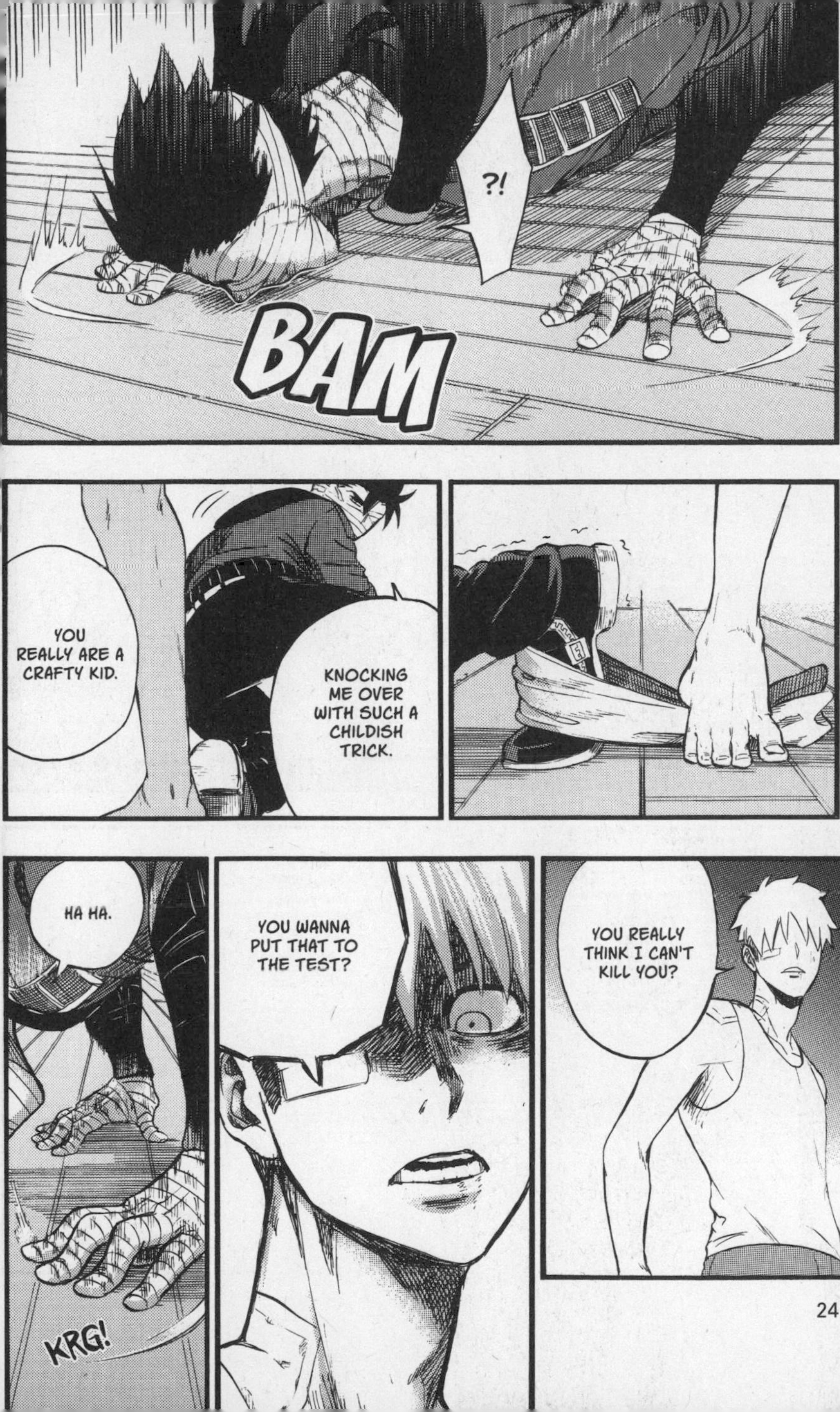
?!
BAM
KNOCKING ME OVER WITH SUCH A CHILDISH TRICK.
YOU REALLY ARE A CRAFTY KID.
YOU REALLY THINK I CAN'T KILL YOU?
YOU WANNA PUT THAT TO THE TEST?
HA HA.
KRG!

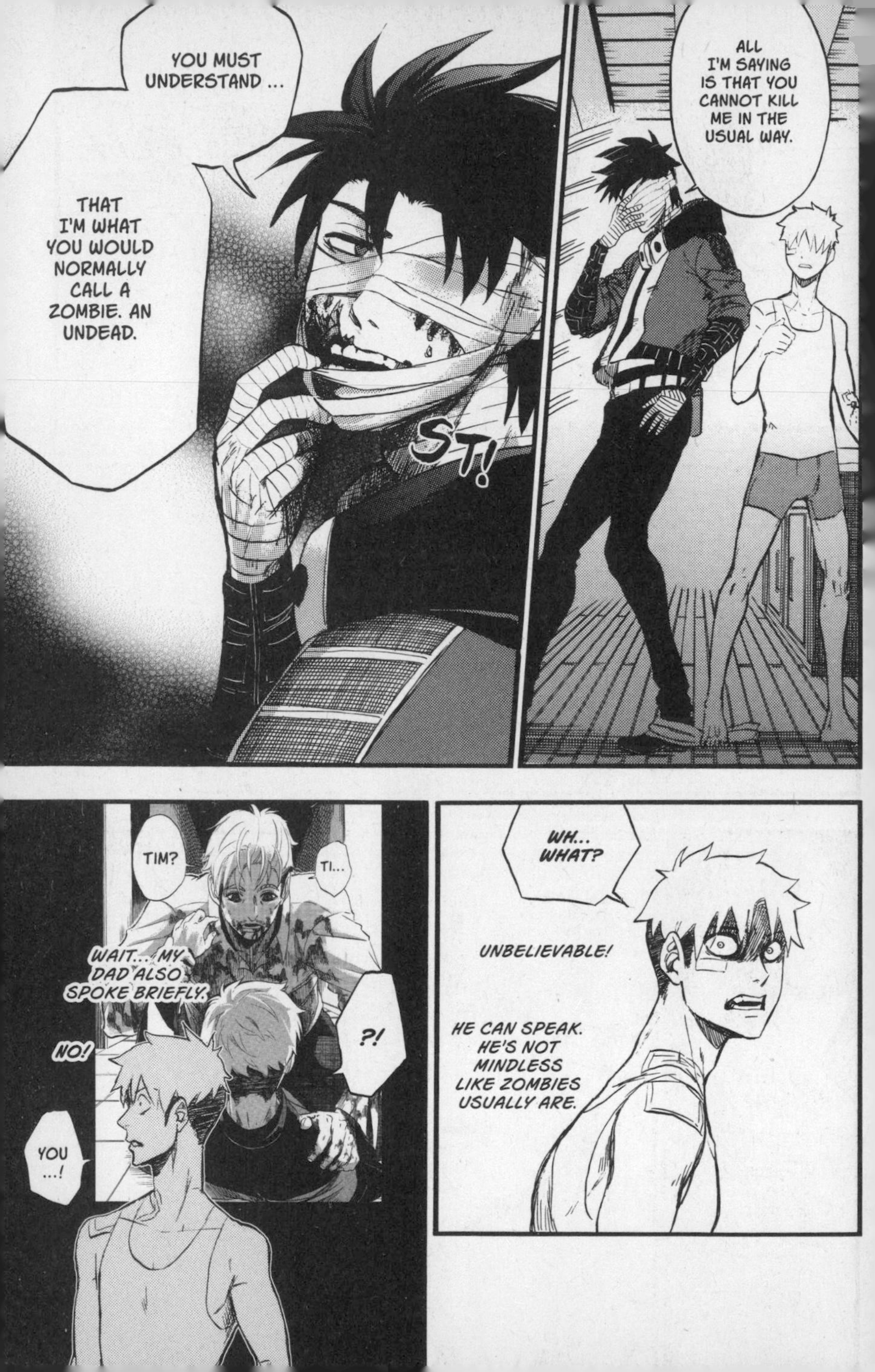
ALL I'M SAYING IS THAT YOU CANNOT KILL ME IN THE USUAL WAY.
YOU MUST UNDERSTAND ...
THAT I'M WHAT YOU WOULD NORMALLY CALL A ZOMBIE. AN UNDEAD.
ST!
WH... WHAT?
UNBELIEVABLE!
HE CAN SPEAK. HE'S NOT MINDLESS LIKE ZOMBIES USUALLY ARE.
TI...
TIM?
WAIT... MY DAD ALSO SPOKE BRIEFLY.
?!
NO!
YOU ...!

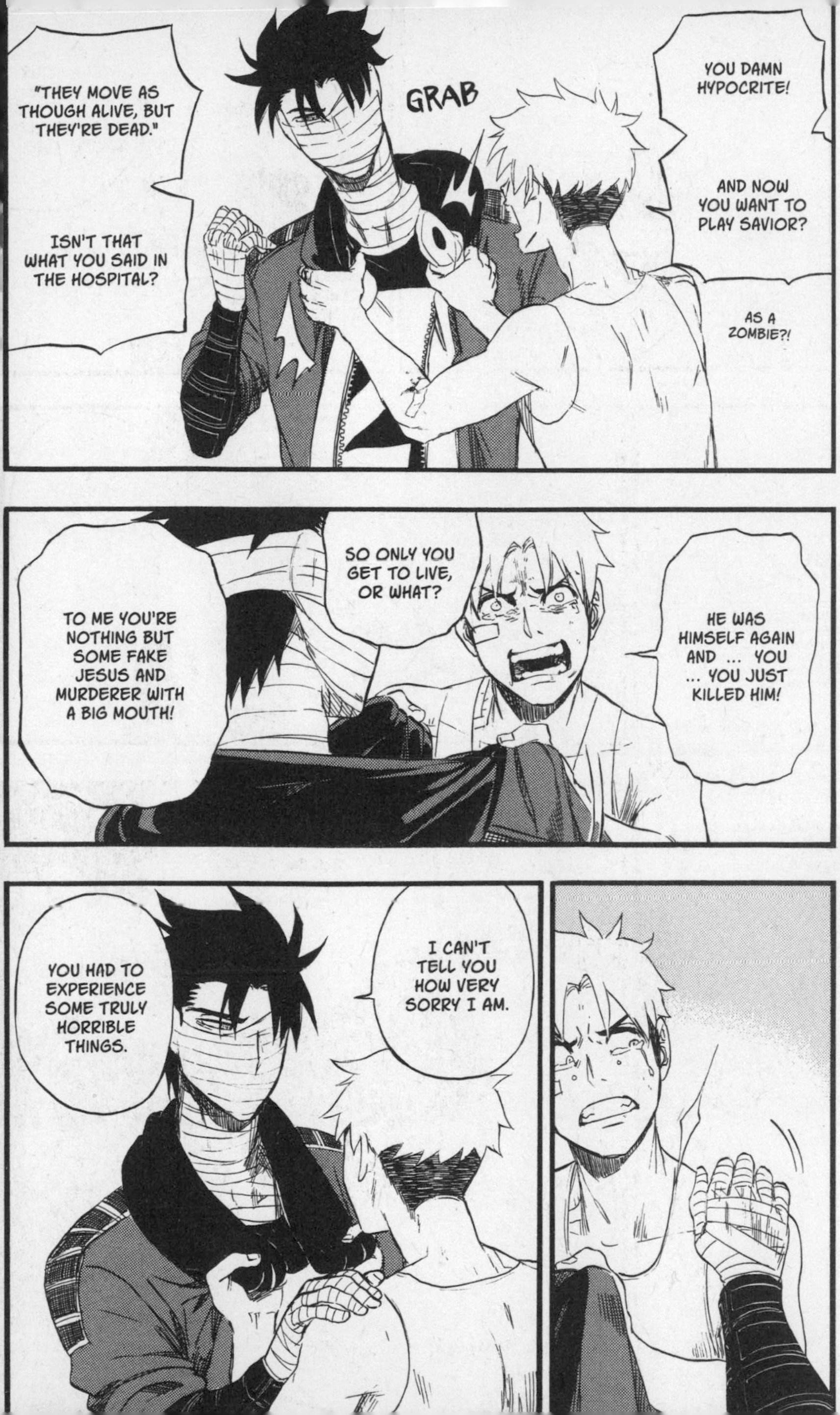
YOU DAMN HYPOCRITE!
AND NOW YOU WANT TO PLAY SAVIOR?
AS A ZOMBIE?!
GRAB
"THEY MOVE AS THOUGH ALIVE, BUT THEY'RE DEAD."
ISN'T THAT WHAT YOU SAID IN THE HOSPITAL?
HE WAS HIMSELF AGAIN AND ... YOU ... YOU JUST KILLED HIM!
SO ONLY YOU GET TO LIVE, OR WHAT?
TO ME YOU'RE NOTHING BUT SOME FAKE JESUS AND MURDERER WITH A BIG MOUTH!
I CAN'T TELL YOU HOW VERY SORRY I AM.
YOU HAD TO EXPERIENCE SOME TRULY HORRIBLE THINGS.

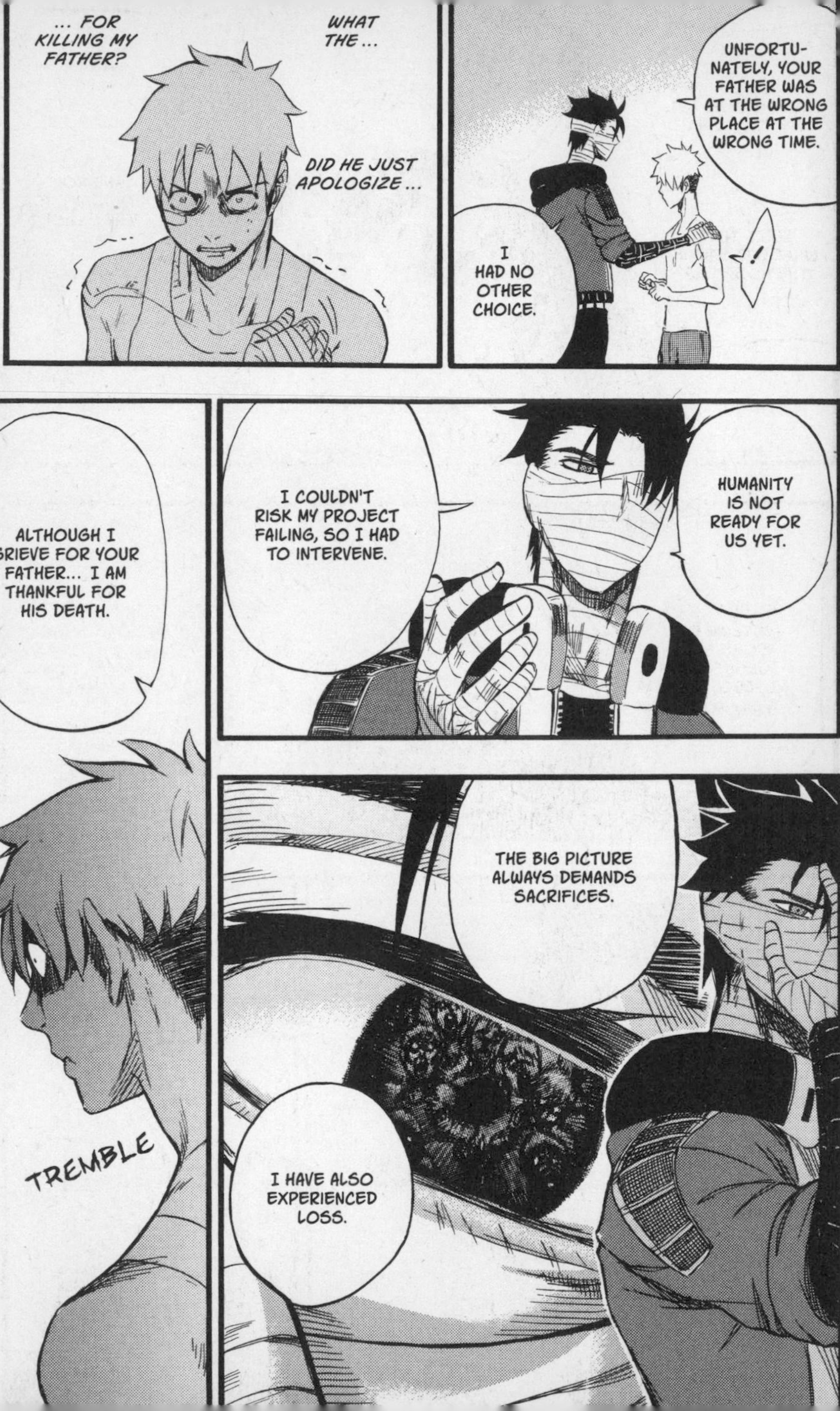
UNFORTUNATELY, YOUR FATHER WAS AT THE WRONG PLACE AT THE WRONG TIME.
!
I HAD NO OTHER CHOICE.
WHAT THE ...
... FOR KILLING MY FATHER?
DID HE JUST APOLOGIZE ...
HUMANITY IS NOT READY FOR US YET.
I COULDN'T RISK MY PROJECT FAILING, SO I HAD TO INTERVENE.
THE BIG PICTURE ALWAYS DEMANDS SACRIFICES.
I HAVE ALSO EXPERIENCED LOSS.
ALTHOUGH I GRIEVE FOR YOUR FATHER... I AM THANKFUL FOR HIS DEATH.
TREMBLE

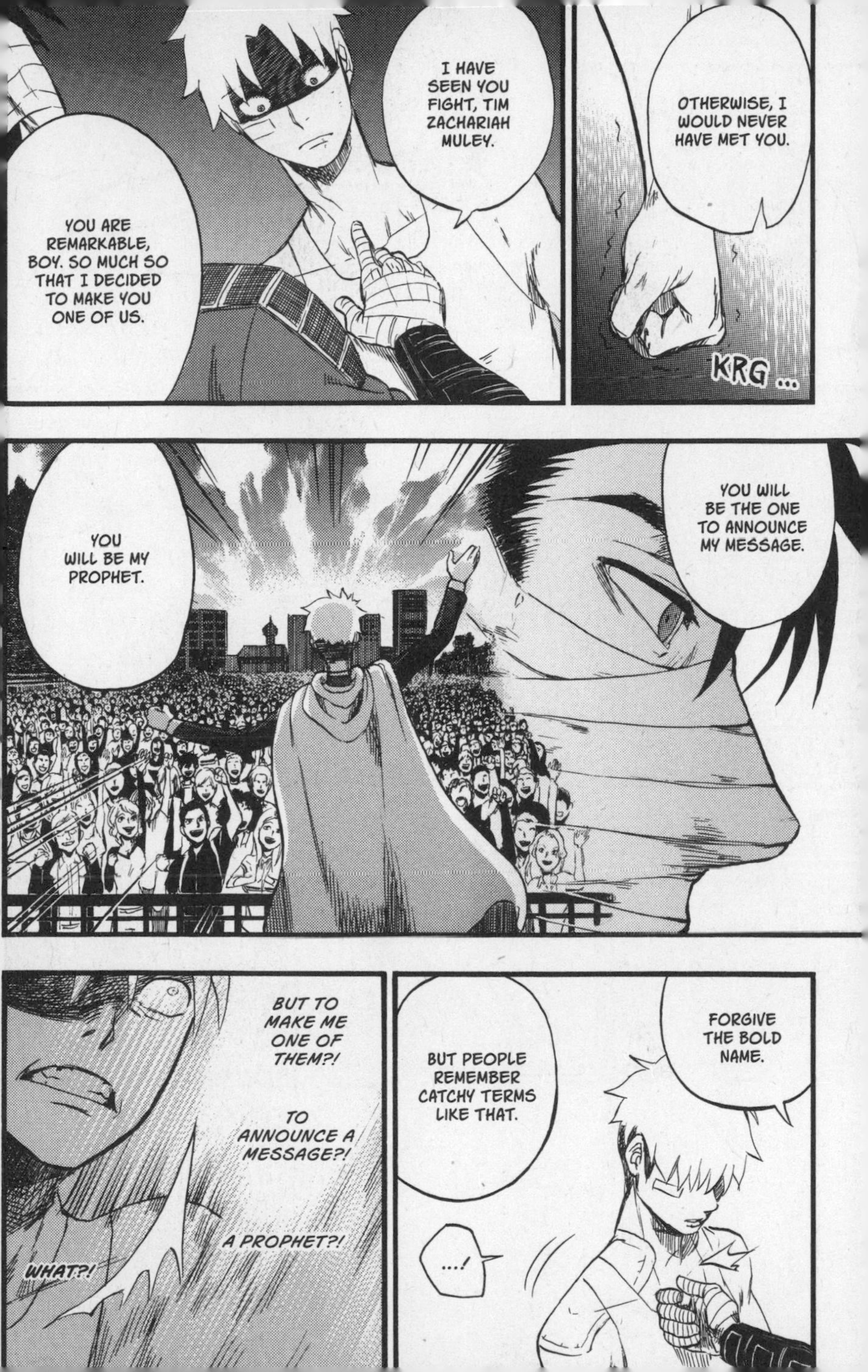
YOU ARE REMARKABLE, BOY. SO MUCH SO THAT I DECIDED TO MAKE YOU ONE OF US.
I HAVE SEEN YOU FIGHT, TIM ZACHARIAH MULEY.
OTHERWISE, I WOULD NEVER HAVE MET YOU.
KRG ...
YOU WILL BE MY PROPHET.
YOU WILL BE THE ONE TO ANNOUNCE MY MESSAGE.
BUT TO MAKE ME ONE OF THEM?!
TO ANNOUNCE A MESSAGE?!
A PROPHET?!
WHAT?!
FORGIVE THE BOLD NAME.
BUT PEOPLE REMEMBER CATCHY TERMS LIKE THAT.
...!

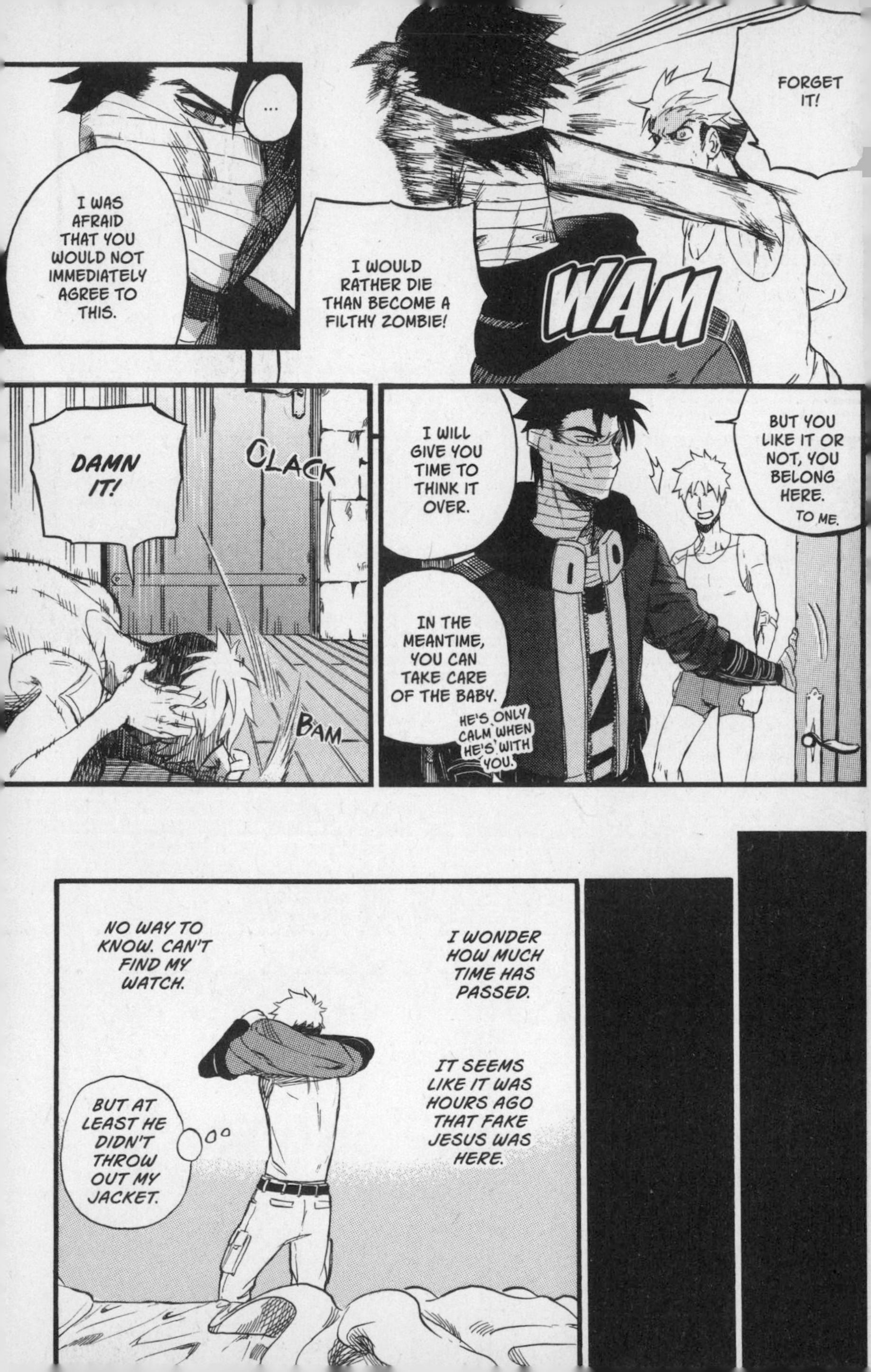
FORGET IT!
I WOULD RATHER DIE THAN BECOME A FILTHY ZOMBIE!
WAM
...
I WAS AFRAID THAT YOU WOULD NOT IMMEDIATELY AGREE TO THIS.
BUT YOU LIKE IT OR NOT, YOU BELONG HERE.
TO ME.
I WILL GIVE YOU TIME TO THINK IT OVER.
IN THE MEANTIME, YOU CAN TAKE CARE OF THE BABY.
HE'S ONLY CALM WHEN HE'S WITH YOU.
CLACK
DAMN IT!
BAM
I WONDER HOW MUCH TIME HAS PASSED.
NO WAY TO KNOW. CAN'T FIND MY WATCH.
IT SEEMS LIKE IT WAS HOURS AGO THAT FAKE JESUS WAS HERE.
BUT AT LEAST HE DIDN'T THROW OUT MY JACKET.

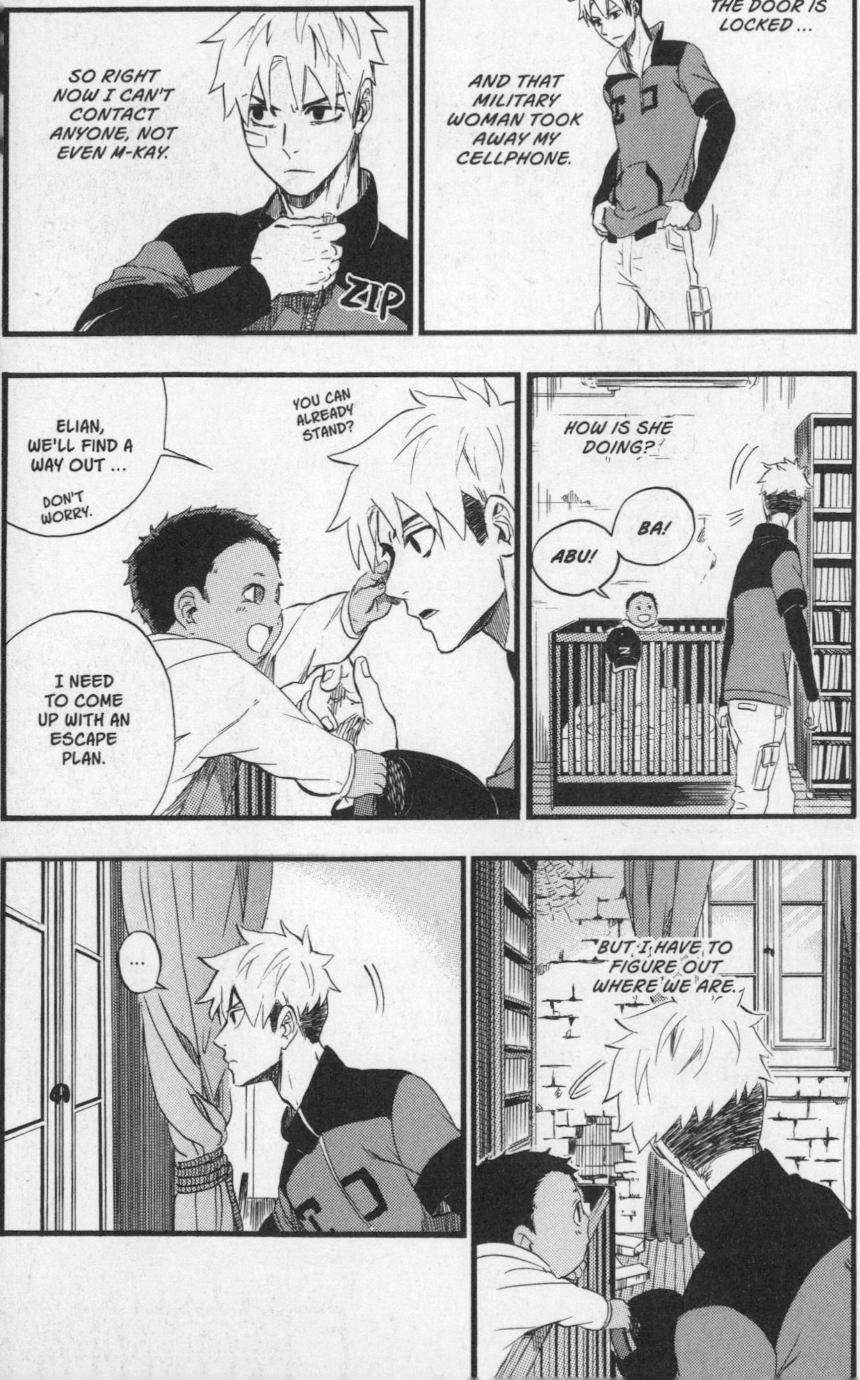
THE DOOR IS LOCKED ...
AND THAT MILITARY WOMAN TOOK AWAY MY CELLPHONE.
SO RIGHT NOW I CAN'T CONTACT ANYONE, NOT EVEN M-KAY.
ZIP
HOW IS SHE DOING?
BA!
ABU!
YOU CAN ALREADY STAND?
ELIAN, WE'LL FIND A WAY OUT ...
DON'T WORRY.
I NEED TO COME UP WITH AN ESCAPE PLAN.
BUT I HAVE TO FIGURE OUT WHERE WE ARE.
...

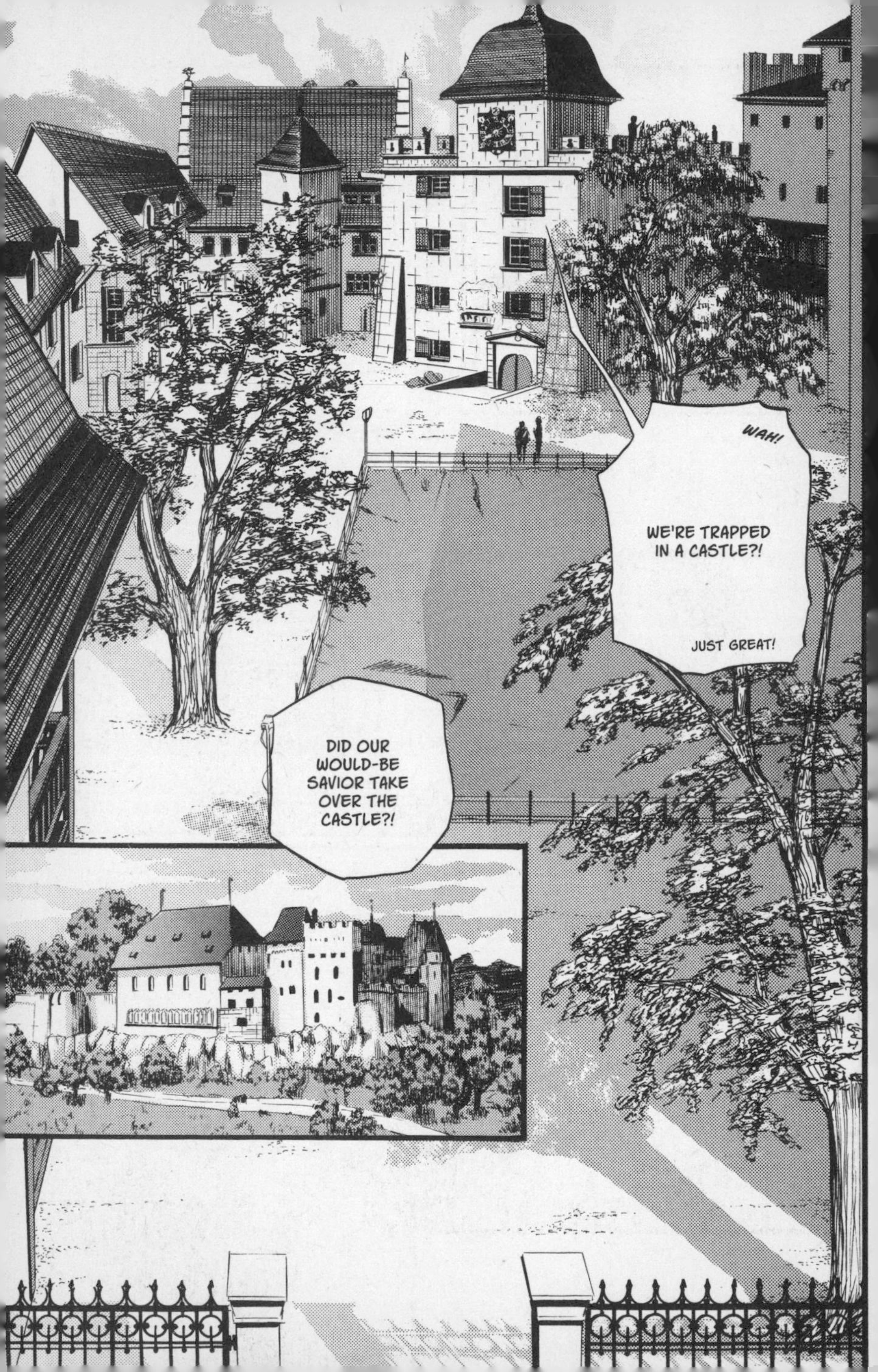
WAH!
WE'RE TRAPPED IN A CASTLE?!
JUST GREAT!
DID OUR WOULD-BE SAVIOR TAKE OVER THE CASTLE?!

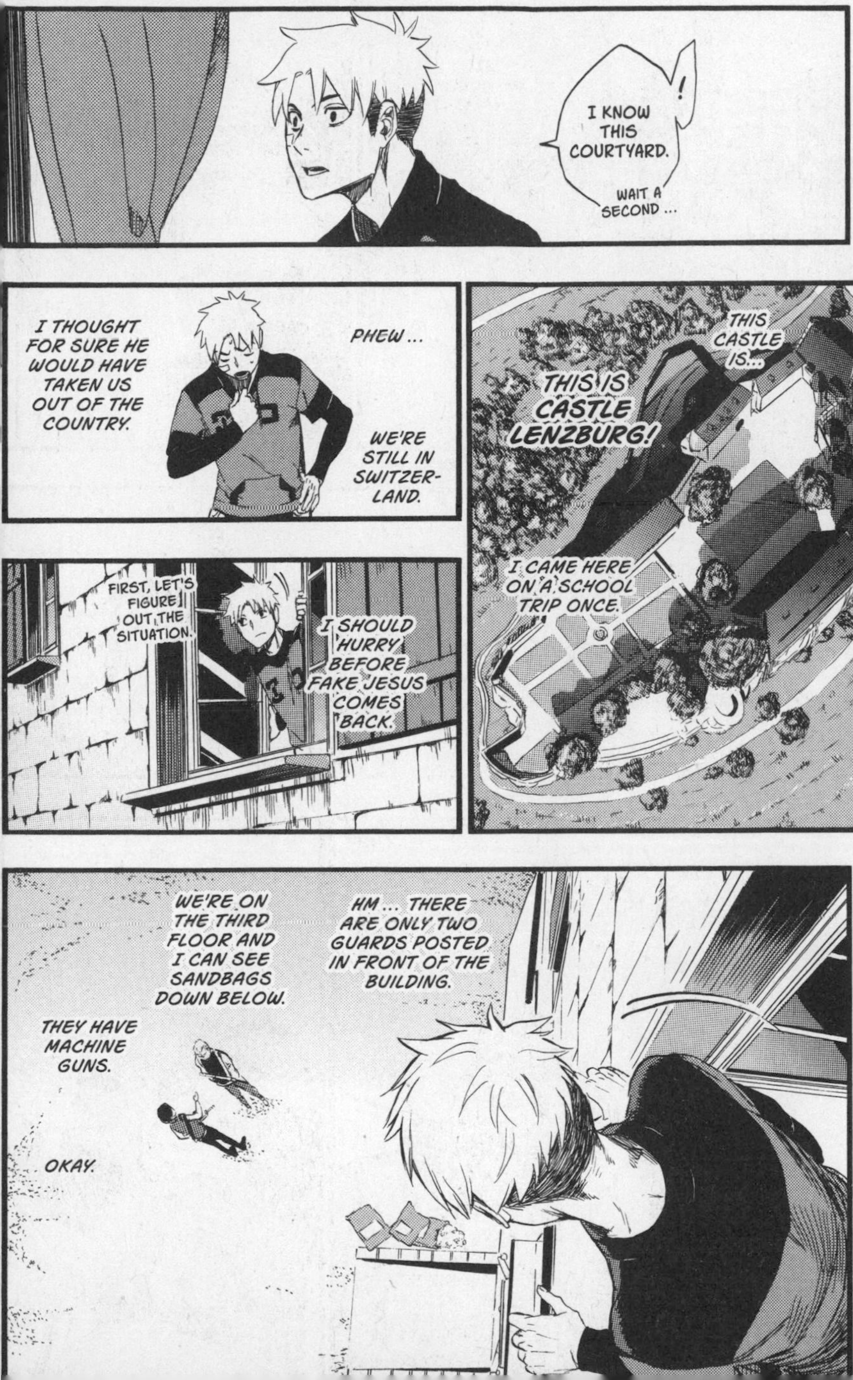
!
I KNOW THIS COURTYARD.
WAIT A SECOND ...
THIS CASTLE IS...
THIS IS CASTLE LENZBURG!
I CAME HERE ON A SCHOOL TRIP ONCE.
PHEW ...
I THOUGHT FOR SURE HE WOULD HAVE TAKEN US OUT OF THE COUNTRY.
WE'RE STILL IN SWITZER-LAND.
I SHOULD HURRY BEFORE FAKE JESUS COMES BACK.
FIRST, LET'S FIGURE OUT THE SITUATION.
HM ... THERE ARE ONLY TWO GUARDS POSTED IN FRONT OF THE BUILDING.
WE'RE ON THE THIRD FLOOR AND I CAN SEE SANDBAGS DOWN BELOW.
THEY HAVE MACHINE GUNS.
OKAY.

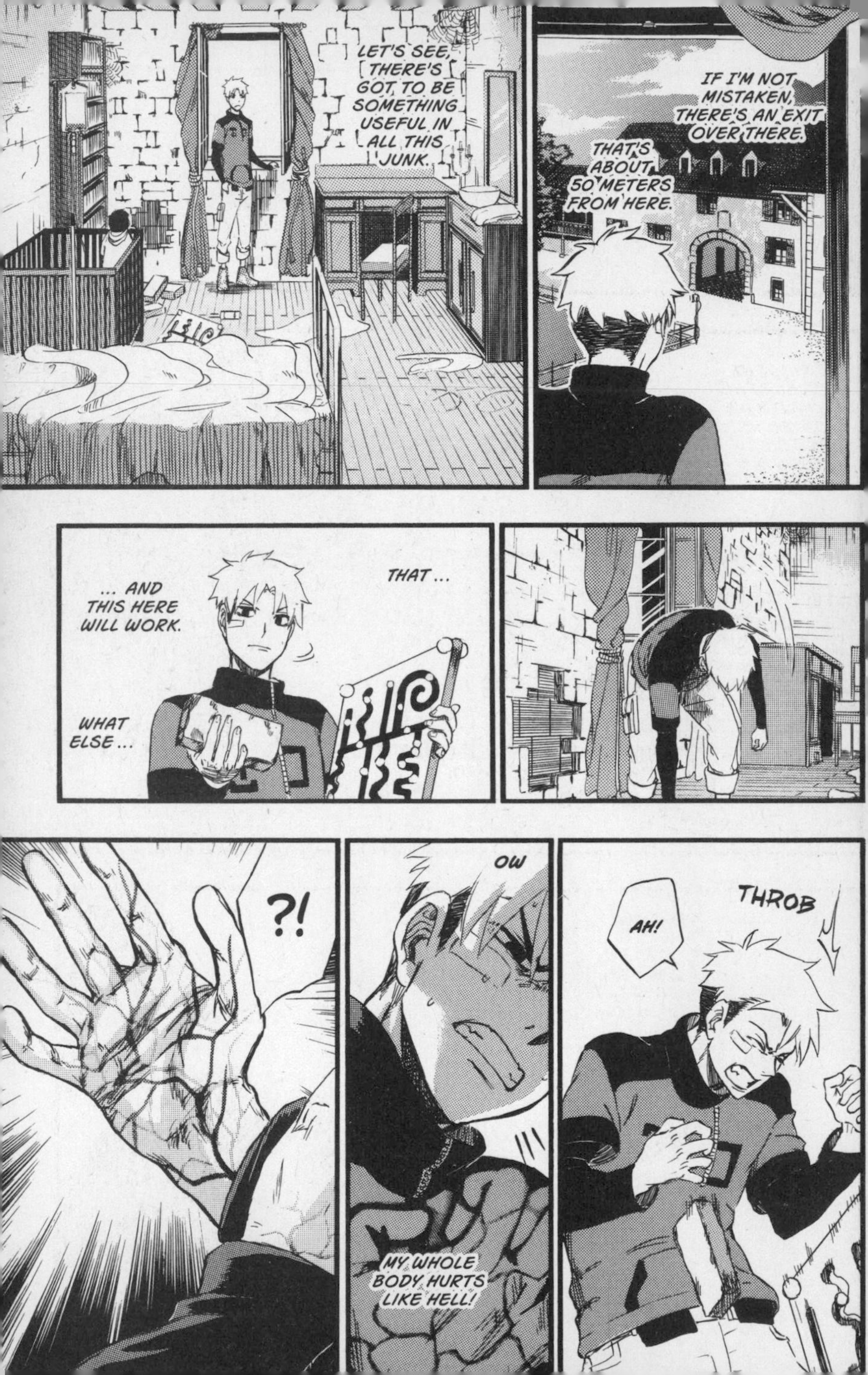
IF I'M NOT MISTAKEN, THERE'S AN EXIT OVER THERE.
THAT'S ABOUT 50 METERS FROM HERE.
LET'S SEE, THERE'S GOT TO BE SOMETHING USEFUL IN ALL THIS JUNK.
THAT ...
... AND THIS HERE WILL WORK.
WHAT ELSE ...
THROB
AH!
OW
MY WHOLE BODY HURTS LIKE HELL!
?!

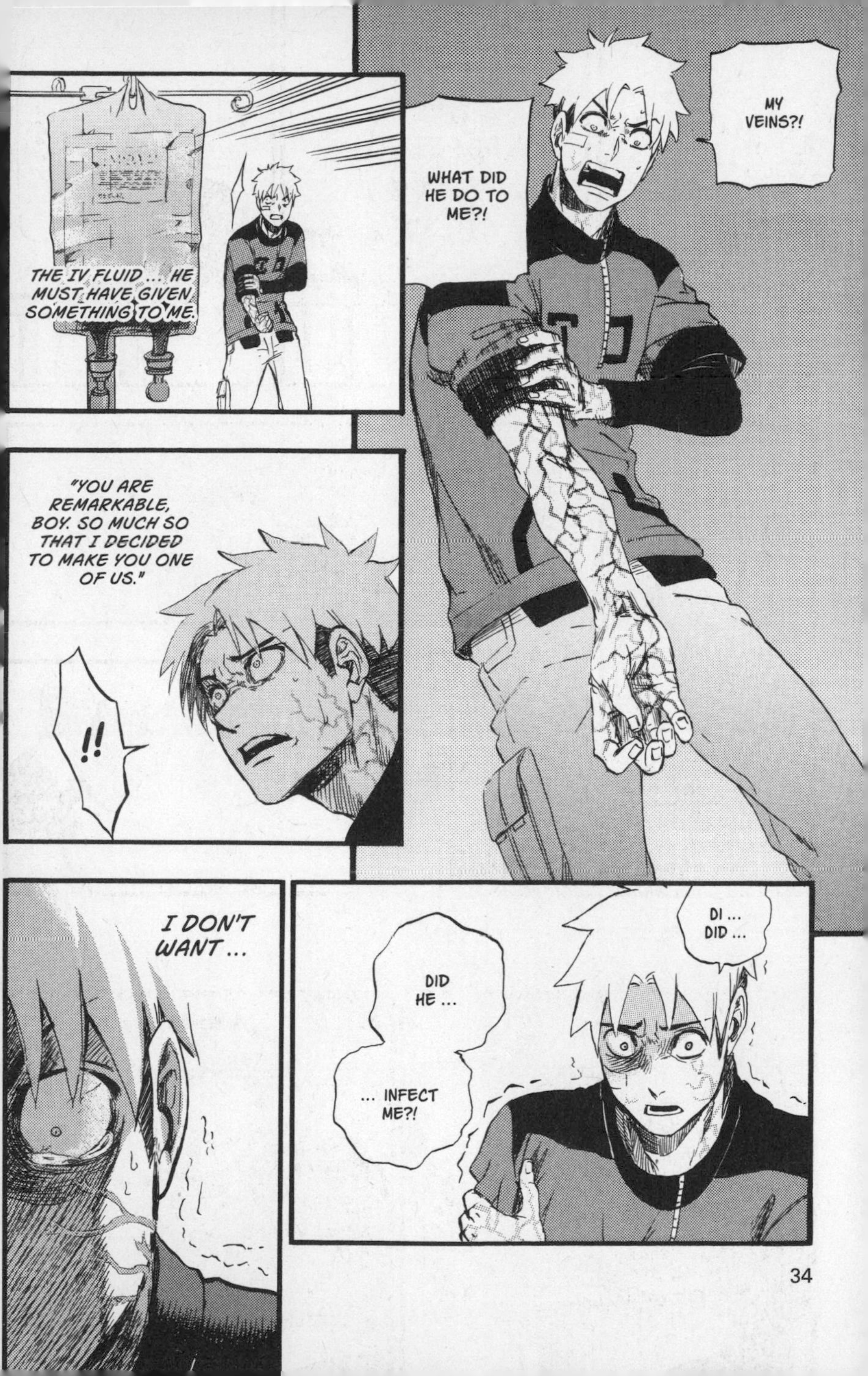

MY VEINS?!
WHAT DID HE DO TO ME?!
THE IV FLUID ... HE MUST HAVE GIVEN SOMETHING TO ME.
"YOU ARE REMARKABLE, BOY. SO MUCH SO THAT I DECIDED TO MAKE YOU ONE OF US."
!!
DI ... DID ...
DID HE ...
... INFECT ME?!
I DON'T WANT ...

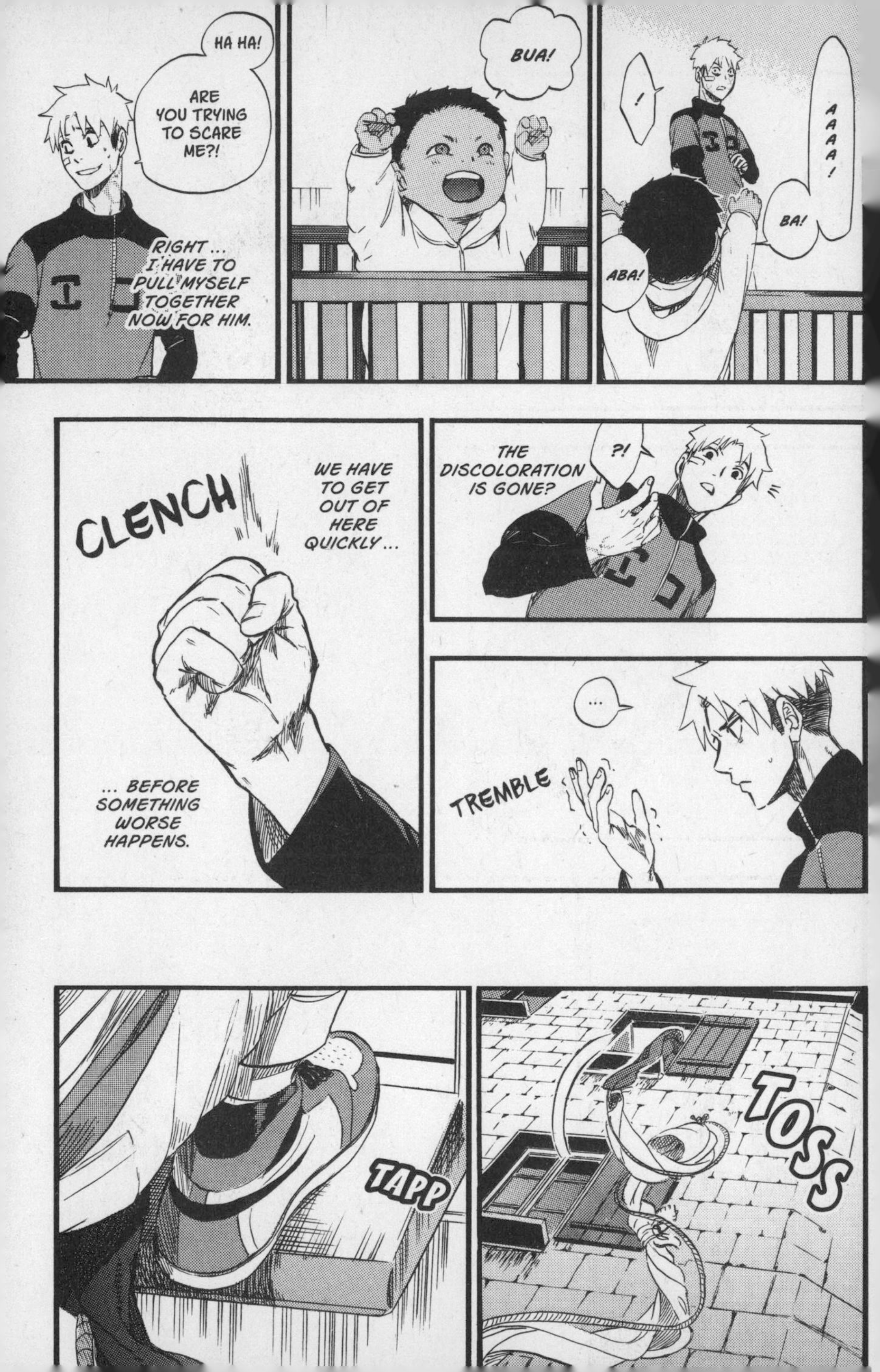
AAAA!
!
BA!
ABA!
BUA!
HA HA!
ARE YOU TRYING TO SCARE ME?!
RIGHT ... I HAVE TO PULL MYSELF TOGETHER NOW FOR HIM.
?!
THE DISCOLORATION IS GONE?
...
TREMBLE
WE HAVE TO GET OUT OF HERE QUICKLY ...
CLENCH
... BEFORE SOMETHING WORSE HAPPENS.
TOSS
TAPP

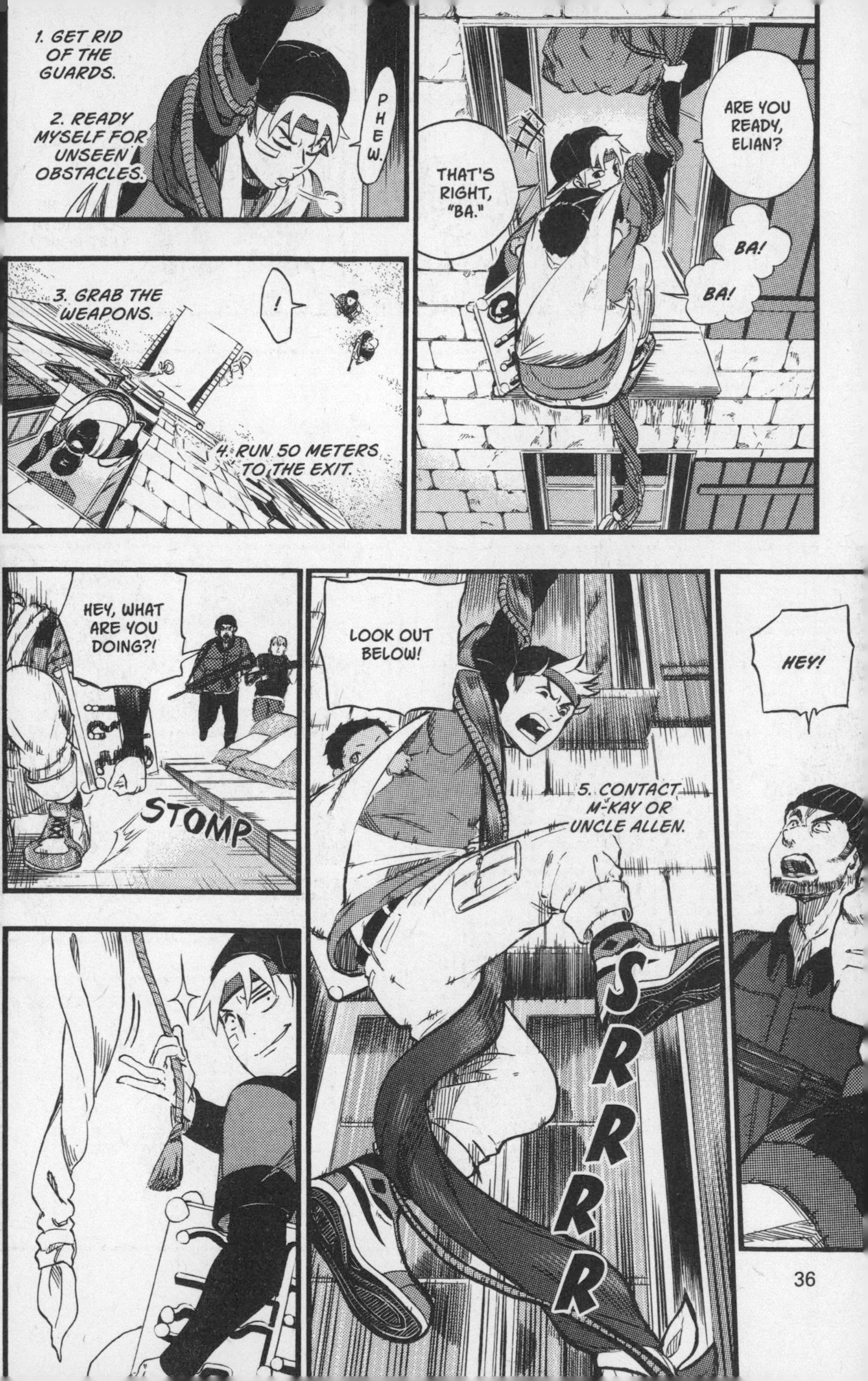
ARE YOU READY, ELIAN?
THAT'S RIGHT, "BA."
BA!
BA!
1. GET RID OF THE GUARDS.
PHEW.
2. READY MYSELF FOR UNSEEN OBSTACLES.
!
3. GRAB THE WEAPONS.
4. RUN 50 METERS TO THE EXIT.
HEY!
LOOK OUT BELOW!
5. CONTACT M-KAY OR UNCLE ALLEN.
SRRRR
HEY, WHAT ARE YOU DOING?!
STOMP

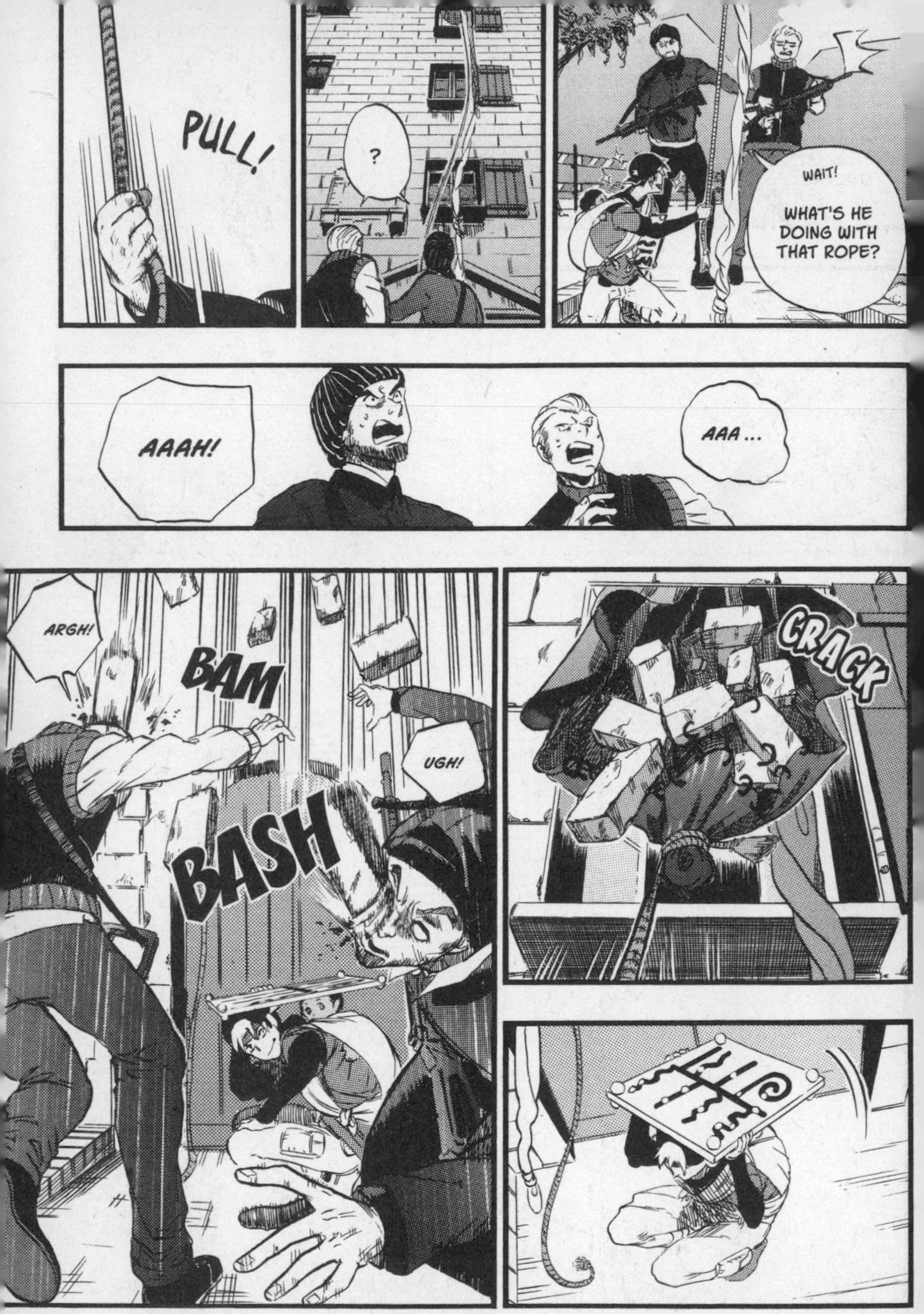
WAIT!
WHAT'S HE DOING WITH THAT ROPE?
?
PULL!
AAA ...
AAAH!
CRACK
ARGH!
BAM
UGH!
BASH

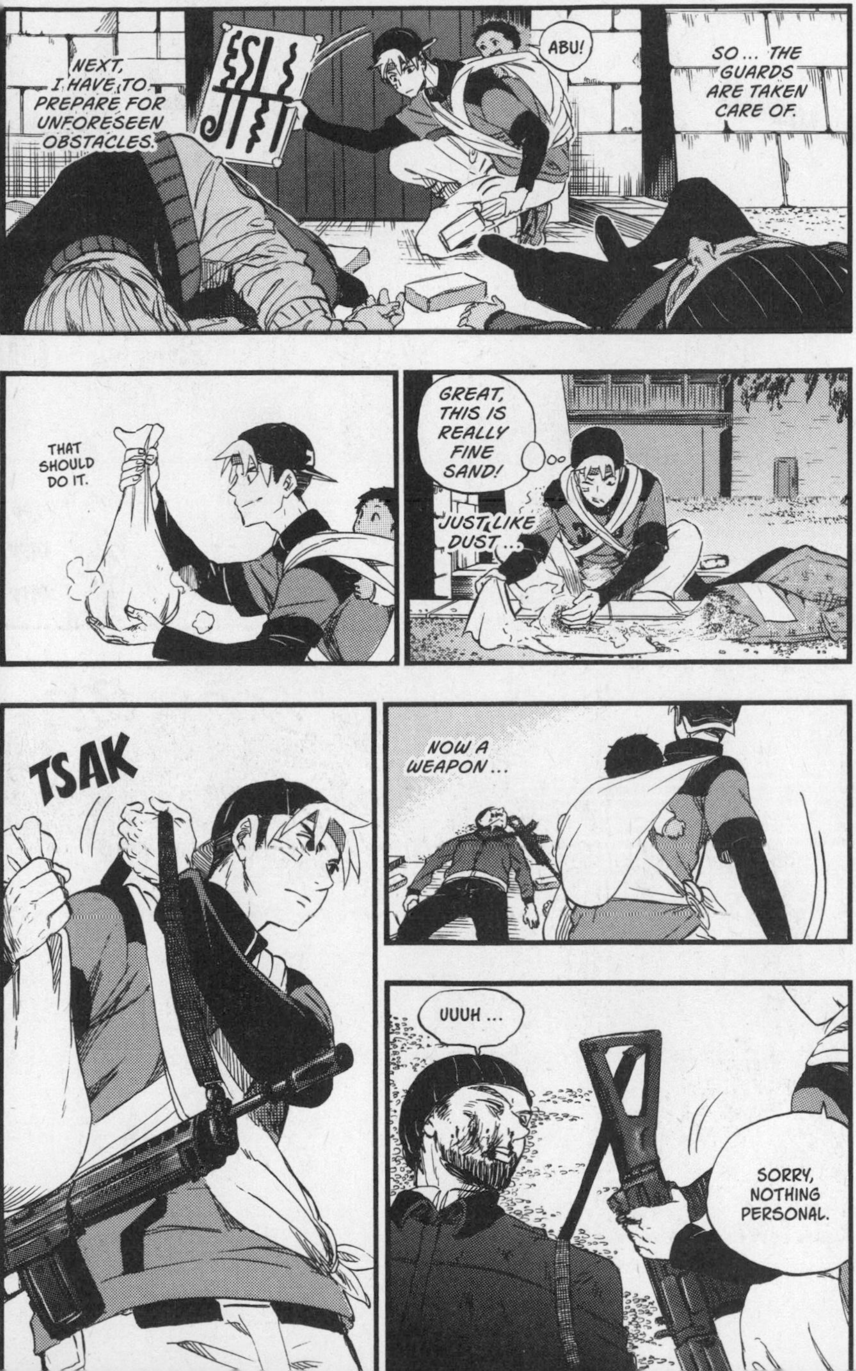
SO ... THE GUARDS ARE TAKEN CARE OF.
ABU!
NEXT, I HAVE TO PREPARE FOR UNFORESEEN OBSTACLES.
GREAT, THIS IS REALLY FINE SAND!
JUST LIKE DUST ...
THAT SHOULD DO IT.
NOW A WEAPON ...
UUUH ...
SORRY, NOTHING PERSONAL.
TSAK

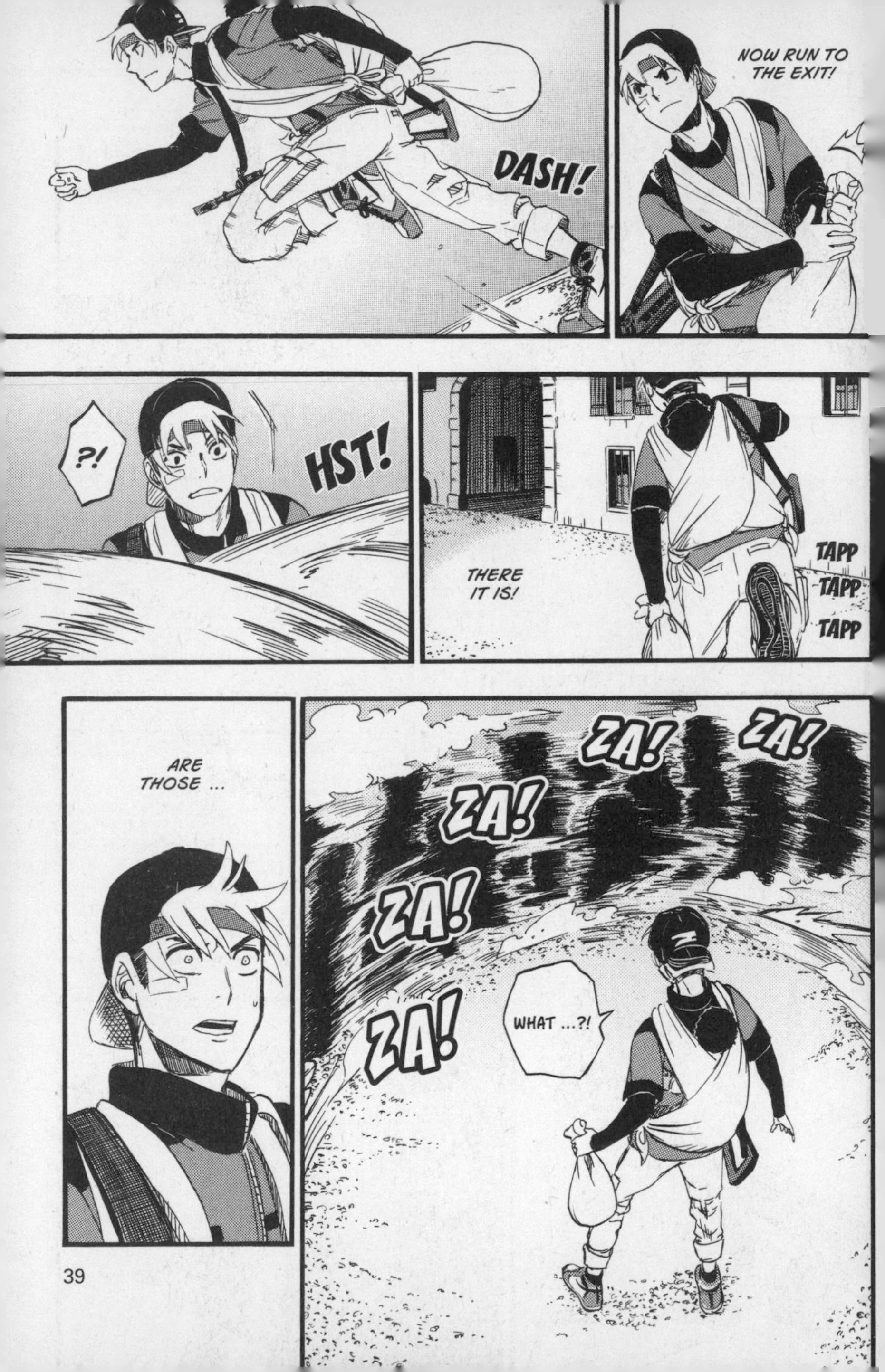
NOW RUN TO THE EXIT!
DASH!
TAPP
TAPP
TAPP
THERE IT IS!
?!
HST!
ZA!
ZA!
ZA!
ZA!
ZA!
WHAT ...?!
ARE THOSE ...

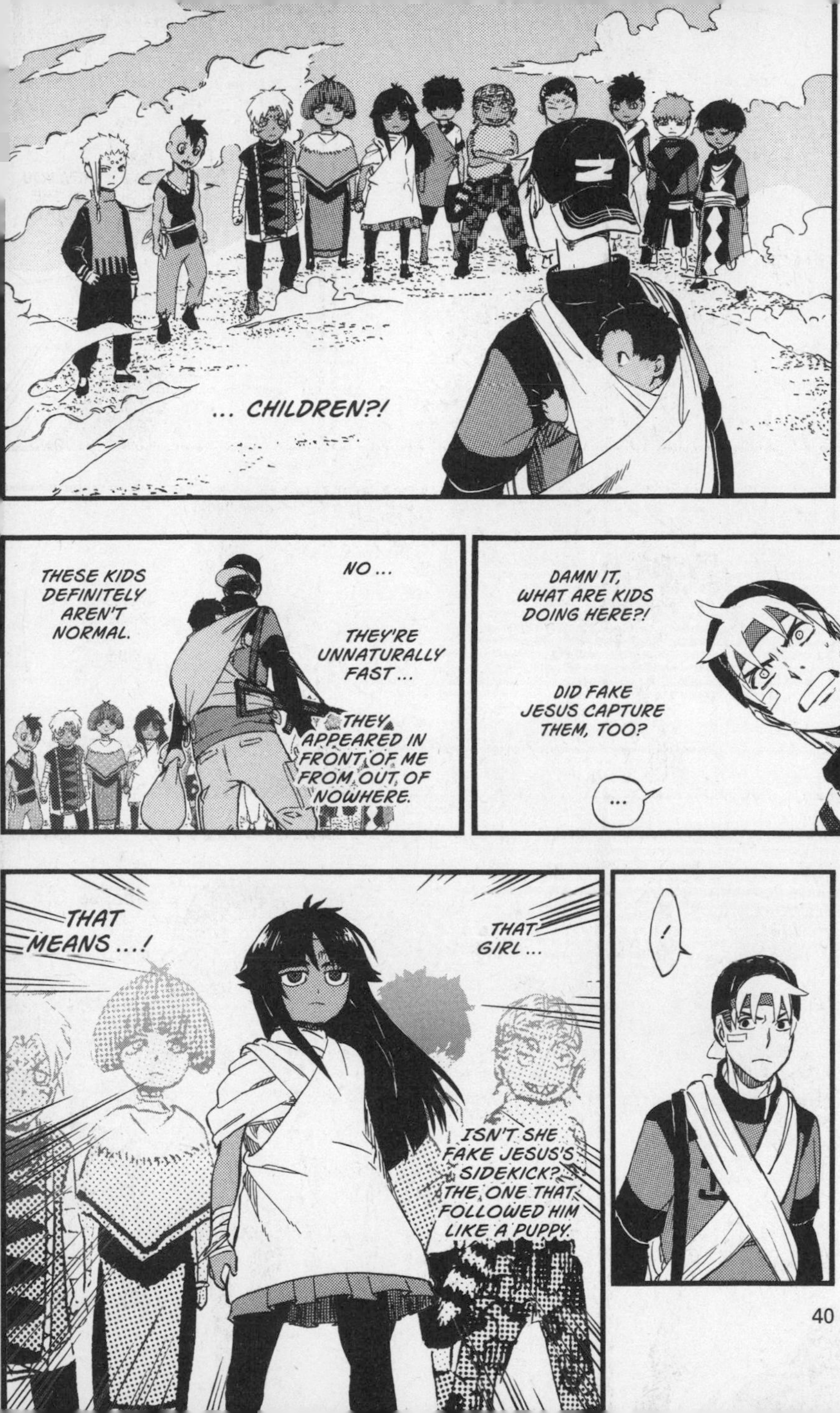
... CHILDREN?!
DAMN IT, WHAT ARE KIDS DOING HERE?!
DID FAKE JESUS CAPTURE THEM, TOO?
...
NO ...
THEY'RE UNNATURALLY FAST ...
THEY APPEARED IN FRONT OF ME FROM OUT OF NOWHERE.
THESE KIDS DEFINITELY AREN'T NORMAL.
!
THAT GIRL ...
ISN'T SHE FAKE JESUS'S SIDEKICK? THE ONE THAT FOLLOWED HIM LIKE A PUPPY.
THAT MEANS ...!

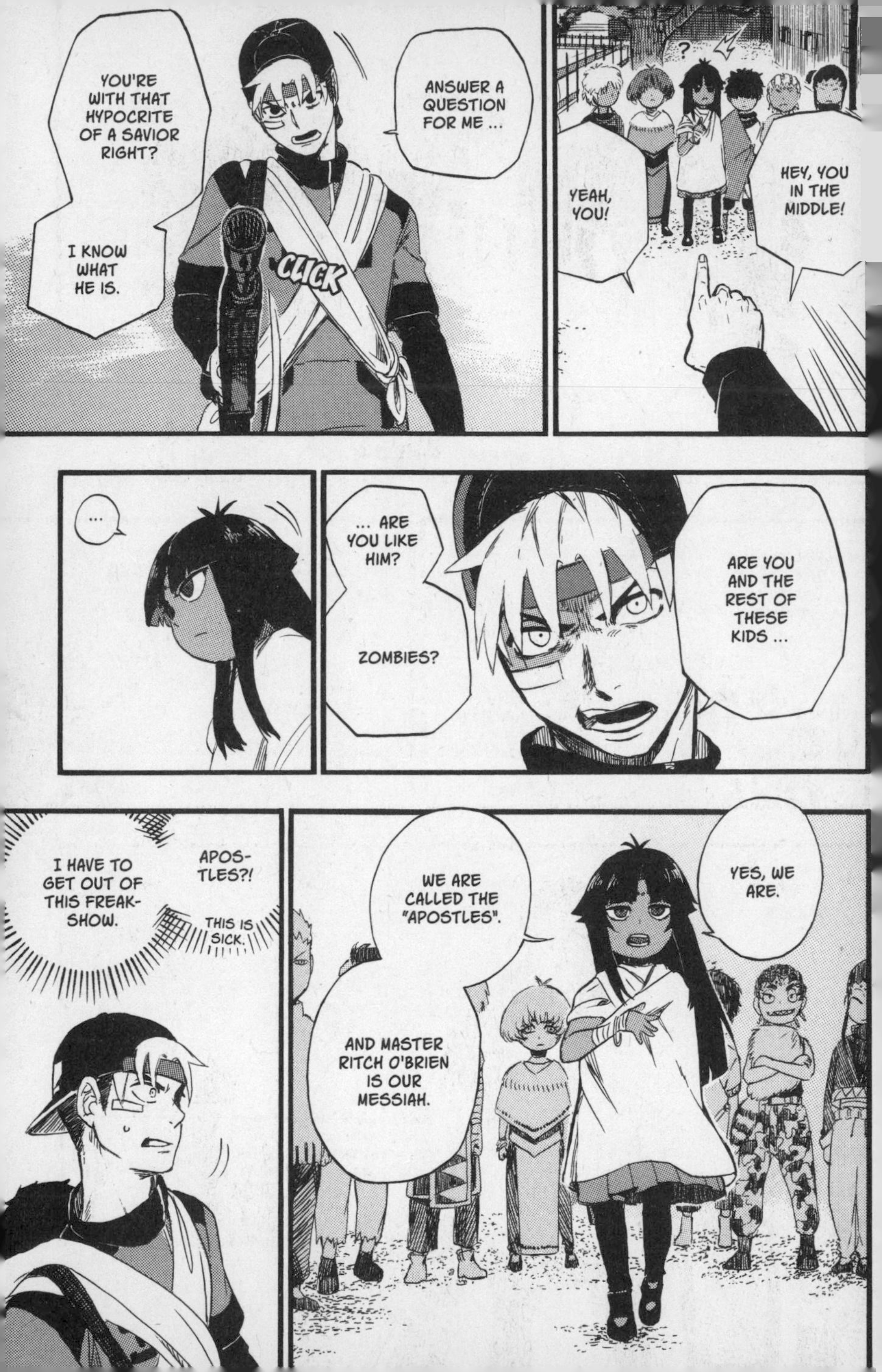
?
HEY, YOU IN THE MIDDLE!
YEAH, YOU!
ANSWER A QUESTION FOR ME ...
YOU'RE WITH THAT HYPOCRITE OF A SAVIOR RIGHT?
CLICK
I KNOW WHAT HE IS.
ARE YOU AND THE REST OF THESE KIDS ...
... ARE YOU LIKE HIM?
ZOMBIES?
...
YES, WE ARE.
WE ARE CALLED THE "APOSTLES".
AND MASTER RITCH O'BRIEN IS OUR MESSIAH.
APOS-TLES?!
THIS IS SICK.
I HAVE TO GET OUT OF THIS FREAK-SHOW.

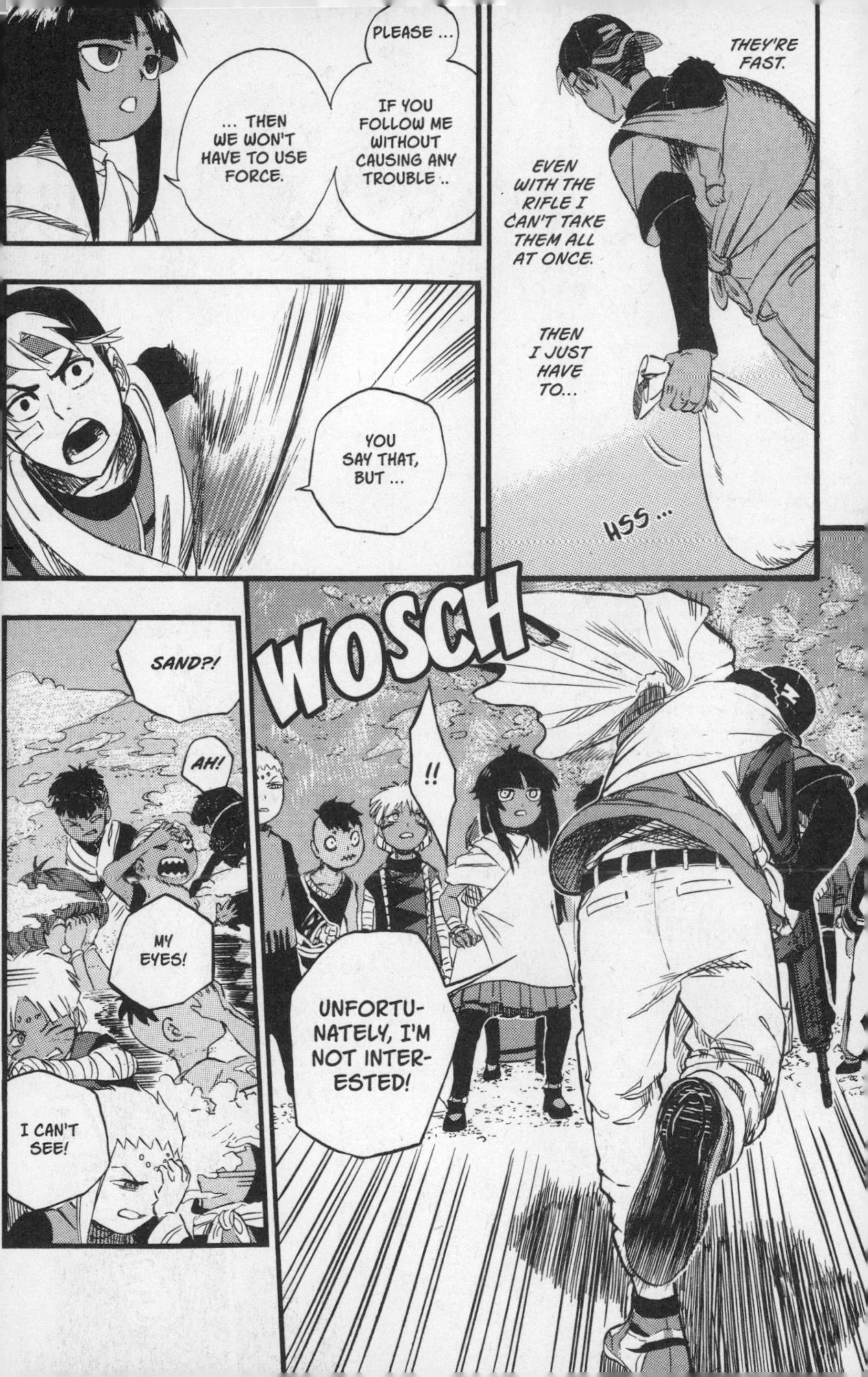
THEY'RE FAST.
EVEN WITH THE RIFLE I CAN'T TAKE THEM ALL AT ONCE.
THEN I JUST HAVE TO...
HSS ...
PLEASE ...
IF YOU FOLLOW ME WITHOUT CAUSING ANY TROUBLE ..
... THEN WE WON'T HAVE TO USE FORCE.
YOU SAY THAT, BUT ...
WOSCH
!!
UNFORTU-NATELY, I'M NOT INTER-ESTED!
SAND?!
AH!
MY EYES!
I CAN'T SEE!

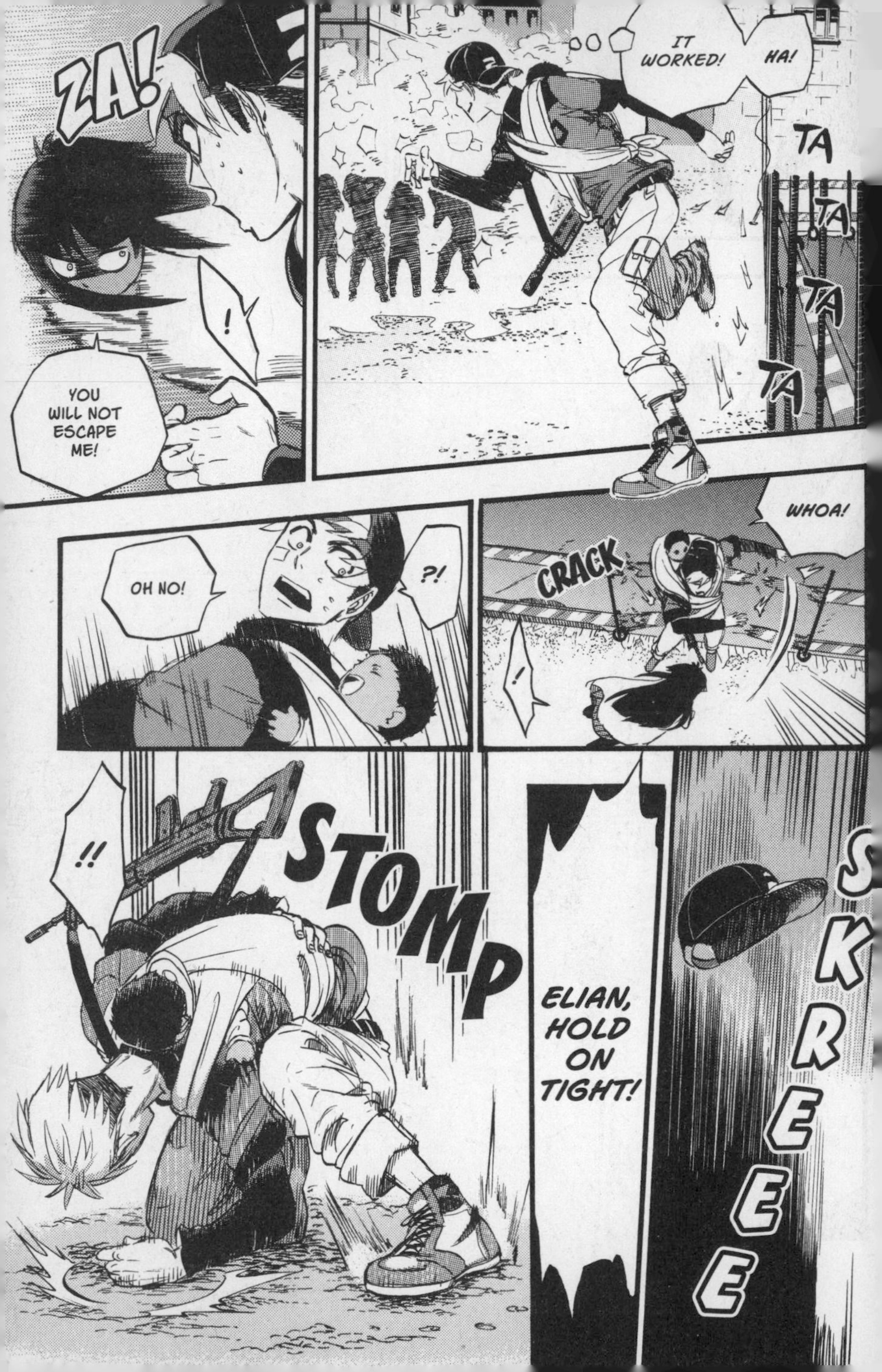
HA!
IT WORKED!
TA
TA
TA
TA
ZA!
!
YOU WILL NOT ESCAPE ME!
WHOA!
CRACK
!
?!
OH NO!
SKREEEE
ELIAN, HOLD ON TIGHT!
STOMP
!!

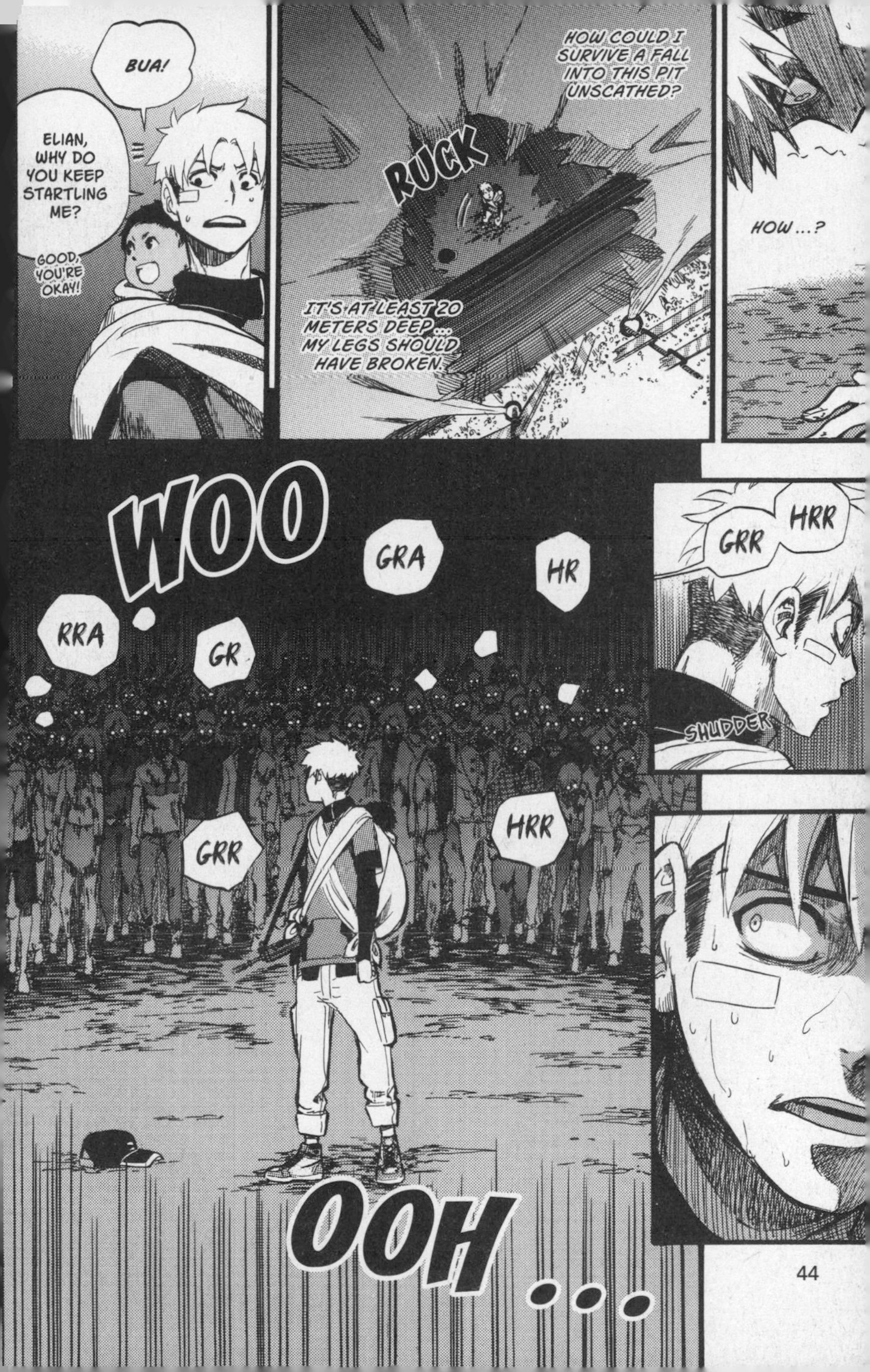
HOW ...?
HOW COULD I SURVIVE A FALL INTO THIS PIT UNSCATHED?
RUCK
IT'S AT LEAST 20 METERS DEEP... MY LEGS SHOULD HAVE BROKEN.
BUA!
ELIAN, WHY DO YOU KEEP STARTLING ME?
GOOD, YOU'RE OKAY!
HRR
GRR
SHUDDER
HR
GRA
WOO
GR
RRA
HRR
GRR
OOH ...

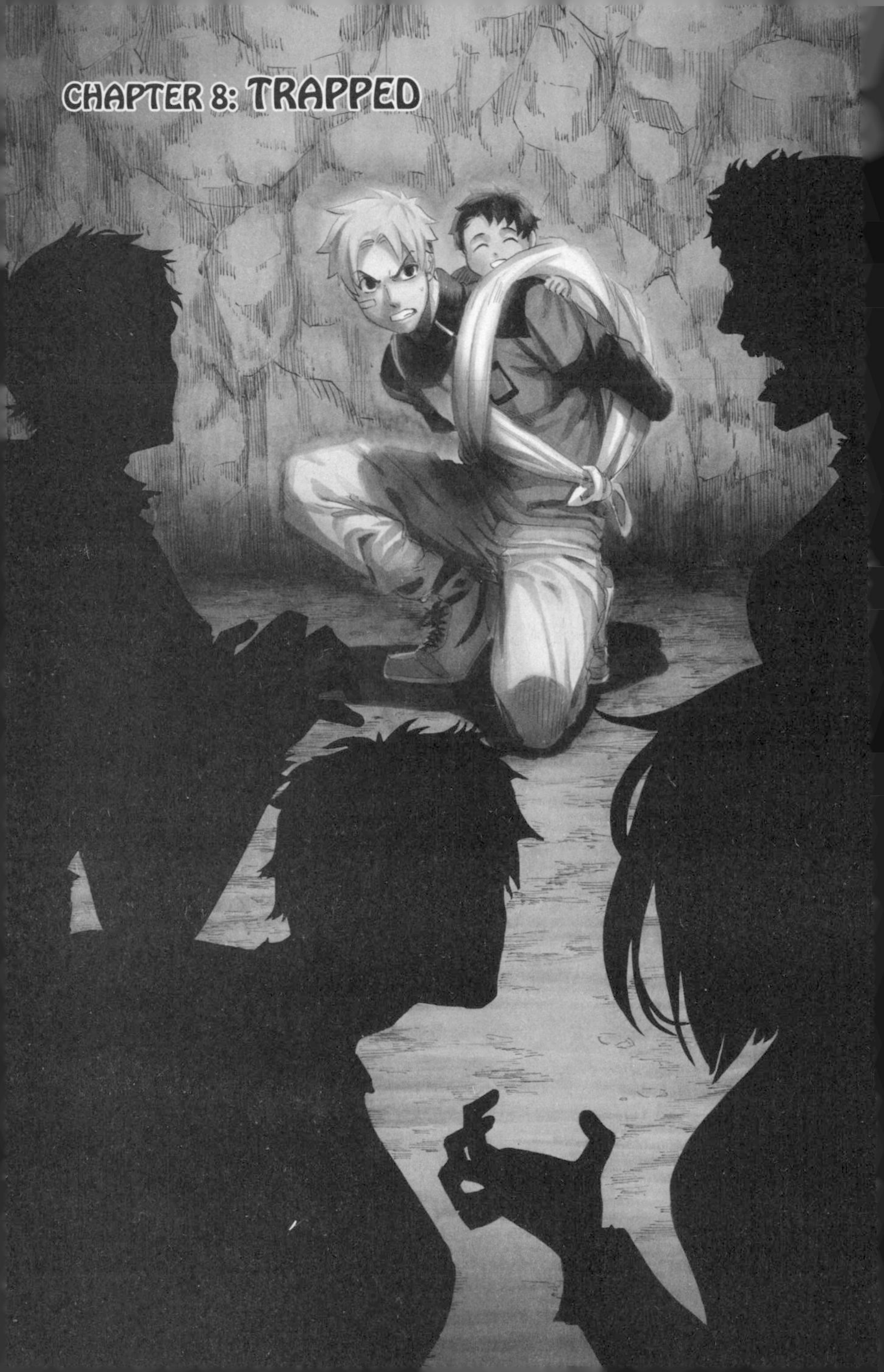
CHAPTER 8: TRAPPED

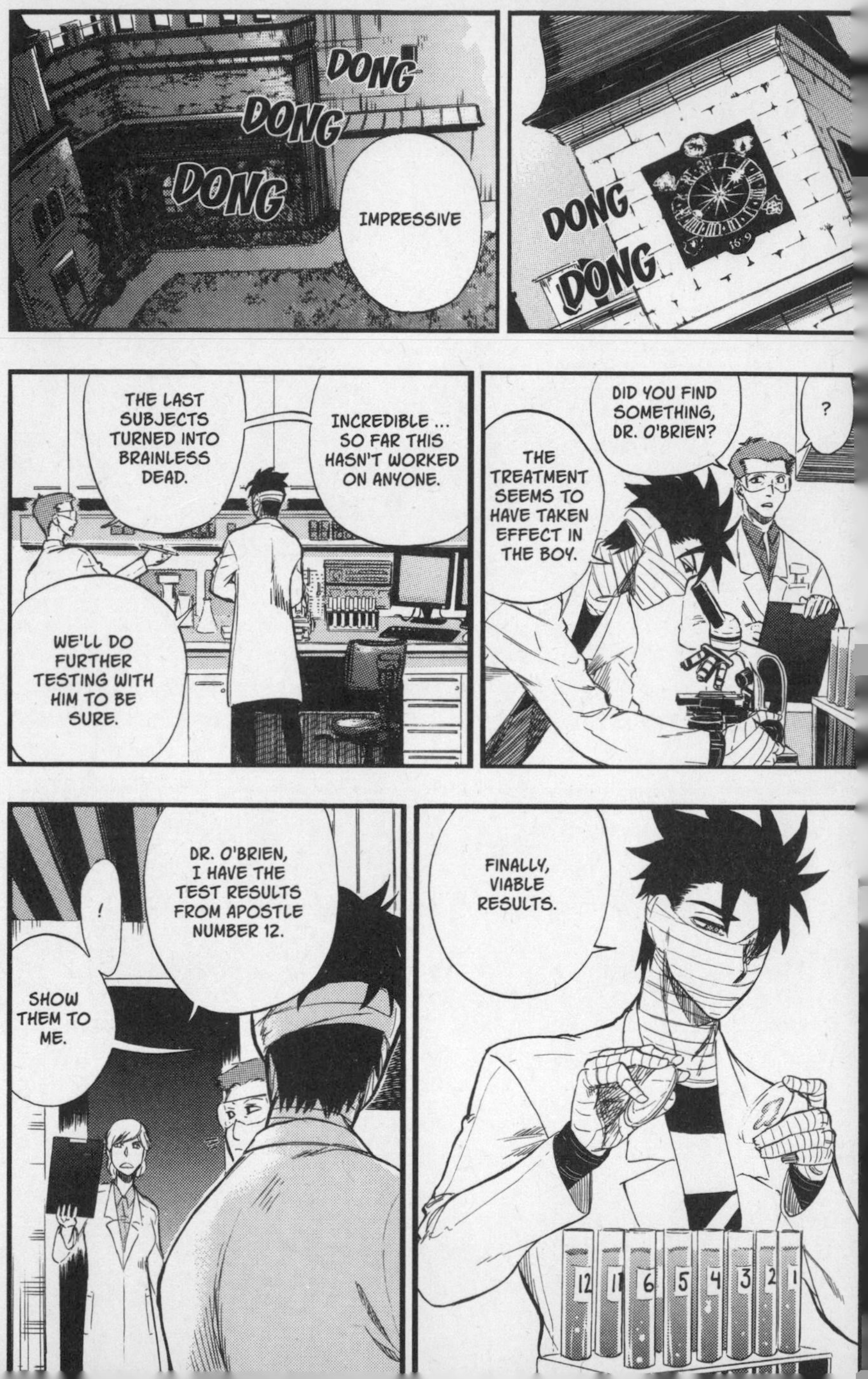
DONG
DONG
DONG
DONG
DONG
IMPRESSIVE
DID YOU FIND SOMETHING, DR. O'BRIEN?
?
THE TREATMENT SEEMS TO HAVE TAKEN EFFECT IN THE BOY.
INCREDIBLE ... SO FAR THIS HASN'T WORKED ON ANYONE.
THE LAST SUBJECTS TURNED INTO BRAINLESS DEAD.
WE'LL DO FURTHER TESTING WITH HIM TO BE SURE.
FINALLY, VIABLE RESULTS.
12 11 6 5 4 3 2 1
DR. O'BRIEN, I HAVE THE TEST RESULTS FROM APOSTLE NUMBER 12.
!
SHOW THEM TO ME.

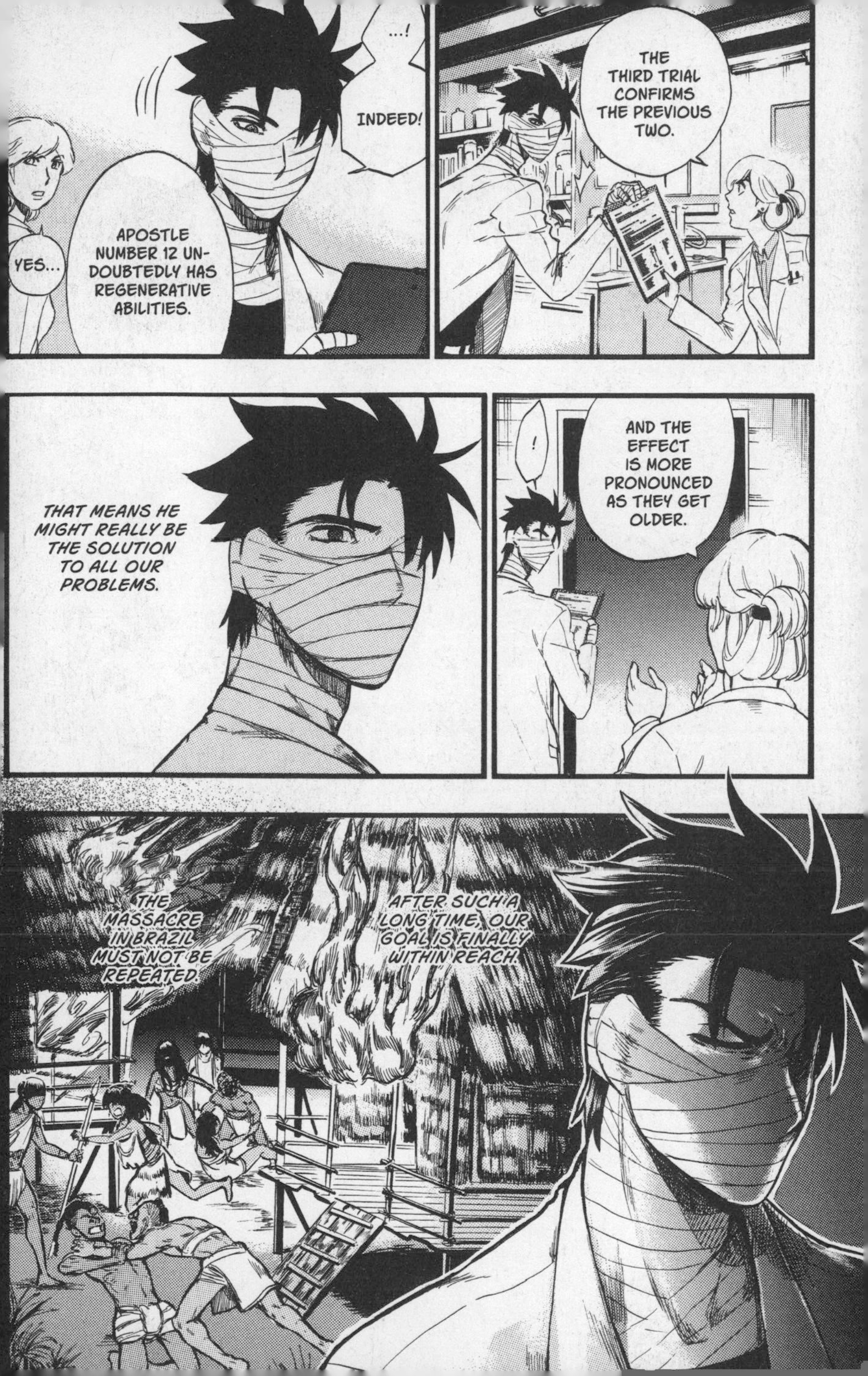
THE THIRD TRIAL CONFIRMS THE PREVIOUS TWO.
...!
INDEED!
APOSTLE NUMBER 12 UN-DOUBTEDLY HAS REGENERATIVE ABILITIES.
YES...
AND THE EFFECT IS MORE PRONOUNCED AS THEY GET OLDER.
!
THAT MEANS HE MIGHT REALLY BE THE SOLUTION TO ALL OUR PROBLEMS.
AFTER SUCH A LONG TIME, OUR GOAL IS FINALLY WITHIN REACH.
THE MASSACRE IN BRAZIL MUST NOT BE REPEATED.

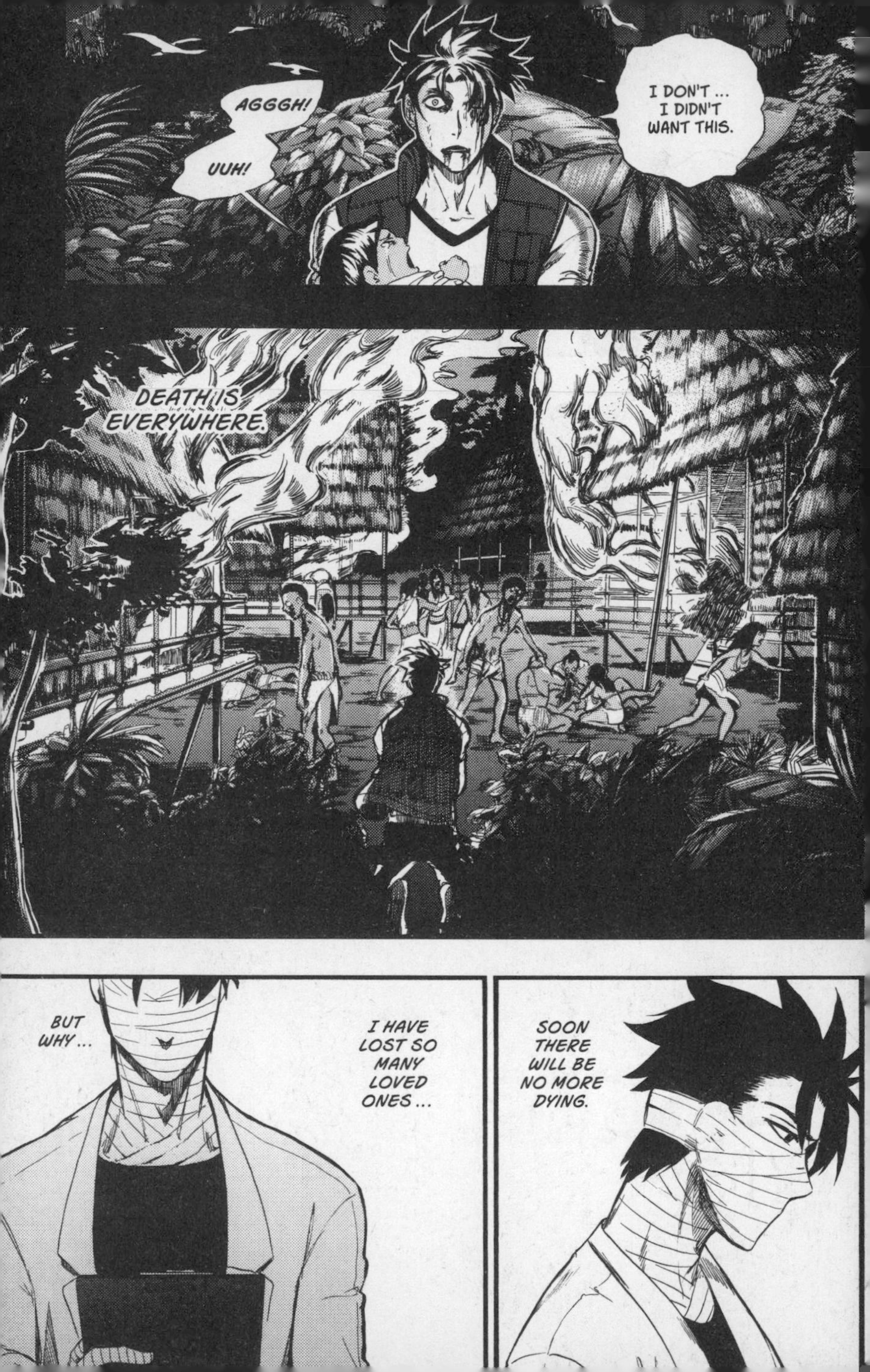
I DON'T ... I DIDN'T WANT THIS.
AGGGH!
UUH!
DEATH IS EVERYWHERE.
SOON THERE WILL BE NO MORE DYING.
I HAVE LOST SO MANY LOVED ONES ...
BUT WHY ...

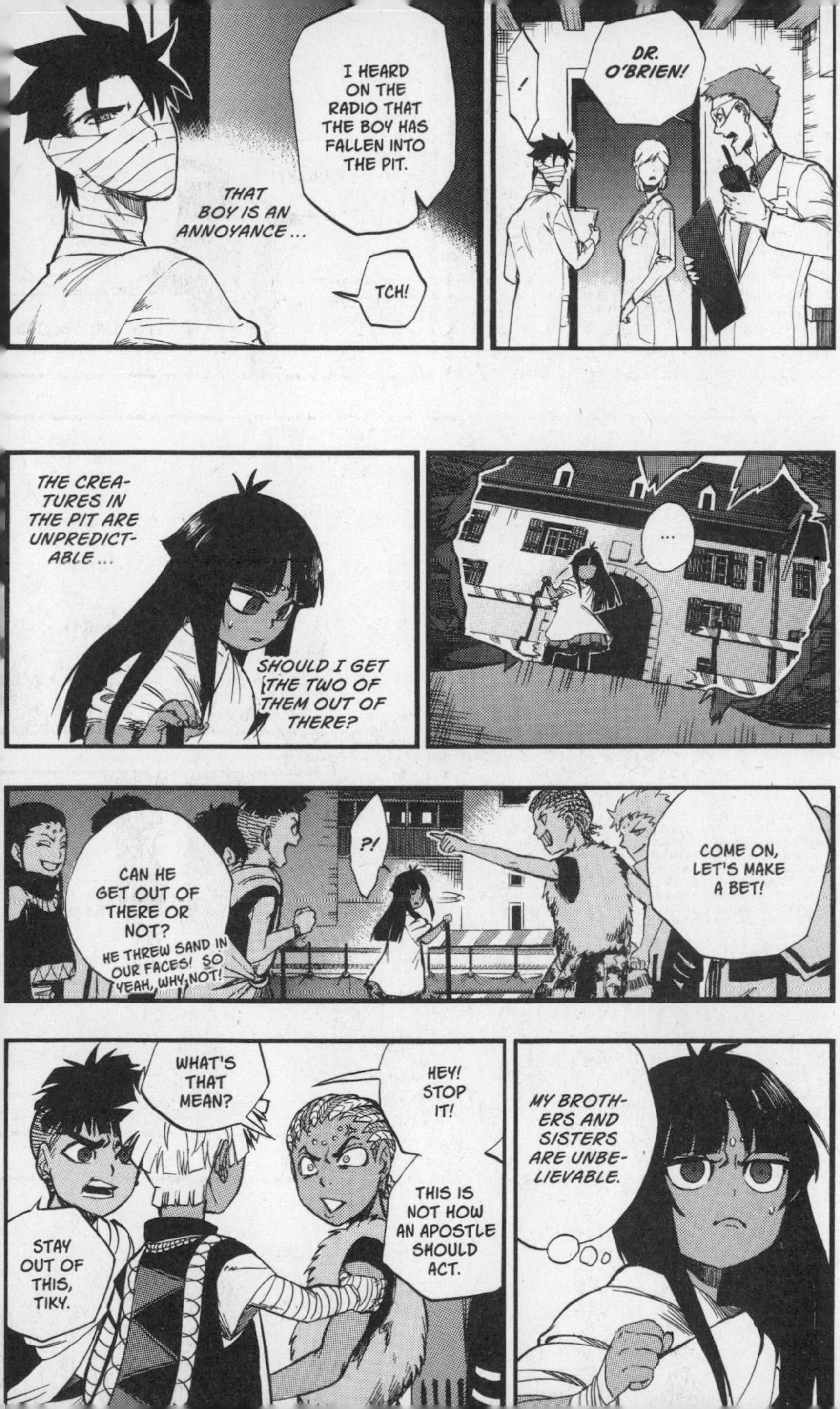
DR. O'BRIEN!
!
I HEARD ON THE RADIO THAT THE BOY HAS FALLEN INTO THE PIT.
THAT BOY IS AN ANNOYANCE ...
TCH!
...
THE CREA-TURES IN THE PIT ARE UNPREDICT-ABLE...
SHOULD I GET THE TWO OF THEM OUT OF THERE?
COME ON, LET'S MAKE A BET!
?!
CAN HE GET OUT OF THERE OR NOT?
HE THREW SAND IN OUR FACES! SO YEAH, WHY NOT!
MY BROTH-ERS AND SISTERS ARE UNBE-LIEVABLE.
HEY! STOP IT!
THIS IS NOT HOW AN APOSTLE SHOULD ACT.
WHAT'S THAT MEAN?
STAY OUT OF THIS, TIKY.

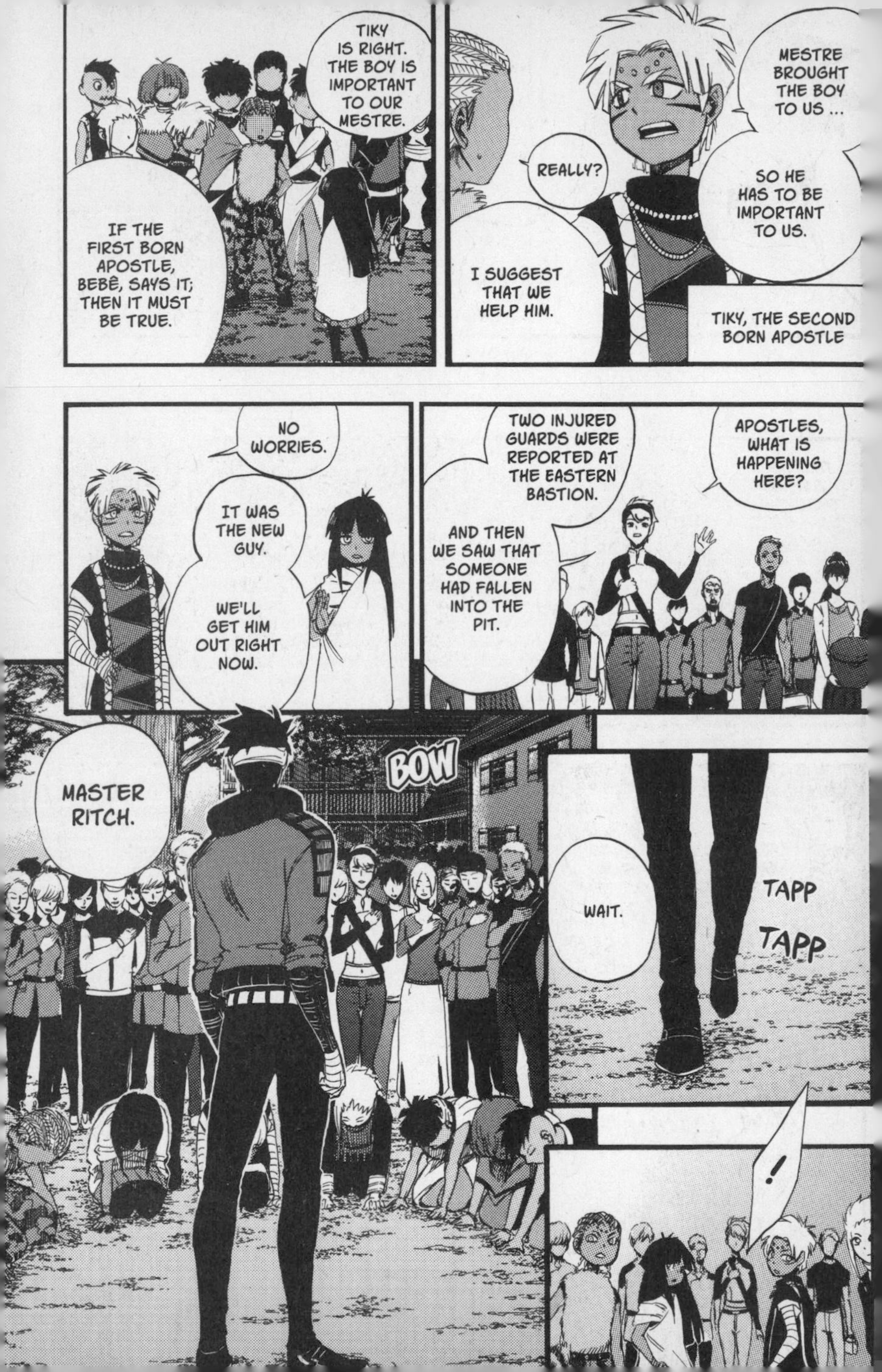
MESTRE BROUGHT THE BOY TO US ...
SO HE HAS TO BE IMPORTANT TO US.
REALLY?
I SUGGEST THAT WE HELP HIM.
TIKY, THE SECOND BORN APOSTLE
TIKY IS RIGHT. THE BOY IS IMPORTANT TO OUR MESTRE.
IF THE FIRST BORN APOSTLE, BEBÊ, SAYS IT; THEN IT MUST BE TRUE.
APOSTLES, WHAT IS HAPPENING HERE?
TWO INJURED GUARDS WERE REPORTED AT THE EASTERN BASTION.
AND THEN WE SAW THAT SOMEONE HAD FALLEN INTO THE PIT.
NO WORRIES.
IT WAS THE NEW GUY.
WE'LL GET HIM OUT RIGHT NOW.
WAIT.
TAPP
TAPP
!
BOW
MASTER RITCH.

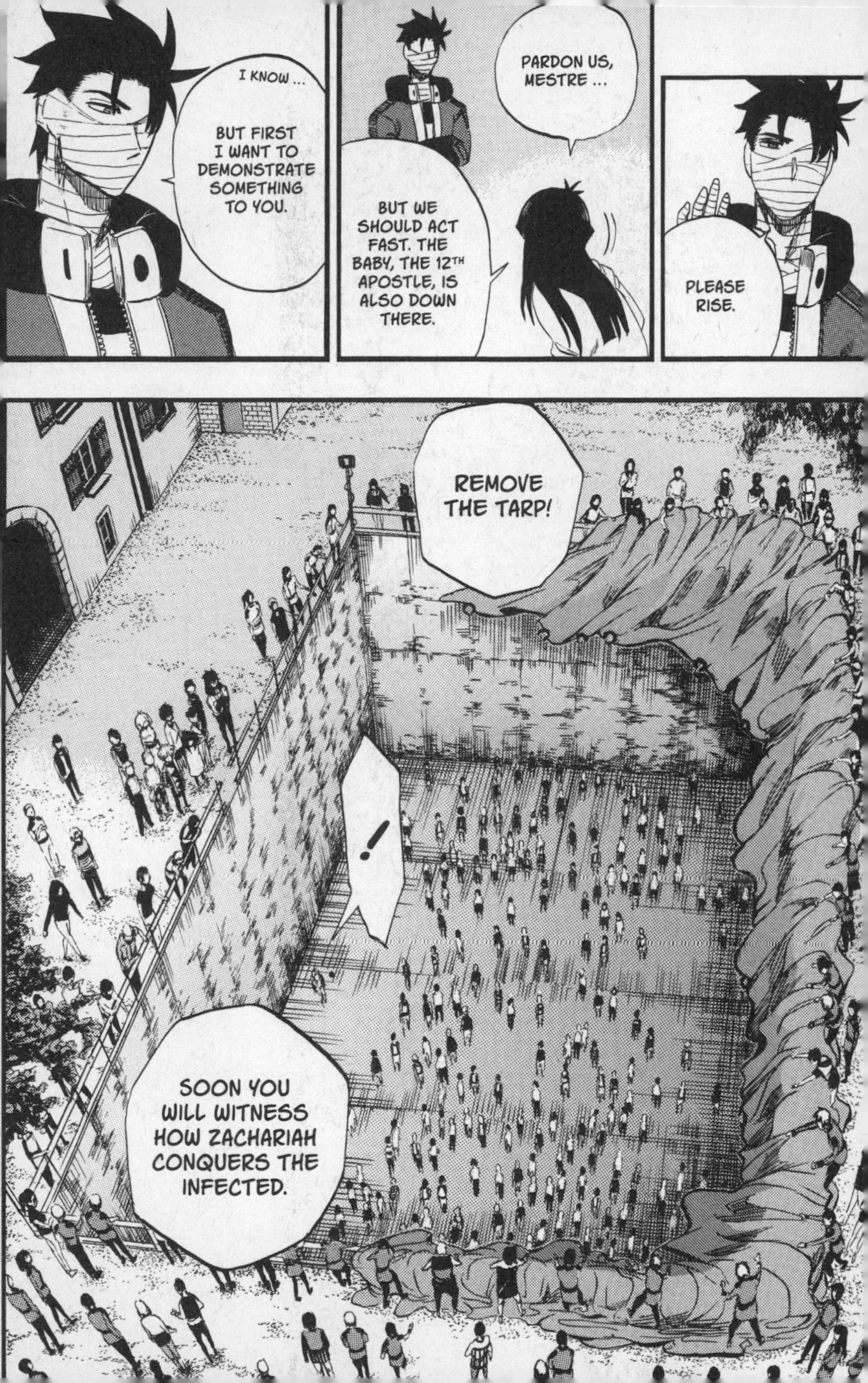
PLEASE RISE.
PARDON US, MESTRE ...
BUT WE SHOULD ACT FAST. THE BABY, THE 12TH APOSTLE, IS ALSO DOWN THERE.
I KNOW ...
BUT FIRST I WANT TO DEMONSTRATE SOMETHING TO YOU.
REMOVE THE TARP!
!
SOON YOU WILL WITNESS HOW ZACHARIAH CONQUERS THE INFECTED.

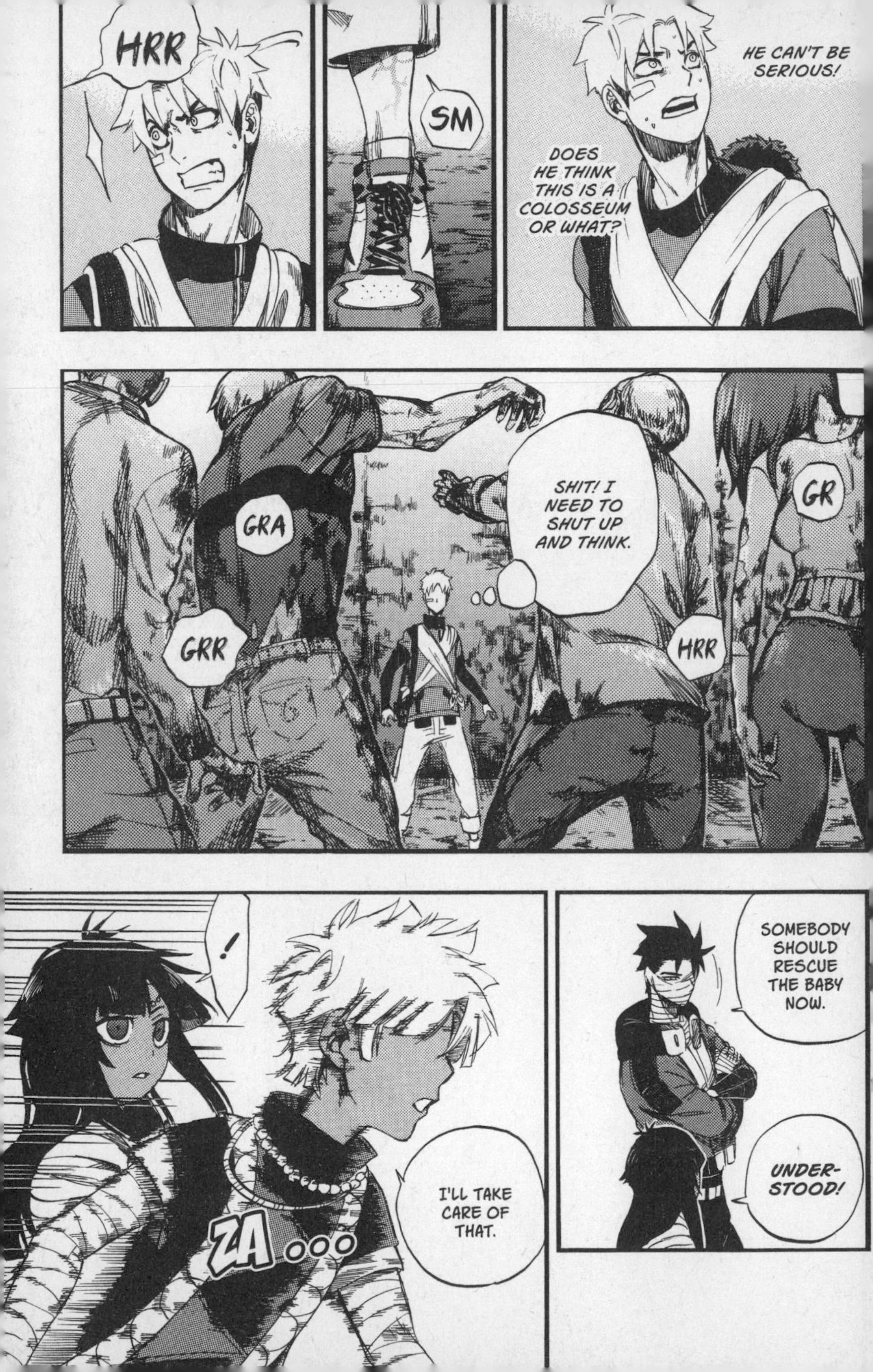
HE CAN'T BE SERIOUS!
DOES HE THINK THIS IS A COLOSSEUM OR WHAT?
SM
HRR
GR
SHIT! I NEED TO SHUT UP AND THINK.
GRA
HRR
GRR
SOMEBODY SHOULD RESCUE THE BABY NOW.
UNDER-STOOD!
!
I'LL TAKE CARE OF THAT.
ZA ...

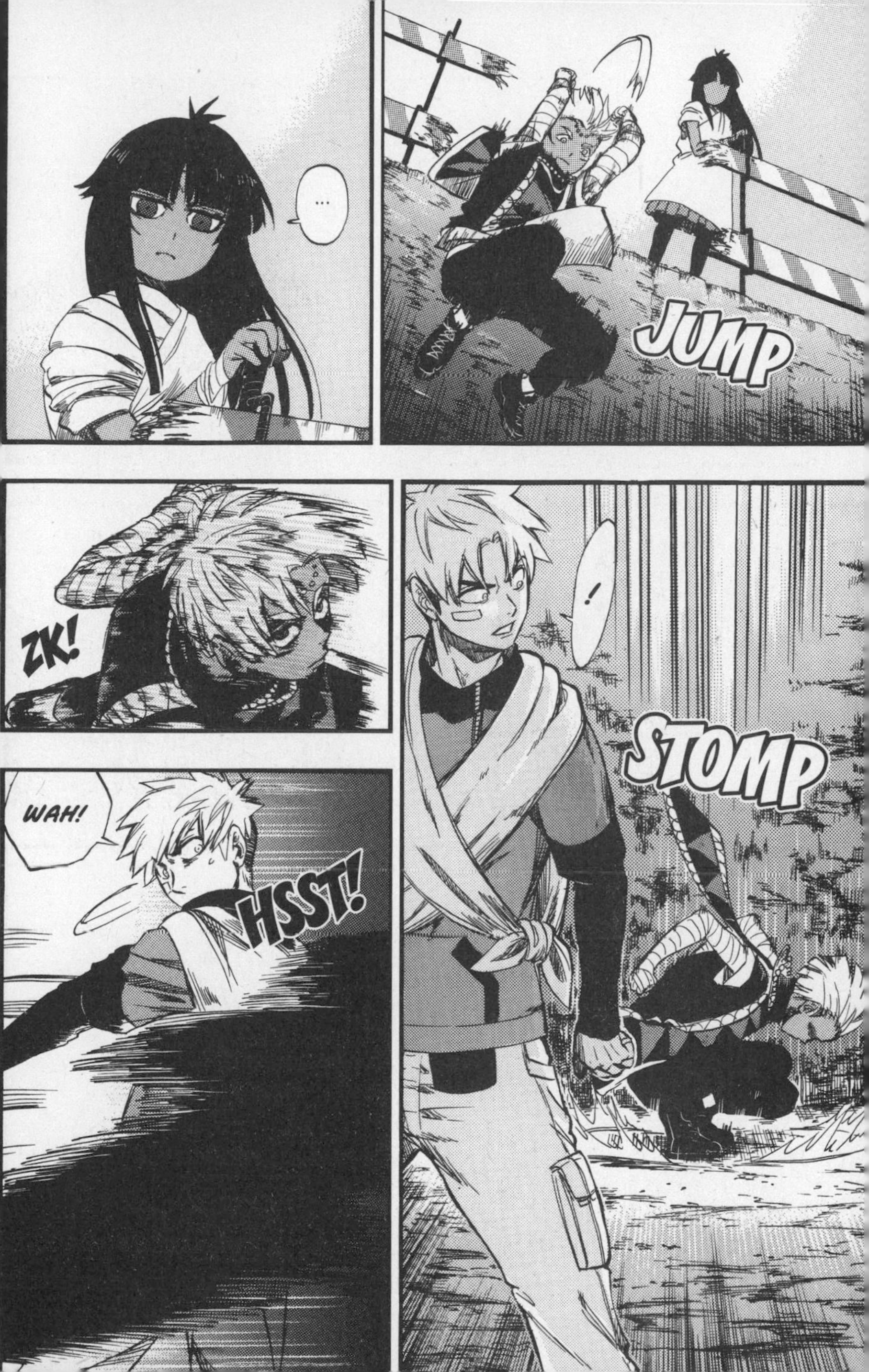
JUMP
...
!
STOMP
ZK!
WAH!
HSST!

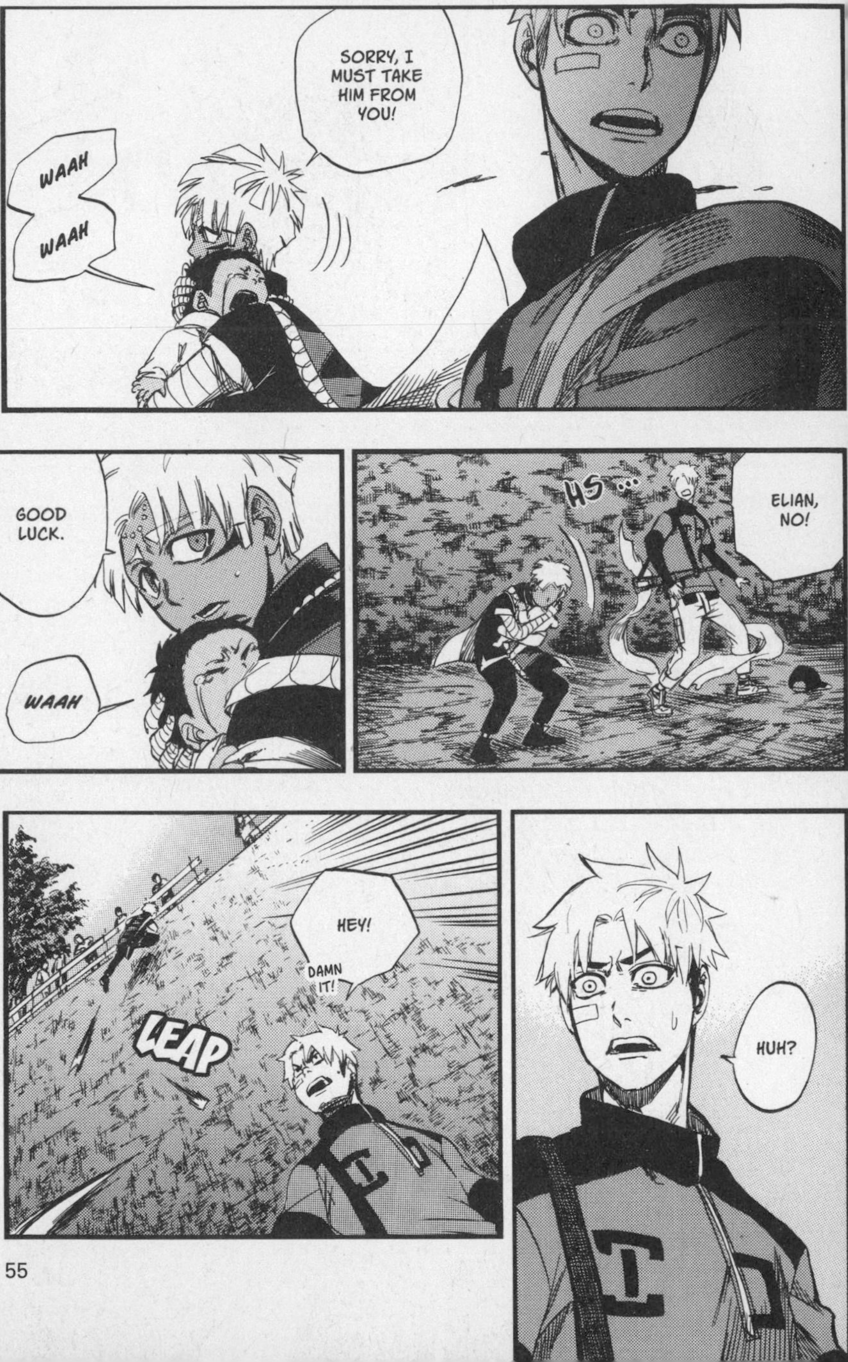
SORRY, I MUST TAKE HIM FROM YOU!
WAAH
WAAH
ELIAN, NO!
HS ...
GOOD LUCK.
WAAH
HUH?
HEY!
DAMN IT!
LEAP

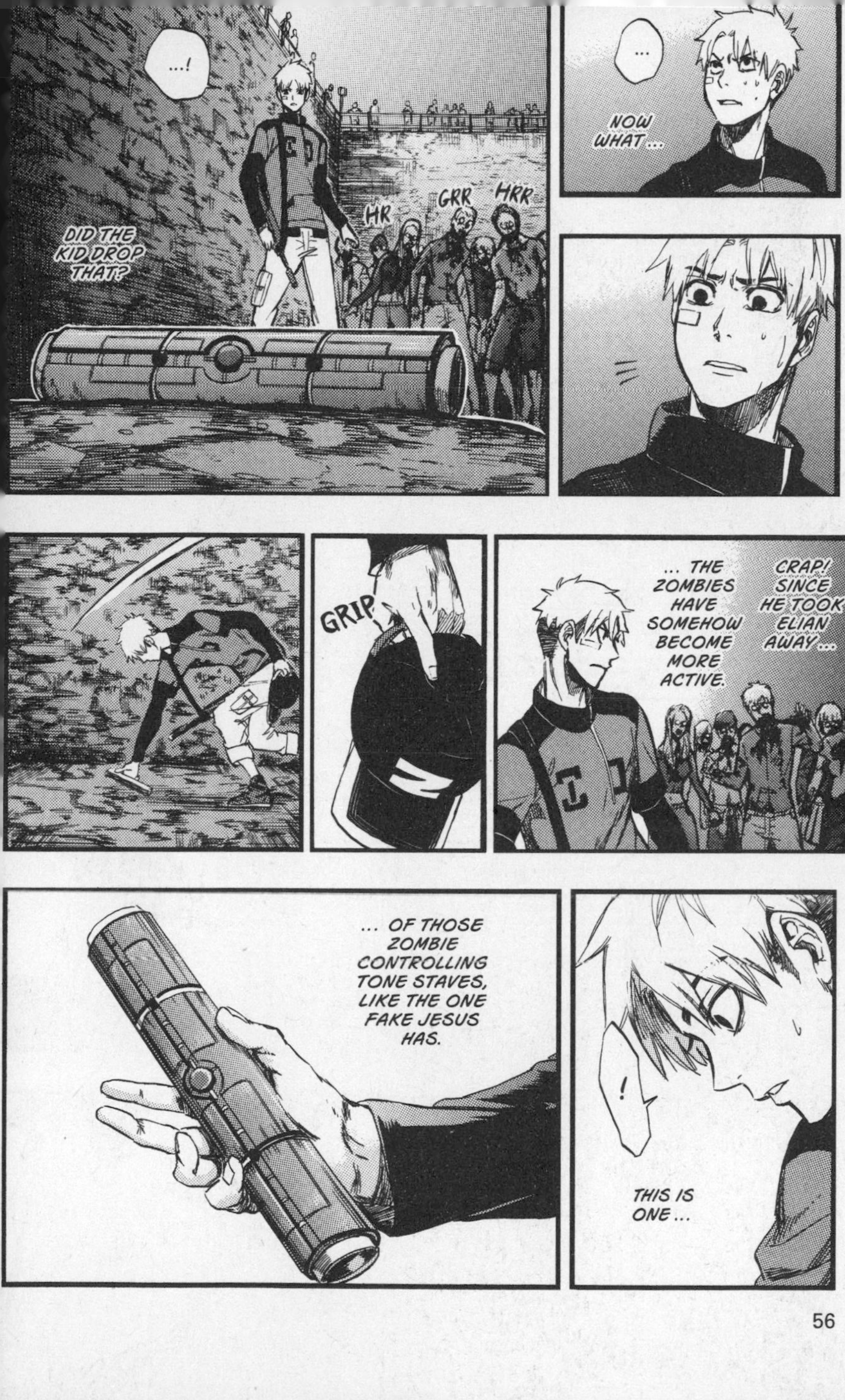
...
NOW WHAT ...
...!
HRR
GRR
HR
DID THE KID DROP THAT?
CRAP! SINCE HE TOOK ELIAN AWAY ...
... THE ZOMBIES HAVE SOMEHOW BECOME MORE ACTIVE.
GRIP
!
THIS IS ONE ...
... OF THOSE ZOMBIE CONTROLLING TONE STAVES, LIKE THE ONE FAKE JESUS HAS.

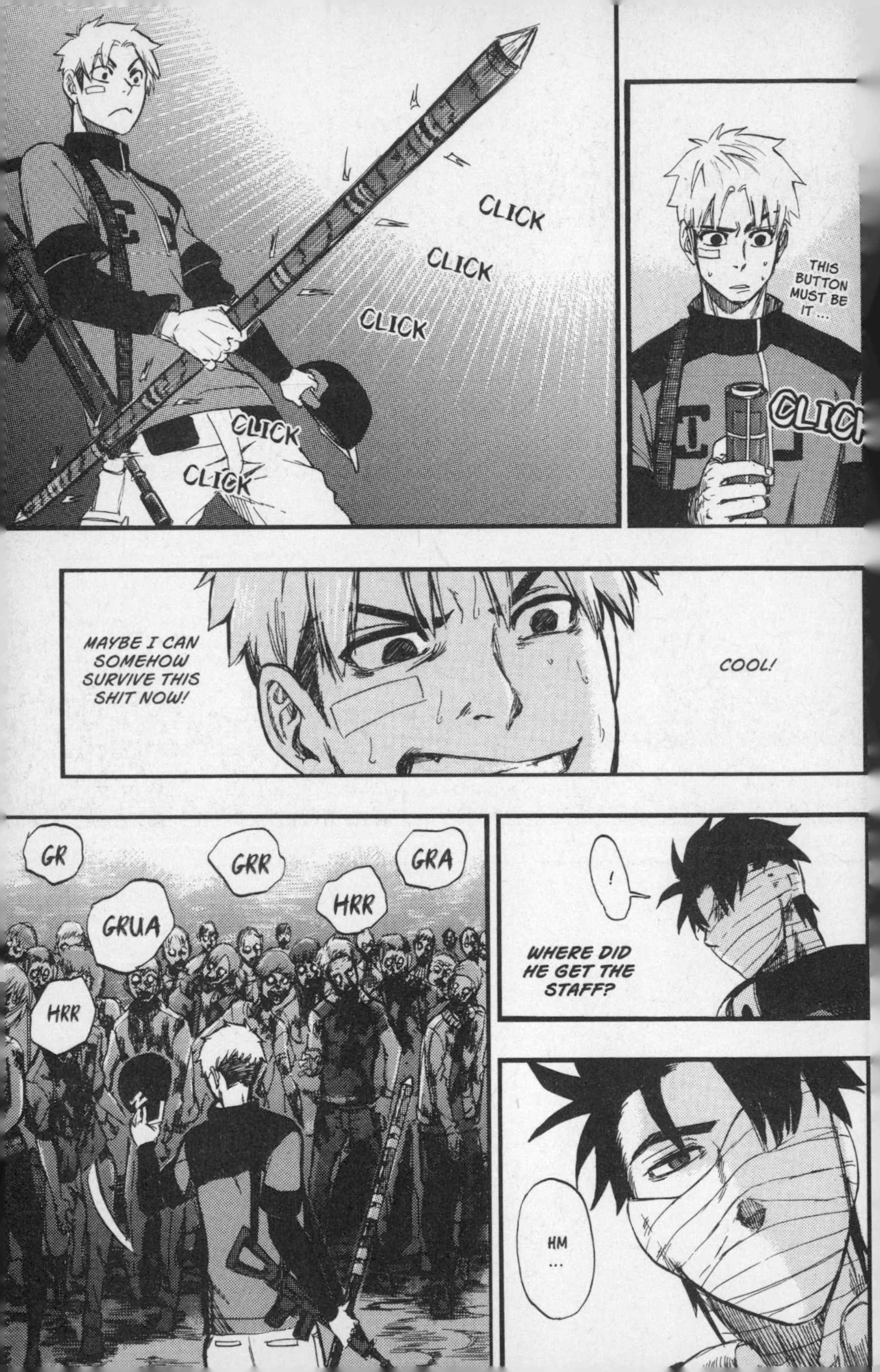
THIS BUTTON MUST BE IT ...
CLICK
CLICK
CLICK
CLICK
CLICK
CLICK
COOL!
MAYBE I CAN SOMEHOW SURVIVE THIS SHIT NOW!
!
WHERE DID HE GET THE STAFF?
HM ...
GRA
GRR
GR
HRR
GRUA
HRR

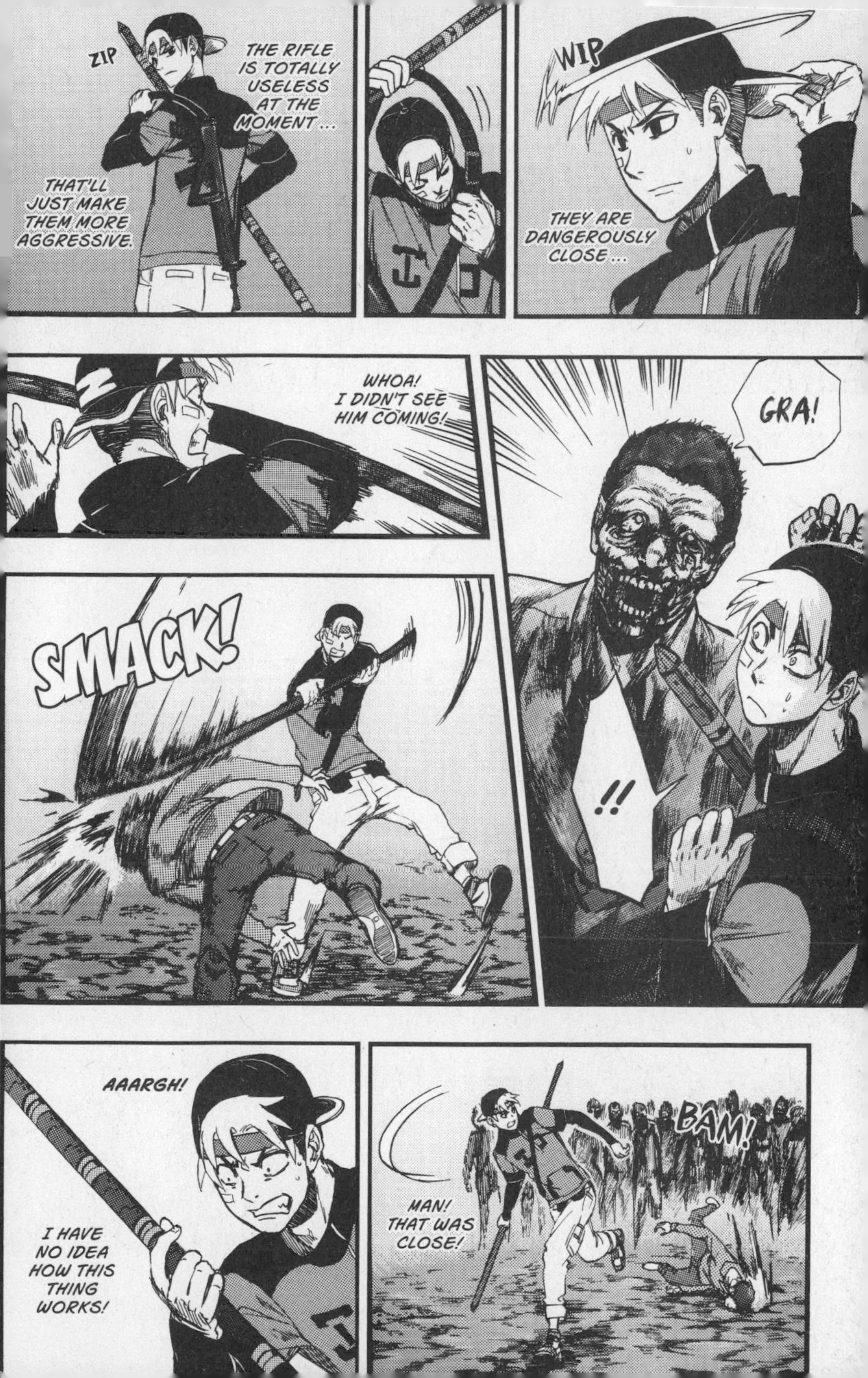
WIP
THEY ARE DANGEROUSLY CLOSE ...
ZIP
THE RIFLE IS TOTALLY USELESS AT THE MOMENT ...
THAT'LL JUST MAKE THEM MORE AGGRESSIVE.
GRA!
!!
WHOA! I DIDN'T SEE HIM COMING!
SMACK!
BAM!
MAN! THAT WAS CLOSE!
AAARGH!
I HAVE NO IDEA HOW THIS THING WORKS!

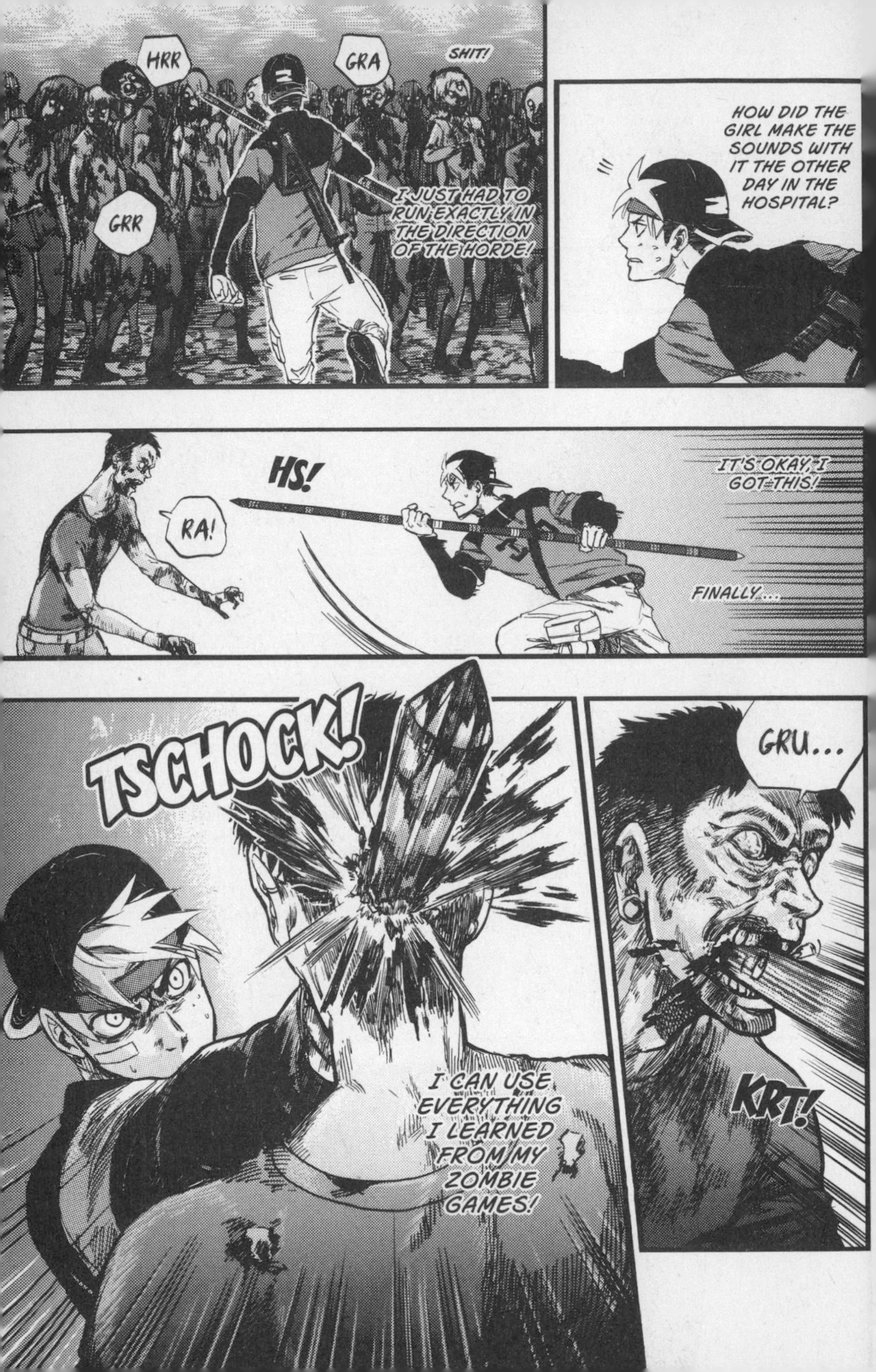
HOW DID THE GIRL MAKE THE SOUNDS WITH IT THE OTHER DAY IN THE HOSPITAL?
SHIT!
GRA
HRR
I JUST HAD TO RUN EXACTLY IN THE DIRECTION OF THE HORDE!
GRR
IT'S OKAY, I GOT THIS!
FINALLY...
HS!
RA!
GRU...
KRT!
TSCHOCK!
I CAN USE EVERYTHING I LEARNED FROM MY ZOMBIE GAMES!

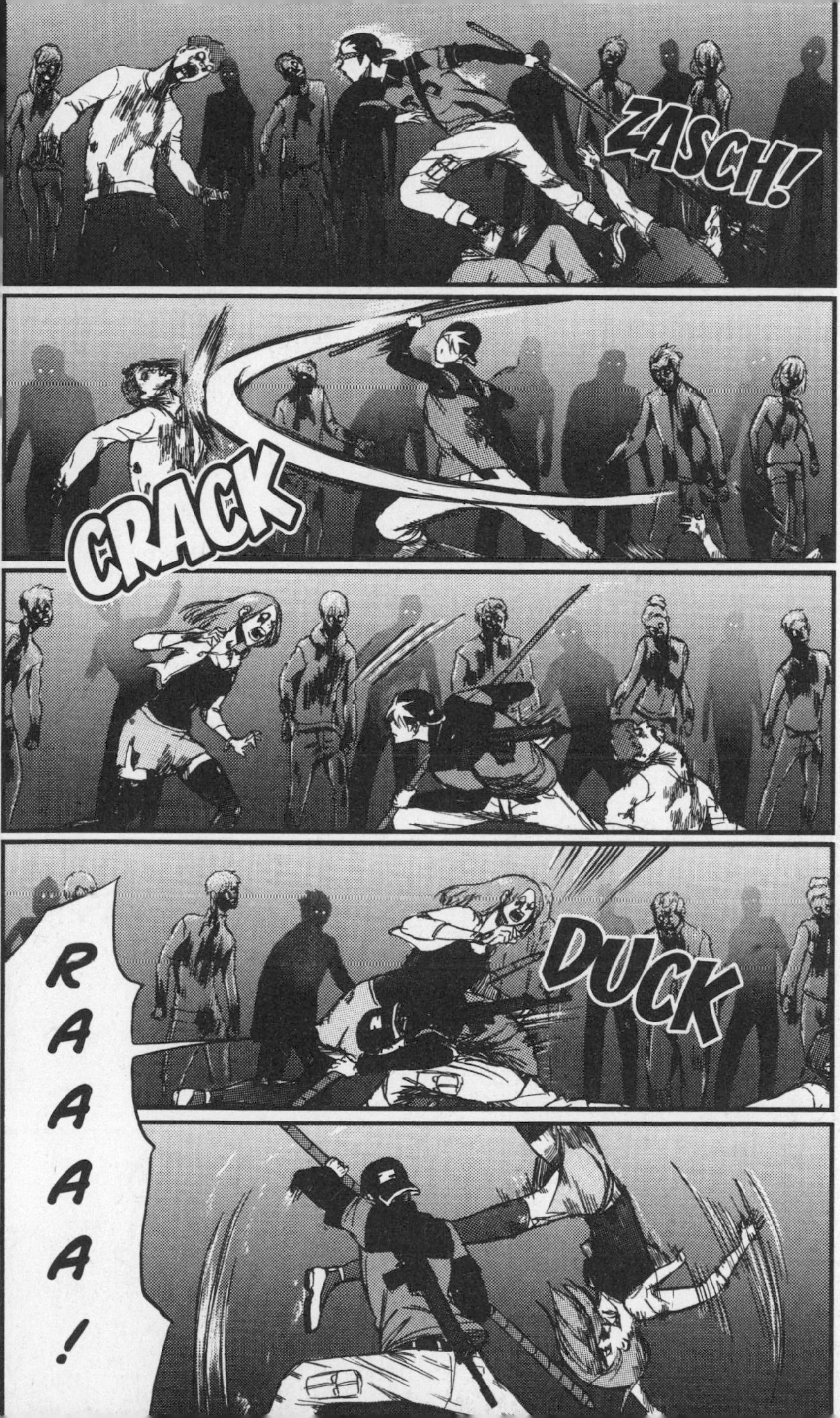
ZASCH!
CRACK
DUCK
RAAAAA!

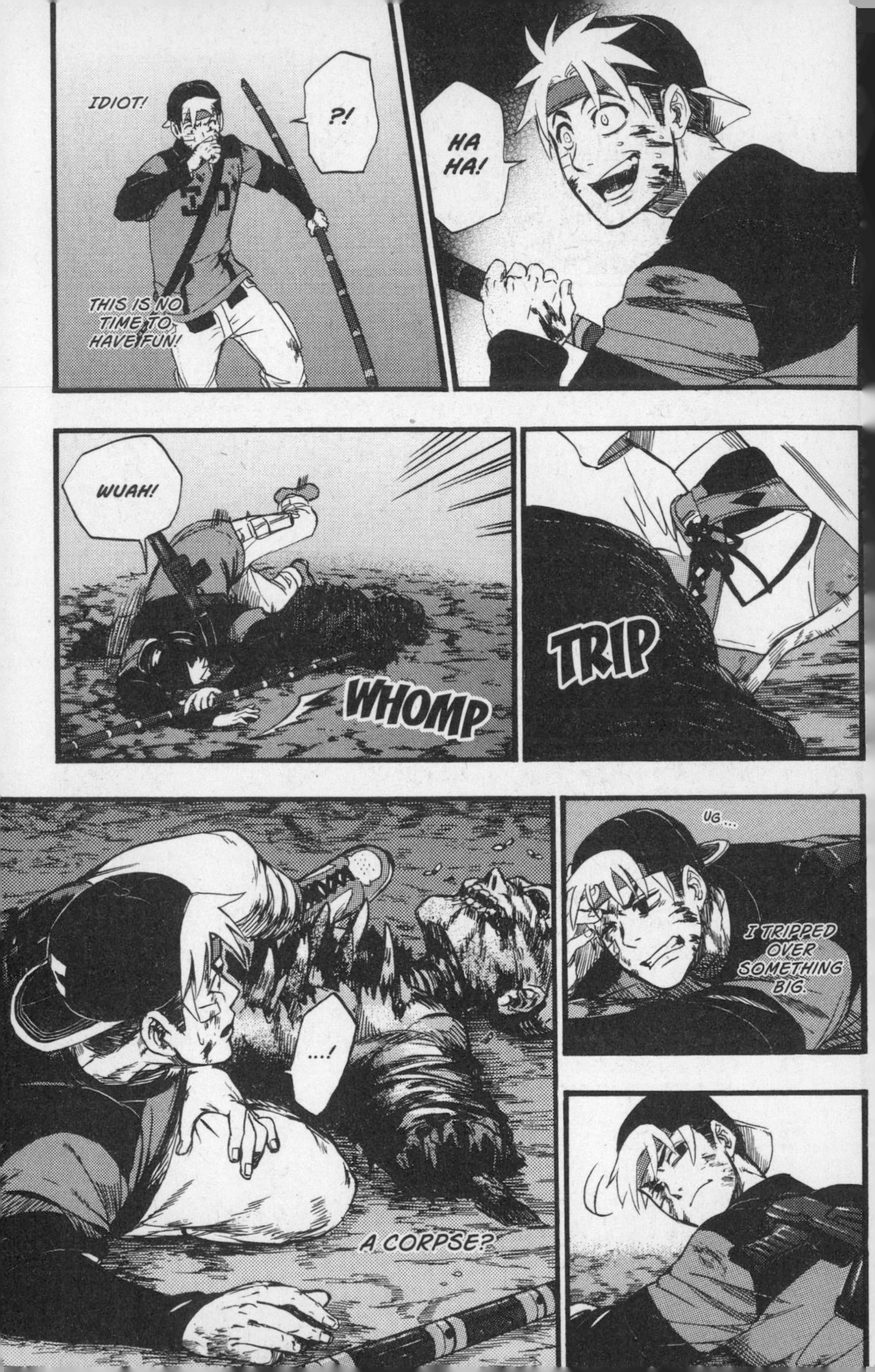
HA HA!
?!
IDIOT!
THIS IS NO TIME TO HAVE FUN!
TRIP
WUAH!
WHOMP
UG ...
I TRIPPED OVER SOMETHING BIG.
...!
A CORPSE?

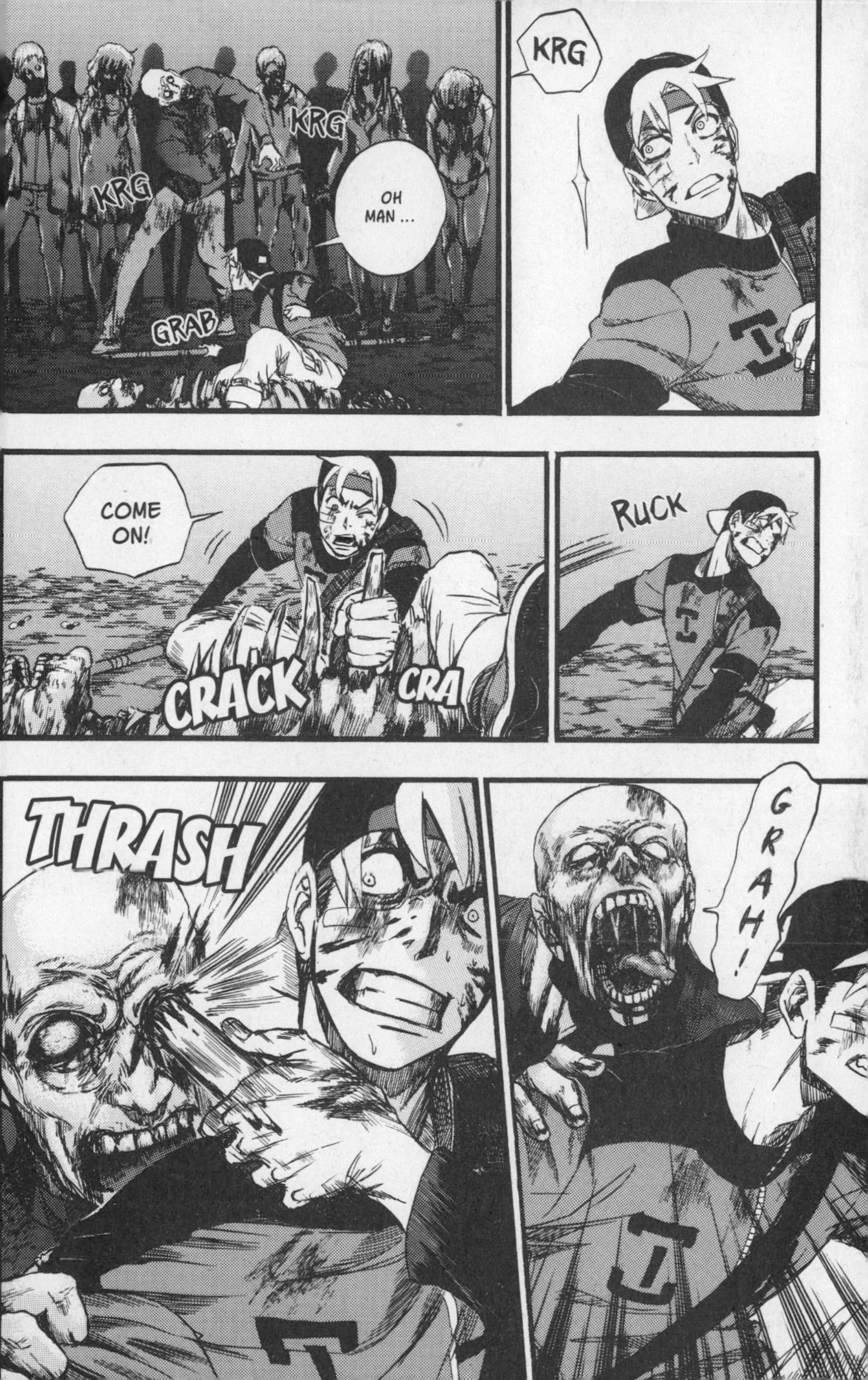
KRG
KRG
OH MAN ...
KRG
GRAB
RUCK
COME ON!
CRA
CRACK
GRAH!
THRASH

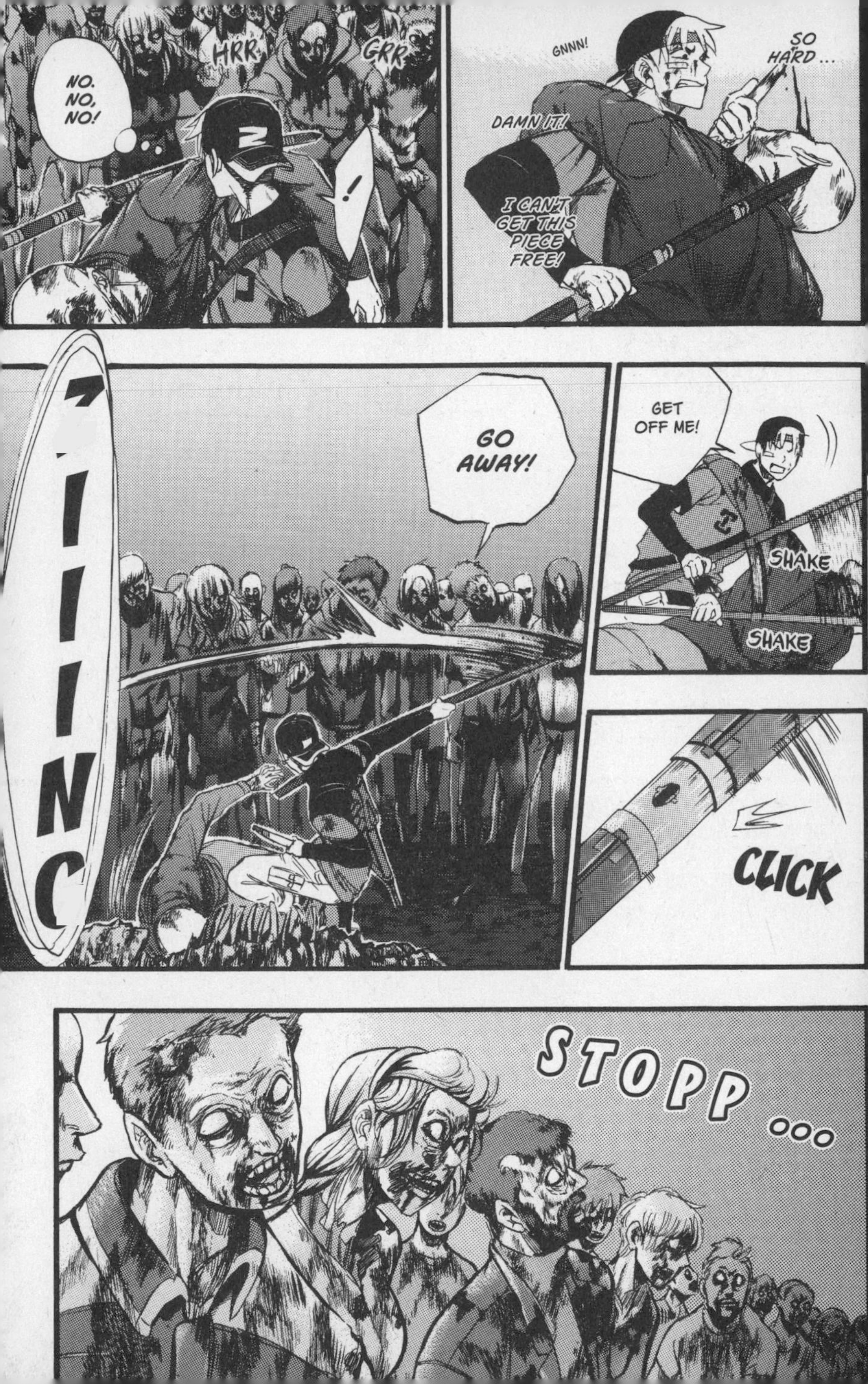
SO HARD...
GNNN!
DAMN IT!
I CAN'T GET THIS PIECE FREE!
GRR
HRR
!
NO. NO, NO!
GET OFF ME!
SHAKE
SHAKE
CLICK
GO AWAY!
ZIINC
STOPP ...

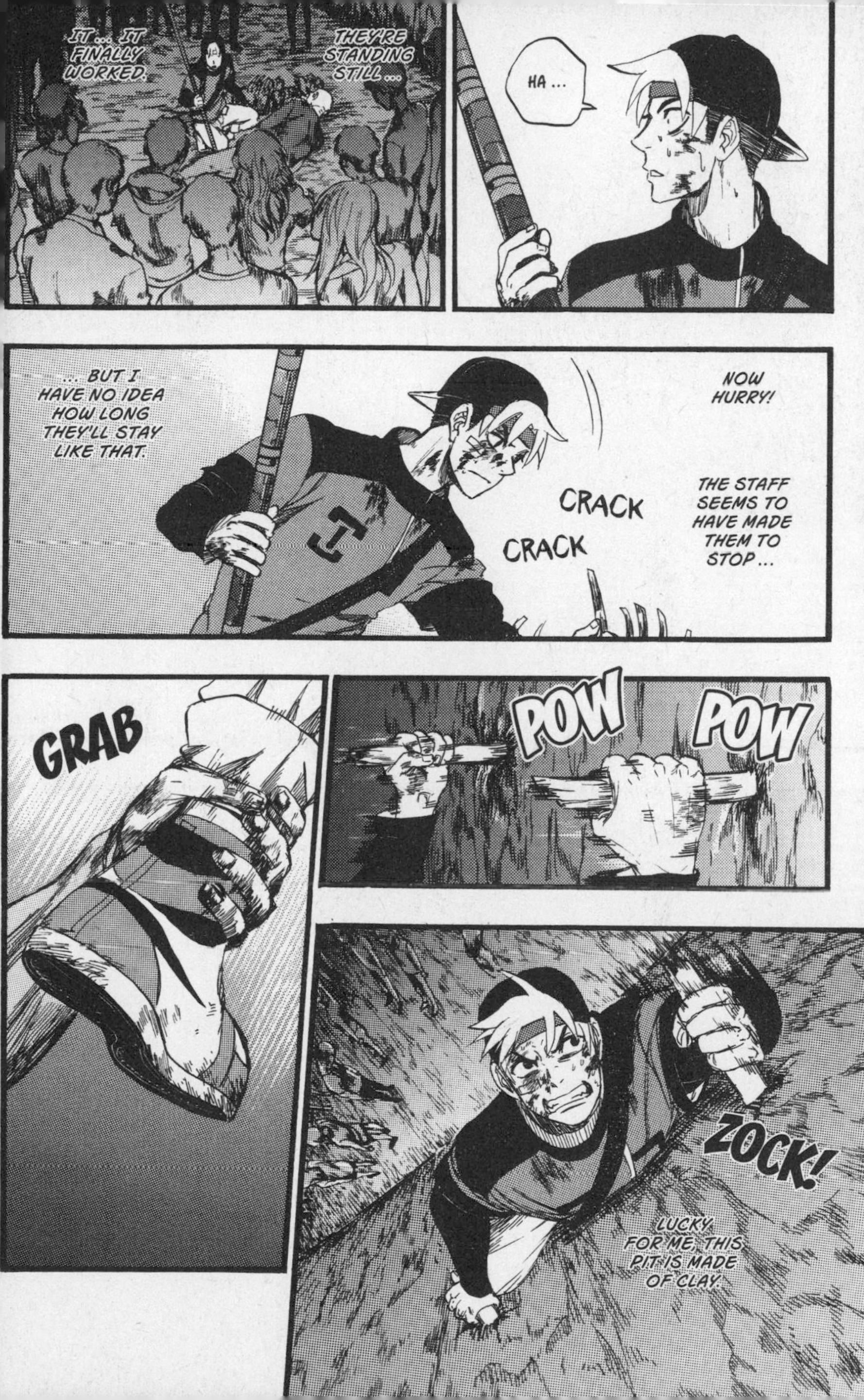
HA ...
THEY'RE STANDING STILL ...
IT ... IT FINALLY WORKED.
NOW HURRY!
THE STAFF SEEMS TO HAVE MADE THEM TO STOP ...
CRACK
CRACK
... BUT I HAVE NO IDEA HOW LONG THEY'LL STAY LIKE THAT.
POW
POW
ZOCK!
LUCKY FOR ME, THIS PIT IS MADE OF CLAY.
GRAB

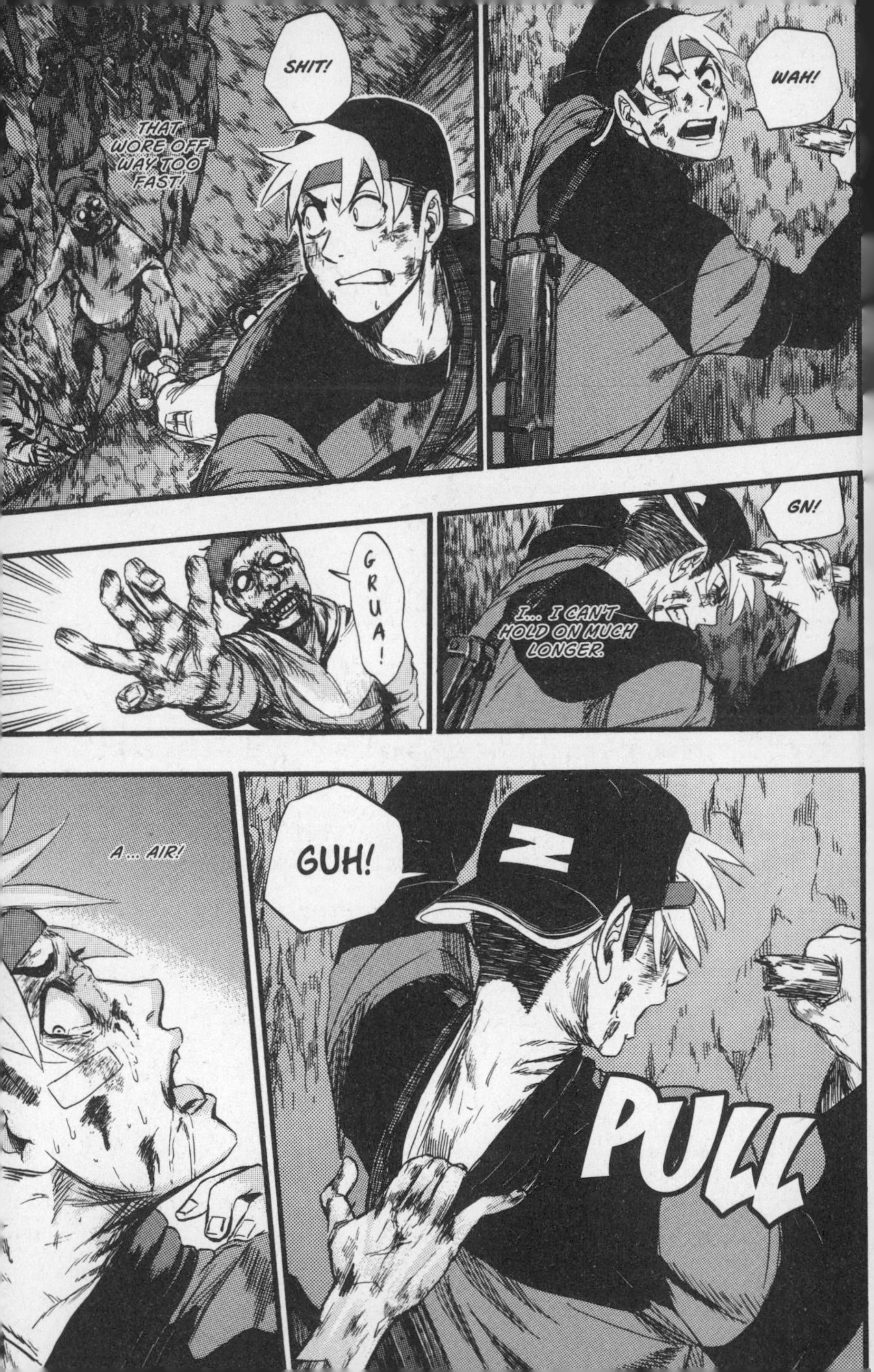
WAH!
SHIT!
THAT WORE OFF WAY TOO FAST!
GN!
I... I CAN'T HOLD ON MUCH LONGER.
GRUA!
GUH!
PULL
A... AIR!

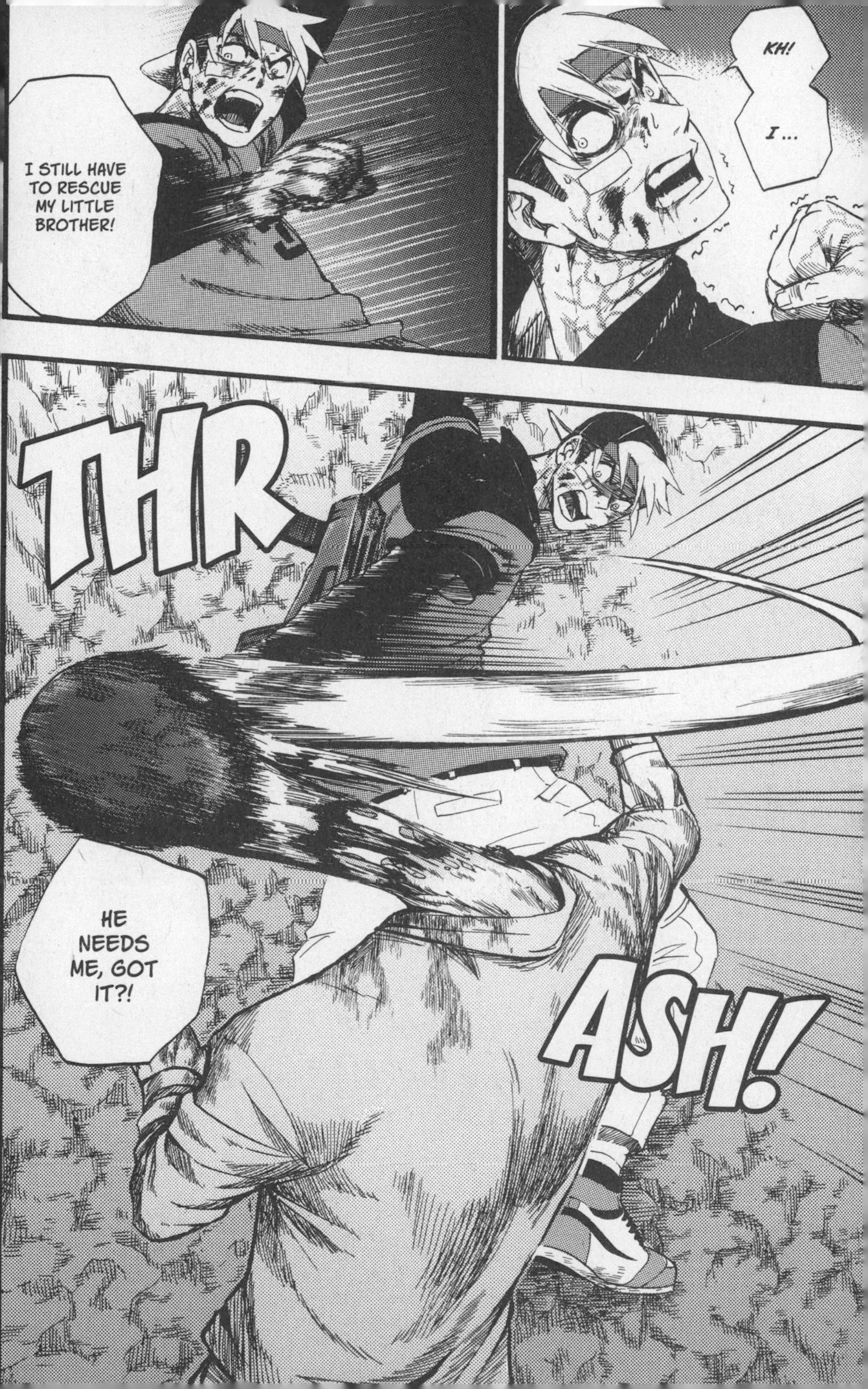
KH!
I...
I STILL HAVE TO RESCUE MY LITTLE BROTHER!
THR
ASH!
HE NEEDS ME, GOT IT?!

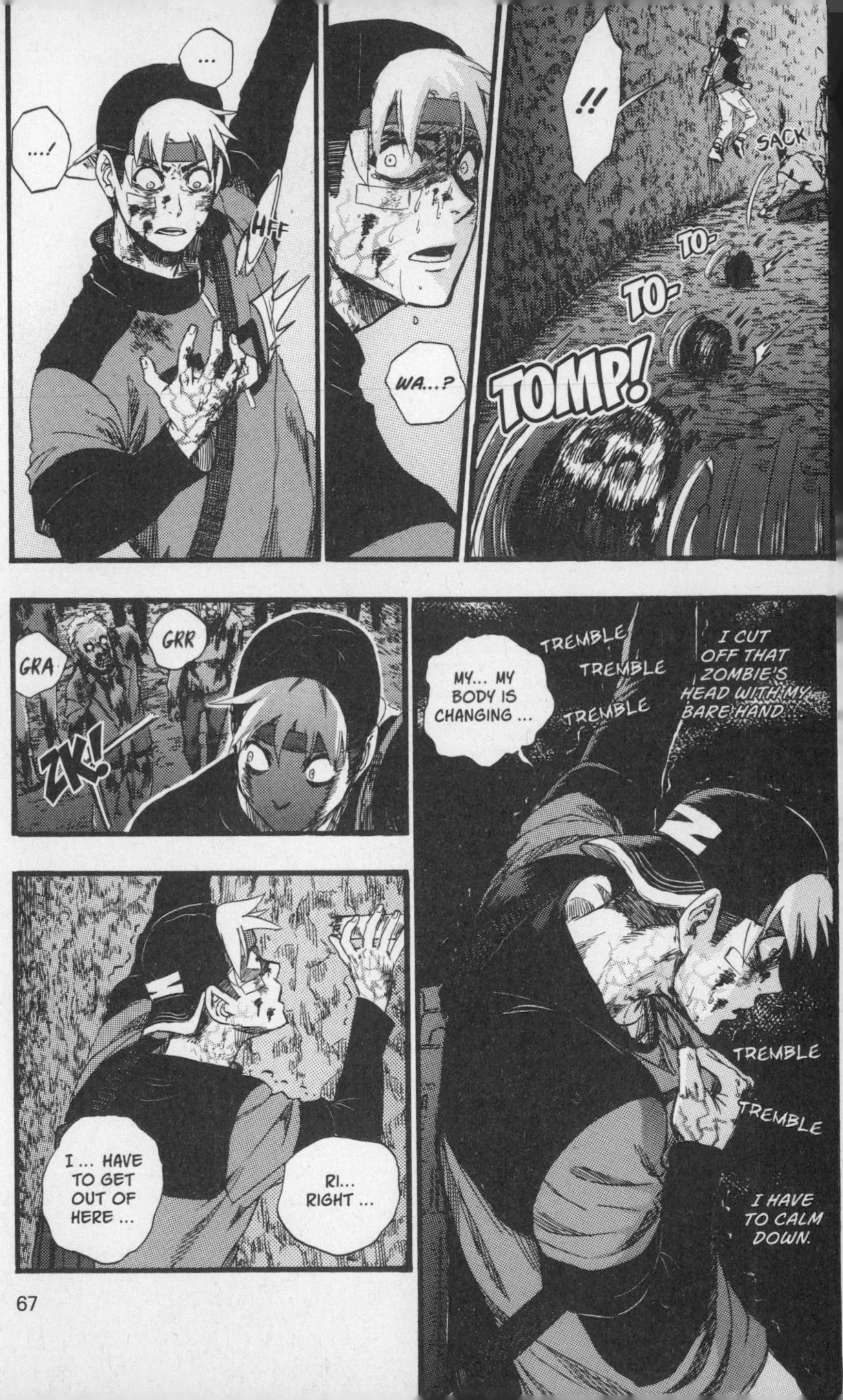
!!
SACK
TO-
TO-
TOMP!
WA...?
...
...!
HFF
I CUT OFF THAT ZOMBIE'S HEAD WITH MY BARE HAND
TREMBLE
TREMBLE
TREMBLE
MY... MY BODY IS CHANGING ...
TREMBLE
TREMBLE
I HAVE TO CALM DOWN.
GRR
GRA
ZK!
RI... RIGHT ...
I ... HAVE TO GET OUT OF HERE ...

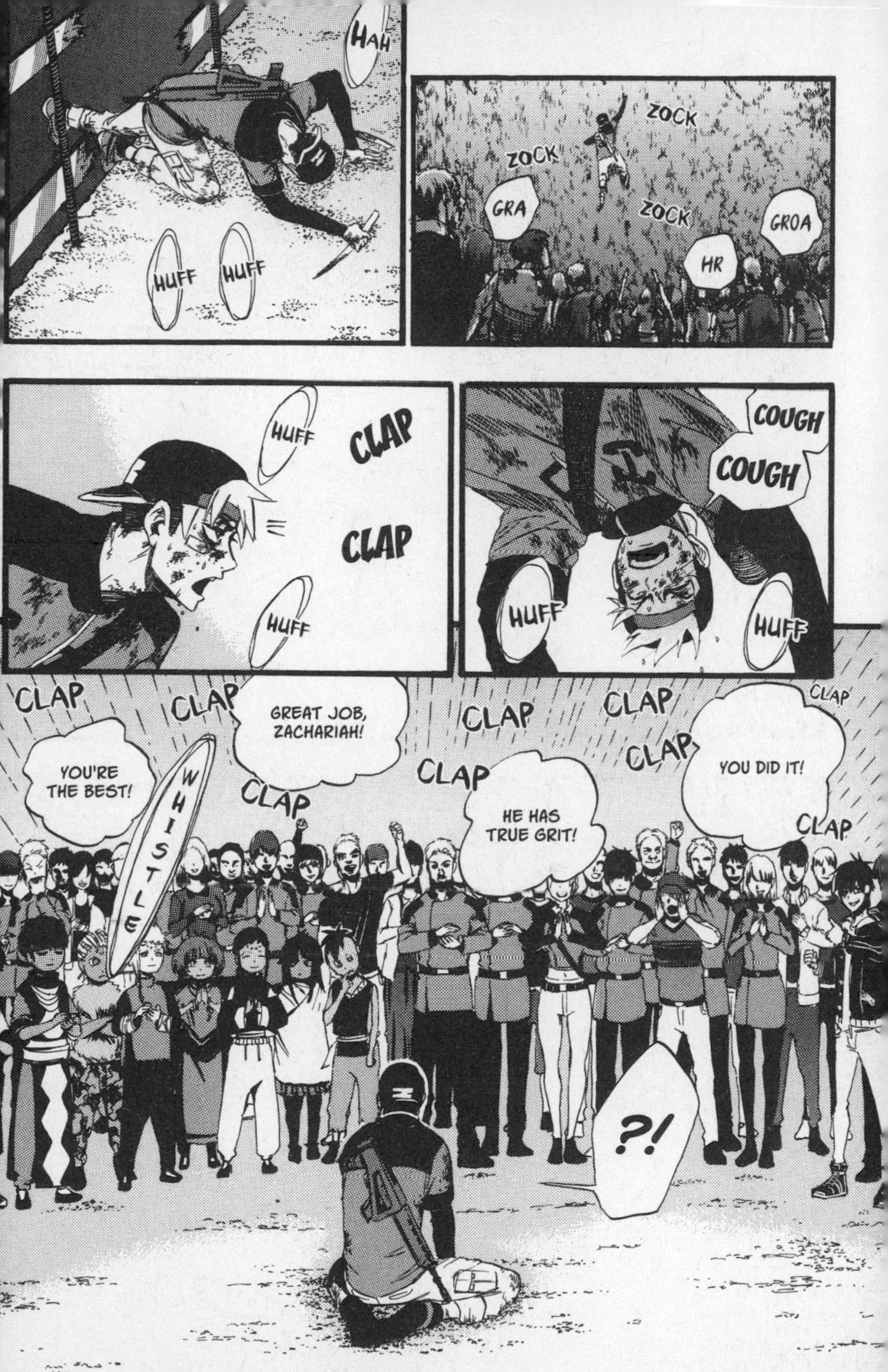
ZOCK
ZOCK
GROA
ZOCK
GRA
HR
HAH
HUFF
HUFF
COUGH
COUGH
HUFF
HUFF
HUFF
CLAP
CLAP
HUFF
CLAP
YOU DID IT!
CLAP
CLAP
CLAP
CLAP
HE HAS TRUE GRIT!
CLAP
CLAP
GREAT JOB, ZACHARIAH!
CLAP
WHISTLE
YOU'RE THE BEST!
CLAP
?!

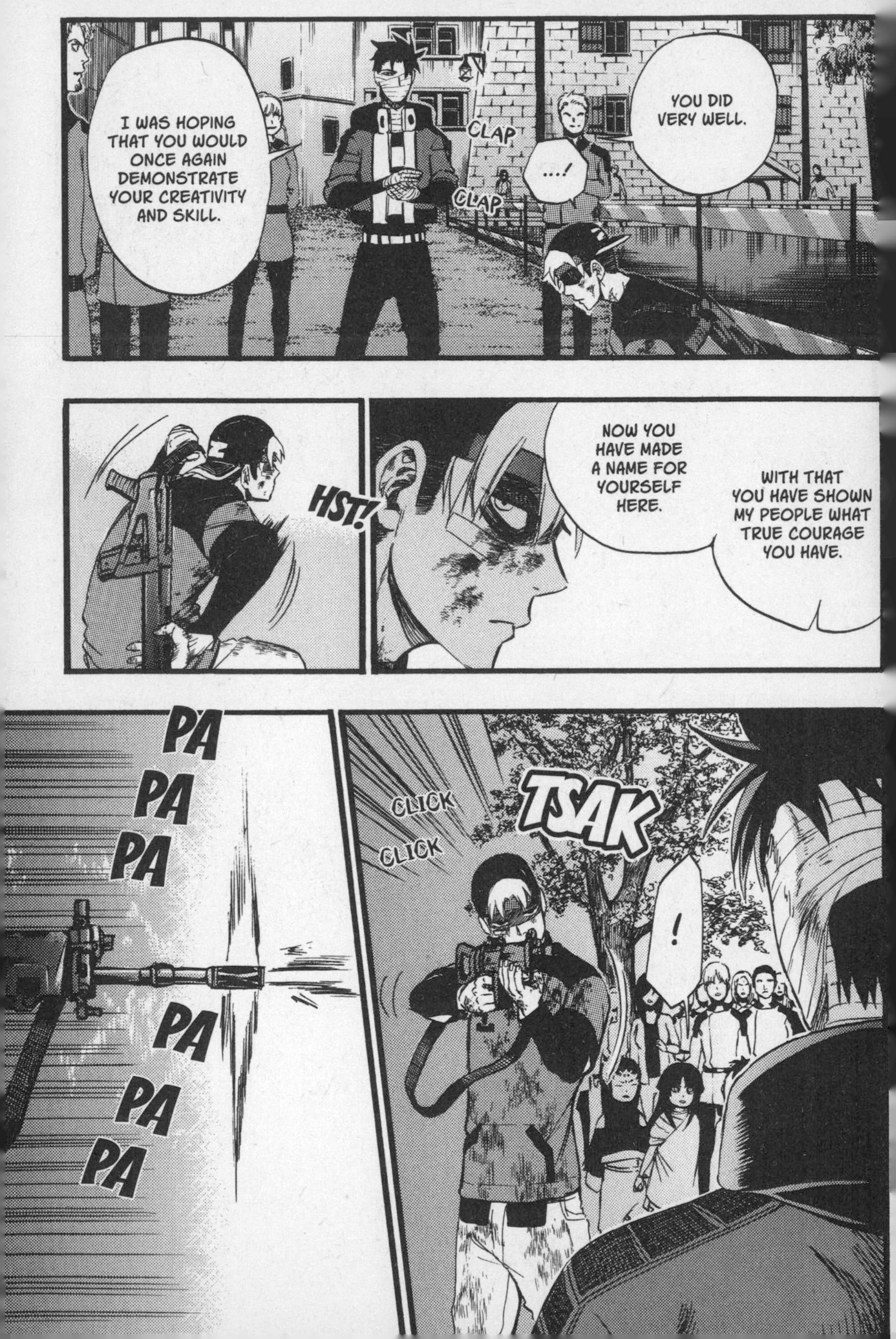
YOU DID VERY WELL.
CLAP
...!
CLAP
I WAS HOPING THAT YOU WOULD ONCE AGAIN DEMONSTRATE YOUR CREATIVITY AND SKILL.
NOW YOU HAVE MADE A NAME FOR YOURSELF HERE.
WITH THAT YOU HAVE SHOWN MY PEOPLE WHAT TRUE COURAGE YOU HAVE.
HST!
TSAK
CLICK
CLICK
!
PA PA PA
PA PA PA

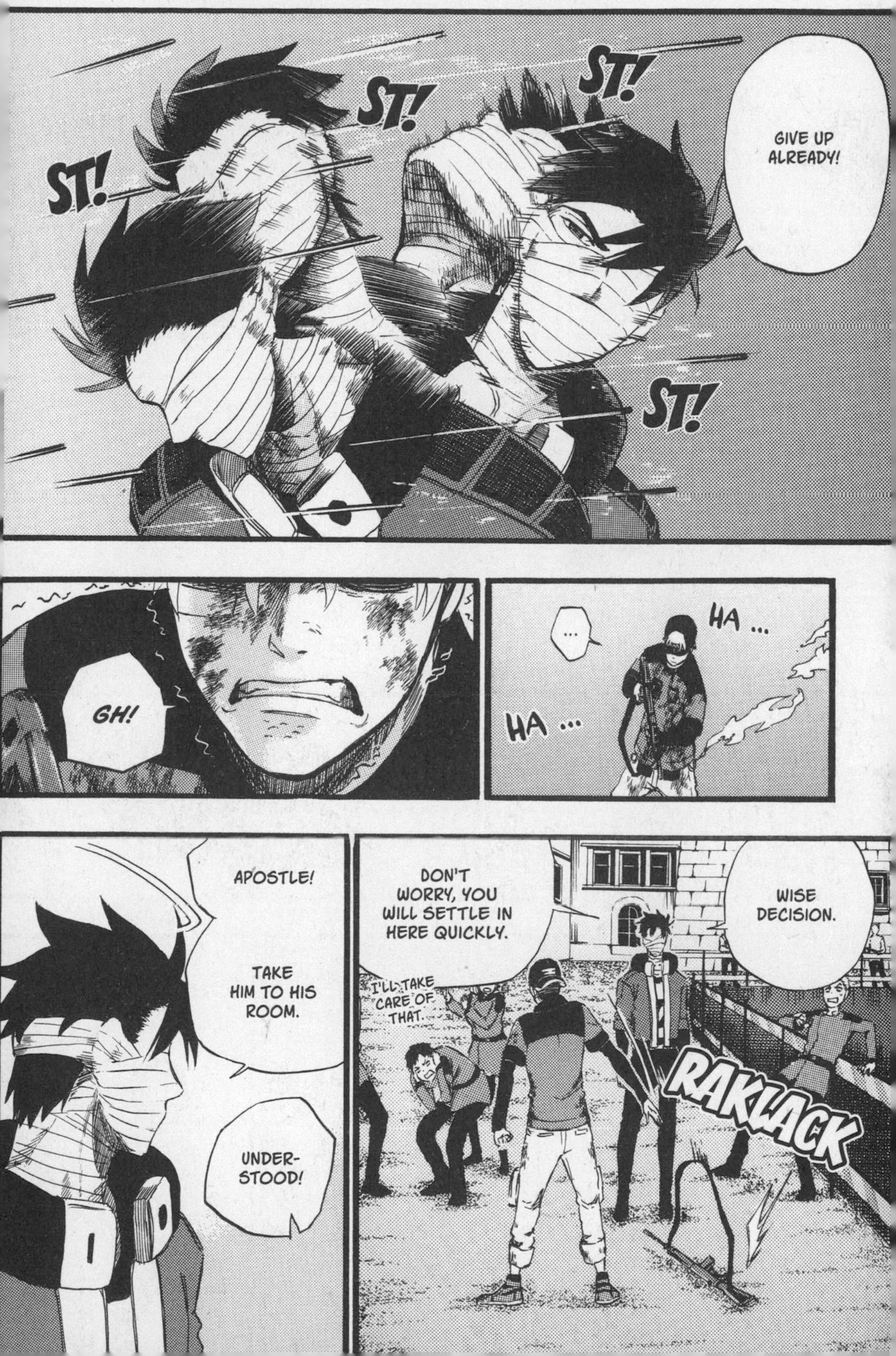
GIVE UP ALREADY!
ST!
ST!
ST!
ST!
...
HA ...
HA ...
GH!
WISE DECISION.
DON'T WORRY, YOU WILL SETTLE IN HERE QUICKLY.
I'LL TAKE CARE OF THAT.
RAKLACK
APOSTLE!
TAKE HIM TO HIS ROOM.
UNDER-STOOD!

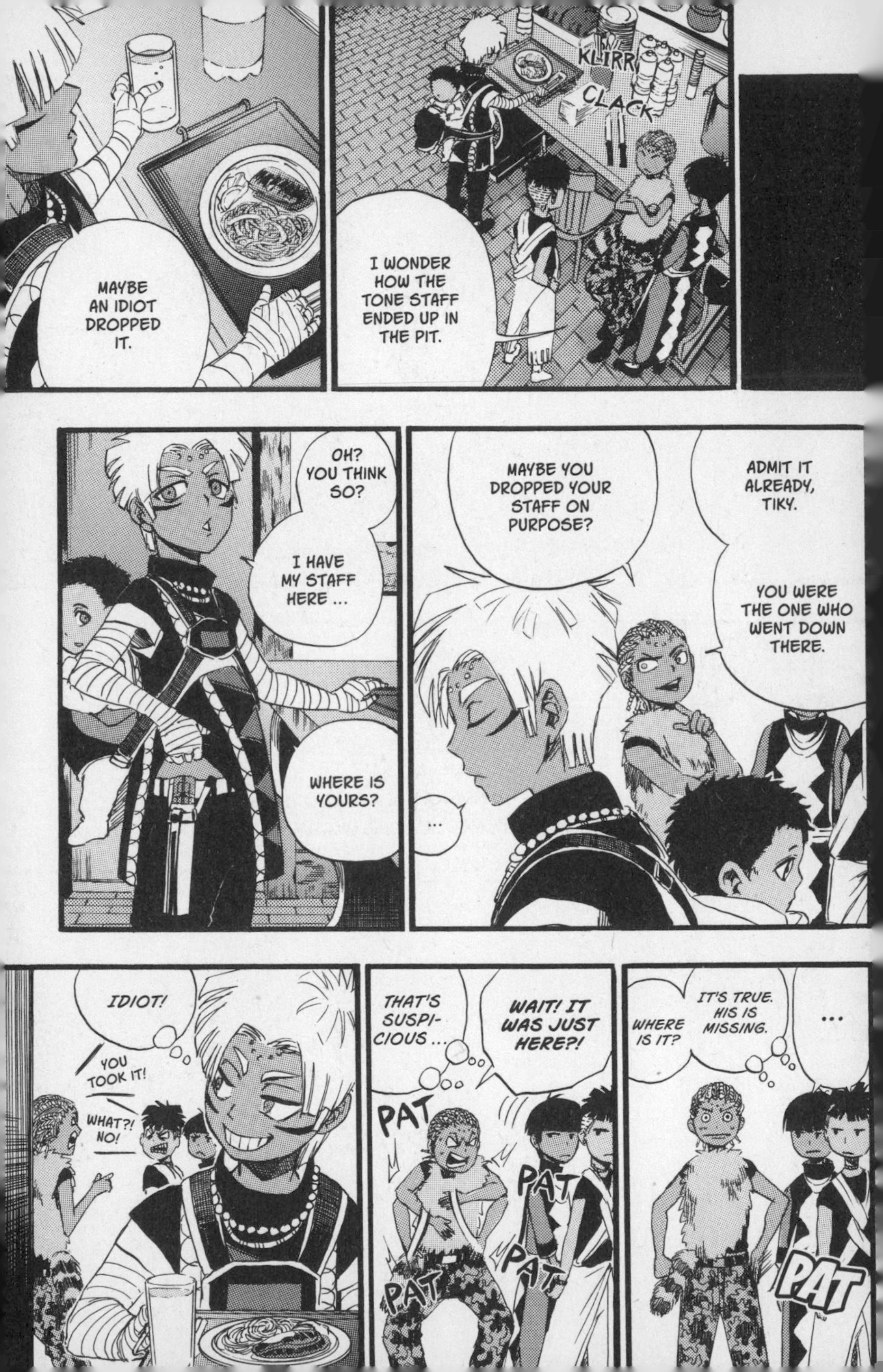
KLIRR
CLACK
I WONDER HOW THE TONE STAFF ENDED UP IN THE PIT.
MAYBE AN IDIOT DROPPED IT.
ADMIT IT ALREADY, TIKY.
YOU WERE THE ONE WHO WENT DOWN THERE.
MAYBE YOU DROPPED YOUR STAFF ON PURPOSE?
...
OH? YOU THINK SO?
I HAVE MY STAFF HERE ...
WHERE IS YOURS?
...
IT'S TRUE. HIS IS MISSING.
WHERE IS IT?
PAT
WAIT! IT WAS JUST HERE?!
THAT'S SUSPICIOUS ...
PAT
PAT
PAT
PAT
IDIOT!
YOU TOOK IT!
WHAT?! NO!

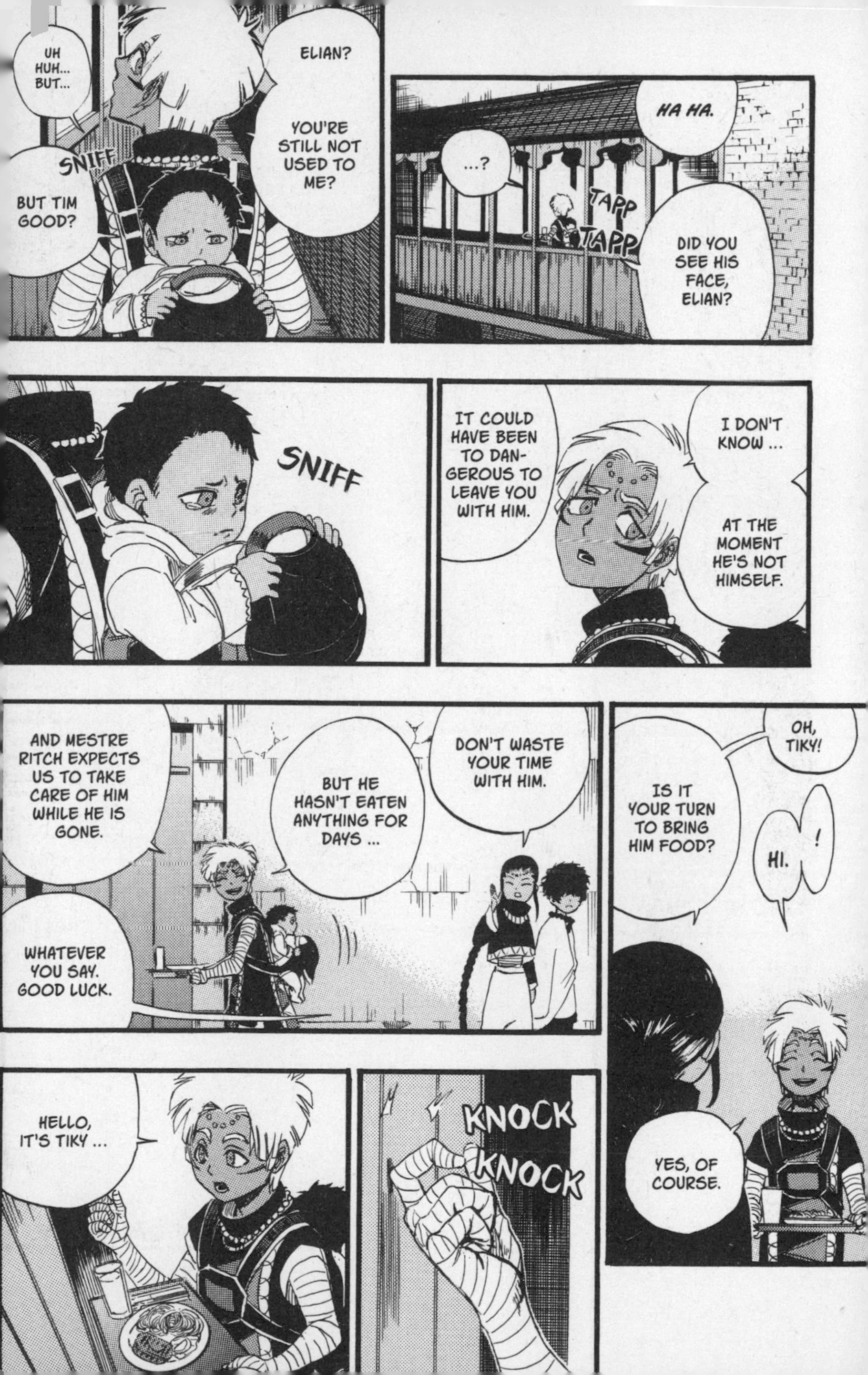
HA HA.
...?
TAPP TAPP
DID YOU SEE HIS FACE, ELIAN?
ELIAN?
YOU'RE STILL NOT USED TO ME?
UH HUH... BUT...
SNIFF
BUT TIM GOOD?
I DON'T KNOW ...
AT THE MOMENT HE'S NOT HIMSELF.
IT COULD HAVE BEEN TO DAN-GEROUS TO LEAVE YOU WITH HIM.
SNIFF
OH, TIKY!
IS IT YOUR TURN TO BRING HIM FOOD?
HI.
!
YES, OF COURSE.
DON'T WASTE YOUR TIME WITH HIM.
BUT HE HASN'T EATEN ANYTHING FOR DAYS ...
AND MESTRE RITCH EXPECTS US TO TAKE CARE OF HIM WHILE HE IS GONE.
WHATEVER YOU SAY. GOOD LUCK.
KNOCK KNOCK
HELLO, IT'S TIKY ...

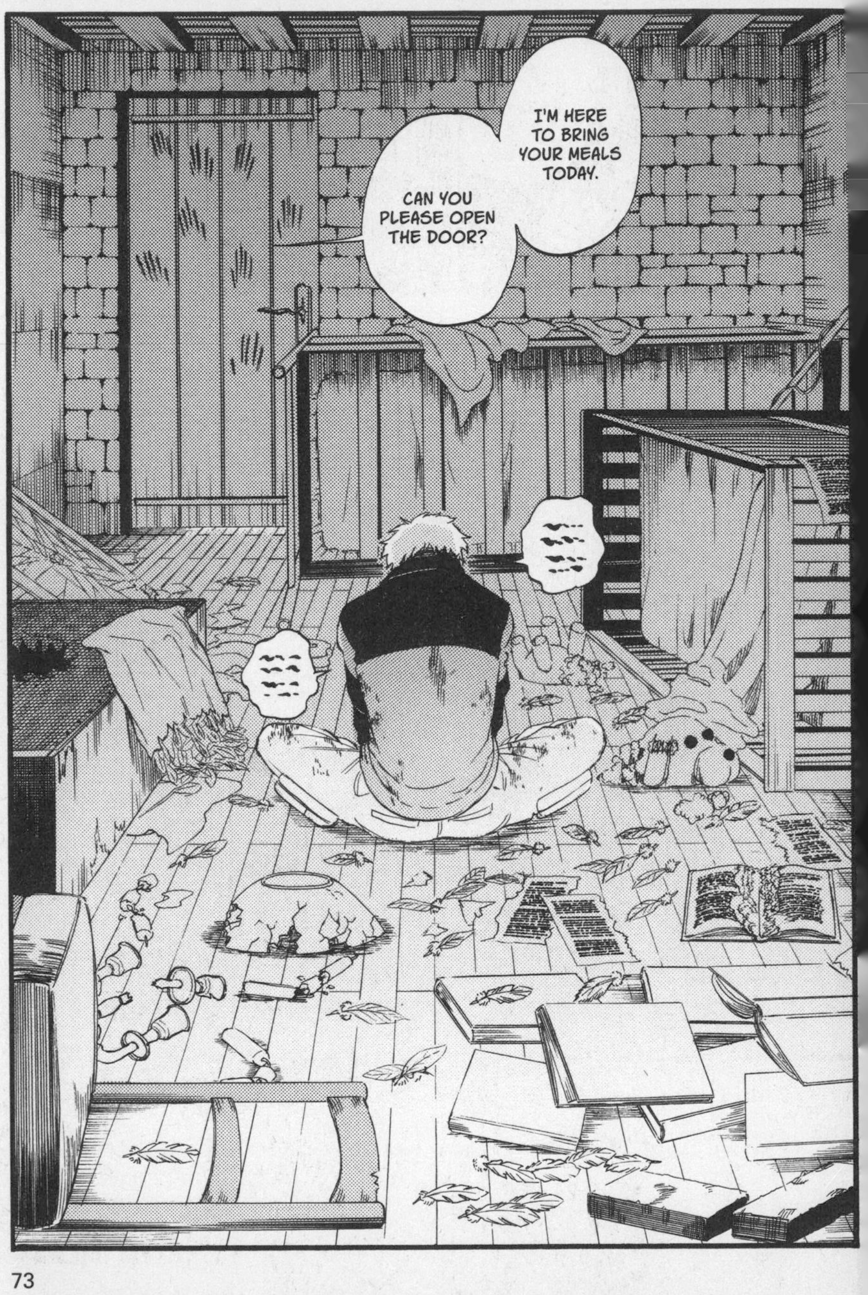
I'M HERE TO BRING YOUR MEALS TODAY.
CAN YOU PLEASE OPEN THE DOOR?

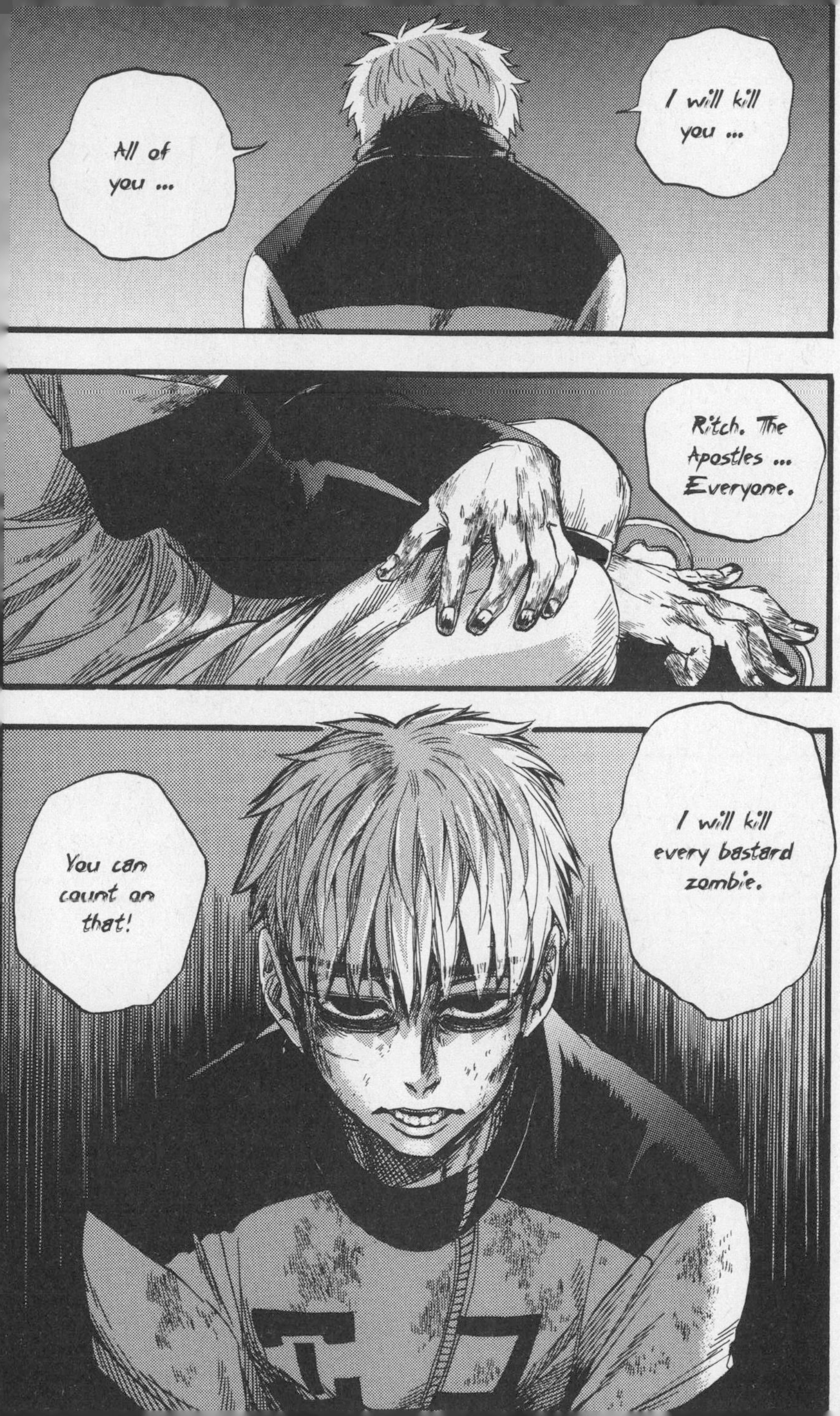
I will kill you ...
All of you ...
Ritch. The Apostles ... Everyone.
I will kill every bastard zombie.
You can count on that!

# CHAPTER 9: REVELATIONS

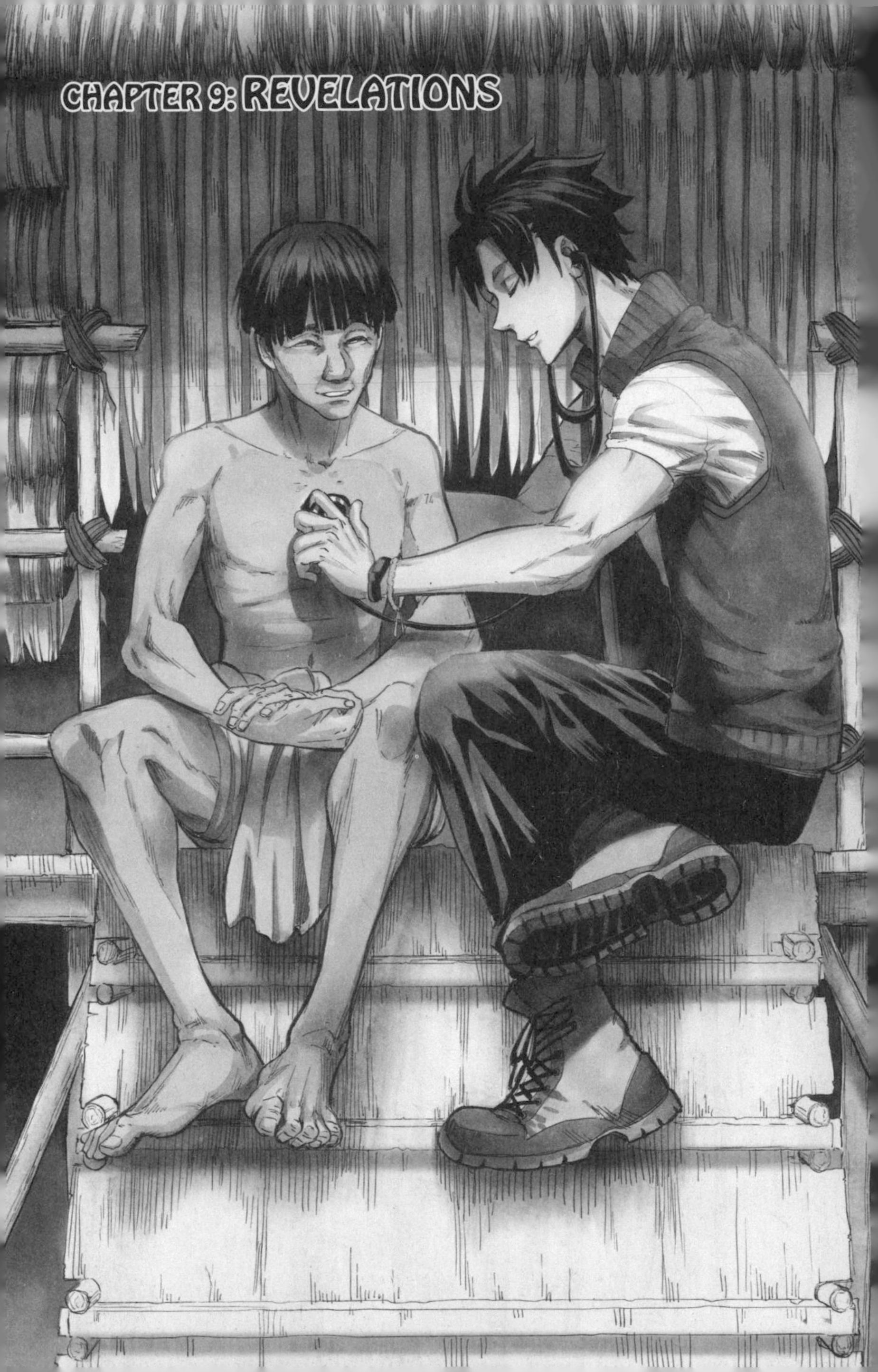

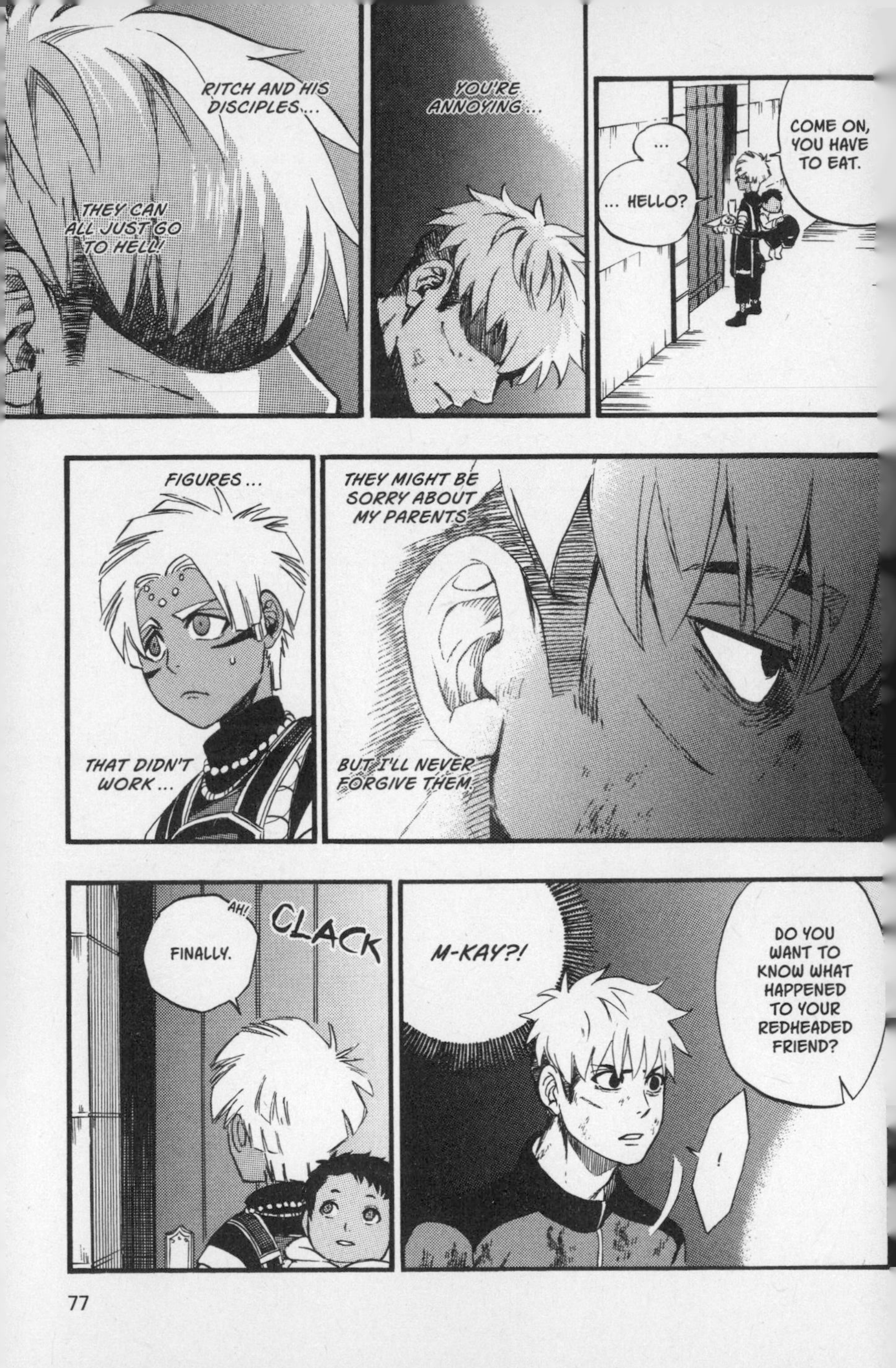
COME ON, YOU HAVE TO EAT.
...
... HELLO?
YOU'RE ANNOYING ...
RITCH AND HIS DISCIPLES ...
THEY CAN ALL JUST GO TO HELL!
THEY MIGHT BE SORRY ABOUT MY PARENTS
BUT I'LL NEVER FORGIVE THEM.
FIGURES ...
THAT DIDN'T WORK ...
DO YOU WANT TO KNOW WHAT HAPPENED TO YOUR REDHEADED FRIEND?
!
M-KAY?!
CLACK
AH!
FINALLY.

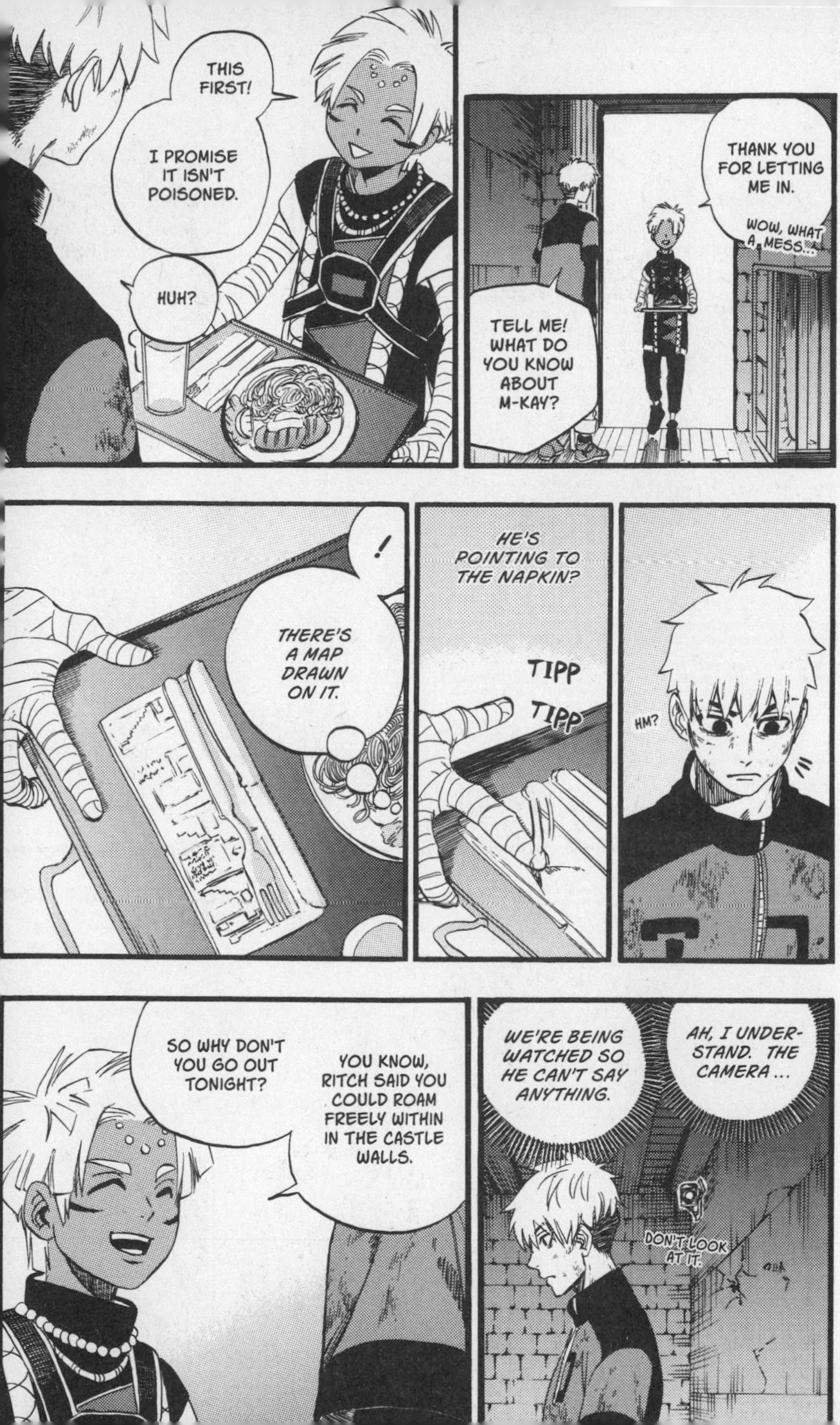
THANK YOU FOR LETTING ME IN.
WOW, WHAT A MESS...
TELL ME! WHAT DO YOU KNOW ABOUT M-KAY?
THIS FIRST!
I PROMISE IT ISN'T POISONED.
HUH?
HM?
HE'S POINTING TO THE NAPKIN?
TIPP
TIPP
!
THERE'S A MAP DRAWN ON IT.
AH, I UNDER-STAND. THE CAMERA ...
WE'RE BEING WATCHED SO HE CAN'T SAY ANYTHING.
DON'T LOOK AT IT.
YOU KNOW, RITCH SAID YOU COULD ROAM FREELY WITHIN IN THE CASTLE WALLS.
SO WHY DON'T YOU GO OUT TONIGHT?

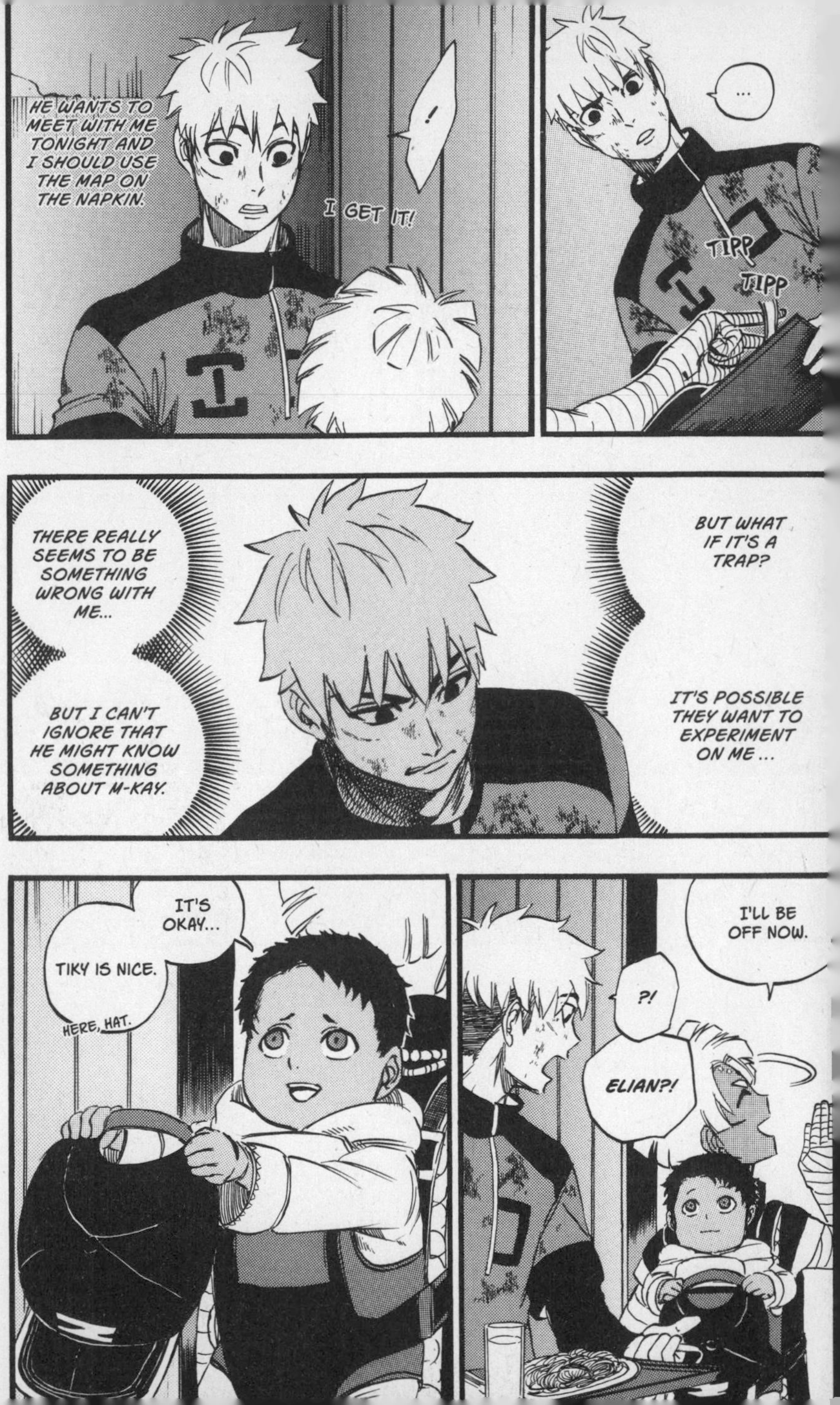
...
TIPP
TIPP
!
HE WANTS TO MEET WITH ME TONIGHT AND I SHOULD USE THE MAP ON THE NAPKIN.
I GET IT!
BUT WHAT IF IT'S A TRAP?
IT'S POSSIBLE THEY WANT TO EXPERIMENT ON ME...
THERE REALLY SEEMS TO BE SOMETHING WRONG WITH ME...
BUT I CAN'T IGNORE THAT HE MIGHT KNOW SOMETHING ABOUT M-KAY.
I'LL BE OFF NOW.
?!
ELIAN?!
IT'S OKAY...
TIKY IS NICE.
HERE, HAT.

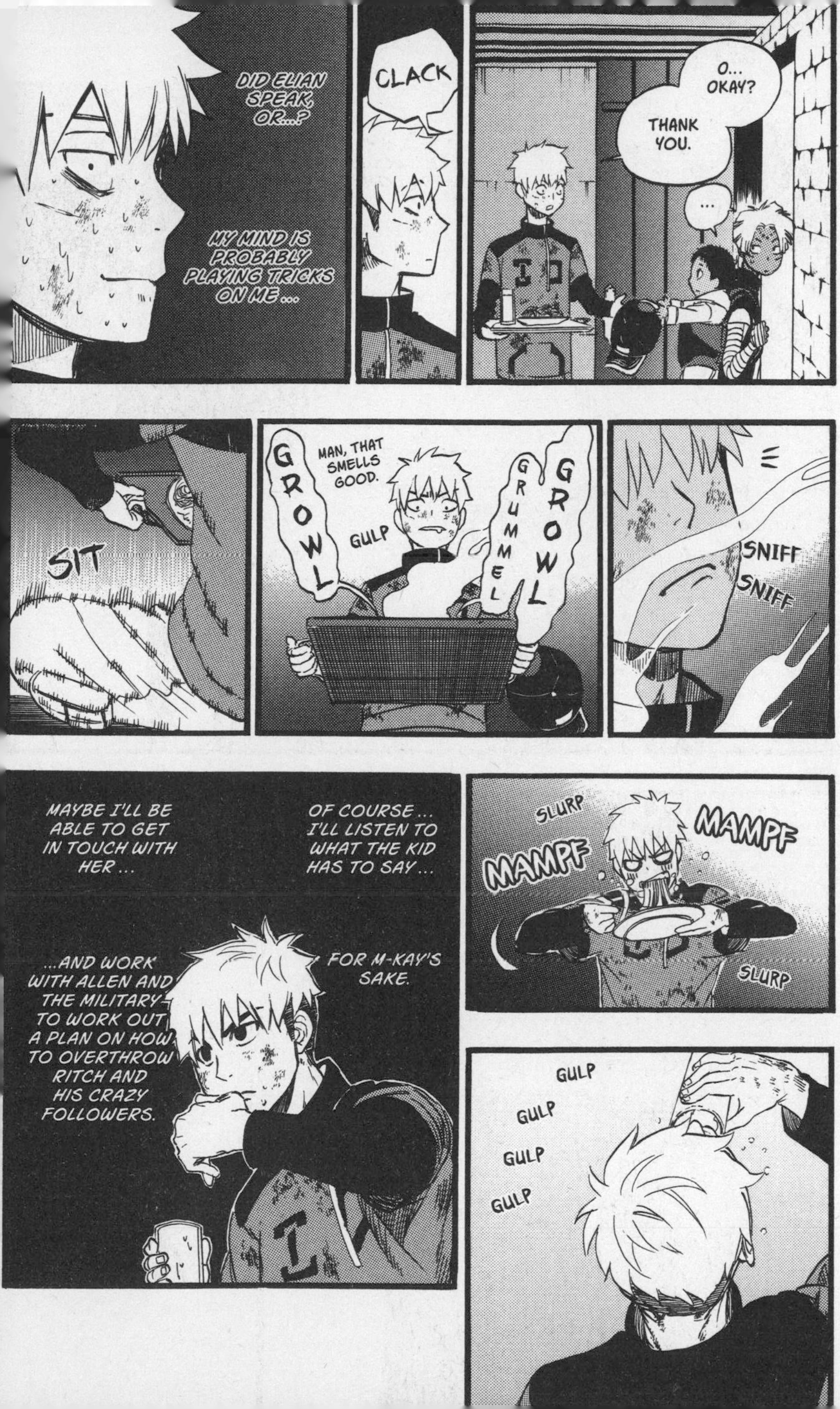
O... OKAY?
THANK YOU.
...
CLACK
DID ELIAN SPEAK, OR...?
MY MIND IS PROBABLY PLAYING TRICKS ON ME...
SNIFF
SNIFF
GROWL
GRUMMEL
MAN, THAT SMELLS GOOD.
GROWL
GULP
SIT
MAMPF
SLURP
MAMPF
SLURP
GULP
GULP
GULP
GULP
OF COURSE... I'LL LISTEN TO WHAT THE KID HAS TO SAY...
MAYBE I'LL BE ABLE TO GET IN TOUCH WITH HER...
FOR M-KAY'S SAKE.
...AND WORK WITH ALLEN AND THE MILITARY-TO WORK OUT A PLAN ON HOW TO OVERTHROW RITCH AND HIS CRAZY FOLLOWERS.

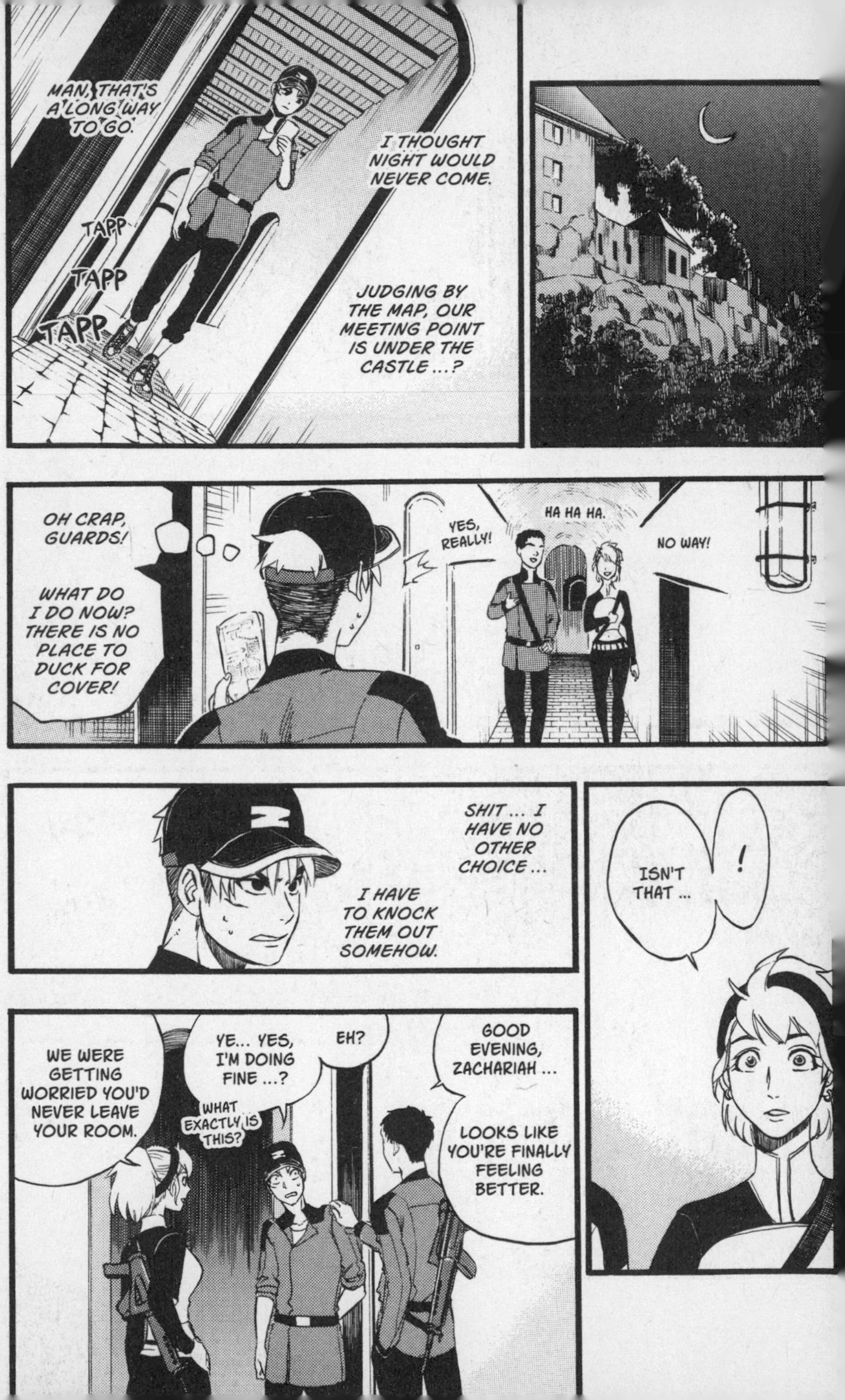
I THOUGHT NIGHT WOULD NEVER COME.
MAN, THAT'S A LONG WAY TO GO.
TAPP
TAPP
TAPP
JUDGING BY THE MAP, OUR MEETING POINT IS UNDER THE CASTLE ...?
NO WAY!
HA HA HA.
YES, REALLY!
OH CRAP, GUARDS!
WHAT DO I DO NOW? THERE IS NO PLACE TO DUCK FOR COVER!
!
ISN'T THAT ...
SHIT ... I HAVE NO OTHER CHOICE ...
I HAVE TO KNOCK THEM OUT SOMEHOW.
GOOD EVENING, ZACHARIAH ...
LOOKS LIKE YOU'RE FINALLY FEELING BETTER.
EH?
YE... YES, I'M DOING FINE ...?
WHAT EXACTLY IS THIS?
WE WERE GETTING WORRIED YOU'D NEVER LEAVE YOUR ROOM.

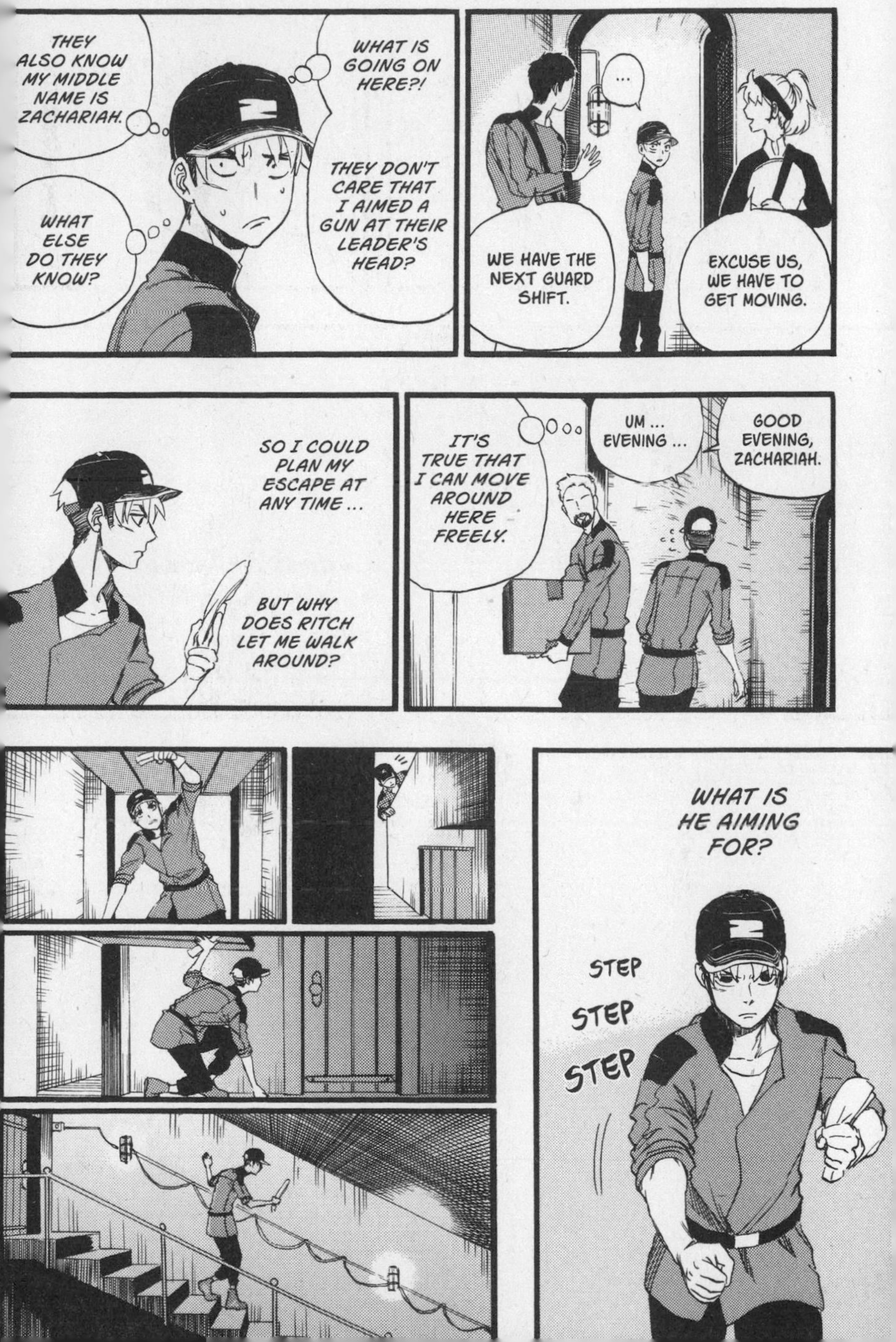
...
EXCUSE US, WE HAVE TO GET MOVING.
WE HAVE THE NEXT GUARD SHIFT.
WHAT IS GOING ON HERE?!
THEY DON'T CARE THAT I AIMED A GUN AT THEIR LEADER'S HEAD?
THEY ALSO KNOW MY MIDDLE NAME IS ZACHARIAH.
WHAT ELSE DO THEY KNOW?
GOOD EVENING, ZACHARIAH.
UM ... EVENING ...
IT'S TRUE THAT I CAN MOVE AROUND HERE FREELY.
SO I COULD PLAN MY ESCAPE AT ANY TIME ...
BUT WHY DOES RITCH LET ME WALK AROUND?
WHAT IS HE AIMING FOR?
STEP
STEP
STEP

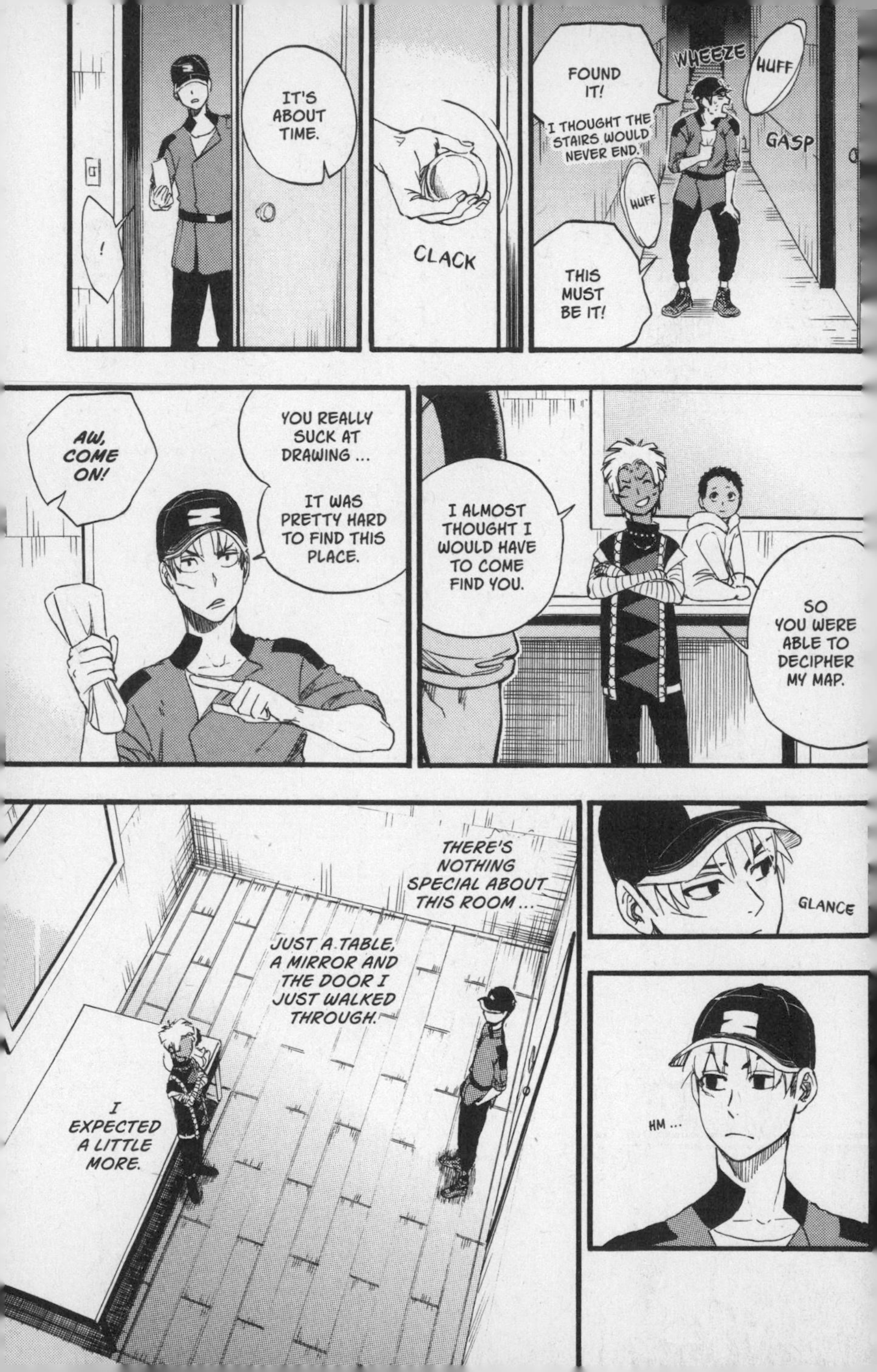
WHEEZE
HUFF
FOUND IT!
I THOUGHT THE STAIRS WOULD NEVER END.
GASP
HUFF
THIS MUST BE IT!
CLACK
IT'S ABOUT TIME.
!
I ALMOST THOUGHT I WOULD HAVE TO COME FIND YOU.
SO YOU WERE ABLE TO DECIPHER MY MAP.
YOU REALLY SUCK AT DRAWING ...
IT WAS PRETTY HARD TO FIND THIS PLACE.
AW, COME ON!
GLANCE
HM ...
THERE'S NOTHING SPECIAL ABOUT THIS ROOM ...
JUST A TABLE, A MIRROR AND THE DOOR I JUST WALKED THROUGH.
I EXPECTED A LITTLE MORE.

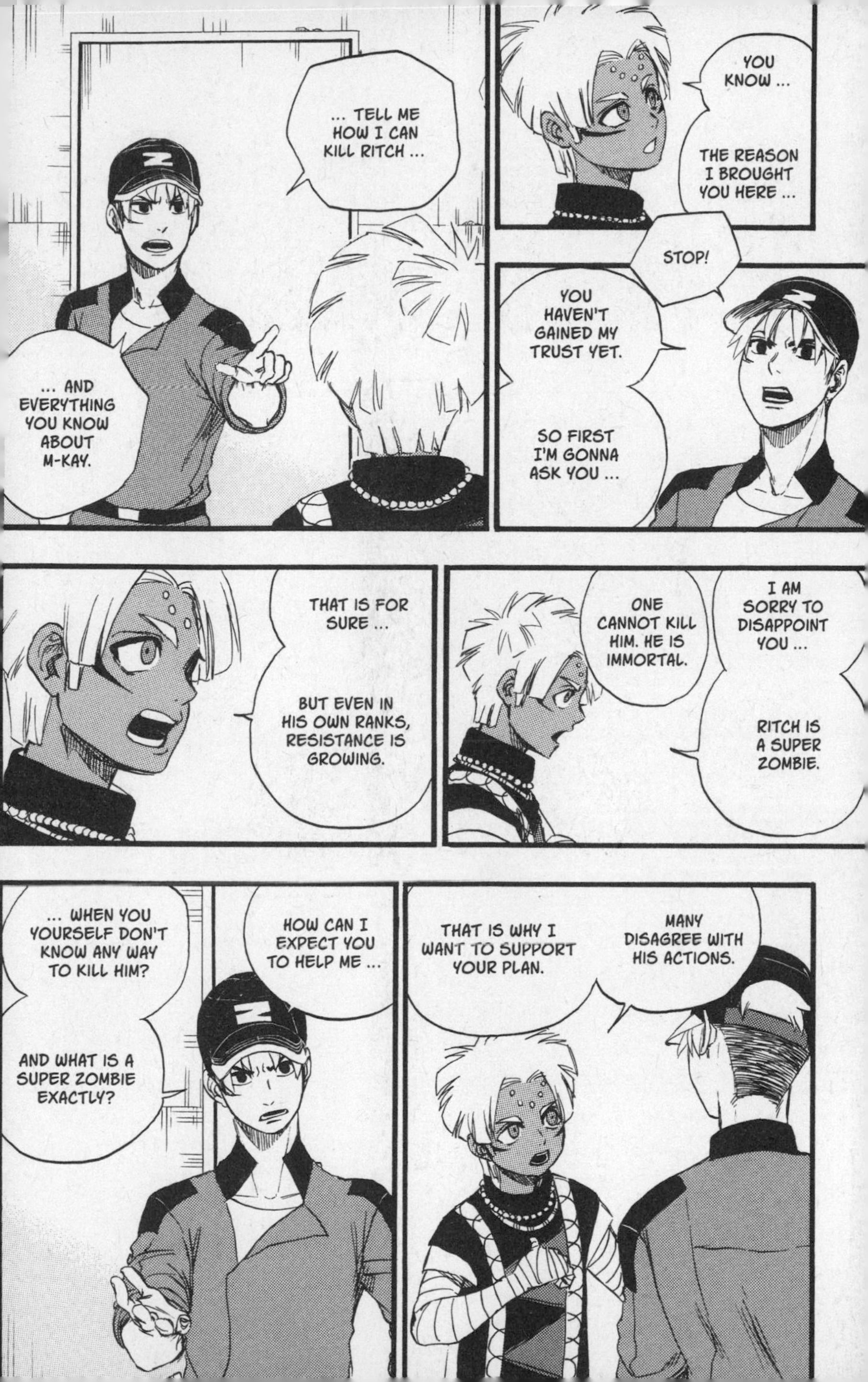
YOU KNOW ...
THE REASON I BROUGHT YOU HERE ...
STOP!
YOU HAVEN'T GAINED MY TRUST YET.
SO FIRST I'M GONNA ASK YOU ...
... TELL ME HOW I CAN KILL RITCH ...
... AND EVERYTHING YOU KNOW ABOUT M-KAY.
I AM SORRY TO DISAPPOINT YOU ...
RITCH IS A SUPER ZOMBIE.
ONE CANNOT KILL HIM. HE IS IMMORTAL.
THAT IS FOR SURE ...
BUT EVEN IN HIS OWN RANKS, RESISTANCE IS GROWING.
MANY DISAGREE WITH HIS ACTIONS.
THAT IS WHY I WANT TO SUPPORT YOUR PLAN.
HOW CAN I EXPECT YOU TO HELP ME ...
... WHEN YOU YOURSELF DON'T KNOW ANY WAY TO KILL HIM?
AND WHAT IS A SUPER ZOMBIE EXACTLY?

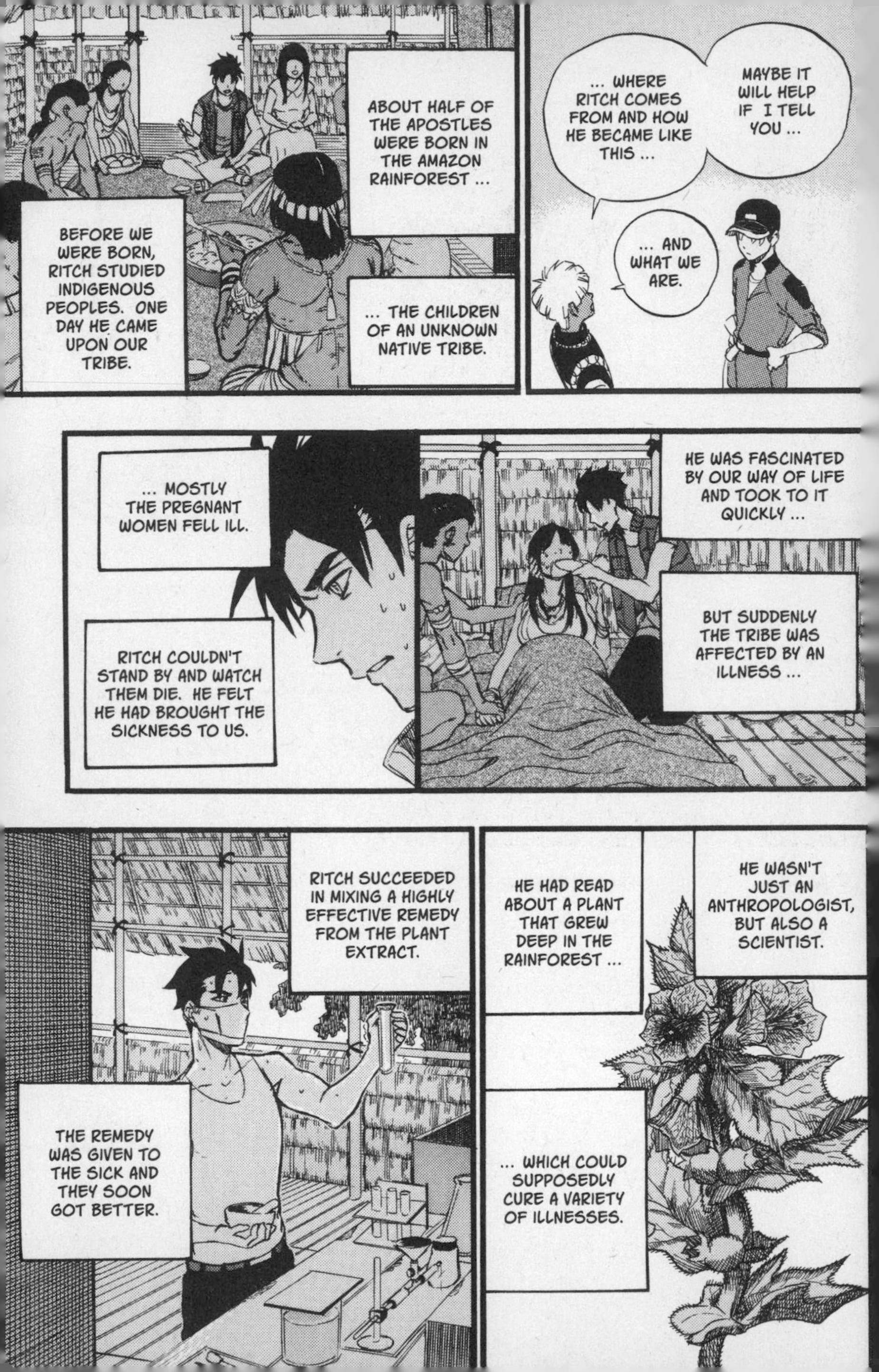
MAYBE IT WILL HELP IF I TELL YOU ...
... WHERE RITCH COMES FROM AND HOW HE BECAME LIKE THIS ...
... AND WHAT WE ARE.
ABOUT HALF OF THE APOSTLES WERE BORN IN THE AMAZON RAINFOREST ...
... THE CHILDREN OF AN UNKNOWN NATIVE TRIBE.
BEFORE WE WERE BORN, RITCH STUDIED INDIGENOUS PEOPLES. ONE DAY HE CAME UPON OUR TRIBE.
HE WAS FASCINATED BY OUR WAY OF LIFE AND TOOK TO IT QUICKLY ...
BUT SUDDENLY THE TRIBE WAS AFFECTED BY AN ILLNESS ...
... MOSTLY THE PREGNANT WOMEN FELL ILL.
RITCH COULDN'T STAND BY AND WATCH THEM DIE. HE FELT HE HAD BROUGHT THE SICKNESS TO US.
HE WASN'T JUST AN ANTHROPOLOGIST, BUT ALSO A SCIENTIST.
HE HAD READ ABOUT A PLANT THAT GREW DEEP IN THE RAINFOREST ...
... WHICH COULD SUPPOSEDLY CURE A VARIETY OF ILLNESSES.
RITCH SUCCEEDED IN MIXING A HIGHLY EFFECTIVE REMEDY FROM THE PLANT EXTRACT.
THE REMEDY WAS GIVEN TO THE SICK AND THEY SOON GOT BETTER.

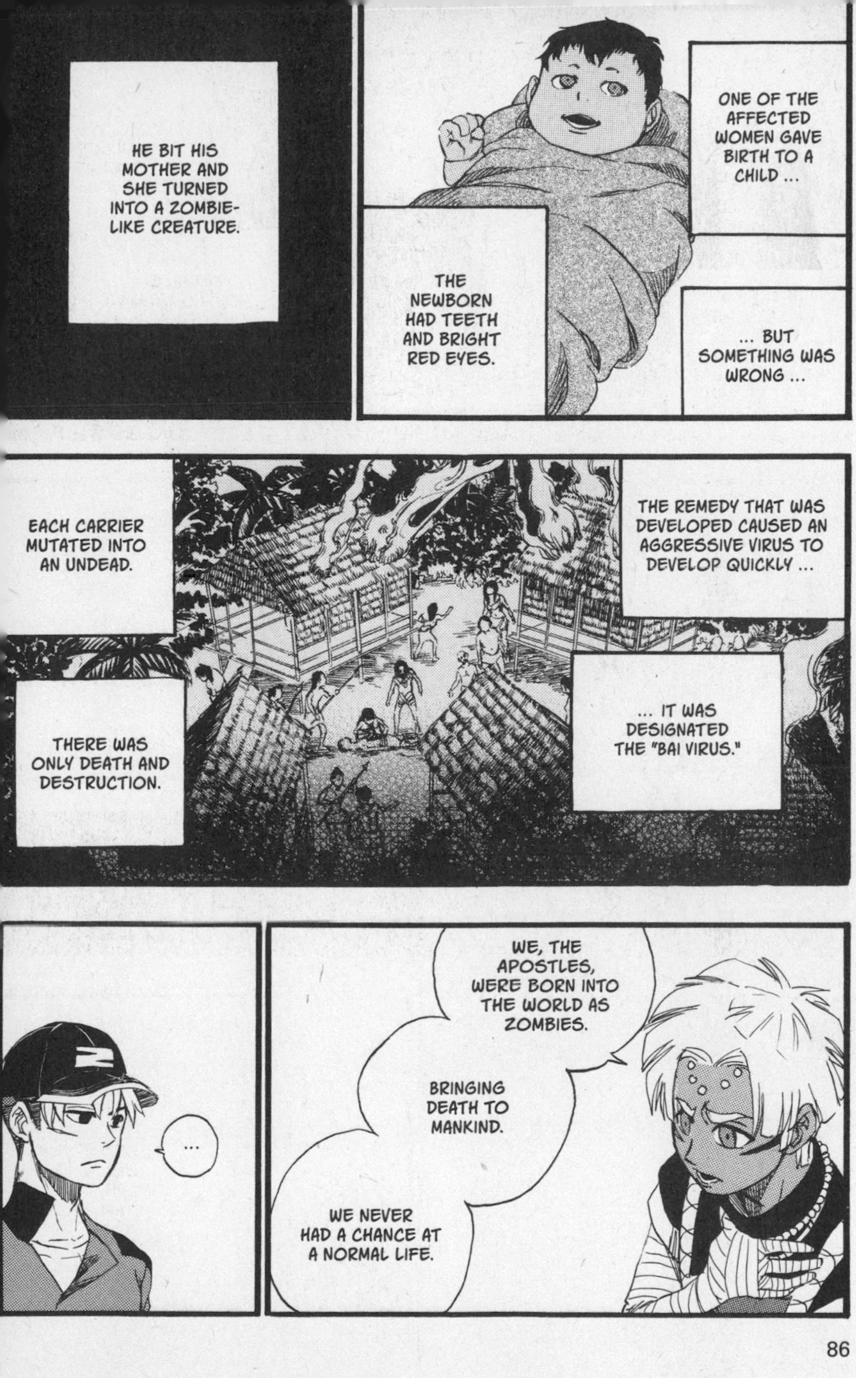
ONE OF THE AFFECTED WOMEN GAVE BIRTH TO A CHILD ...
... BUT SOMETHING WAS WRONG ...
THE NEWBORN HAD TEETH AND BRIGHT RED EYES.
HE BIT HIS MOTHER AND SHE TURNED INTO A ZOMBIE-LIKE CREATURE.
THE REMEDY THAT WAS DEVELOPED CAUSED AN AGGRESSIVE VIRUS TO DEVELOP QUICKLY ...
... IT WAS DESIGNATED THE "BAI VIRUS."
EACH CARRIER MUTATED INTO AN UNDEAD.
THERE WAS ONLY DEATH AND DESTRUCTION.
WE, THE APOSTLES, WERE BORN INTO THE WORLD AS ZOMBIES.
BRINGING DEATH TO MANKIND.
WE NEVER HAD A CHANCE AT A NORMAL LIFE.
...

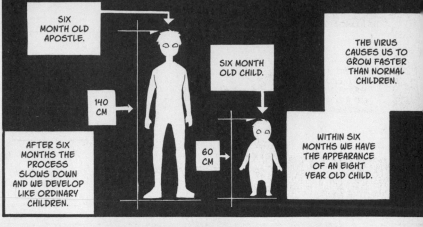

THE VIRUS CAUSES US TO GROW FASTER THAN NORMAL CHILDREN.
WITHIN SIX MONTHS WE HAVE THE APPEARANCE OF AN EIGHT YEAR OLD CHILD.
SIX MONTH OLD CHILD.
60 CM
SIX MONTH OLD APOSTLE.
140 CM
AFTER SIX MONTHS THE PROCESS SLOWS DOWN AND WE DEVELOP LIKE ORDINARY CHILDREN.
OUR BRAIN CELLS ALSO DEVELOP RAPIDLY.
OUR PERCEPTION IS ENORMOUS.
SIX MONTH OLD APOSTLE
17 YEAR OLD TEENAGER
I'M NOT EXAGGERATING WHEN I SAY THAT OUR BRAIN WORKS 30 TIMES FASTER.
AFTER SIX MONTHS, WE HAVE THE COGNITION OF A 17 YEAR OLD.
BUT THIS DEVELOPMENT DOES NOT STOP.
OUR PERCEPTION WILL ALWAYS BE ABOVE AVERAGE.
STOP! HANG ON!
BEFORE YOU KEEP TALKING ABOUT CONFUSING STUFF ...
LET ME DIGEST THE FIRST PART.
AH... HE'S OVER-WHELMED.

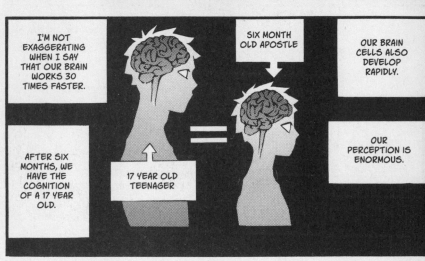

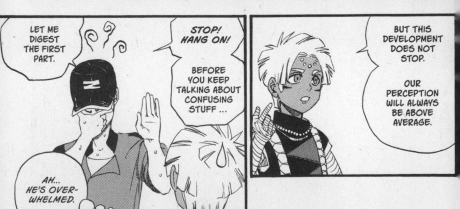

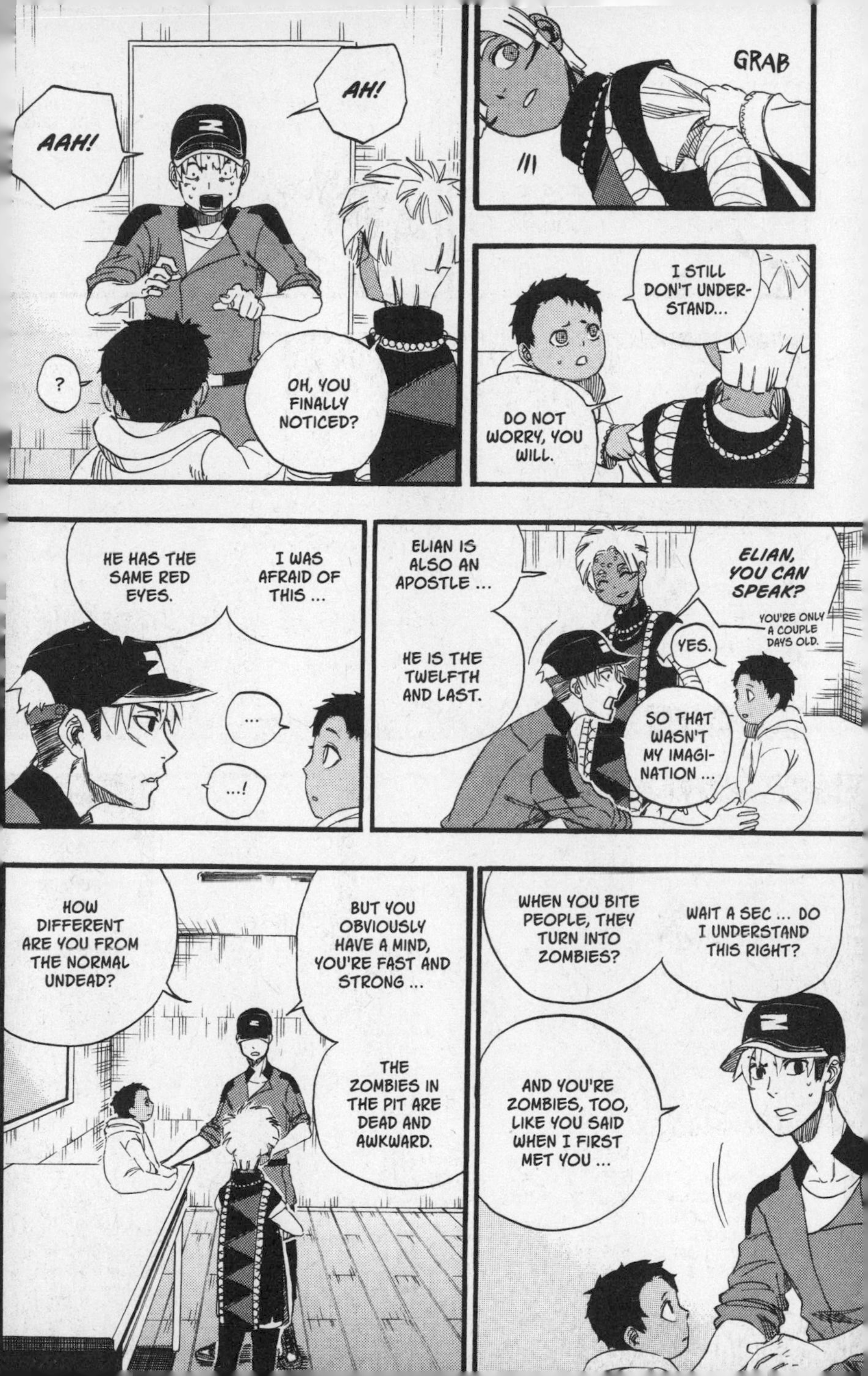
GRAB
///
I STILL DON'T UNDER-STAND...
DO NOT WORRY, YOU WILL.
AH!
AAH!
OH, YOU FINALLY NOTICED?
?
ELIAN, YOU CAN SPEAK?
YOU'RE ONLY A COUPLE DAYS OLD.
ELIAN IS ALSO AN APOSTLE ...
YES.
HE IS THE TWELFTH AND LAST.
SO THAT WASN'T MY IMAGI-NATION ...
I WAS AFRAID OF THIS ...
HE HAS THE SAME RED EYES.
...
...!
WAIT A SEC ... DO I UNDERSTAND THIS RIGHT?
WHEN YOU BITE PEOPLE, THEY TURN INTO ZOMBIES?
AND YOU'RE ZOMBIES, TOO, LIKE YOU SAID WHEN I FIRST MET YOU ...
BUT YOU OBVIOUSLY HAVE A MIND, YOU'RE FAST AND STRONG ...
HOW DIFFERENT ARE YOU FROM THE NORMAL UNDEAD?
THE ZOMBIES IN THE PIT ARE DEAD AND AWKWARD.

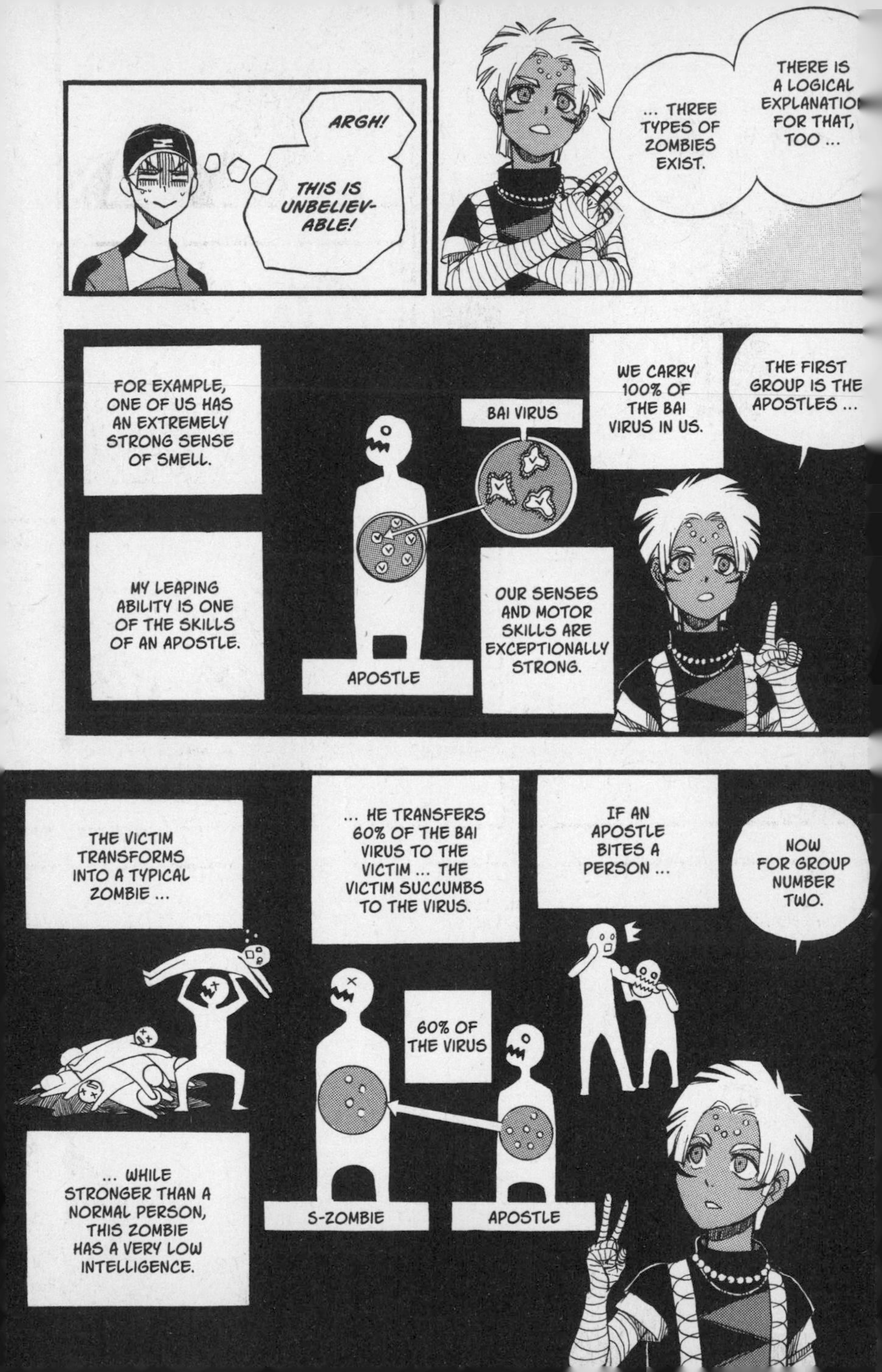
THERE IS A LOGICAL EXPLANATION FOR THAT, TOO ...
... THREE TYPES OF ZOMBIES EXIST.
ARGH!
THIS IS UNBELIEV-ABLE!
THE FIRST GROUP IS THE APOSTLES ...
WE CARRY 100% OF THE BAI VIRUS IN US.
BAI VIRUS
OUR SENSES AND MOTOR SKILLS ARE EXCEPTIONALLY STRONG.
FOR EXAMPLE, ONE OF US HAS AN EXTREMELY STRONG SENSE OF SMELL.
MY LEAPING ABILITY IS ONE OF THE SKILLS OF AN APOSTLE.
APOSTLE
NOW FOR GROUP NUMBER TWO.
IF AN APOSTLE BITES A PERSON ...
... HE TRANSFERS 60% OF THE BAI VIRUS TO THE VICTIM ... THE VICTIM SUCCUMBS TO THE VIRUS.
THE VICTIM TRANSFORMS INTO A TYPICAL ZOMBIE ...
60% OF THE VIRUS
APOSTLE
S-ZOMBIE
... WHILE STRONGER THAN A NORMAL PERSON, THIS ZOMBIE HAS A VERY LOW INTELLIGENCE.

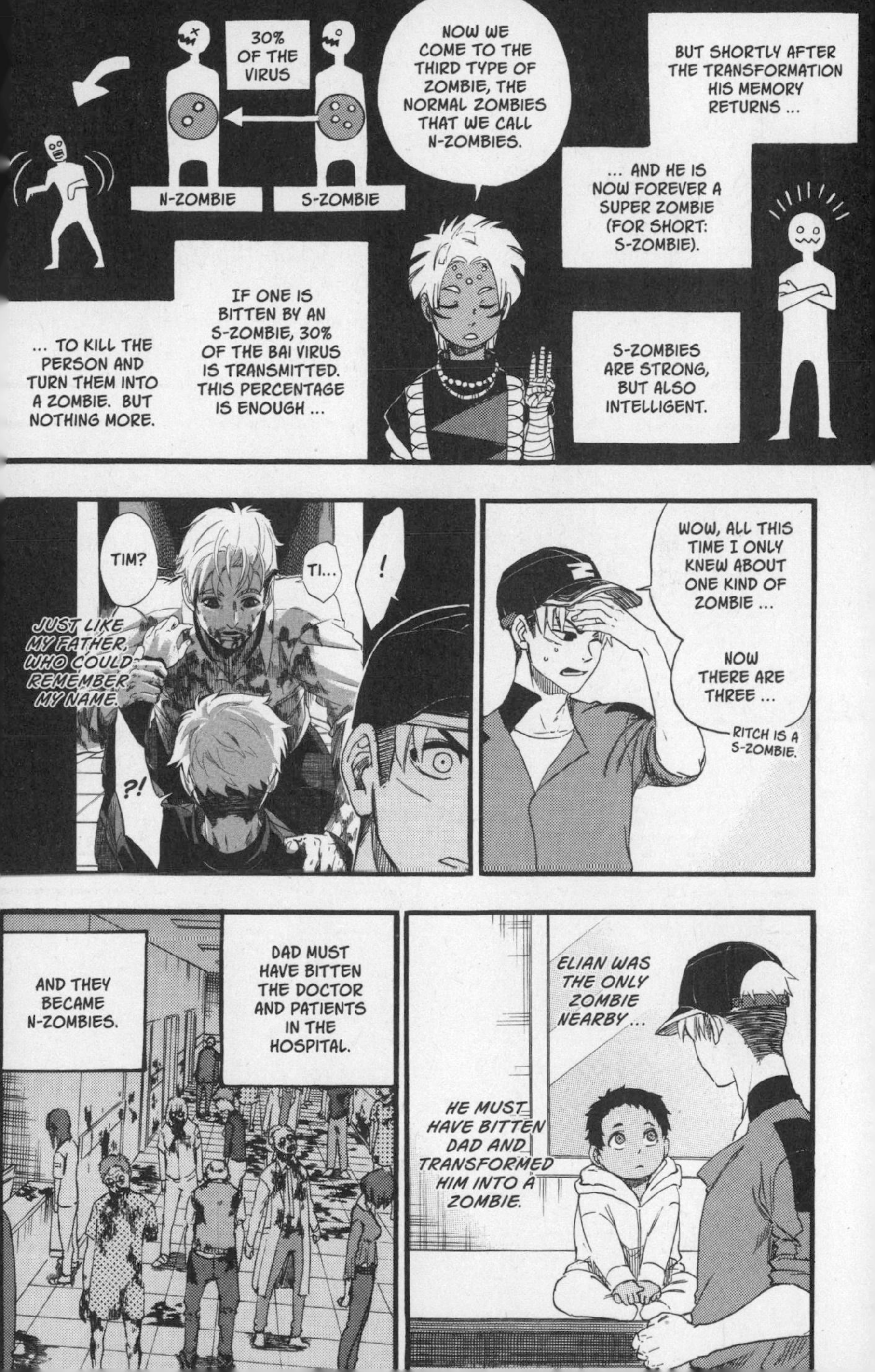
BUT SHORTLY AFTER THE TRANSFORMATION HIS MEMORY RETURNS ...
... AND HE IS NOW FOREVER A SUPER ZOMBIE (FOR SHORT: S-ZOMBIE).
S-ZOMBIES ARE STRONG, BUT ALSO INTELLIGENT.
NOW WE COME TO THE THIRD TYPE OF ZOMBIE, THE NORMAL ZOMBIES THAT WE CALL N-ZOMBIES.
30% OF THE VIRUS
S-ZOMBIE
N-ZOMBIE
IF ONE IS BITTEN BY AN S-ZOMBIE, 30% OF THE BAI VIRUS IS TRANSMITTED. THIS PERCENTAGE IS ENOUGH ...
... TO KILL THE PERSON AND TURN THEM INTO A ZOMBIE. BUT NOTHING MORE.
WOW, ALL THIS TIME I ONLY KNEW ABOUT ONE KIND OF ZOMBIE ...
NOW THERE ARE THREE ...
RITCH IS A S-ZOMBIE.
!
TI...
TIM?
?!
JUST LIKE MY FATHER, WHO COULD REMEMBER MY NAME.
ELIAN WAS THE ONLY ZOMBIE NEARBY ...
HE MUST HAVE BITTEN DAD AND TRANSFORMED HIM INTO A ZOMBIE.
DAD MUST HAVE BITTEN THE DOCTOR AND PATIENTS IN THE HOSPITAL.
AND THEY BECAME N-ZOMBIES.

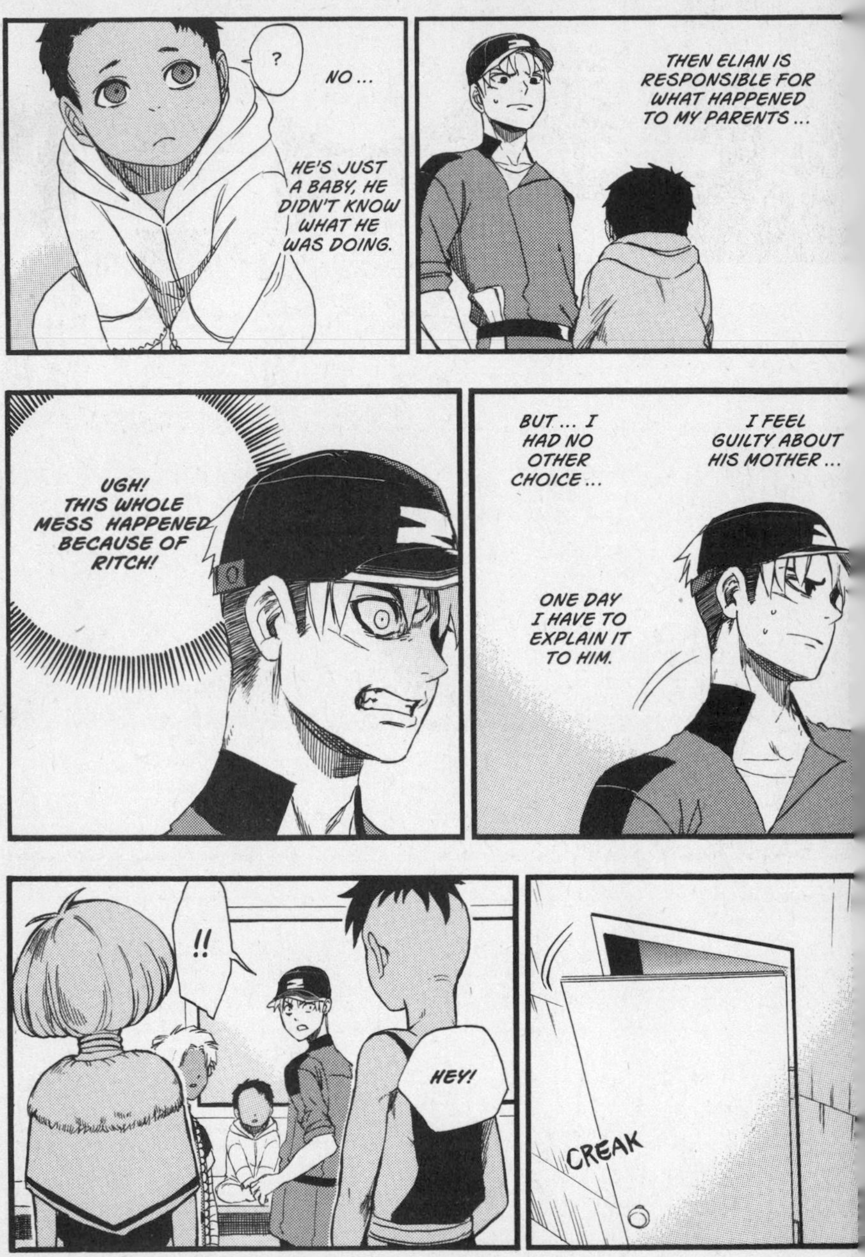
THEN ELIAN IS RESPONSIBLE FOR WHAT HAPPENED TO MY PARENTS ...
?
NO ...
HE'S JUST A BABY, HE DIDN'T KNOW WHAT HE WAS DOING.
I FEEL GUILTY ABOUT HIS MOTHER ...
BUT ... I HAD NO OTHER CHOICE ...
ONE DAY I HAVE TO EXPLAIN IT TO HIM.
UGH! THIS WHOLE MESS HAPPENED BECAUSE OF RITCH!
CREAK
HEY!
!!

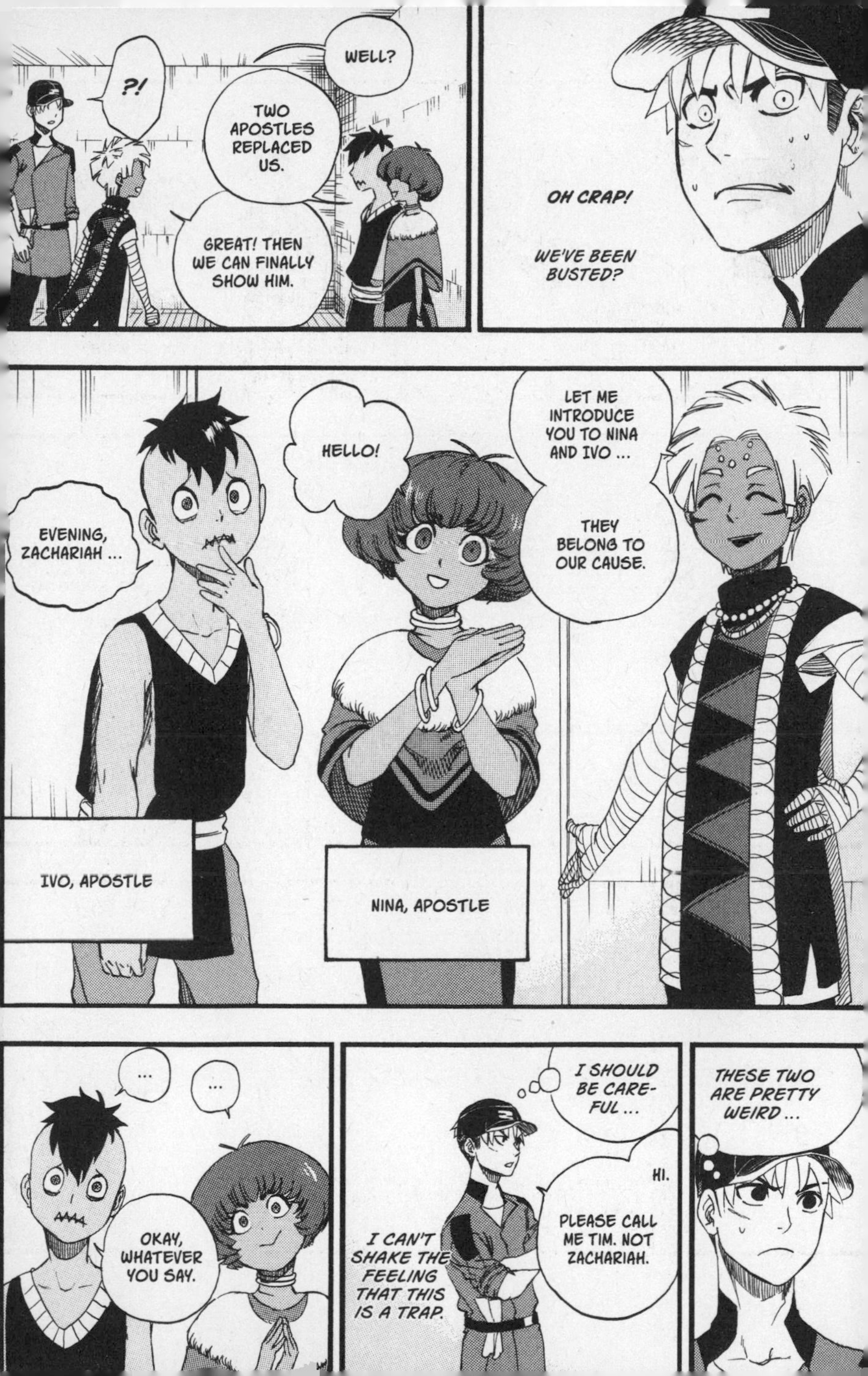
OH CRAP!
WE'VE BEEN BUSTED?
WELL?
?!
TWO APOSTLES REPLACED US.
GREAT! THEN WE CAN FINALLY SHOW HIM.
LET ME INTRODUCE YOU TO NINA AND IVO ...
THEY BELONG TO OUR CAUSE.
HELLO!
EVENING, ZACHARIAH ...
NINA, APOSTLE
IVO, APOSTLE
THESE TWO ARE PRETTY WEIRD ...
I SHOULD BE CARE-FUL ...
HI.
PLEASE CALL ME TIM. NOT ZACHARIAH.
I CAN'T SHAKE THE FEELING THAT THIS IS A TRAP.
...
...
OKAY, WHATEVER YOU SAY.

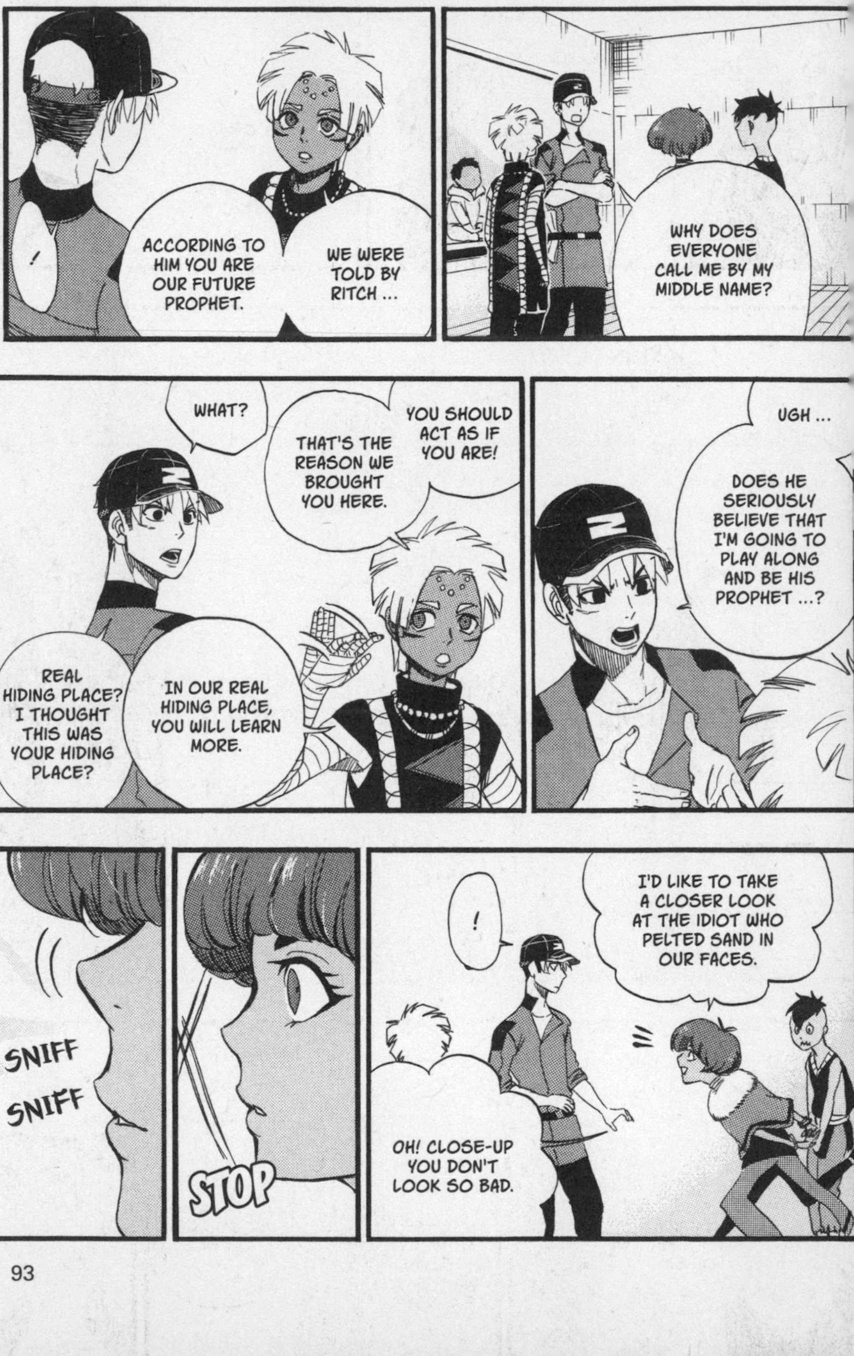
WHY DOES EVERYONE CALL ME BY MY MIDDLE NAME?
WE WERE TOLD BY RITCH ...
ACCORDING TO HIM YOU ARE OUR FUTURE PROPHET.
!
UGH ...
DOES HE SERIOUSLY BELIEVE THAT I'M GOING TO PLAY ALONG AND BE HIS PROPHET ...?
YOU SHOULD ACT AS IF YOU ARE!
WHAT?
THAT'S THE REASON WE BROUGHT YOU HERE.
IN OUR REAL HIDING PLACE, YOU WILL LEARN MORE.
REAL HIDING PLACE? I THOUGHT THIS WAS YOUR HIDING PLACE?
I'D LIKE TO TAKE A CLOSER LOOK AT THE IDIOT WHO PELTED SAND IN OUR FACES.
!
OH! CLOSE-UP YOU DON'T LOOK SO BAD.
STOP
SNIFF
SNIFF

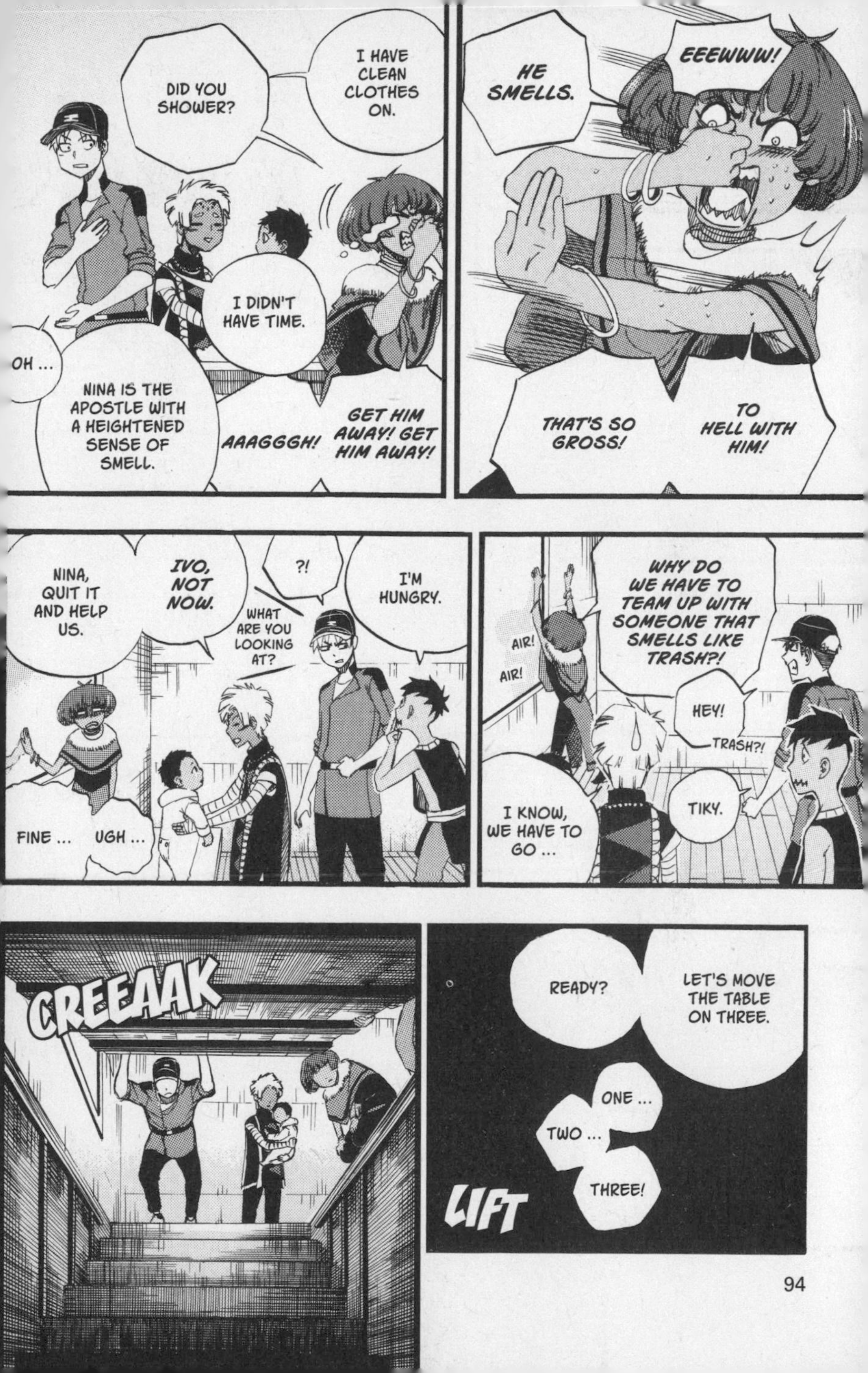
EEEWWW!
HE SMELLS.
TO HELL WITH HIM!
THAT'S SO GROSS!
I HAVE CLEAN CLOTHES ON.
DID YOU SHOWER?
I DIDN'T HAVE TIME.
GET HIM AWAY! GET HIM AWAY!
AAAGGGH!
NINA IS THE APOSTLE WITH A HEIGHTENED SENSE OF SMELL.
OH ...
WHY DO WE HAVE TO TEAM UP WITH SOMEONE THAT SMELLS LIKE TRASH?!
AIR!
AIR!
HEY!
TRASH?!
TIKY.
I KNOW, WE HAVE TO GO ...
I'M HUNGRY.
?!
WHAT ARE YOU LOOKING AT?
IVO, NOT NOW.
NINA, QUIT IT AND HELP US.
UGH ...
FINE ...
LET'S MOVE THE TABLE ON THREE.
READY?
ONE ...
TWO ...
THREE!
LIFT
CREEAAK

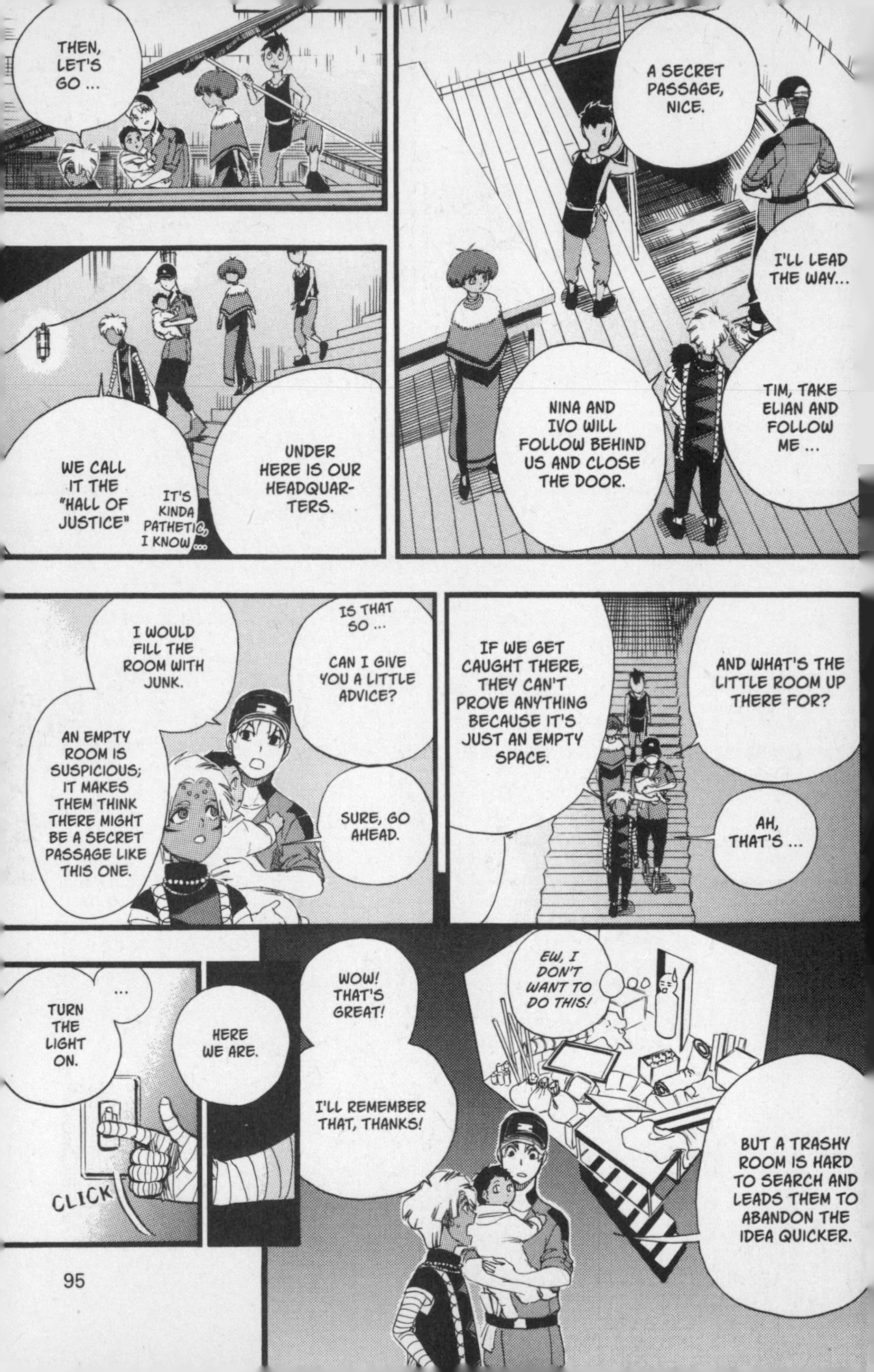
A SECRET PASSAGE, NICE.
I'LL LEAD THE WAY...
TIM, TAKE ELIAN AND FOLLOW ME ...
NINA AND IVO WILL FOLLOW BEHIND US AND CLOSE THE DOOR.
THEN, LET'S GO ...
UNDER HERE IS OUR HEADQUARTERS.
WE CALL IT THE "HALL OF JUSTICE"
IT'S KINDA PATHETIC, I KNOW...
AND WHAT'S THE LITTLE ROOM UP THERE FOR?
AH, THAT'S ...
IF WE GET CAUGHT THERE, THEY CAN'T PROVE ANYTHING BECAUSE IT'S JUST AN EMPTY SPACE.
IS THAT SO ...
CAN I GIVE YOU A LITTLE ADVICE?
SURE, GO AHEAD.
I WOULD FILL THE ROOM WITH JUNK.
AN EMPTY ROOM IS SUSPICIOUS; IT MAKES THEM THINK THERE MIGHT BE A SECRET PASSAGE LIKE THIS ONE.
EW, I DON'T WANT TO DO THIS!
BUT A TRASHY ROOM IS HARD TO SEARCH AND LEADS THEM TO ABANDON THE IDEA QUICKER.
WOW! THAT'S GREAT!
I'LL REMEMBER THAT, THANKS!
HERE WE ARE.
...
TURN THE LIGHT ON.
CLICK

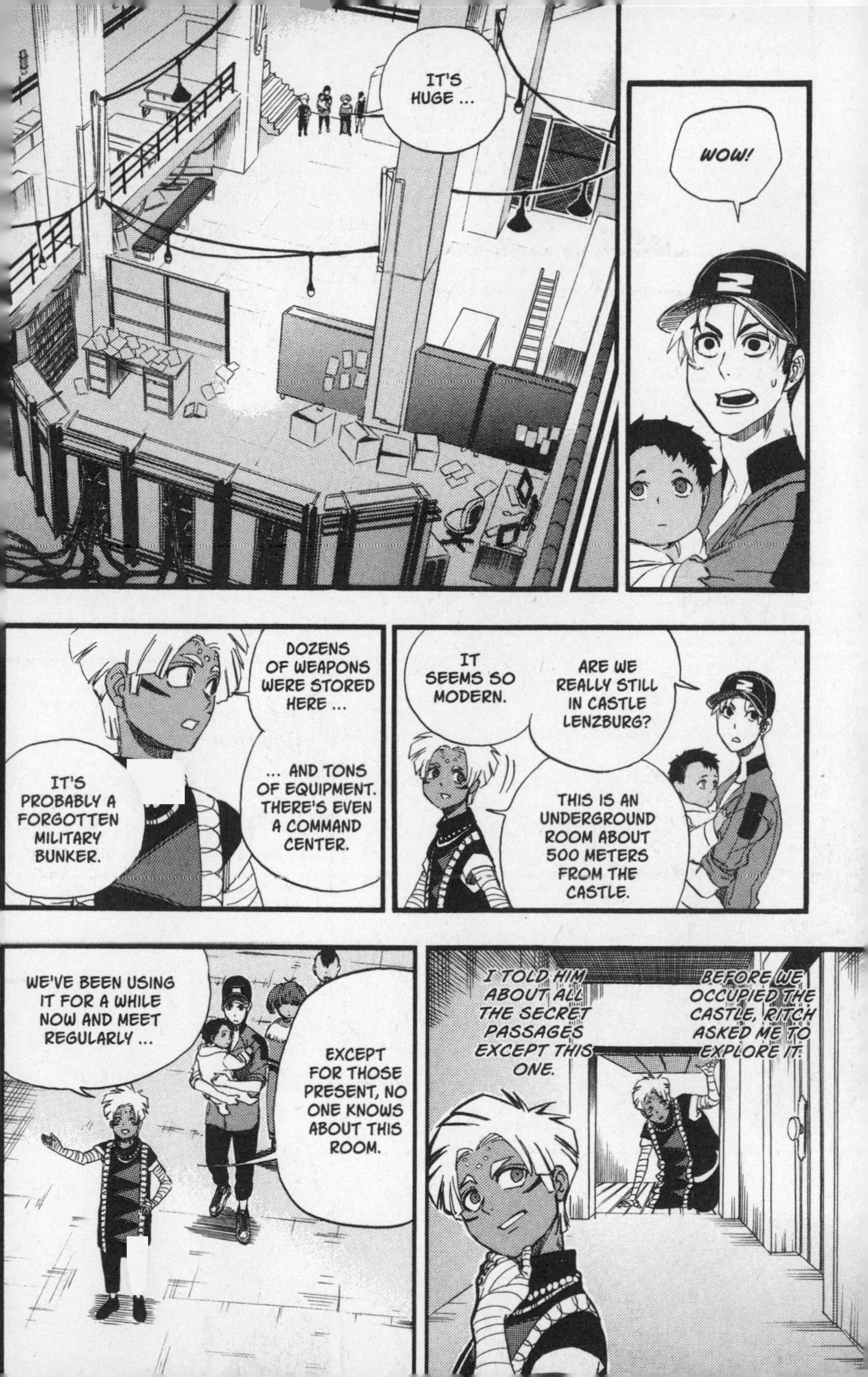
WOW!
IT'S HUGE ...
ARE WE REALLY STILL IN CASTLE LENZBURG?
IT SEEMS SO MODERN.
THIS IS AN UNDERGROUND ROOM ABOUT 500 METERS FROM THE CASTLE.
DOZENS OF WEAPONS WERE STORED HERE ...
... AND TONS OF EQUIPMENT. THERE'S EVEN A COMMAND CENTER.
IT'S PROBABLY A FORGOTTEN MILITARY BUNKER.
BEFORE WE OCCUPIED THE CASTLE, RITCH ASKED ME TO EXPLORE IT.
I TOLD HIM ABOUT ALL THE SECRET PASSAGES EXCEPT THIS ONE.
WE'VE BEEN USING IT FOR A WHILE NOW AND MEET REGULARLY ...
EXCEPT FOR THOSE PRESENT, NO ONE KNOWS ABOUT THIS ROOM.

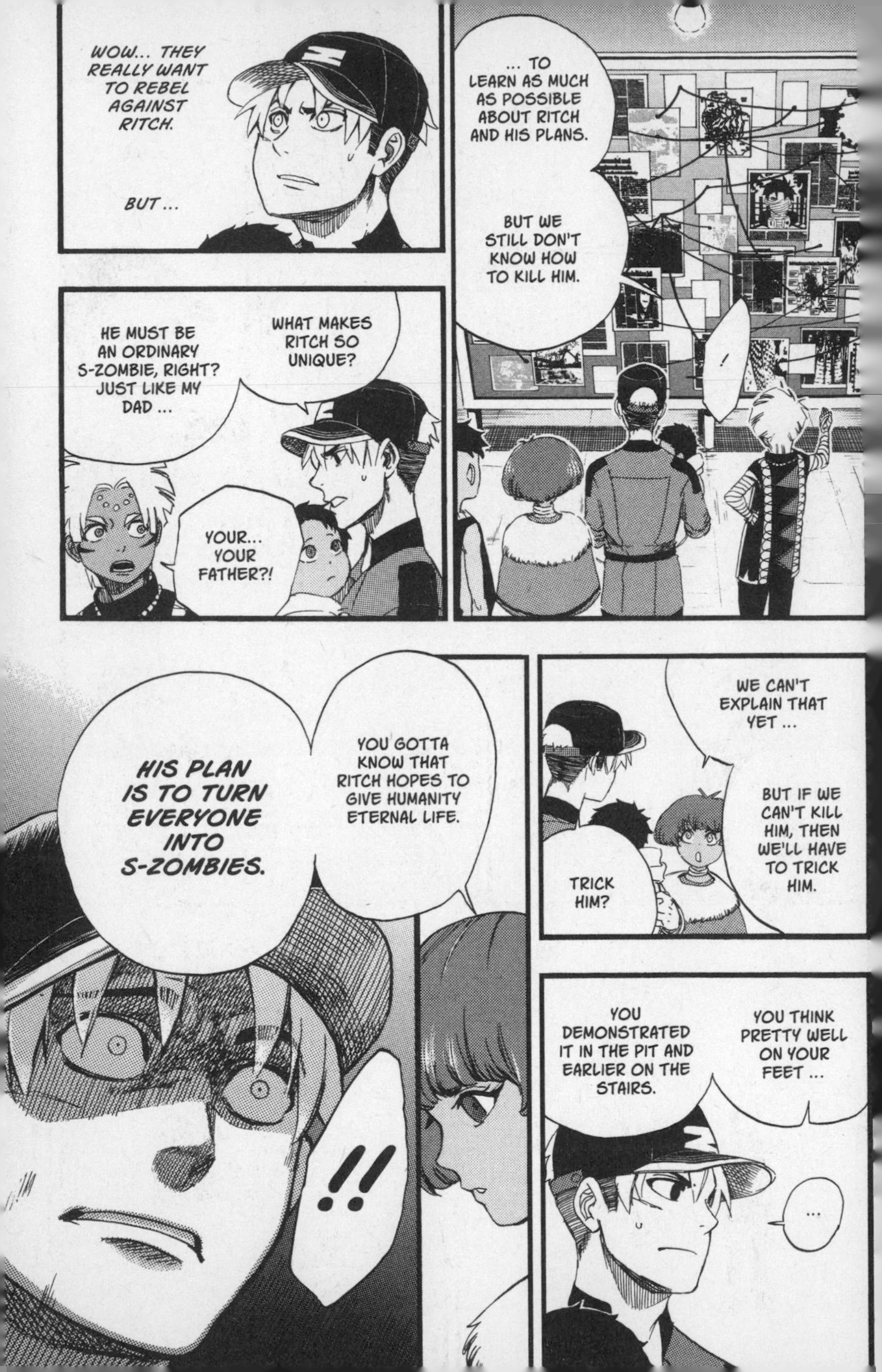
... TO LEARN AS MUCH AS POSSIBLE ABOUT RITCH AND HIS PLANS.
BUT WE STILL DON'T KNOW HOW TO KILL HIM.
!
WOW... THEY REALLY WANT TO REBEL AGAINST RITCH.
BUT ...
WHAT MAKES RITCH SO UNIQUE?
HE MUST BE AN ORDINARY S-ZOMBIE, RIGHT? JUST LIKE MY DAD ...
YOUR... YOUR FATHER?!
WE CAN'T EXPLAIN THAT YET ...
BUT IF WE CAN'T KILL HIM, THEN WE'LL HAVE TO TRICK HIM.
TRICK HIM?
YOU THINK PRETTY WELL ON YOUR FEET ...
YOU DEMONSTRATED IT IN THE PIT AND EARLIER ON THE STAIRS.
...
YOU GOTTA KNOW THAT RITCH HOPES TO GIVE HUMANITY ETERNAL LIFE.
HIS PLAN IS TO TURN EVERYONE INTO S-ZOMBIES.
!!

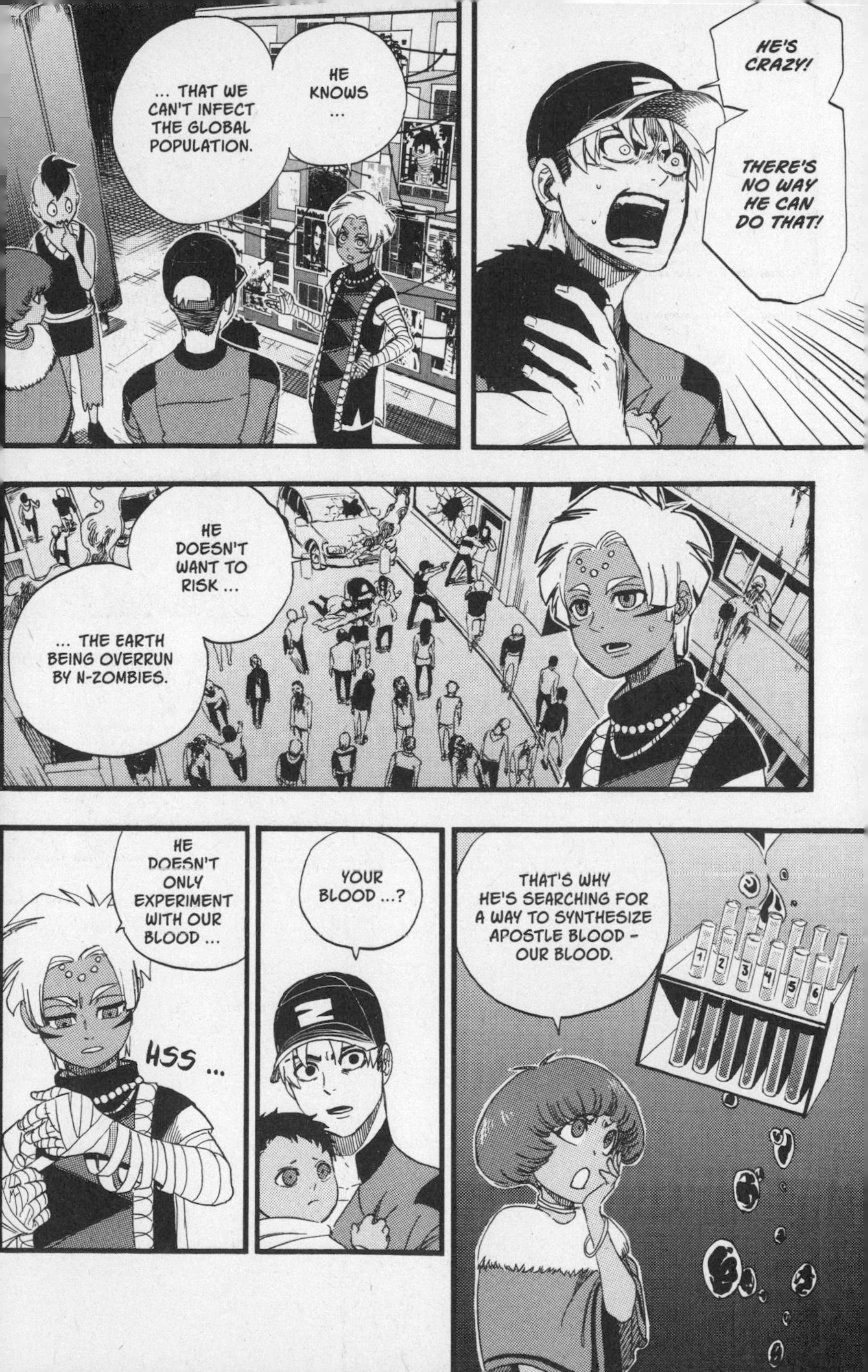
HE'S CRAZY!
THERE'S NO WAY HE CAN DO THAT!
HE KNOWS ...
... THAT WE CAN'T INFECT THE GLOBAL POPULATION.
HE DOESN'T WANT TO RISK ...
... THE EARTH BEING OVERRUN BY N-ZOMBIES.
THAT'S WHY HE'S SEARCHING FOR A WAY TO SYNTHESIZE APOSTLE BLOOD - OUR BLOOD.
YOUR BLOOD ...?
HE DOESN'T ONLY EXPERIMENT WITH OUR BLOOD ...
HSS ...

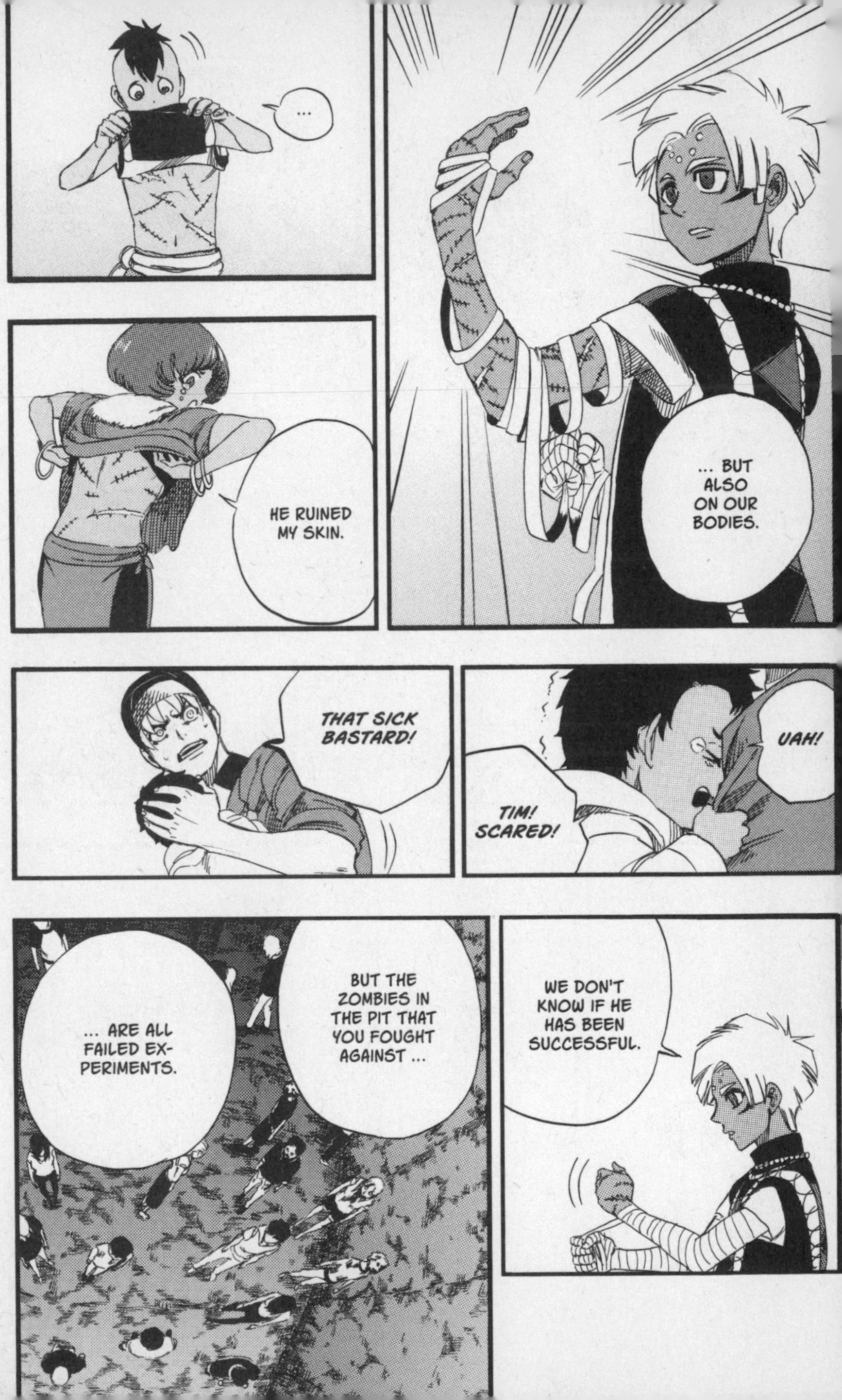
... BUT ALSO ON OUR BODIES.
...
HE RUINED MY SKIN.
UAH!
TIM! SCARED!
THAT SICK BASTARD!
WE DON'T KNOW IF HE HAS BEEN SUCCESSFUL.
BUT THE ZOMBIES IN THE PIT THAT YOU FOUGHT AGAINST ...
... ARE ALL FAILED EX-
PERIMENTS.

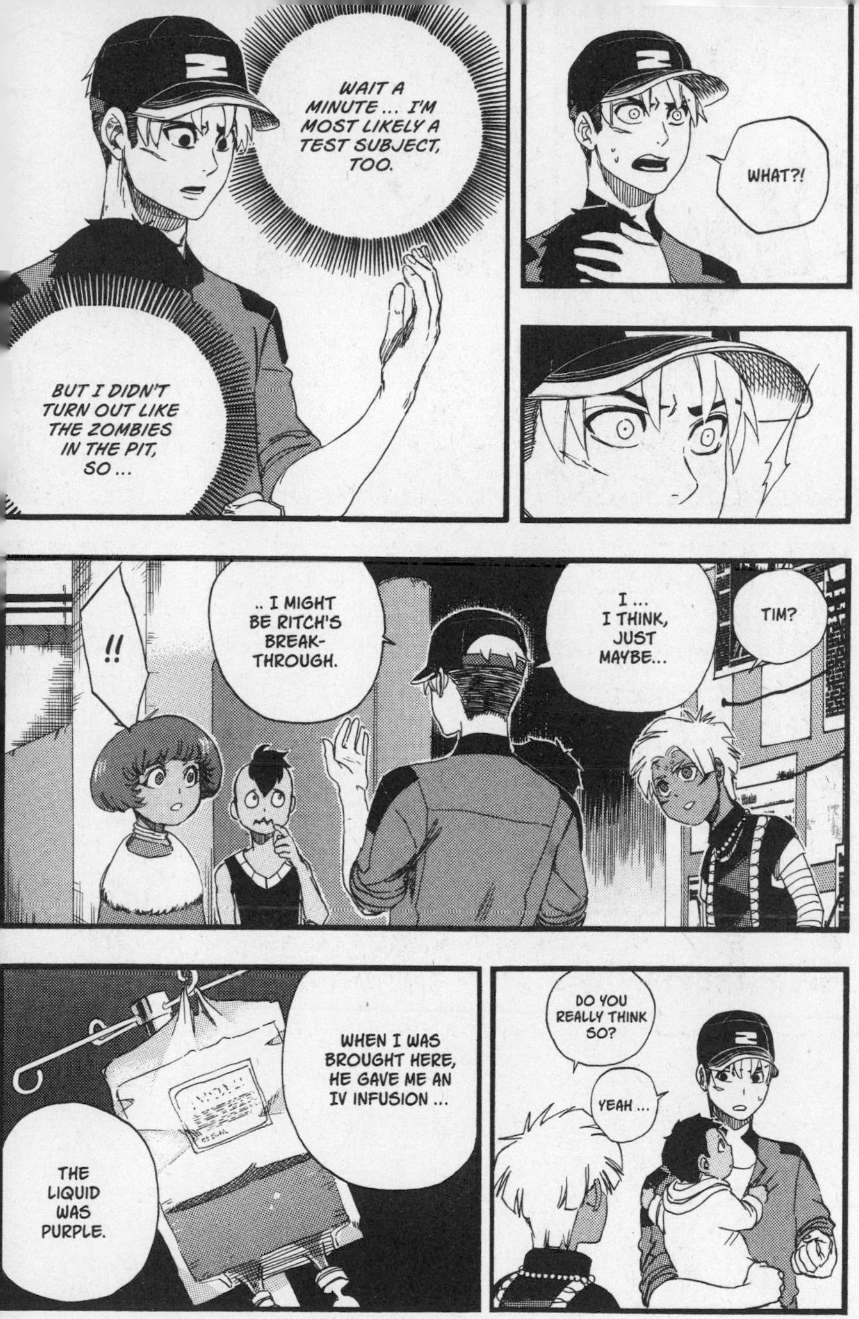
WHAT?!
WAIT A MINUTE ... I'M MOST LIKELY A TEST SUBJECT, TOO.
BUT I DIDN'T TURN OUT LIKE THE ZOMBIES IN THE PIT, SO ...
TIM?
I ... I THINK, JUST MAYBE...
.. I MIGHT BE RITCH'S BREAK-THROUGH.
!!
DO YOU REALLY THINK SO?
YEAH ...
WHEN I WAS BROUGHT HERE, HE GAVE ME AN IV INFUSION ...
THE LIQUID WAS PURPLE.

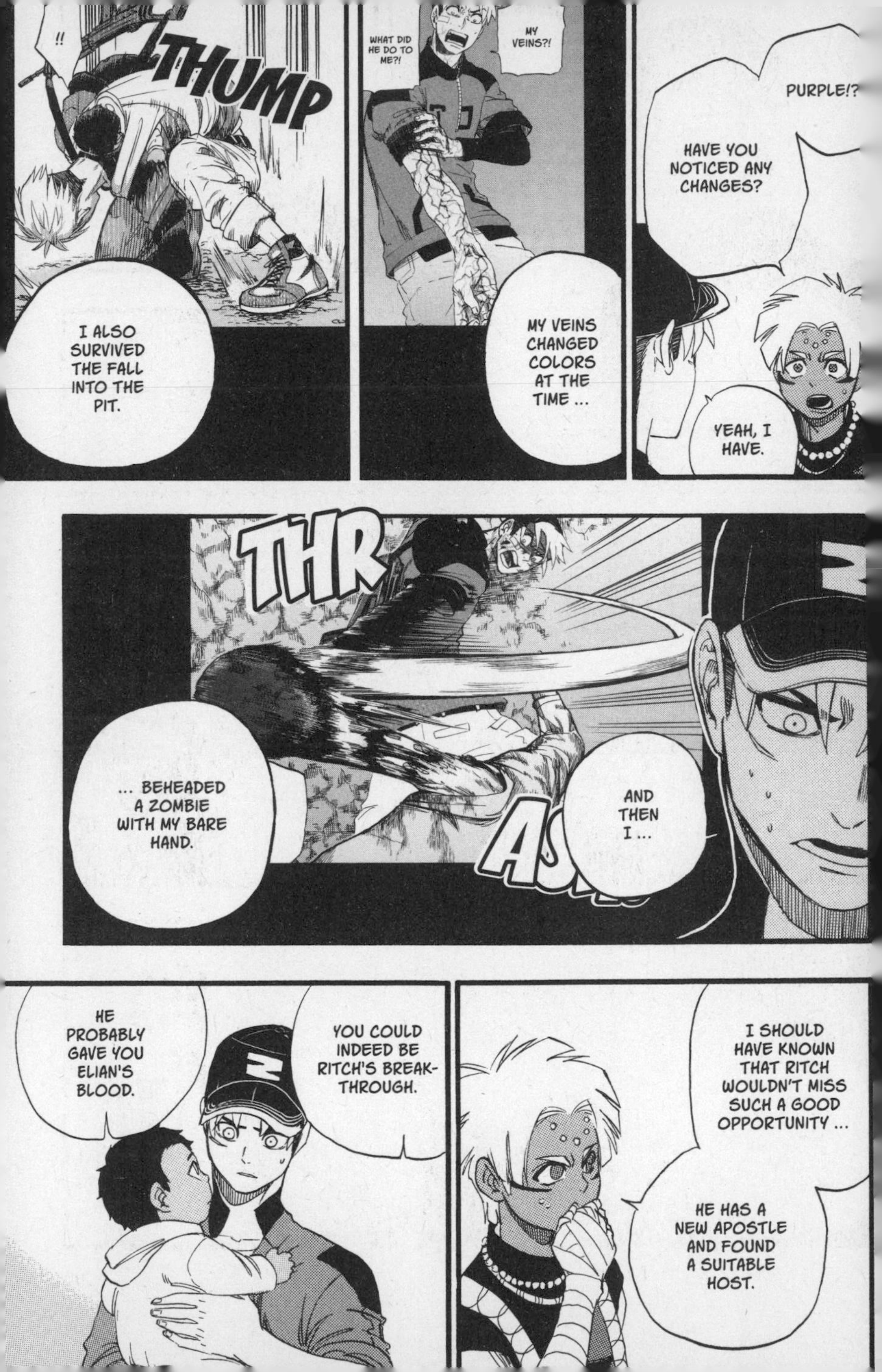
HAVE YOU NOTICED ANY CHANGES?
YEAH, I HAVE.
MY VEINS?!
WHAT DID HE DO TO ME?!
PURPLE!?
MY VEINS CHANGED COLORS AT THE TIME ...
!!
THUMP
I ALSO SURVIVED THE FALL INTO THE PIT.
AND THEN I ...
THR
... BEHEADED A ZOMBIE WITH MY BARE HAND.
I SHOULD HAVE KNOWN THAT RITCH WOULDN'T MISS SUCH A GOOD OPPORTUNITY ...
HE HAS A NEW APOSTLE AND FOUND A SUITABLE HOST.
YOU COULD INDEED BE RITCH'S BREAK-THROUGH.
HE PROBABLY GAVE YOU ELIAN'S BLOOD.

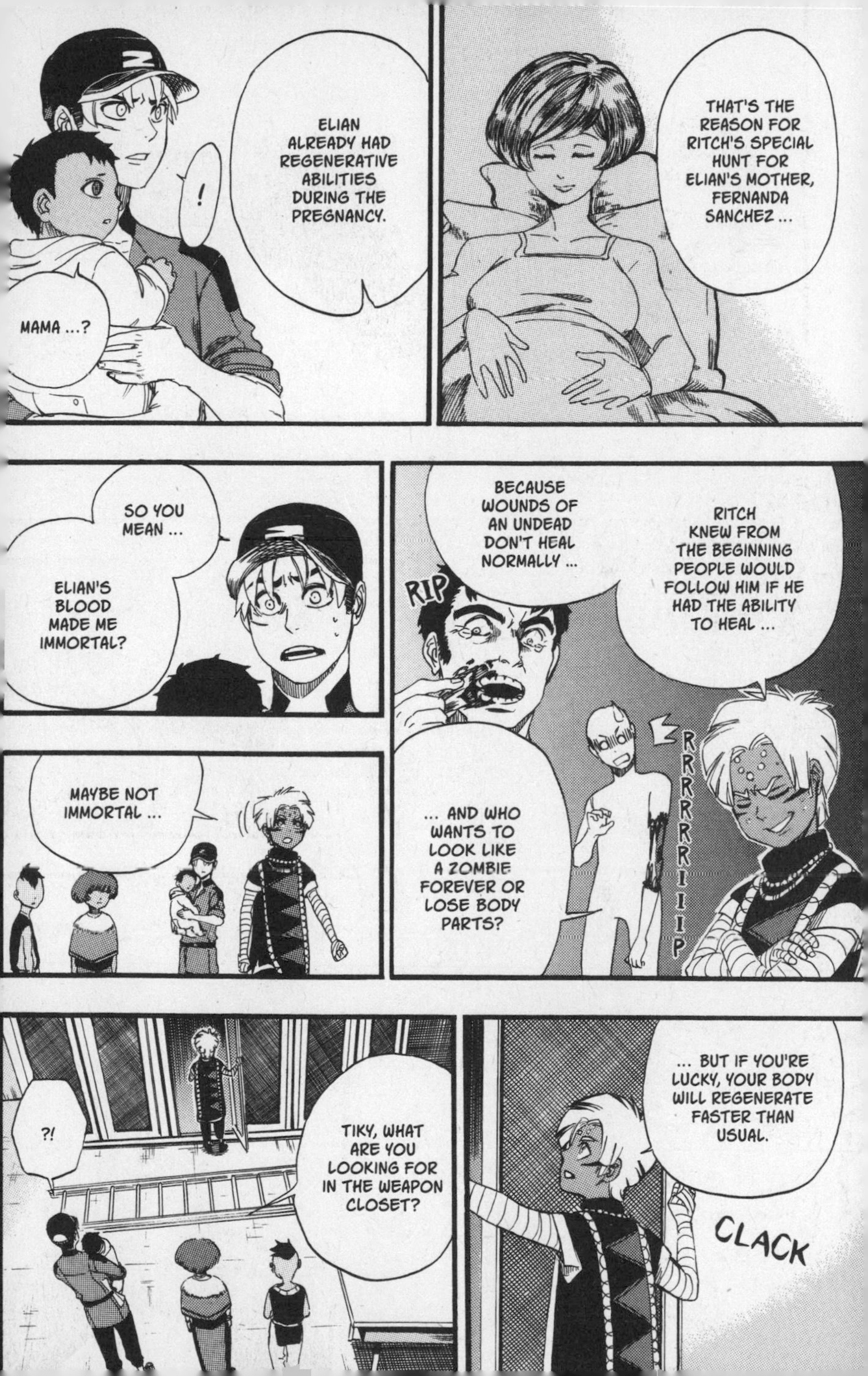
THAT'S THE REASON FOR RITCH'S SPECIAL HUNT FOR ELIAN'S MOTHER, FERNANDA SANCHEZ ...
ELIAN ALREADY HAD REGENERATIVE ABILITIES DURING THE PREGNANCY.
!
MAMA ...?
RITCH KNEW FROM THE BEGINNING PEOPLE WOULD FOLLOW HIM IF HE HAD THE ABILITY TO HEAL ...
BECAUSE WOUNDS OF AN UNDEAD DON'T HEAL NORMALLY ...
RIP
RRRRRIIIP
... AND WHO WANTS TO LOOK LIKE A ZOMBIE FOREVER OR LOSE BODY PARTS?
SO YOU MEAN ...
ELIAN'S BLOOD MADE ME IMMORTAL?
MAYBE NOT IMMORTAL ...
... BUT IF YOU'RE LUCKY, YOUR BODY WILL REGENERATE FASTER THAN USUAL.
CLACK
?!
TIKY, WHAT ARE YOU LOOKING FOR IN THE WEAPON CLOSET?

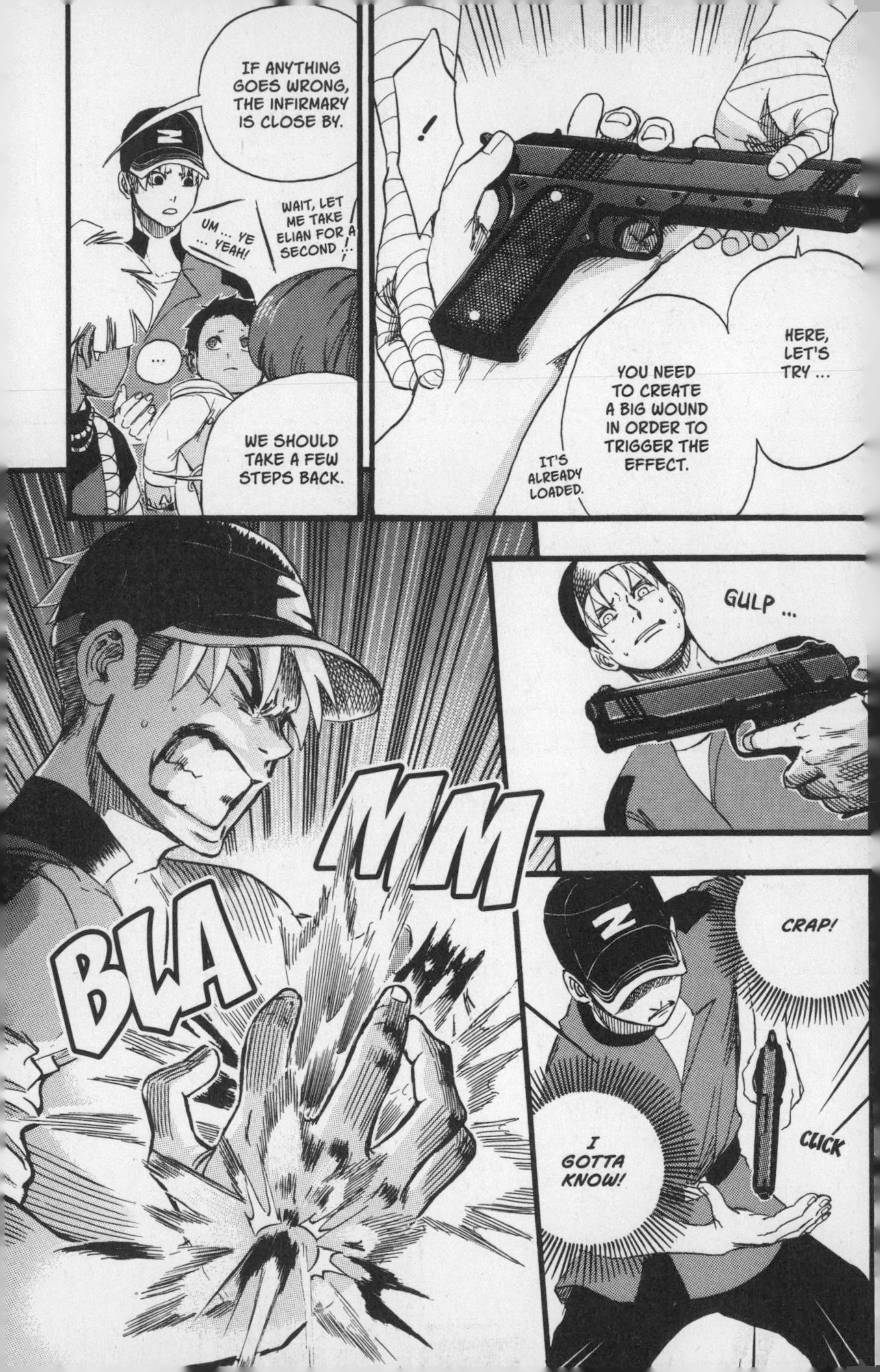
!
HERE, LET'S TRY ...
YOU NEED TO CREATE A BIG WOUND IN ORDER TO TRIGGER THE EFFECT.
IT'S ALREADY LOADED.
IF ANYTHING GOES WRONG, THE INFIRMARY IS CLOSE BY.
WAIT, LET ME TAKE ELIAN FOR A SECOND ...
UM ... YE ... YEAH!
...
WE SHOULD TAKE A FEW STEPS BACK.
GULP ...
CRAP!
CLICK
I GOTTA KNOW!
BLAMM

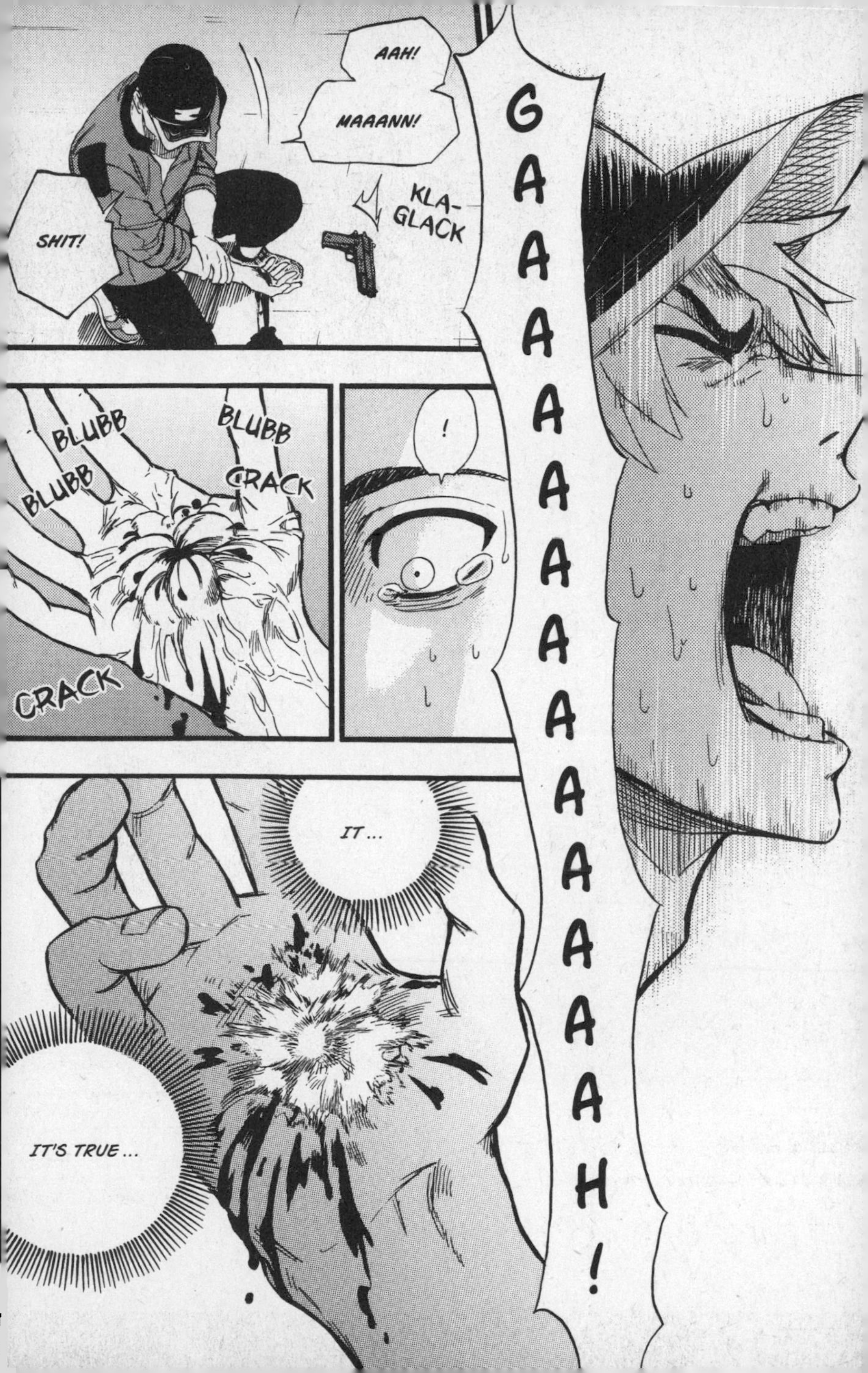
GAAAAAAAAAAAAAAAH!
AAH!
MAAANN!
KLA-GLACK
SHIT!
!
BLUBB
BLUBB
BLUBB
CRACK
CRACK
IT...
IT'S TRUE...

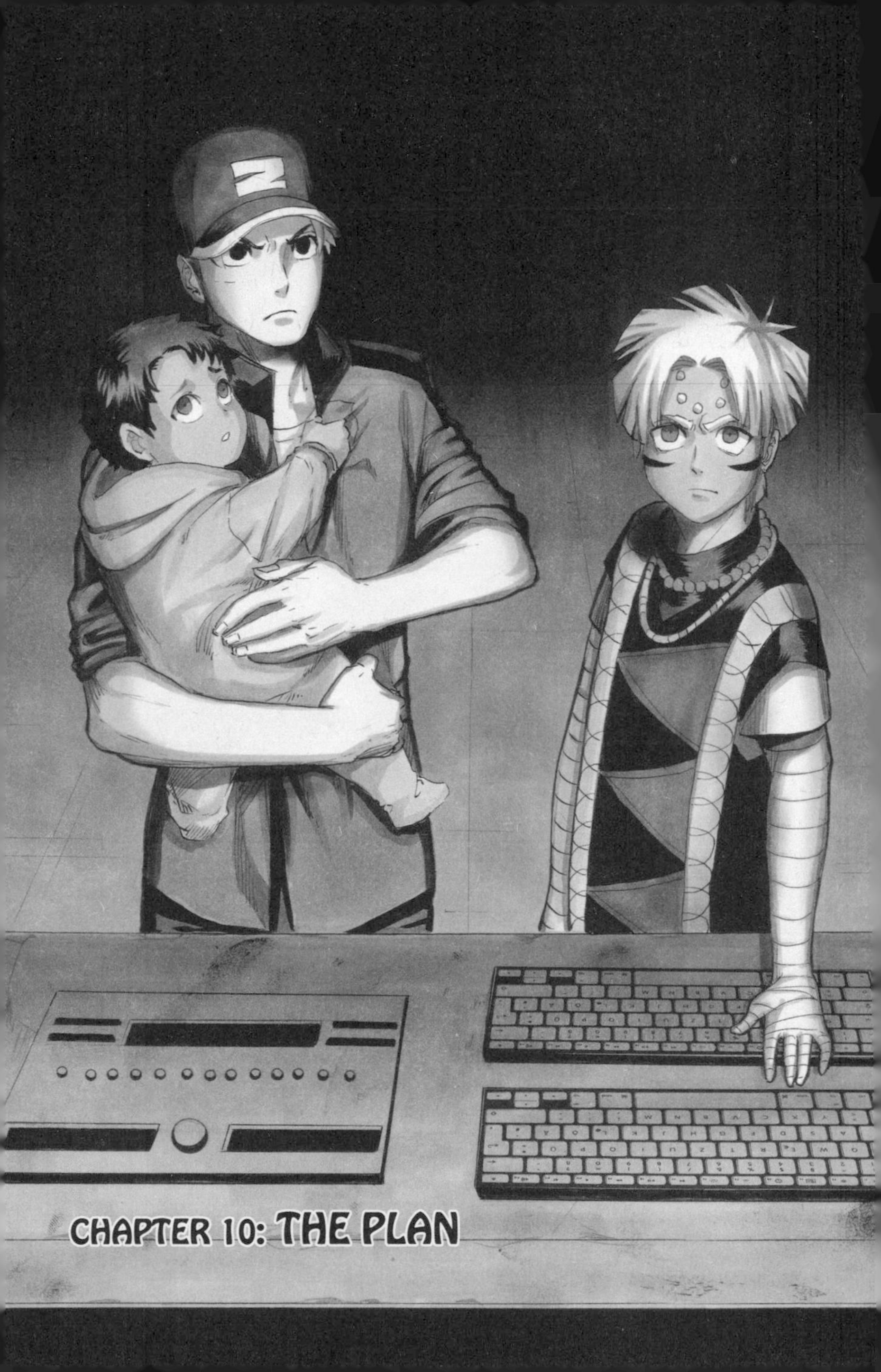
CHAPTER 10: THE PLAN

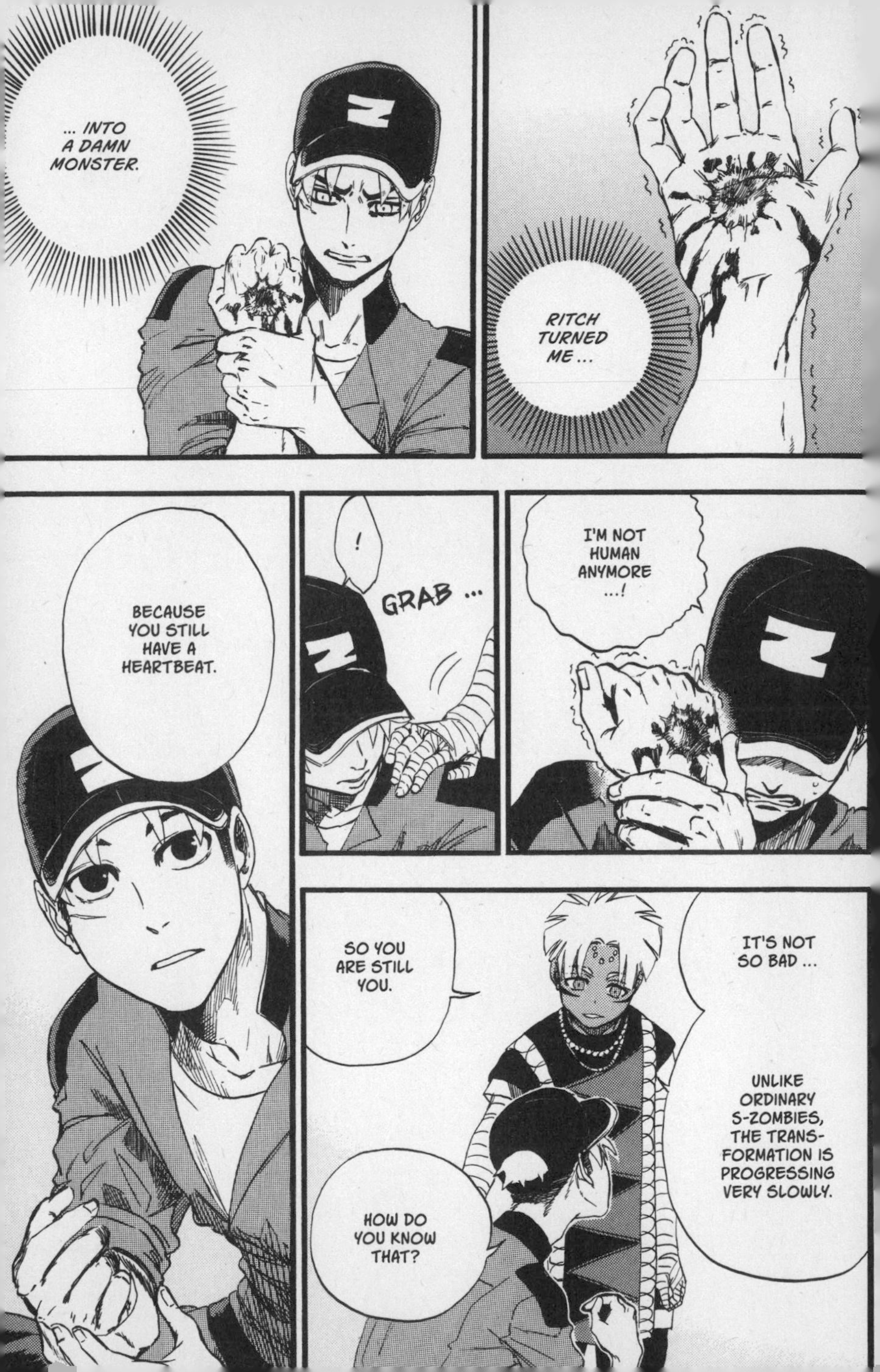
RITCH TURNED ME ...
... INTO A DAMN MONSTER.
I'M NOT HUMAN ANYMORE ...!
!
GRAB ...
IT'S NOT SO BAD ...
UNLIKE ORDINARY S-ZOMBIES, THE TRANS-FORMATION IS PROGRESSING VERY SLOWLY.
SO YOU ARE STILL YOU.
HOW DO YOU KNOW THAT?
BECAUSE YOU STILL HAVE A HEARTBEAT.

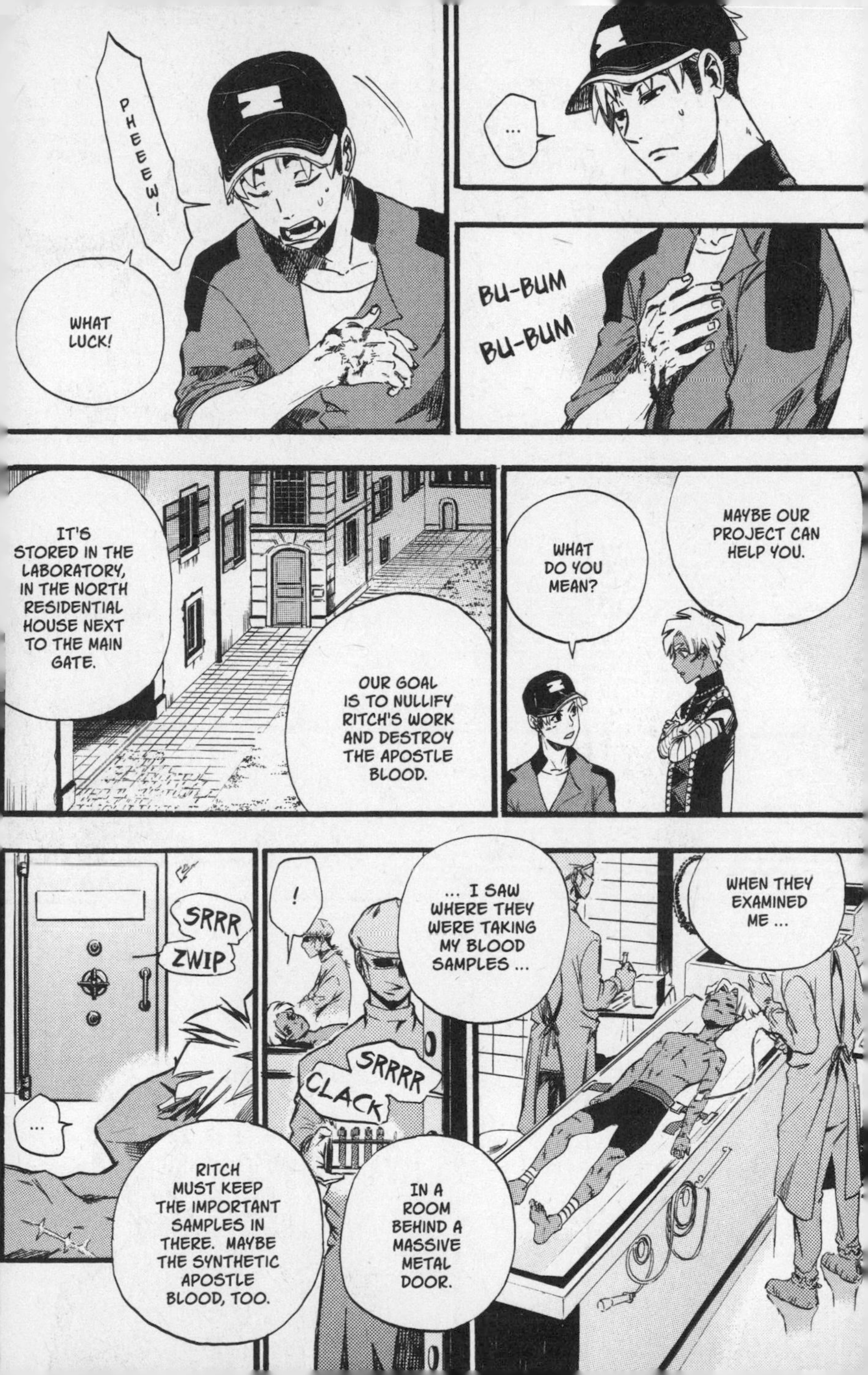
...
BU-BUM
BU-BUM
PHEEEW!
WHAT LUCK!
MAYBE OUR PROJECT CAN HELP YOU.
WHAT DO YOU MEAN?
OUR GOAL IS TO NULLIFY RITCH'S WORK AND DESTROY THE APOSTLE BLOOD.
IT'S STORED IN THE LABORATORY, IN THE NORTH RESIDENTIAL HOUSE NEXT TO THE MAIN GATE.
WHEN THEY EXAMINED ME ...
... I SAW WHERE THEY WERE TAKING MY BLOOD SAMPLES ...
IN A ROOM BEHIND A MASSIVE METAL DOOR.
!
SRRRR
CLACK
RITCH MUST KEEP THE IMPORTANT SAMPLES IN THERE. MAYBE THE SYNTHETIC APOSTLE BLOOD, TOO.
SRRR
ZWIP
...

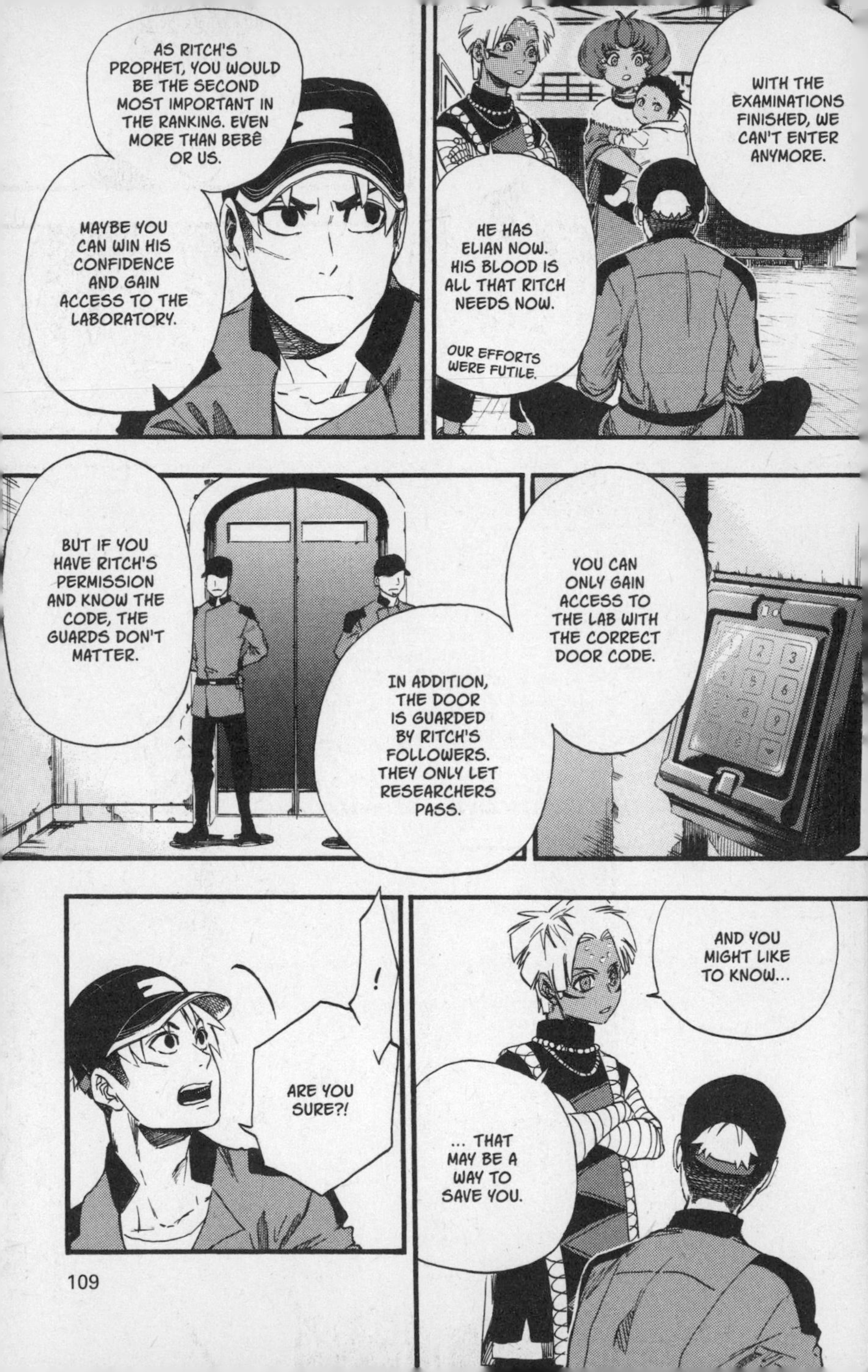
WITH THE EXAMINATIONS FINISHED, WE CAN'T ENTER ANYMORE.
HE HAS ELIAN NOW. HIS BLOOD IS ALL THAT RITCH NEEDS NOW.
OUR EFFORTS WERE FUTILE.
AS RITCH'S PROPHET, YOU WOULD BE THE SECOND MOST IMPORTANT IN THE RANKING. EVEN MORE THAN BEBÊ OR US.
MAYBE YOU CAN WIN HIS CONFIDENCE AND GAIN ACCESS TO THE LABORATORY.
YOU CAN ONLY GAIN ACCESS TO THE LAB WITH THE CORRECT DOOR CODE.
IN ADDITION, THE DOOR IS GUARDED BY RITCH'S FOLLOWERS. THEY ONLY LET RESEARCHERS PASS.
BUT IF YOU HAVE RITCH'S PERMISSION AND KNOW THE CODE, THE GUARDS DON'T MATTER.
AND YOU MIGHT LIKE TO KNOW...
... THAT MAY BE A WAY TO SAVE YOU.
!
ARE YOU SURE?!

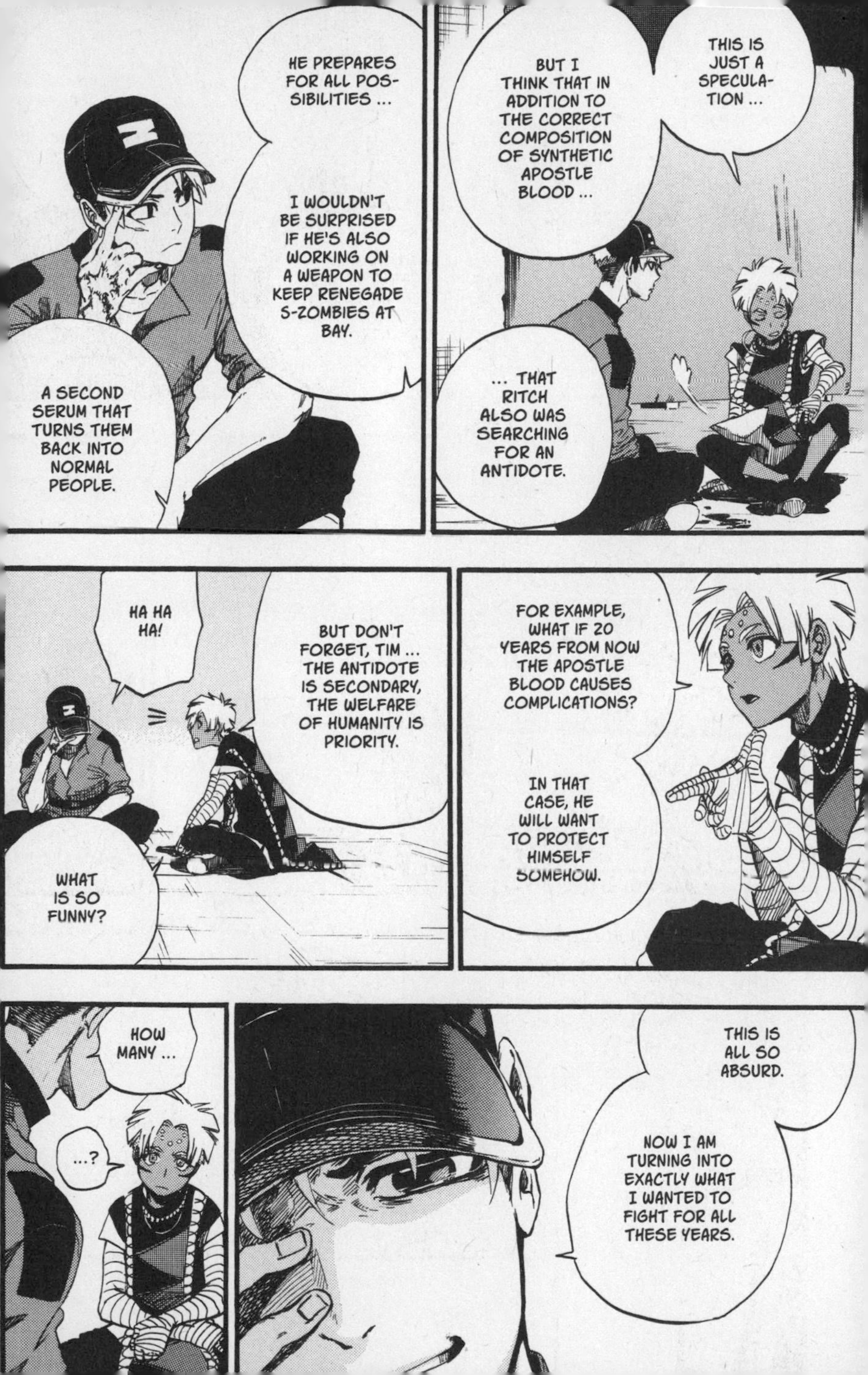
THIS IS JUST A SPECULATION ...
BUT I THINK THAT IN ADDITION TO THE CORRECT COMPOSITION OF SYNTHETIC APOSTLE BLOOD ...
... THAT RITCH ALSO WAS SEARCHING FOR AN ANTIDOTE.
HE PREPARES FOR ALL POSSIBILITIES ...
I WOULDN'T BE SURPRISED IF HE'S ALSO WORKING ON A WEAPON TO KEEP RENEGADE S-ZOMBIES AT BAY.
A SECOND SERUM THAT TURNS THEM BACK INTO NORMAL PEOPLE.
FOR EXAMPLE, WHAT IF 20 YEARS FROM NOW THE APOSTLE BLOOD CAUSES COMPLICATIONS?
IN THAT CASE, HE WILL WANT TO PROTECT HIMSELF SOMEHOW.
BUT DON'T FORGET, TIM ... THE ANTIDOTE IS SECONDARY, THE WELFARE OF HUMANITY IS PRIORITY.
HA HA HA!
WHAT IS SO FUNNY?
THIS IS ALL SO ABSURD.
NOW I AM TURNING INTO EXACTLY WHAT I WANTED TO FIGHT FOR ALL THESE YEARS.
HOW MANY ...
...?

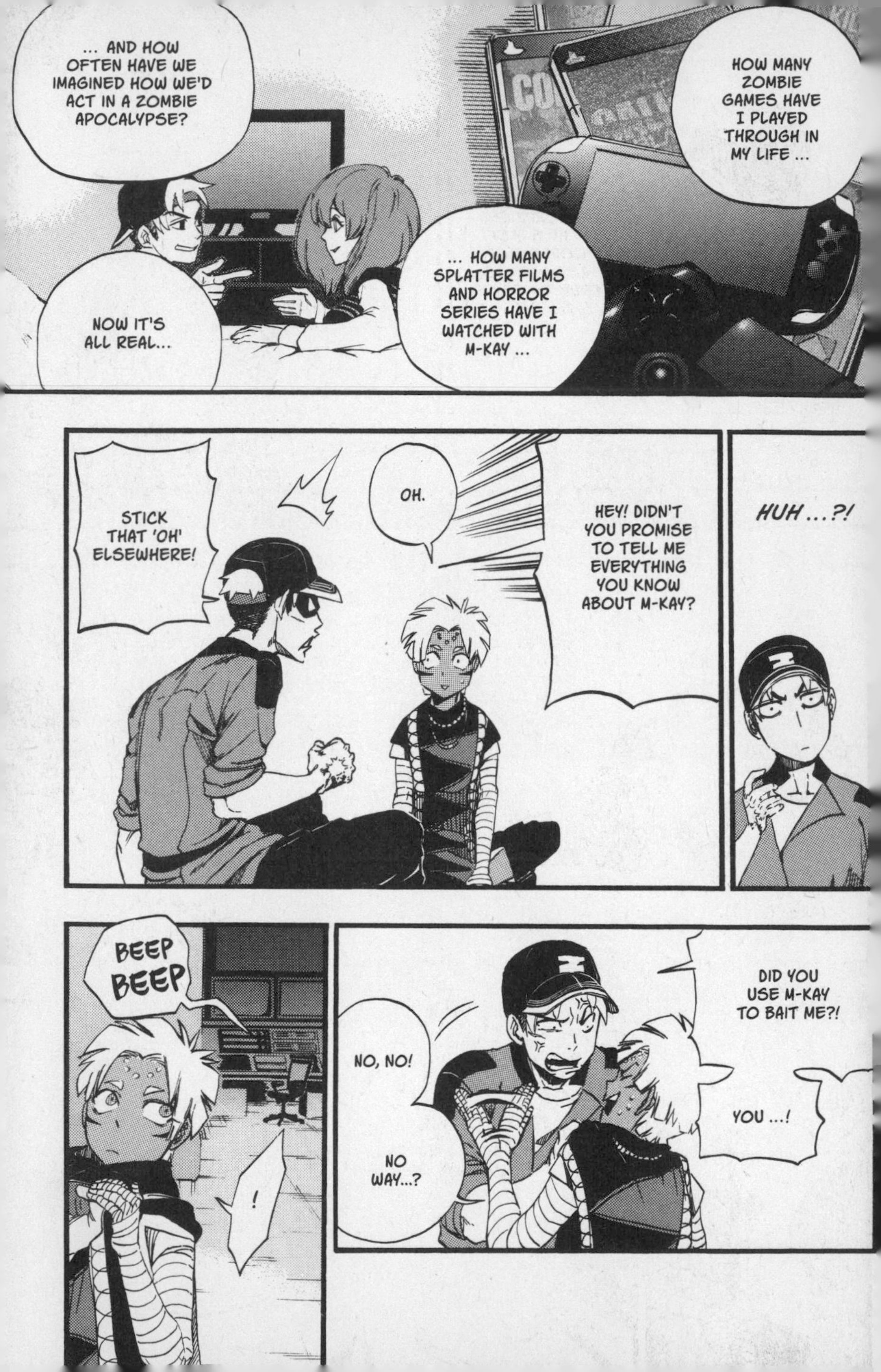
HOW MANY ZOMBIE GAMES HAVE I PLAYED THROUGH IN MY LIFE ...
... HOW MANY SPLATTER FILMS AND HORROR SERIES HAVE I WATCHED WITH M-KAY ...
... AND HOW OFTEN HAVE WE IMAGINED HOW WE'D ACT IN A ZOMBIE APOCALYPSE?
NOW IT'S ALL REAL...
HUH ...?!
HEY! DIDN'T YOU PROMISE TO TELL ME EVERYTHING YOU KNOW ABOUT M-KAY?
OH.
STICK THAT 'OH' ELSEWHERE!
DID YOU USE M-KAY TO BAIT ME?!
YOU ...!
NO, NO!
NO WAY...?
BEEP BEEP
!

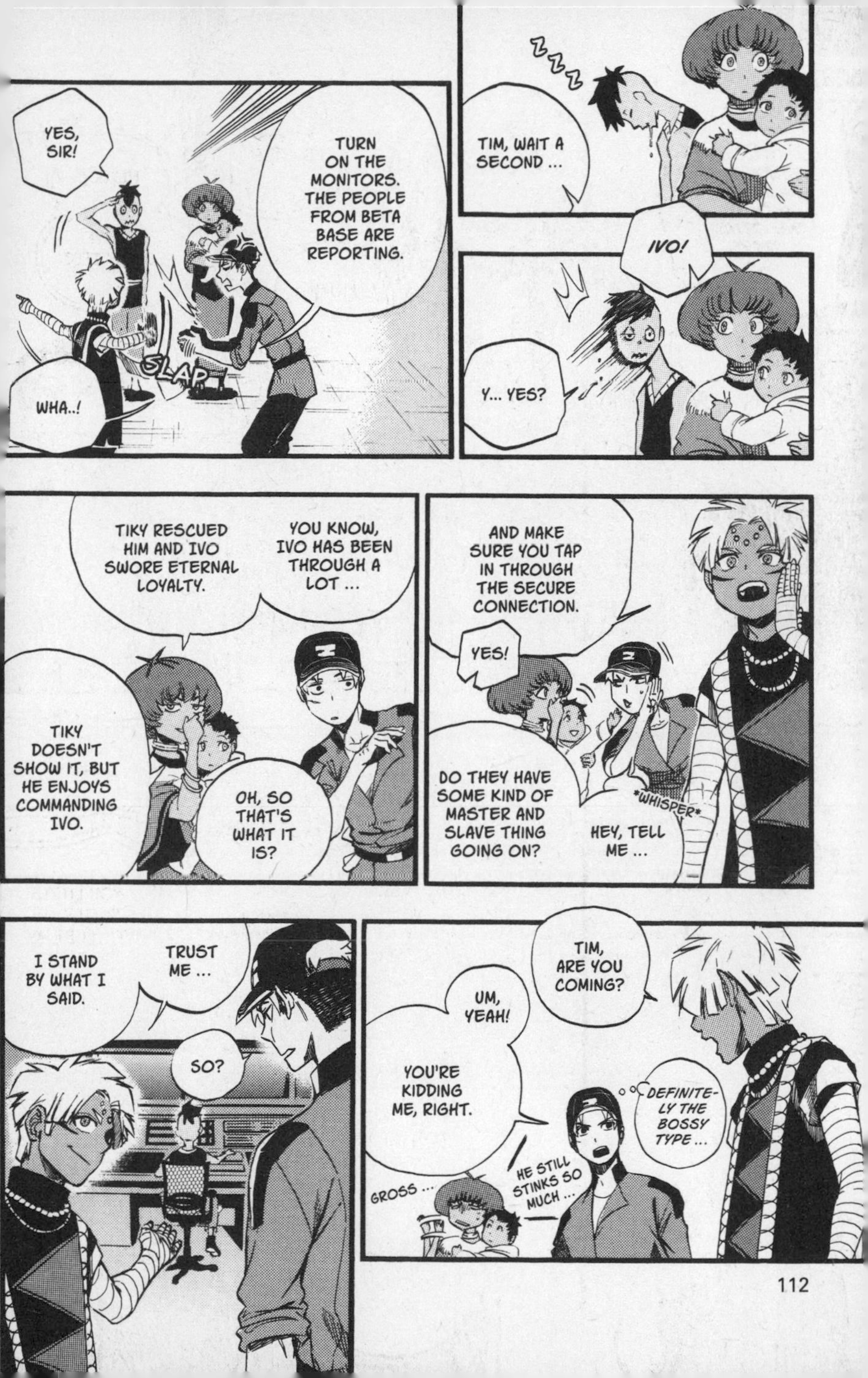
ZZZ
TIM, WAIT A SECOND ...
IVO!
Y... YES?
TURN ON THE MONITORS. THE PEOPLE FROM BETA BASE ARE REPORTING.
YES, SIR!
SLAP
WHA..!
AND MAKE SURE YOU TAP IN THROUGH THE SECURE CONNECTION.
YES!
*WHISPER*
HEY, TELL ME ...
DO THEY HAVE SOME KIND OF MASTER AND SLAVE THING GOING ON?
YOU KNOW, IVO HAS BEEN THROUGH A LOT ...
TIKY RESCUED HIM AND IVO SWORE ETERNAL LOYALTY.
OH, SO THAT'S WHAT IT IS?
TIKY DOESN'T SHOW IT, BUT HE ENJOYS COMMANDING IVO.
TIM, ARE YOU COMING?
UM, YEAH!
DEFINITE-LY THE BOSSY TYPE ...
YOU'RE KIDDING ME, RIGHT.
HE STILL STINKS SO MUCH ...
GROSS ...
TRUST ME ...
I STAND BY WHAT I SAID.
SO?

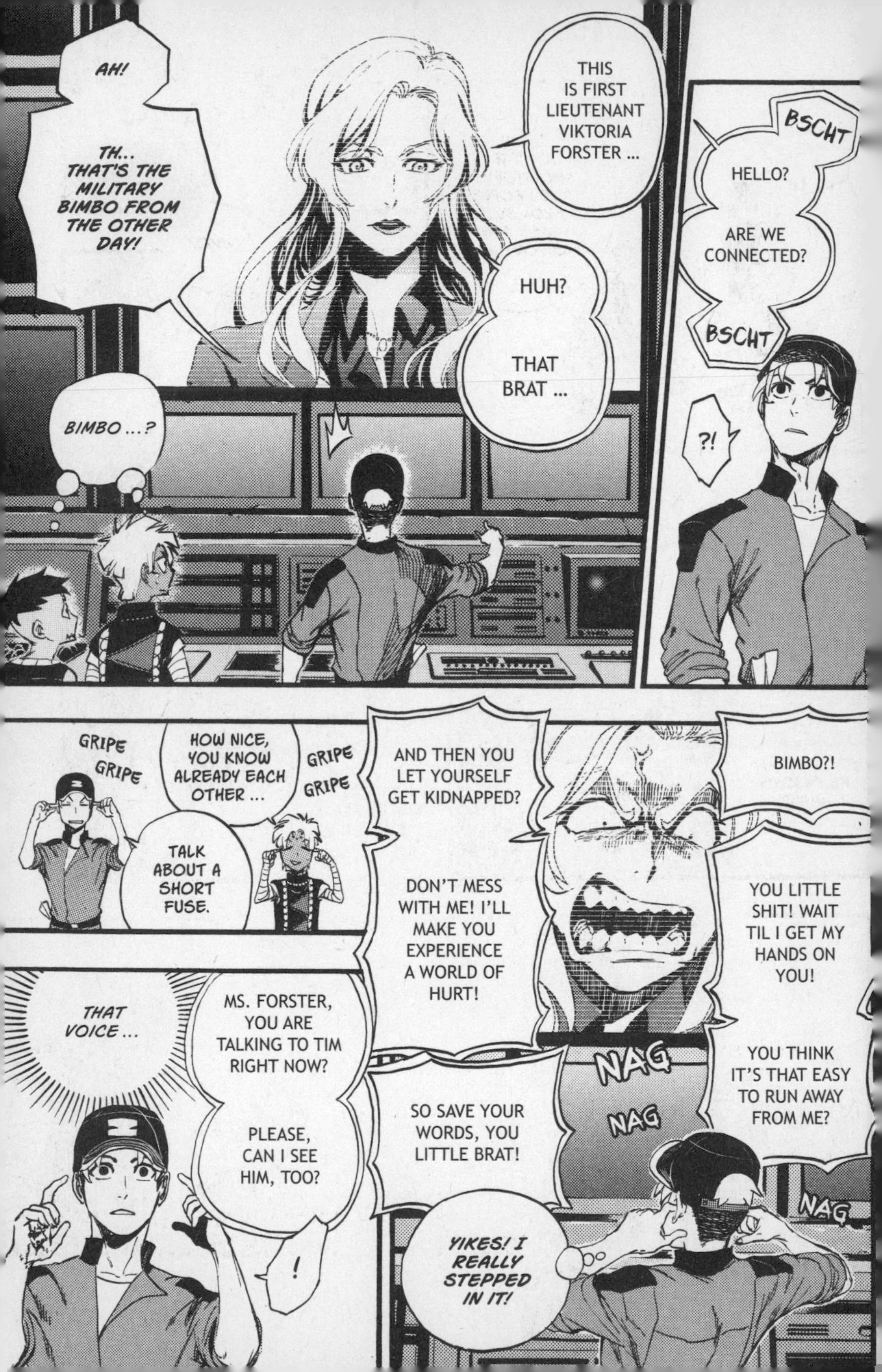

BSCHT
HELLO?
ARE WE CONNECTED?
BSCHT
?!
THIS IS FIRST LIEUTENANT VIKTORIA FORSTER ...
HUH?
THAT BRAT ...
AH!
TH... THAT'S THE MILITARY BIMBO FROM THE OTHER DAY!
BIMBO ...?
BIMBO?!
AND THEN YOU LET YOURSELF GET KIDNAPPED?
YOU LITTLE SHIT! WAIT TIL I GET MY HANDS ON YOU!
DON'T MESS WITH ME! I'LL MAKE YOU EXPERIENCE A WORLD OF HURT!
YOU THINK IT'S THAT EASY TO RUN AWAY FROM ME?
SO SAVE YOUR WORDS, YOU LITTLE BRAT!
NAG
NAG
NAG
YIKES! I REALLY STEPPED IN IT!
GRIPE GRIPE
HOW NICE, YOU KNOW ALREADY EACH OTHER ...
GRIPE GRIPE
TALK ABOUT A SHORT FUSE.
MS. FORSTER, YOU ARE TALKING TO TIM RIGHT NOW?
THAT VOICE ...
PLEASE, CAN I SEE HIM, TOO?
!

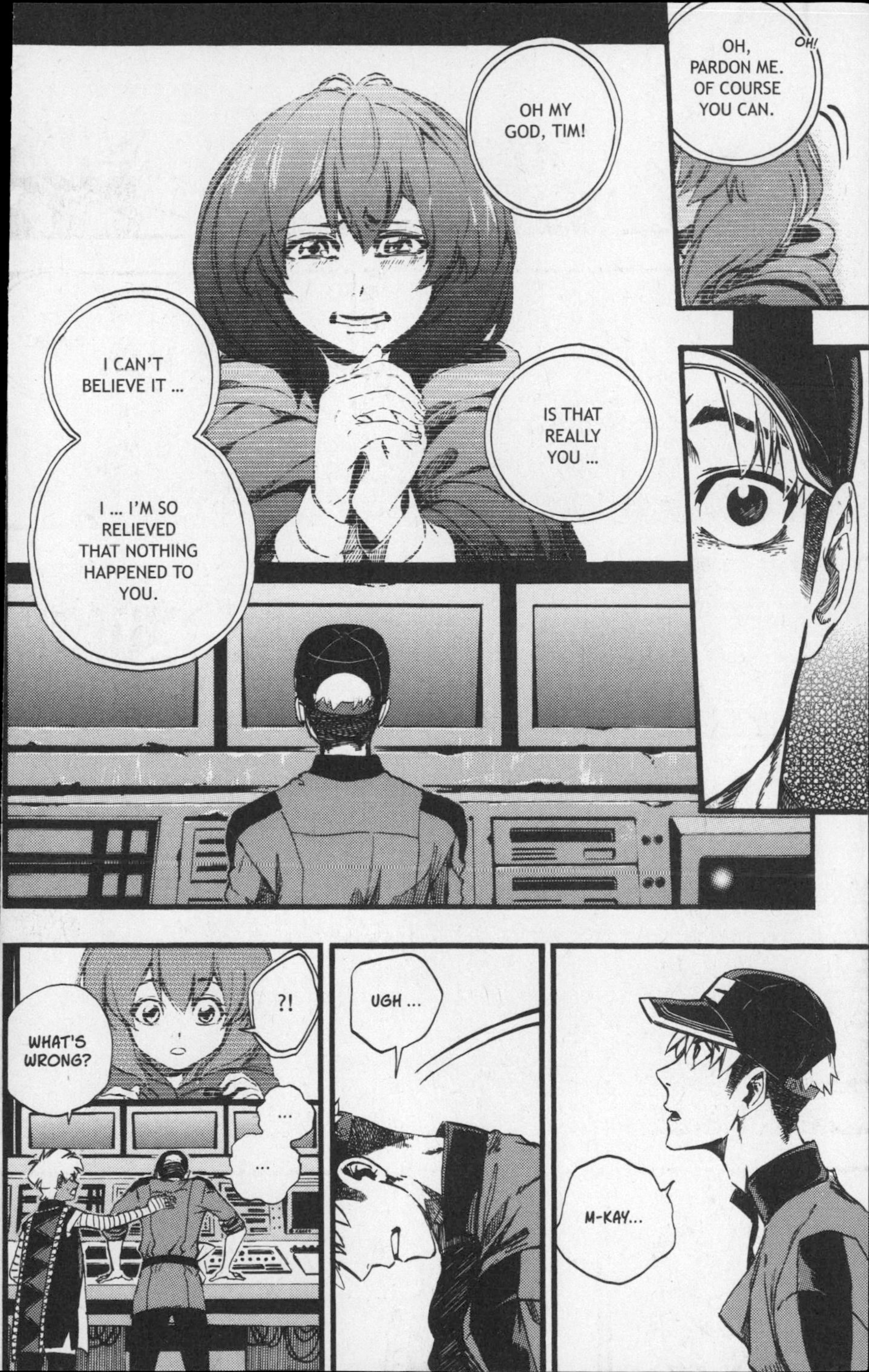
OH!
OH, PARDON ME. OF COURSE YOU CAN.
OH MY GOD, TIM!
IS THAT REALLY YOU ...
I CAN'T BELIEVE IT ...
I ... I'M SO RELIEVED THAT NOTHING HAPPENED TO YOU.
M-KAY...
UGH ...
?!
WHAT'S WRONG?
...
...

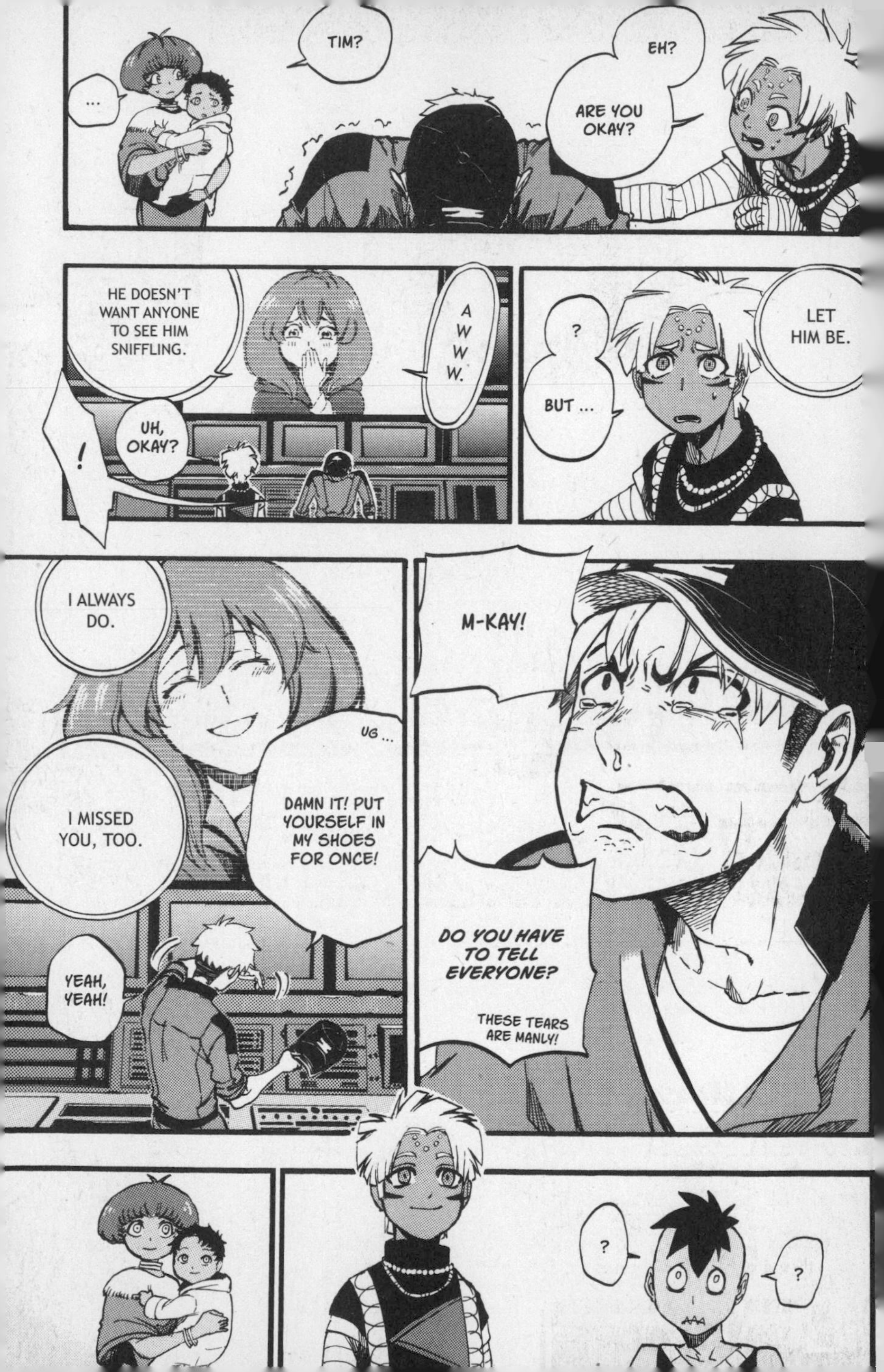
EH?
ARE YOU OKAY?
TIM?
...
LET HIM BE.
?
BUT ...
AWWW.
HE DOESN'T WANT ANYONE TO SEE HIM SNIFFLING.
UH, OKAY?
!
M-KAY!
DO YOU HAVE TO TELL EVERYONE?
THESE TEARS ARE MANLY!
I ALWAYS DO.
UG ...
DAMN IT! PUT YOURSELF IN MY SHOES FOR ONCE!
I MISSED YOU, TOO.
YEAH, YEAH!
?
?

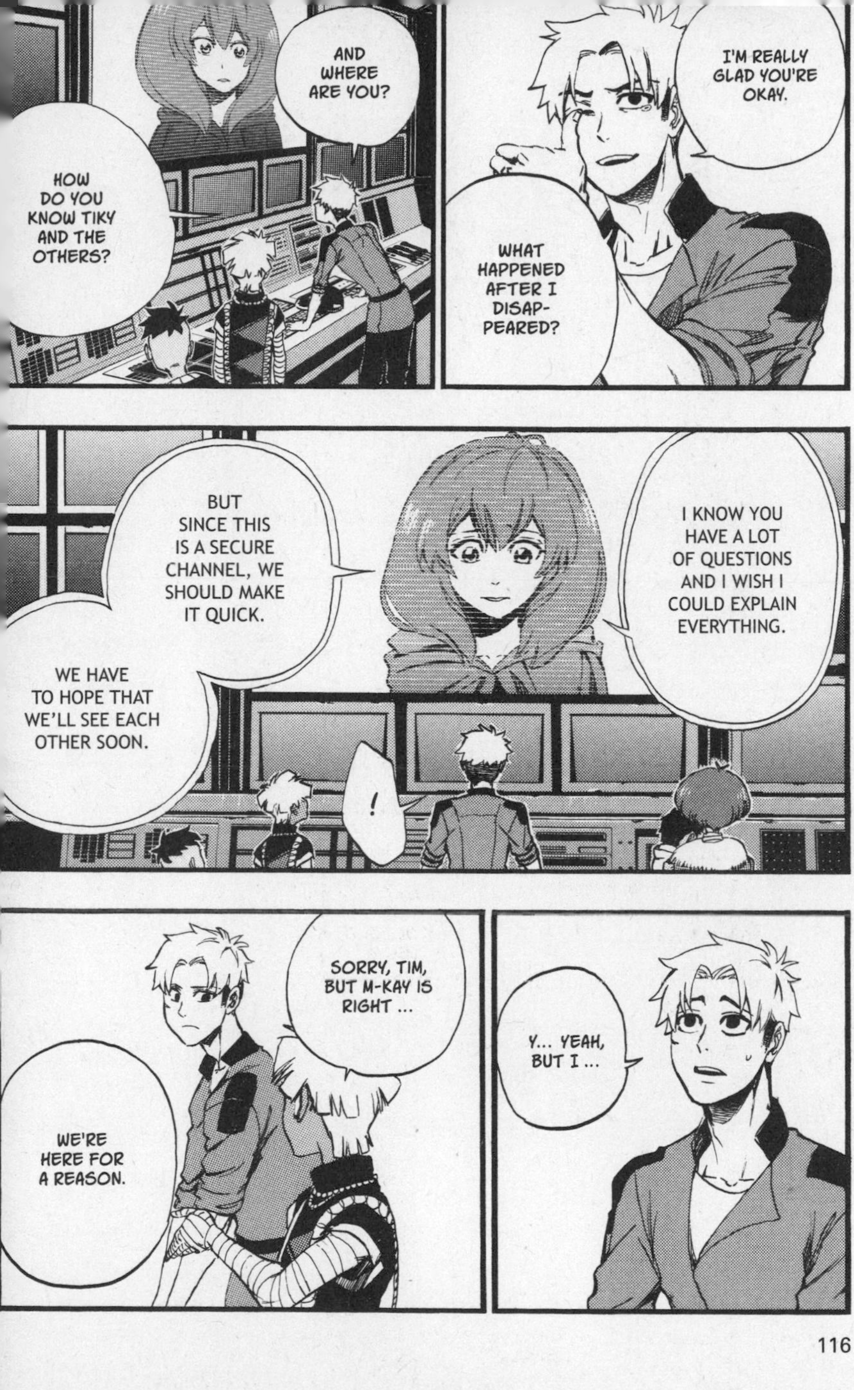
I'M REALLY GLAD YOU'RE OKAY.
WHAT HAPPENED AFTER I DISAP-PEARED?
AND WHERE ARE YOU?
HOW DO YOU KNOW TIKY AND THE OTHERS?
I KNOW YOU HAVE A LOT OF QUESTIONS AND I WISH I COULD EXPLAIN EVERYTHING.
BUT SINCE THIS IS A SECURE CHANNEL, WE SHOULD MAKE IT QUICK.
WE HAVE TO HOPE THAT WE'LL SEE EACH OTHER SOON.
!
Y... YEAH, BUT I ...
SORRY, TIM, BUT M-KAY IS RIGHT ...
WE'RE HERE FOR A REASON.

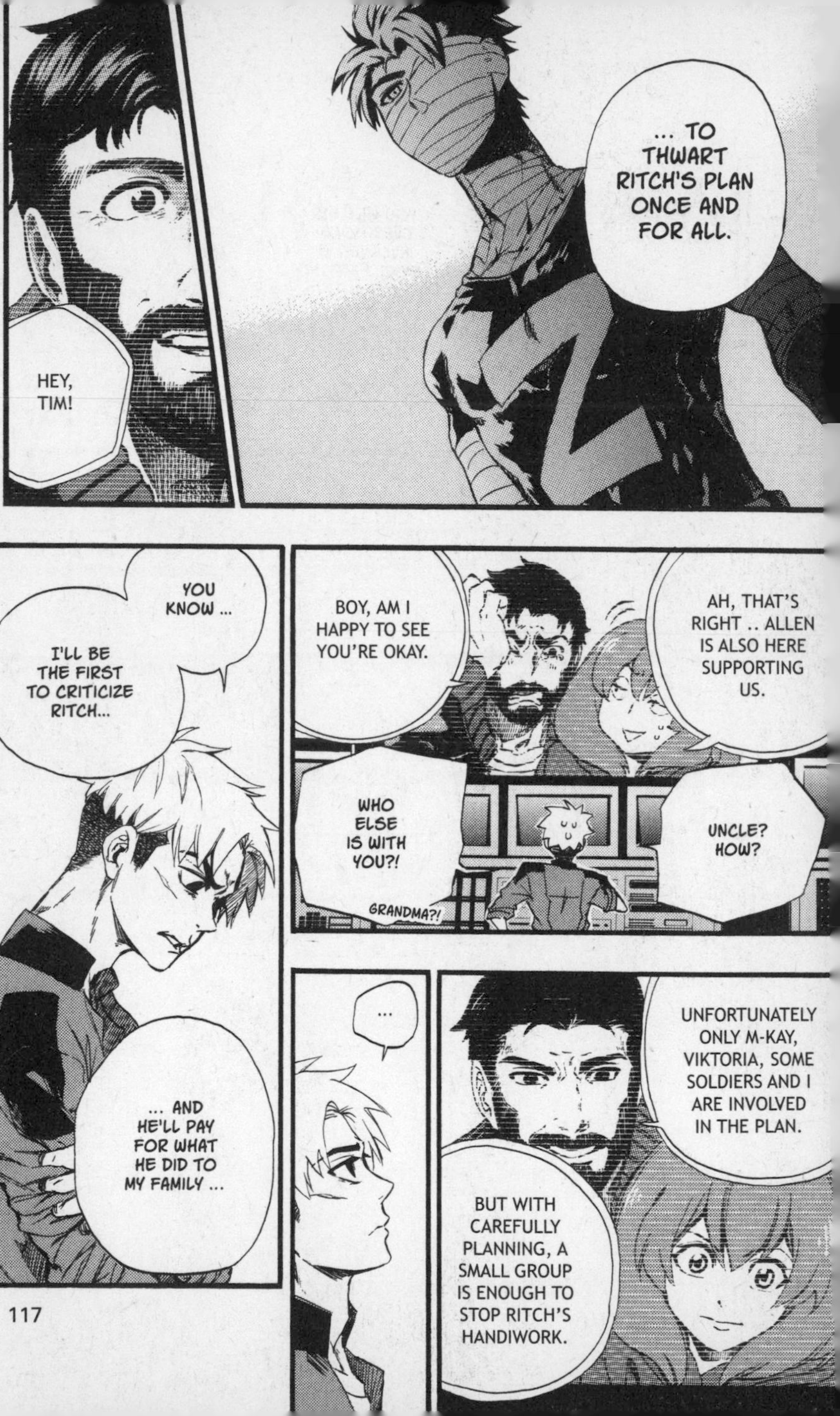
... TO THWART RITCH'S PLAN ONCE AND FOR ALL.
HEY, TIM!
AH, THAT'S RIGHT .. ALLEN IS ALSO HERE SUPPORTING US.
BOY, AM I HAPPY TO SEE YOU'RE OKAY.
UNCLE? HOW?
WHO ELSE IS WITH YOU?!
GRANDMA?!
UNFORTUNATELY ONLY M-KAY, VIKTORIA, SOME SOLDIERS AND I ARE INVOLVED IN THE PLAN.
BUT WITH CAREFULLY PLANNING, A SMALL GROUP IS ENOUGH TO STOP RITCH'S HANDIWORK.
...
YOU KNOW ...
I'LL BE THE FIRST TO CRITICIZE RITCH...
... AND HE'LL PAY FOR WHAT HE DID TO MY FAMILY ...

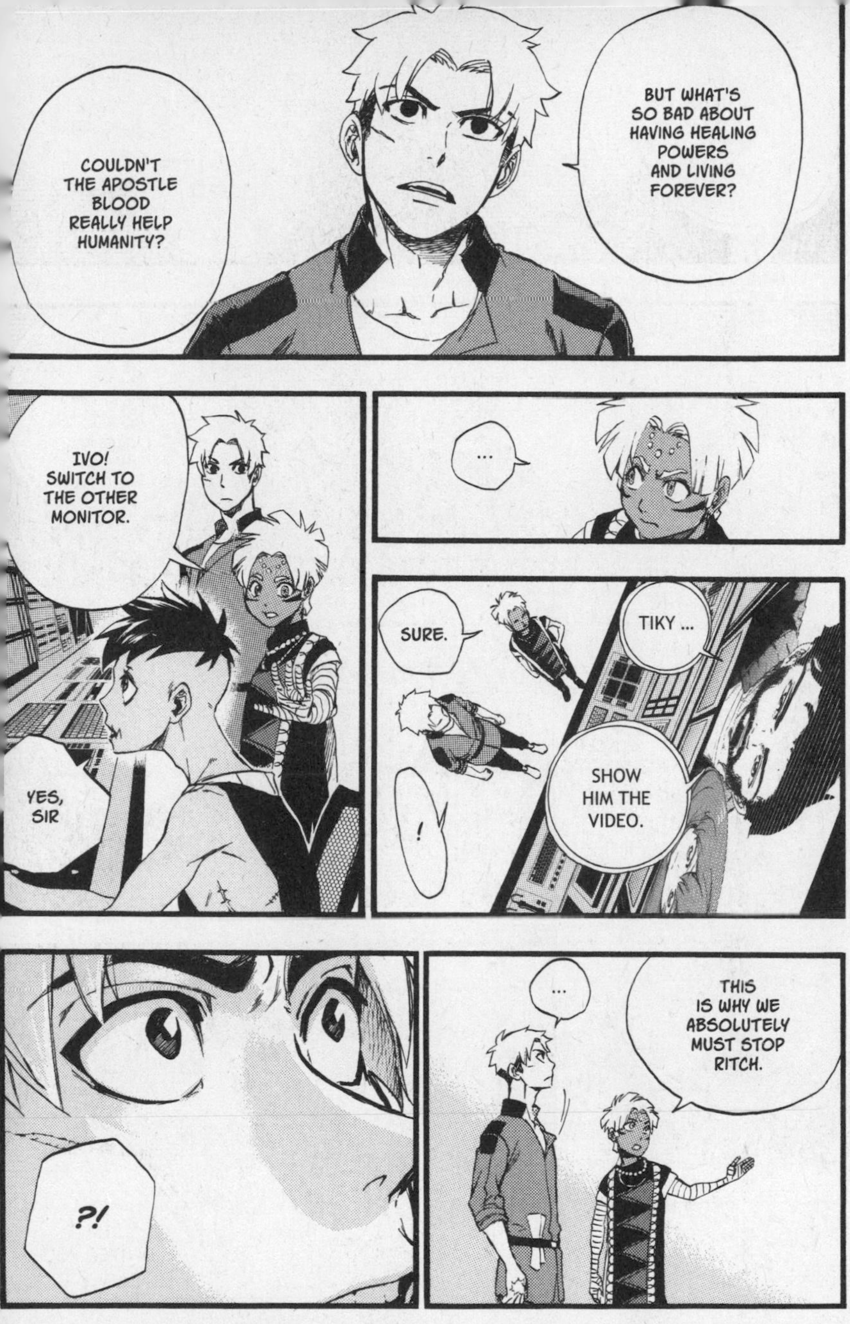
BUT WHAT'S SO BAD ABOUT HAVING HEALING POWERS AND LIVING FOREVER?
COULDN'T THE APOSTLE BLOOD REALLY HELP HUMANITY?
...
TIKY ...
SURE.
SHOW HIM THE VIDEO.
!
IVO! SWITCH TO THE OTHER MONITOR.
YES, SIR
THIS IS WHY WE ABSOLUTELY MUST STOP RITCH.
...
?!

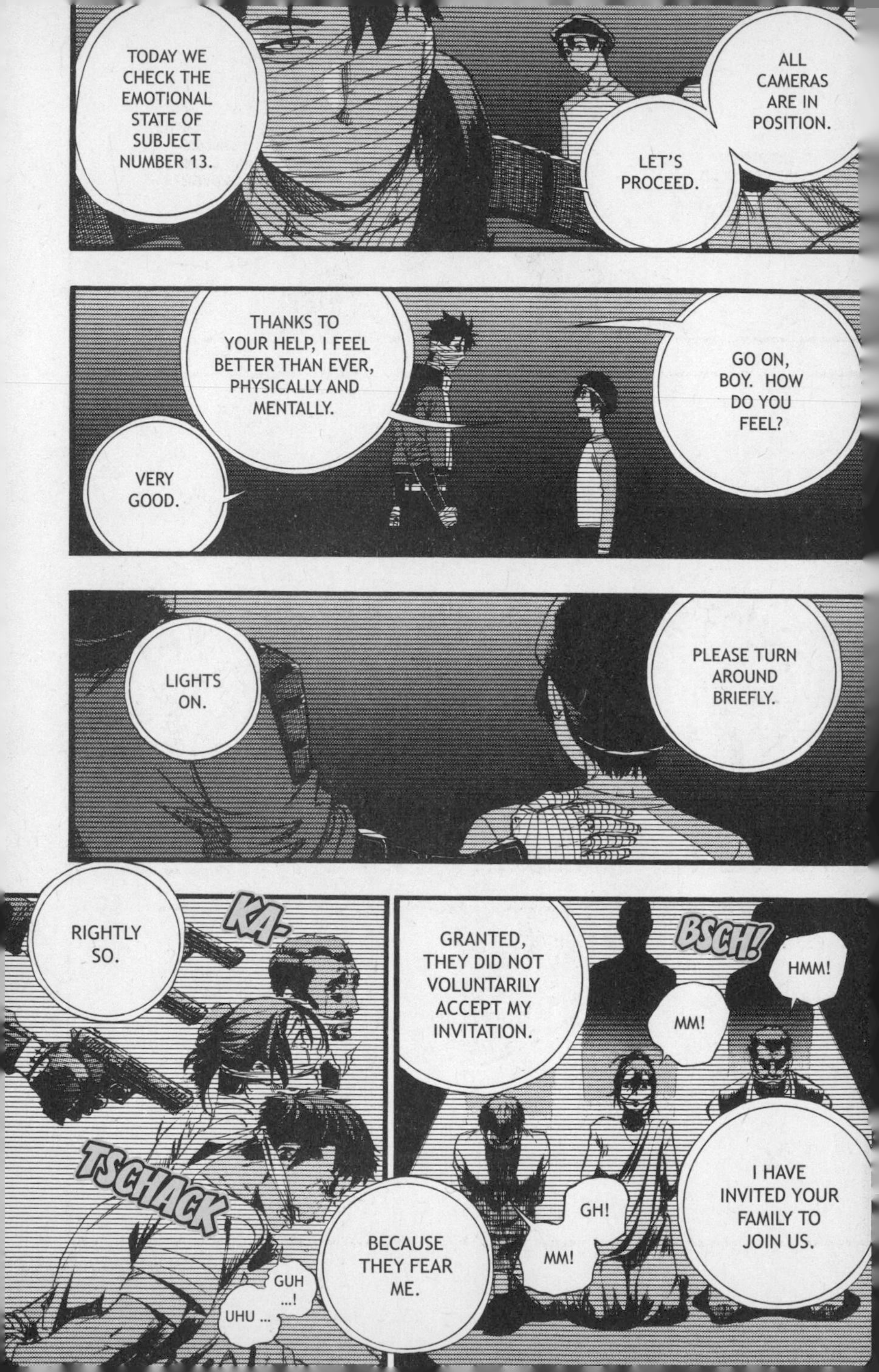
ALL CAMERAS ARE IN POSITION.
LET'S PROCEED.
TODAY WE CHECK THE EMOTIONAL STATE OF SUBJECT NUMBER 13.
GO ON, BOY. HOW DO YOU FEEL?
THANKS TO YOUR HELP, I FEEL BETTER THAN EVER, PHYSICALLY AND MENTALLY.
VERY GOOD.
PLEASE TURN AROUND BRIEFLY.
LIGHTS ON.
BSCH!
HMM!
MM!
I HAVE INVITED YOUR FAMILY TO JOIN US.
GRANTED, THEY DID NOT VOLUNTARILY ACCEPT MY INVITATION.
GH!
MM!
BECAUSE THEY FEAR ME.
KA-
RIGHTLY SO.
TSCHACK
GUH ...!
UHU ...

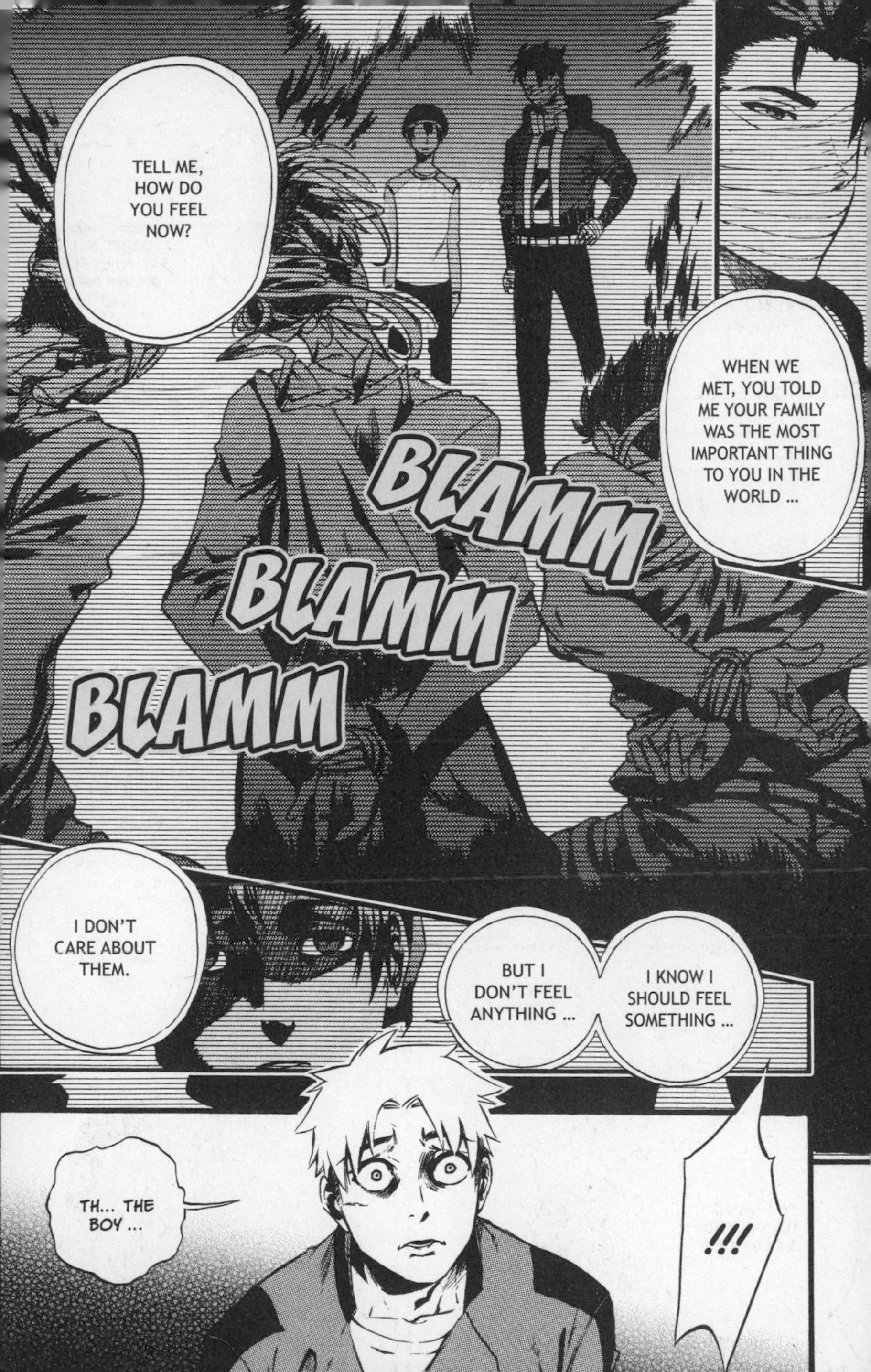
WHEN WE MET, YOU TOLD ME YOUR FAMILY WAS THE MOST IMPORTANT THING TO YOU IN THE WORLD ...
TELL ME, HOW DO YOU FEEL NOW?
BLAMM
BLAMM
BLAMM
I KNOW I SHOULD FEEL SOMETHING ...
BUT I DON'T FEEL ANYTHING ...
I DON'T CARE ABOUT THEM.
!!!
TH... THE BOY ...

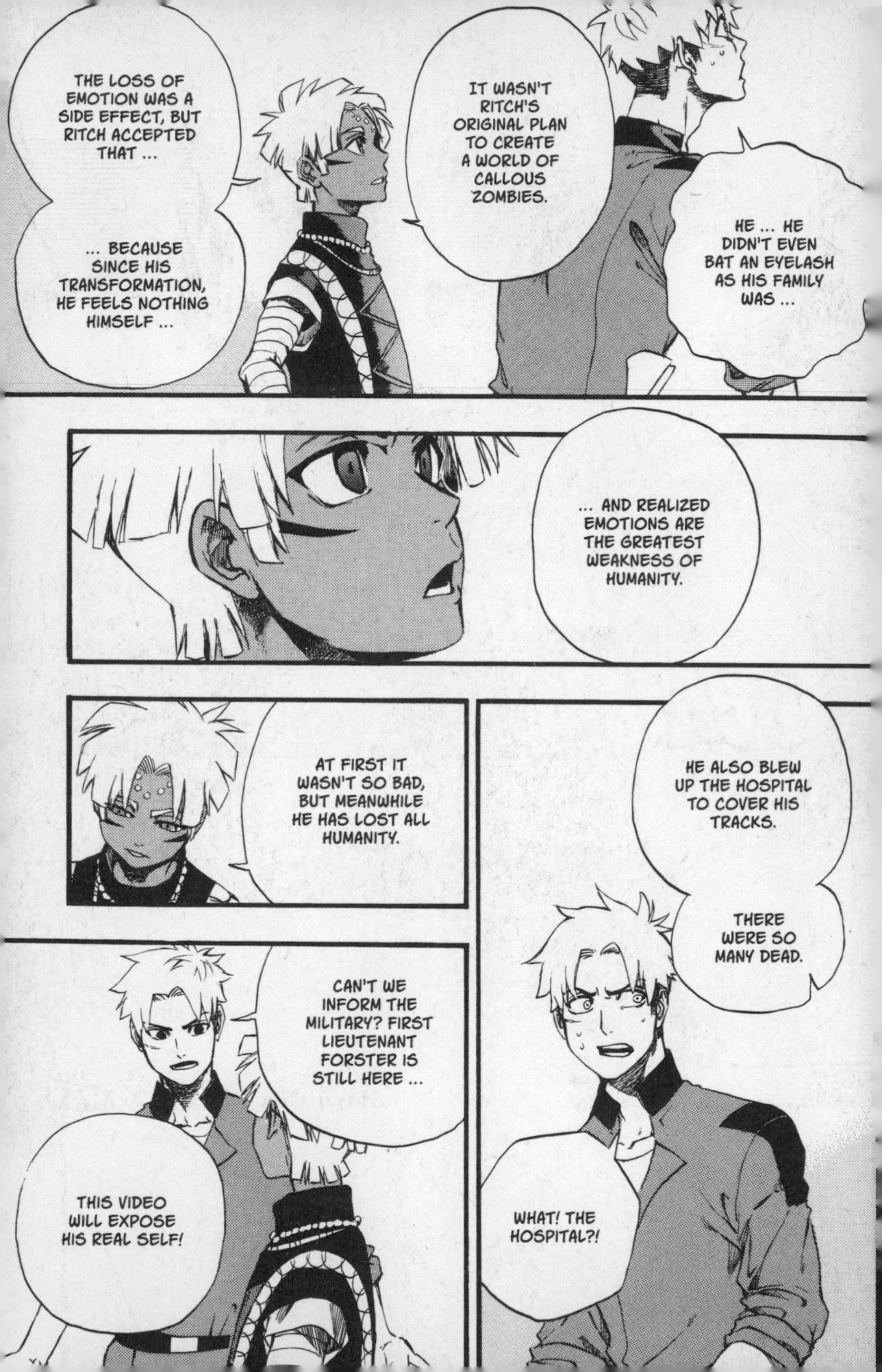
HE ... HE DIDN'T EVEN BAT AN EYELASH AS HIS FAMILY WAS ...
IT WASN'T RITCH'S ORIGINAL PLAN TO CREATE A WORLD OF CALLOUS ZOMBIES.
THE LOSS OF EMOTION WAS A SIDE EFFECT, BUT RITCH ACCEPTED THAT ...
... BECAUSE SINCE HIS TRANSFORMATION, HE FEELS NOTHING HIMSELF ...
... AND REALIZED EMOTIONS ARE THE GREATEST WEAKNESS OF HUMANITY.
HE ALSO BLEW UP THE HOSPITAL TO COVER HIS TRACKS.
THERE WERE SO MANY DEAD.
WHAT! THE HOSPITAL?!
AT FIRST IT WASN'T SO BAD, BUT MEANWHILE HE HAS LOST ALL HUMANITY.
CAN'T WE INFORM THE MILITARY? FIRST LIEUTENANT FORSTER IS STILL HERE ...
THIS VIDEO WILL EXPOSE HIS REAL SELF!

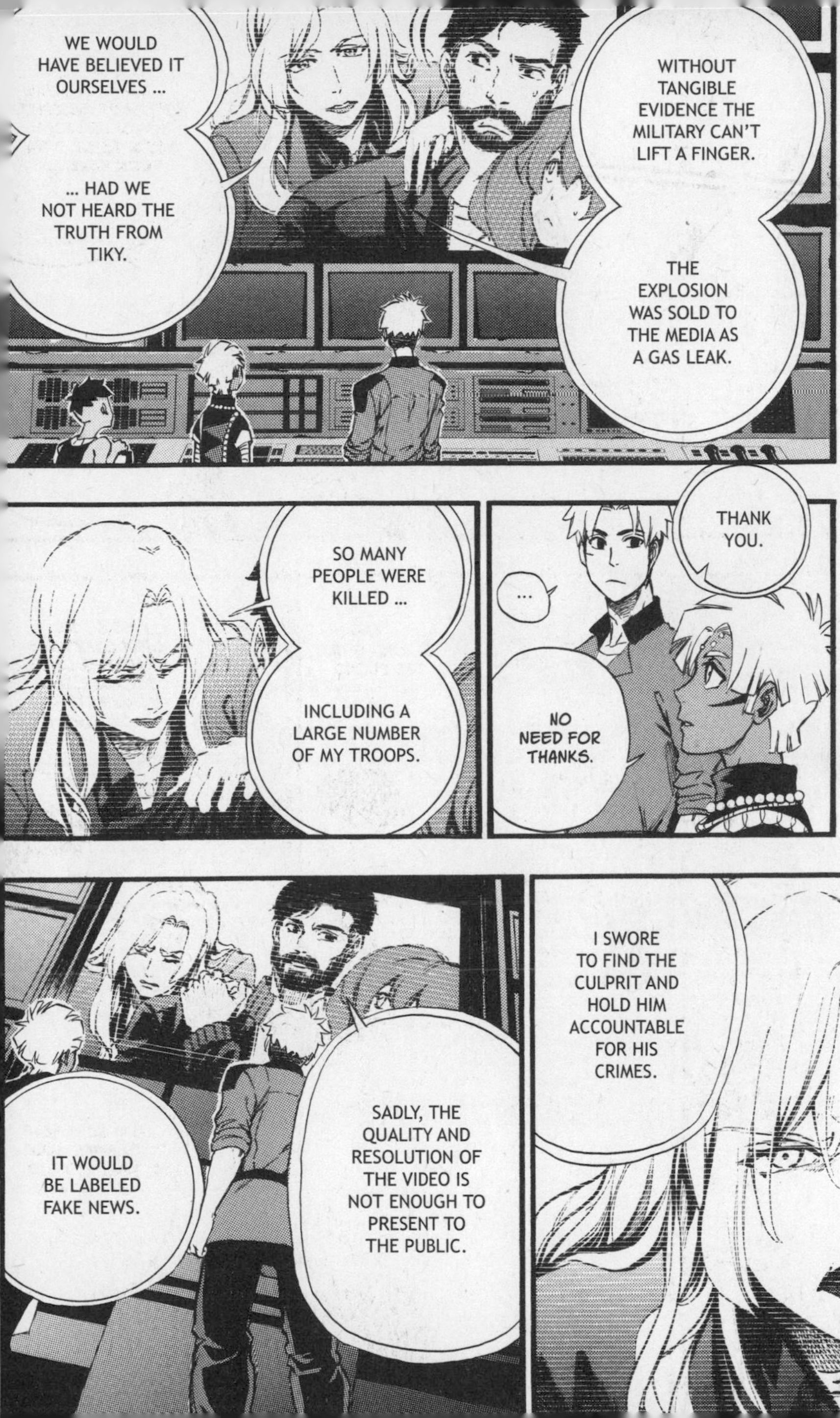
WITHOUT TANGIBLE EVIDENCE THE MILITARY CAN'T LIFT A FINGER.
THE EXPLOSION WAS SOLD TO THE MEDIA AS A GAS LEAK.
WE WOULD HAVE BELIEVED IT OURSELVES ...
... HAD WE NOT HEARD THE TRUTH FROM TIKY.
THANK YOU.
...
NO NEED FOR THANKS.
SO MANY PEOPLE WERE KILLED ...
INCLUDING A LARGE NUMBER OF MY TROOPS.
I SWORE TO FIND THE CULPRIT AND HOLD HIM ACCOUNTABLE FOR HIS CRIMES.
SADLY, THE QUALITY AND RESOLUTION OF THE VIDEO IS NOT ENOUGH TO PRESENT TO THE PUBLIC.
IT WOULD BE LABELED FAKE NEWS.

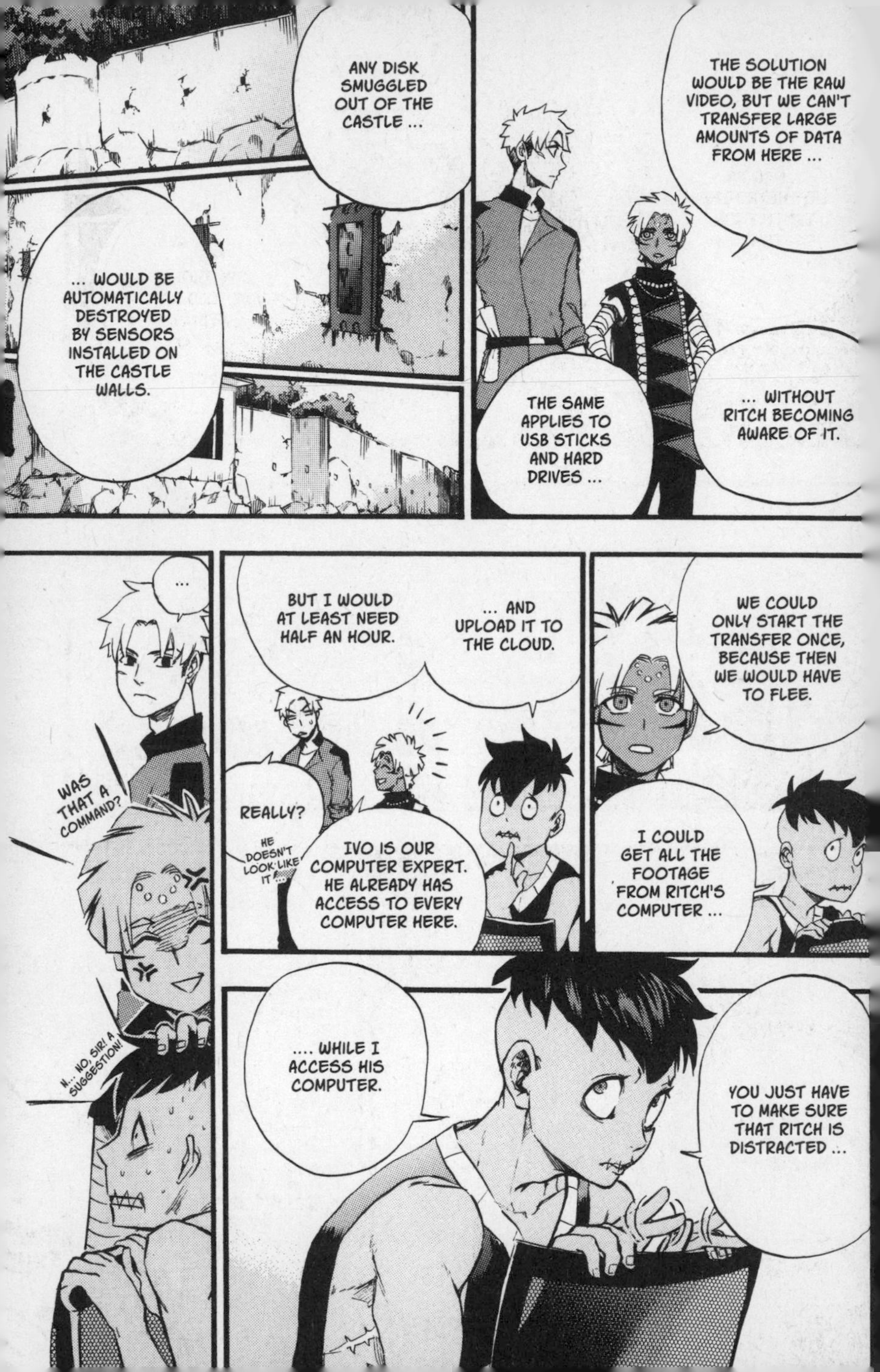
THE SOLUTION WOULD BE THE RAW VIDEO, BUT WE CAN'T TRANSFER LARGE AMOUNTS OF DATA FROM HERE ...
... WITHOUT RITCH BECOMING AWARE OF IT.
THE SAME APPLIES TO USB STICKS AND HARD DRIVES ...
ANY DISK SMUGGLED OUT OF THE CASTLE ...
... WOULD BE AUTOMATICALLY DESTROYED BY SENSORS INSTALLED ON THE CASTLE WALLS.
WE COULD ONLY START THE TRANSFER ONCE, BECAUSE THEN WE WOULD HAVE TO FLEE.
I COULD GET ALL THE FOOTAGE FROM RITCH'S COMPUTER ...
... AND UPLOAD IT TO THE CLOUD.
BUT I WOULD AT LEAST NEED HALF AN HOUR.
IVO IS OUR COMPUTER EXPERT. HE ALREADY HAS ACCESS TO EVERY COMPUTER HERE.
REALLY?
HE DOESN'T LOOK LIKE IT ...
YOU JUST HAVE TO MAKE SURE THAT RITCH IS DISTRACTED ...
.... WHILE I ACCESS HIS COMPUTER.
...
WAS THAT A COMMAND?
N... NO, SIR! A SUGGESTION!

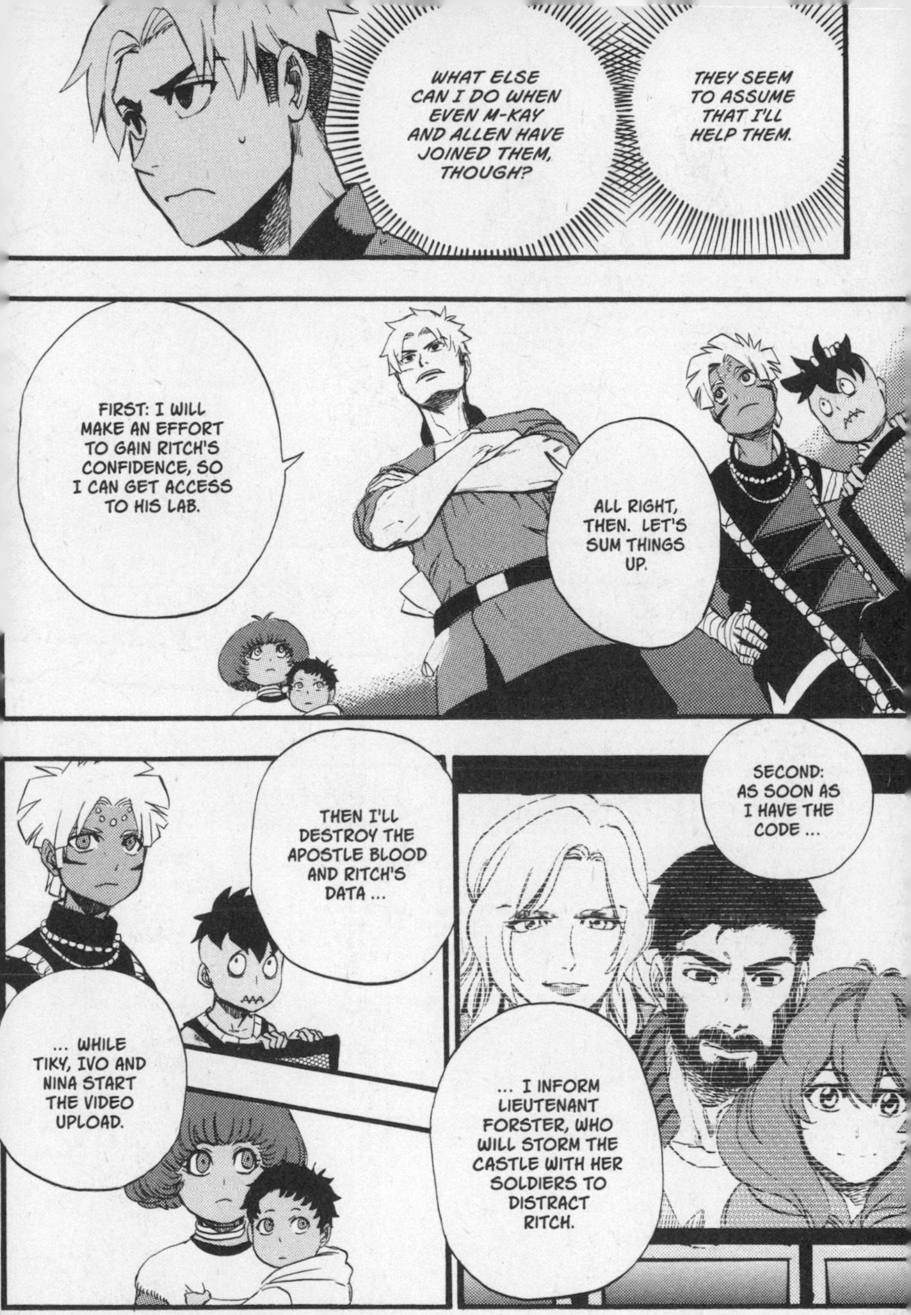
THEY SEEM TO ASSUME THAT I'LL HELP THEM.
WHAT ELSE CAN I DO WHEN EVEN M-KAY AND ALLEN HAVE JOINED THEM, THOUGH?
ALL RIGHT, THEN. LET'S SUM THINGS UP.
FIRST: I WILL MAKE AN EFFORT TO GAIN RITCH'S CONFIDENCE, SO I CAN GET ACCESS TO HIS LAB.
SECOND: AS SOON AS I HAVE THE CODE ...
... I INFORM LIEUTENANT FORSTER, WHO WILL STORM THE CASTLE WITH HER SOLDIERS TO DISTRACT RITCH.
THEN I'LL DESTROY THE APOSTLE BLOOD AND RITCH'S DATA ...
... WHILE TIKY, IVO AND NINA START THE VIDEO UPLOAD.

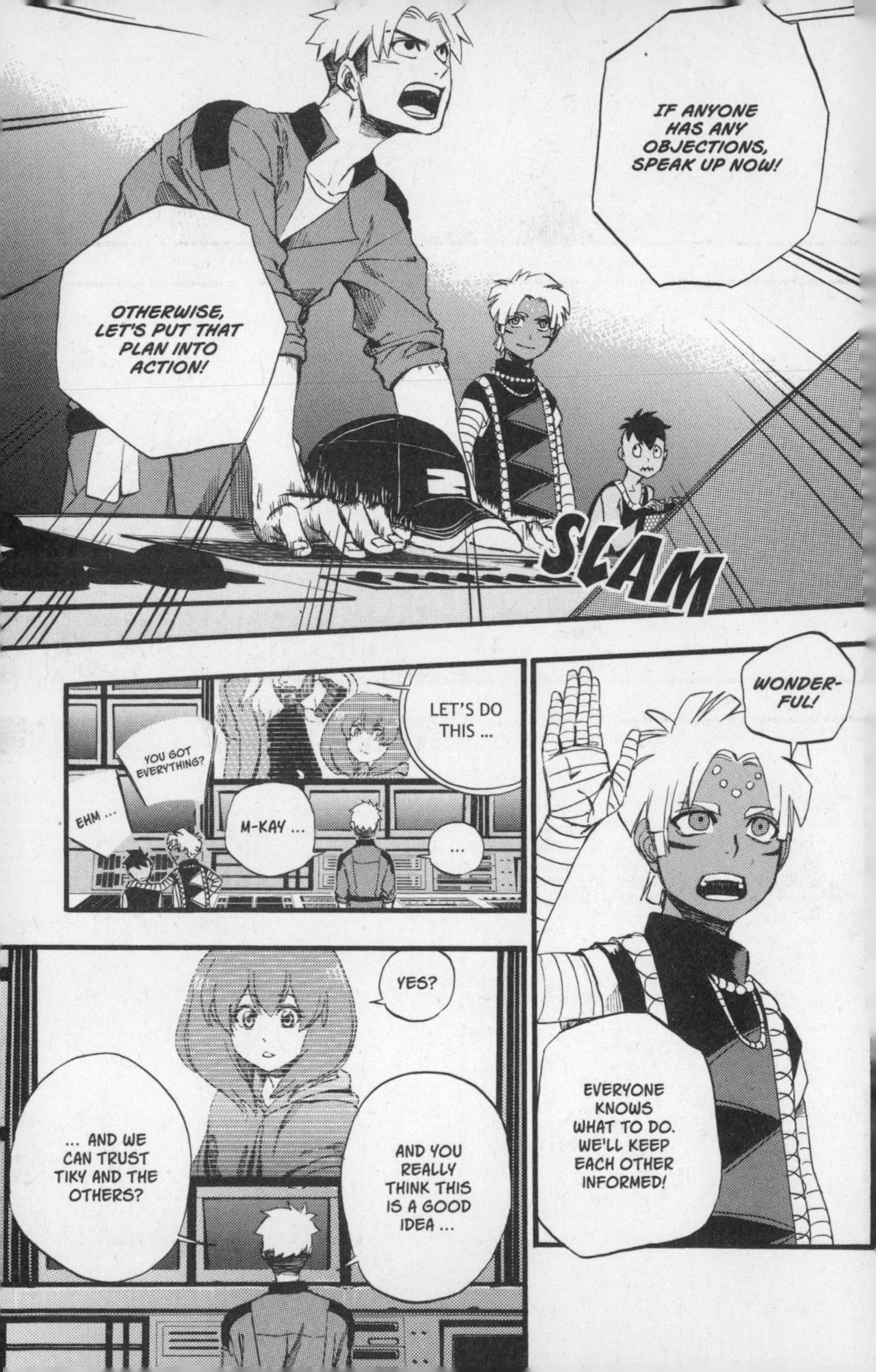
IF ANYONE HAS ANY OBJECTIONS, SPEAK UP NOW!
OTHERWISE, LET'S PUT THAT PLAN INTO ACTION!
SLAM
WONDER-FUL!
EVERYONE KNOWS WHAT TO DO. WE'LL KEEP EACH OTHER INFORMED!
LET'S DO THIS ...
YOU GOT EVERYTHING?
M-KAY ...
...
EHM ...
YES?
AND YOU REALLY THINK THIS IS A GOOD IDEA ...
... AND WE CAN TRUST TIKY AND THE OTHERS?

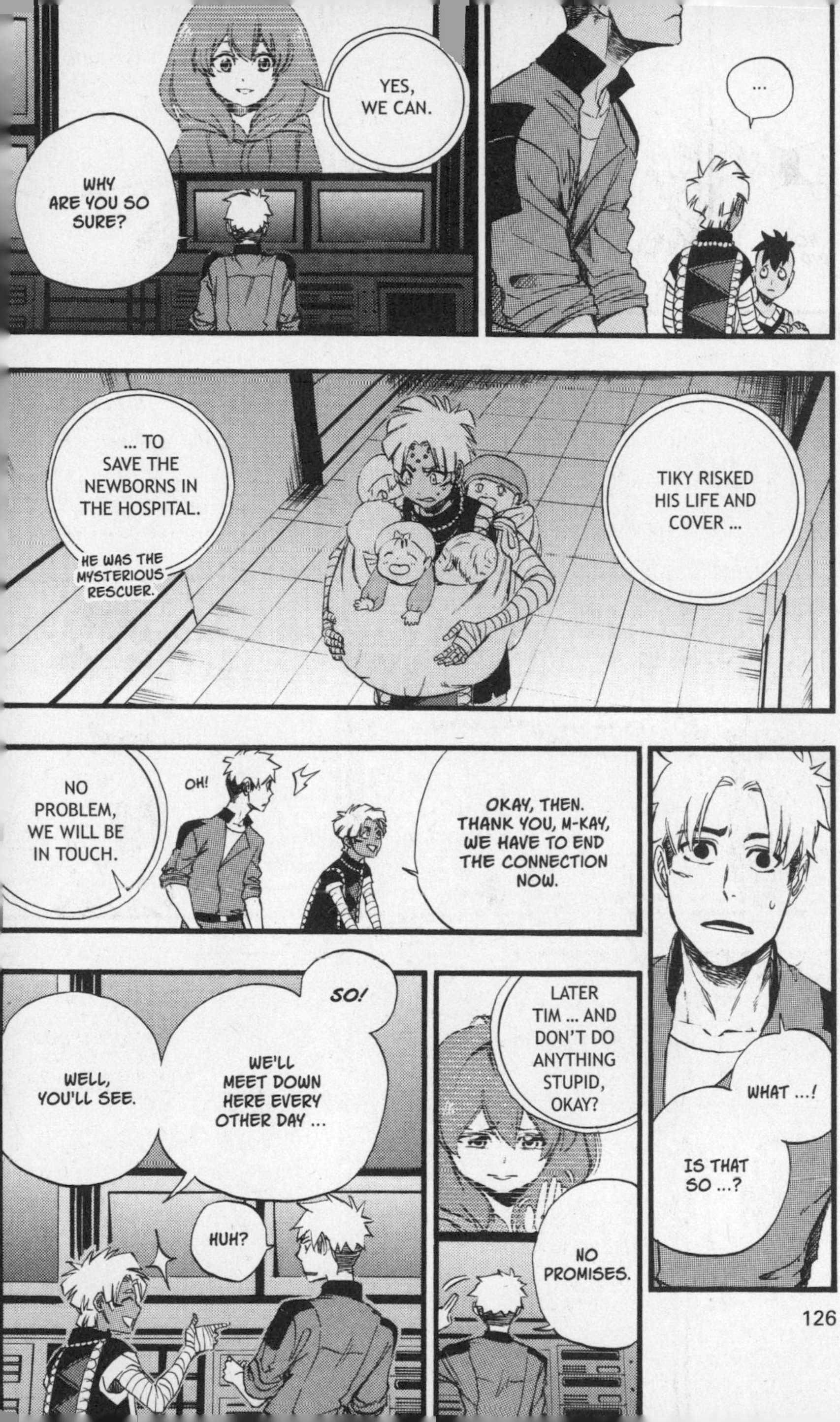
...
YES, WE CAN.
WHY ARE YOU SO SURE?
TIKY RISKED HIS LIFE AND COVER ...
... TO SAVE THE NEWBORNS IN THE HOSPITAL.
HE WAS THE MYSTERIOUS RESCUER.
WHAT ...!
IS THAT SO ...?
OKAY, THEN. THANK YOU, M-KAY, WE HAVE TO END THE CONNECTION NOW.
OH!
NO PROBLEM, WE WILL BE IN TOUCH.
LATER TIM ... AND DON'T DO ANYTHING STUPID, OKAY?
NO PROMISES.
SO!
WE'LL MEET DOWN HERE EVERY OTHER DAY ...
WELL, YOU'LL SEE.
HUH?

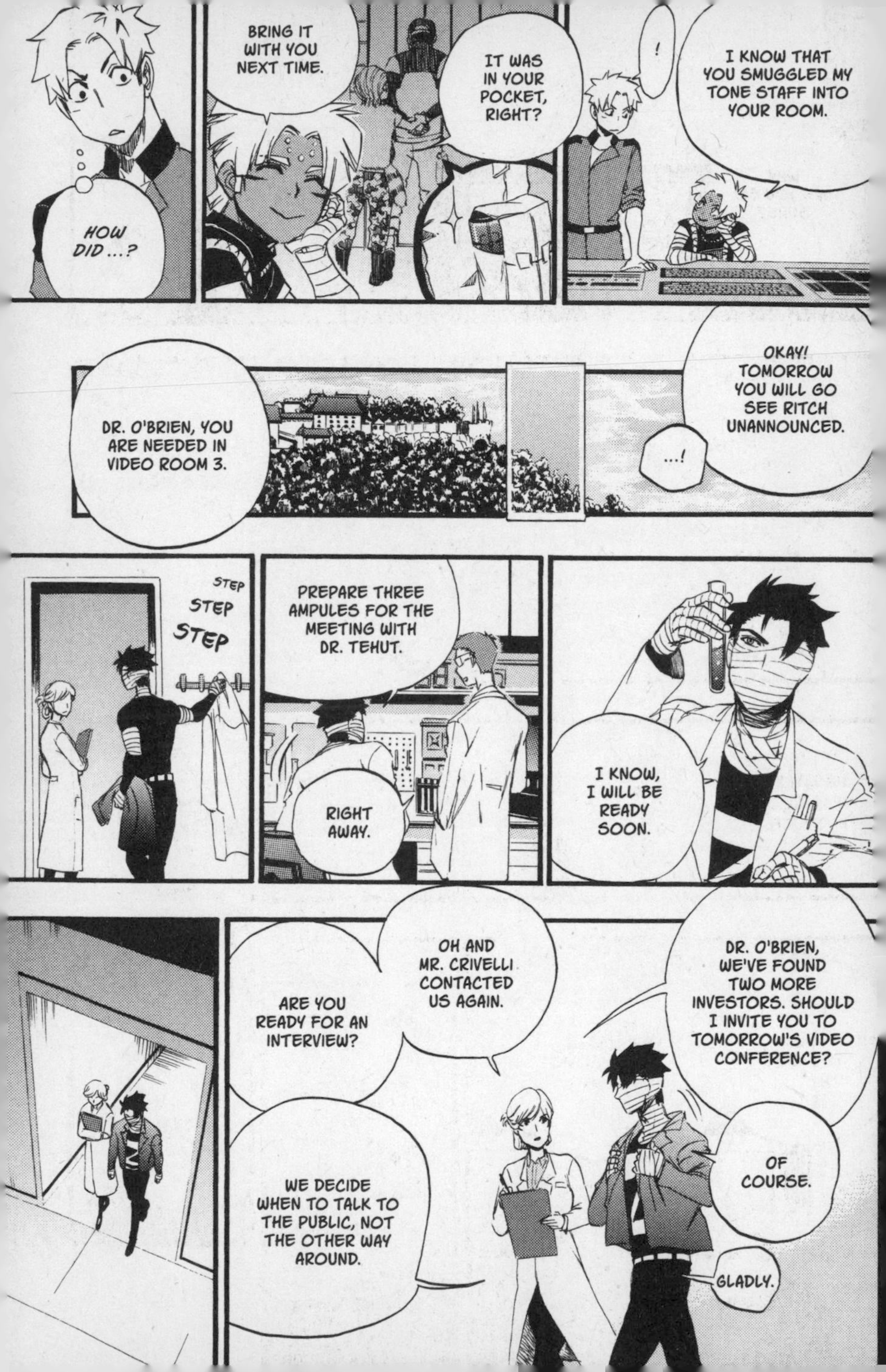
I KNOW THAT YOU SMUGGLED MY TONE STAFF INTO YOUR ROOM.
!
IT WAS IN YOUR POCKET, RIGHT?
BRING IT WITH YOU NEXT TIME.
HOW DID...?
OKAY! TOMORROW YOU WILL GO SEE RITCH UNANNOUNCED.
...!
DR. O'BRIEN, YOU ARE NEEDED IN VIDEO ROOM 3.
I KNOW, I WILL BE READY SOON.
PREPARE THREE AMPULES FOR THE MEETING WITH DR. TEHUT.
RIGHT AWAY.
STEP
STEP
STEP
DR. O'BRIEN, WE'VE FOUND TWO MORE INVESTORS. SHOULD I INVITE YOU TO TOMORROW'S VIDEO CONFERENCE?
OF COURSE.
OH AND MR. CRIVELLI CONTACTED US AGAIN.
ARE YOU READY FOR AN INTERVIEW?
WE DECIDE WHEN TO TALK TO THE PUBLIC, NOT THE OTHER WAY AROUND.
GLADLY.

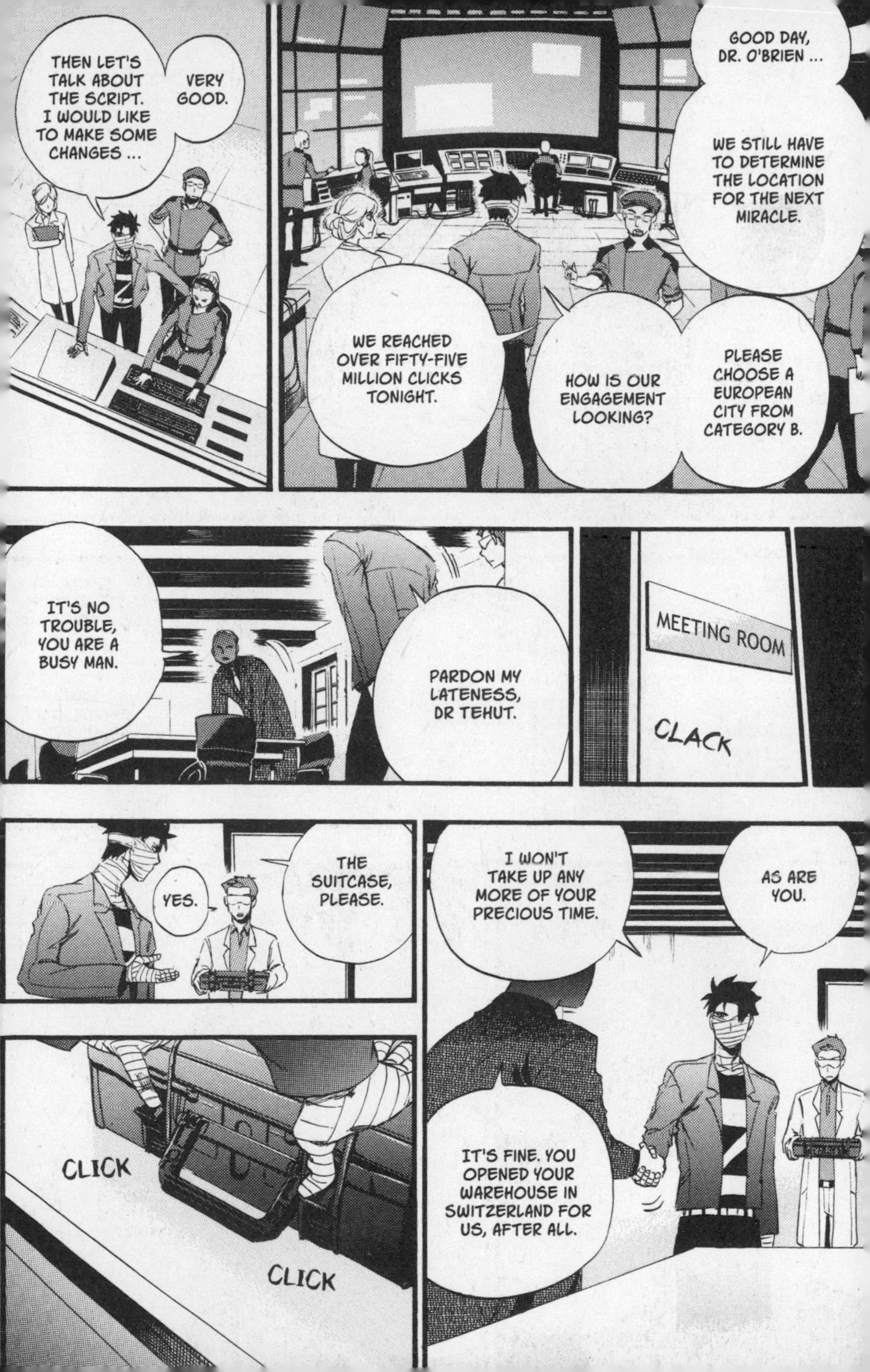
GOOD DAY, DR. O'BRIEN ...
WE STILL HAVE TO DETERMINE THE LOCATION FOR THE NEXT MIRACLE.
PLEASE CHOOSE A EUROPEAN CITY FROM CATEGORY B.
HOW IS OUR ENGAGEMENT LOOKING?
WE REACHED OVER FIFTY-FIVE MILLION CLICKS TONIGHT.
VERY GOOD.
THEN LET'S TALK ABOUT THE SCRIPT. I WOULD LIKE TO MAKE SOME CHANGES ...
MEETING ROOM
CLACK
PARDON MY LATENESS, DR TEHUT.
IT'S NO TROUBLE, YOU ARE A BUSY MAN.
AS ARE YOU.
I WON'T TAKE UP ANY MORE OF YOUR PRECIOUS TIME.
IT'S FINE. YOU OPENED YOUR WAREHOUSE IN SWITZERLAND FOR US, AFTER ALL.
THE SUITCASE, PLEASE.
YES.
CLICK
CLICK

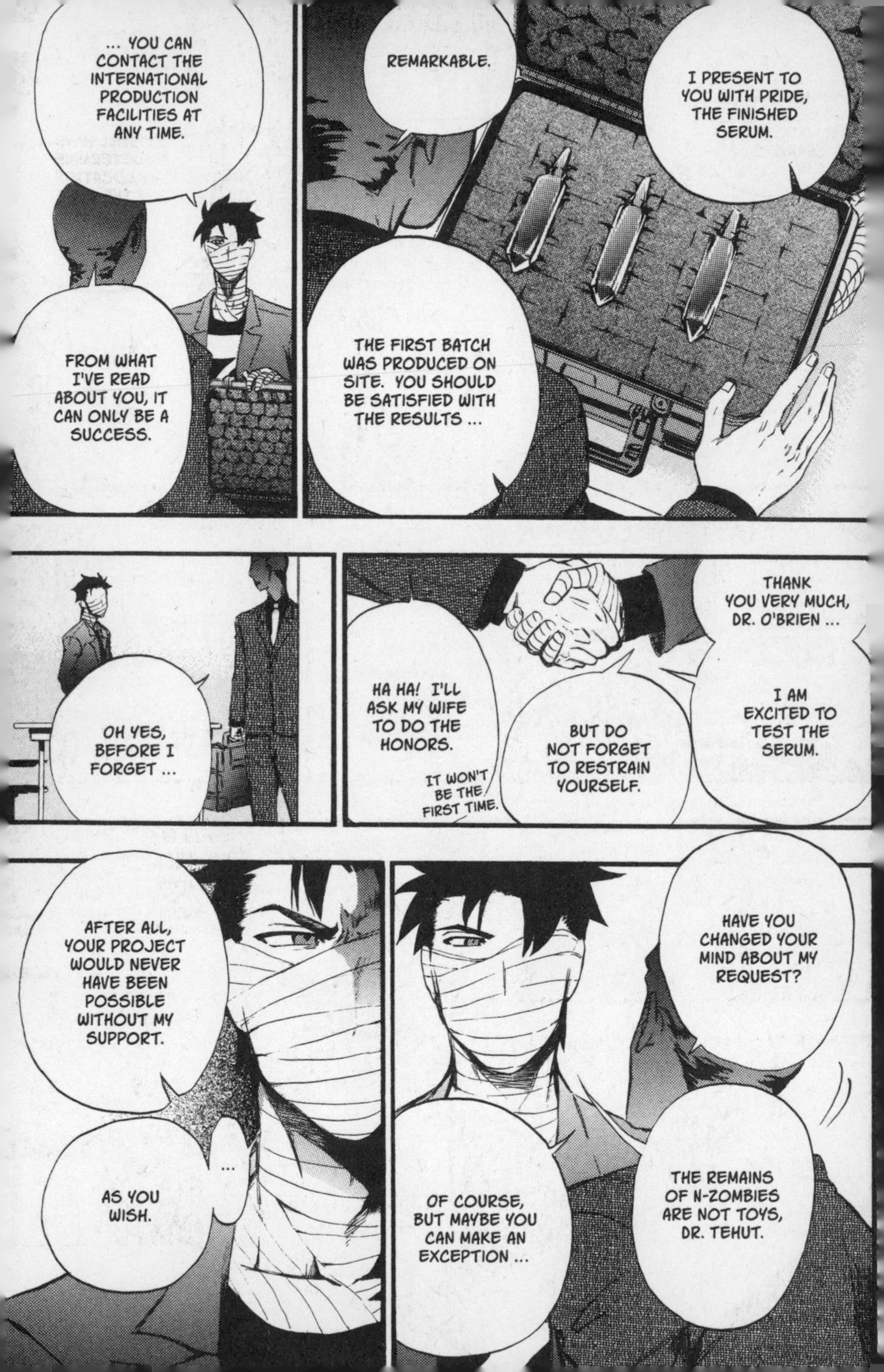
I PRESENT TO YOU WITH PRIDE, THE FINISHED SERUM.
REMARKABLE.
THE FIRST BATCH WAS PRODUCED ON SITE. YOU SHOULD BE SATISFIED WITH THE RESULTS ...
... YOU CAN CONTACT THE INTERNATIONAL PRODUCTION FACILITIES AT ANY TIME.
FROM WHAT I'VE READ ABOUT YOU, IT CAN ONLY BE A SUCCESS.
THANK YOU VERY MUCH, DR. O'BRIEN ...
I AM EXCITED TO TEST THE SERUM.
BUT DO NOT FORGET TO RESTRAIN YOURSELF.
HA HA! I'LL ASK MY WIFE TO DO THE HONORS.
IT WON'T BE THE FIRST TIME.
OH YES, BEFORE I FORGET ...
HAVE YOU CHANGED YOUR MIND ABOUT MY REQUEST?
THE REMAINS OF N-ZOMBIES ARE NOT TOYS, DR. TEHUT.
OF COURSE, BUT MAYBE YOU CAN MAKE AN EXCEPTION ...
AFTER ALL, YOUR PROJECT WOULD NEVER HAVE BEEN POSSIBLE WITHOUT MY SUPPORT.
...
AS YOU WISH.

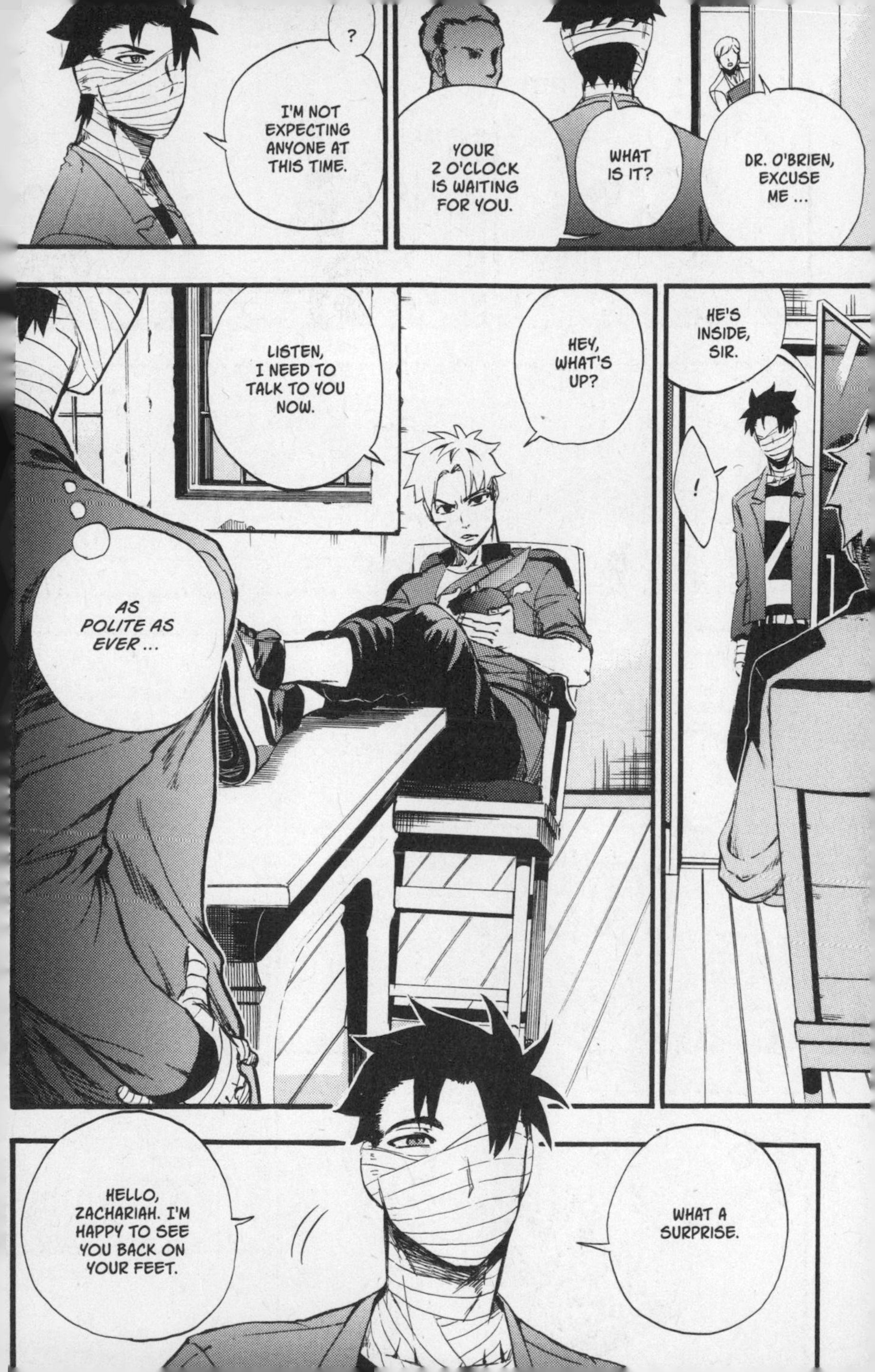
DR. O'BRIEN, EXCUSE ME ...
WHAT IS IT?
YOUR 2 O'CLOCK IS WAITING FOR YOU.
?
I'M NOT EXPECTING ANYONE AT THIS TIME.
HE'S INSIDE, SIR.
!
HEY, WHAT'S UP?
LISTEN, I NEED TO TALK TO YOU NOW.
AS POLITE AS EVER ...
WHAT A SURPRISE.
HELLO, ZACHARIAH. I'M HAPPY TO SEE YOU BACK ON YOUR FEET.

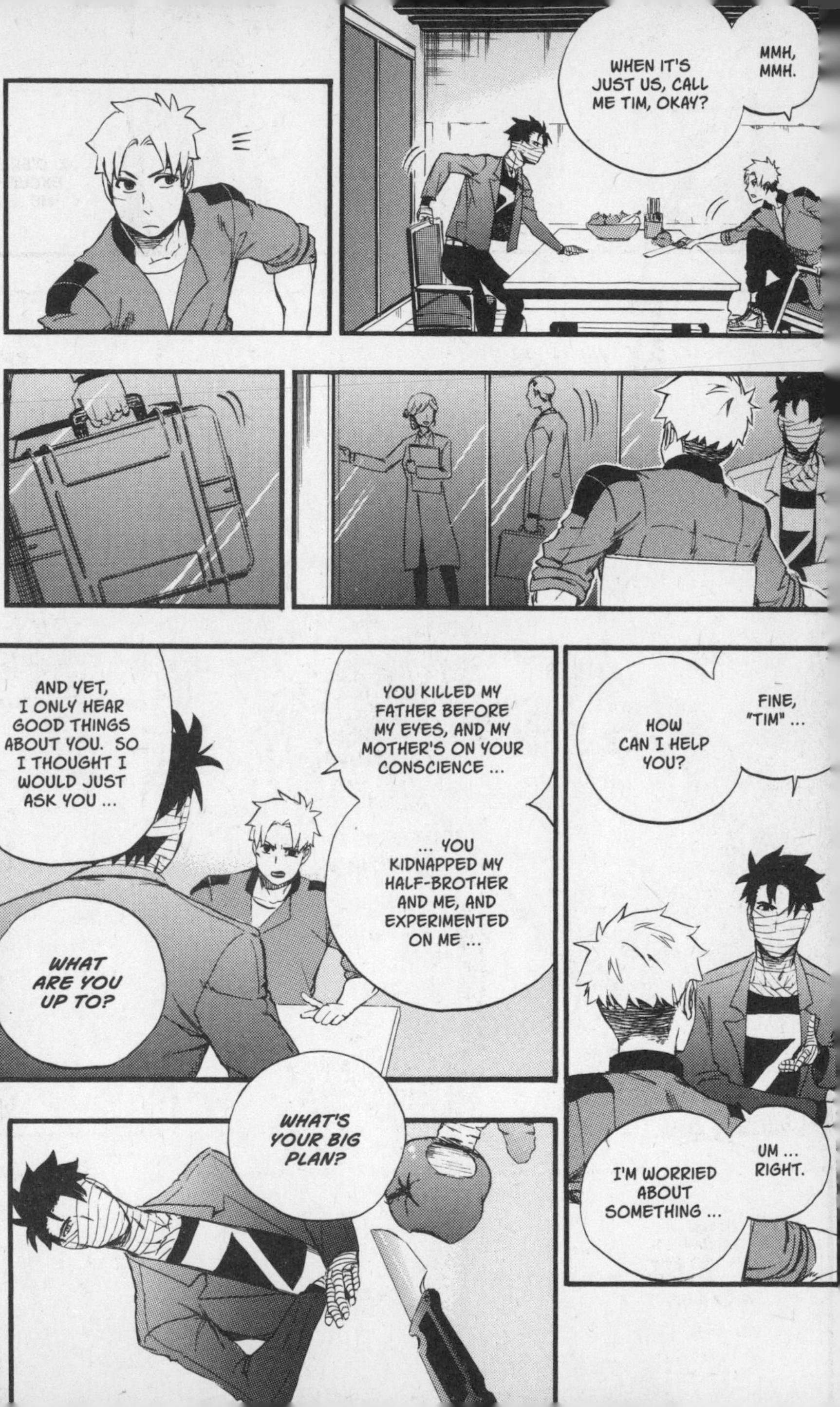
MMH, MMH.
WHEN IT'S JUST US, CALL ME TIM, OKAY?
FINE, "TIM" ...
HOW CAN I HELP YOU?
UM ... RIGHT.
I'M WORRIED ABOUT SOMETHING ...
YOU KILLED MY FATHER BEFORE MY EYES, AND MY MOTHER'S ON YOUR CONSCIENCE ...
... YOU KIDNAPPED MY HALF-BROTHER AND ME, AND EXPERIMENTED ON ME ...
AND YET, I ONLY HEAR GOOD THINGS ABOUT YOU. SO I THOUGHT I WOULD JUST ASK YOU ...
WHAT ARE YOU UP TO?
WHAT'S YOUR BIG PLAN?

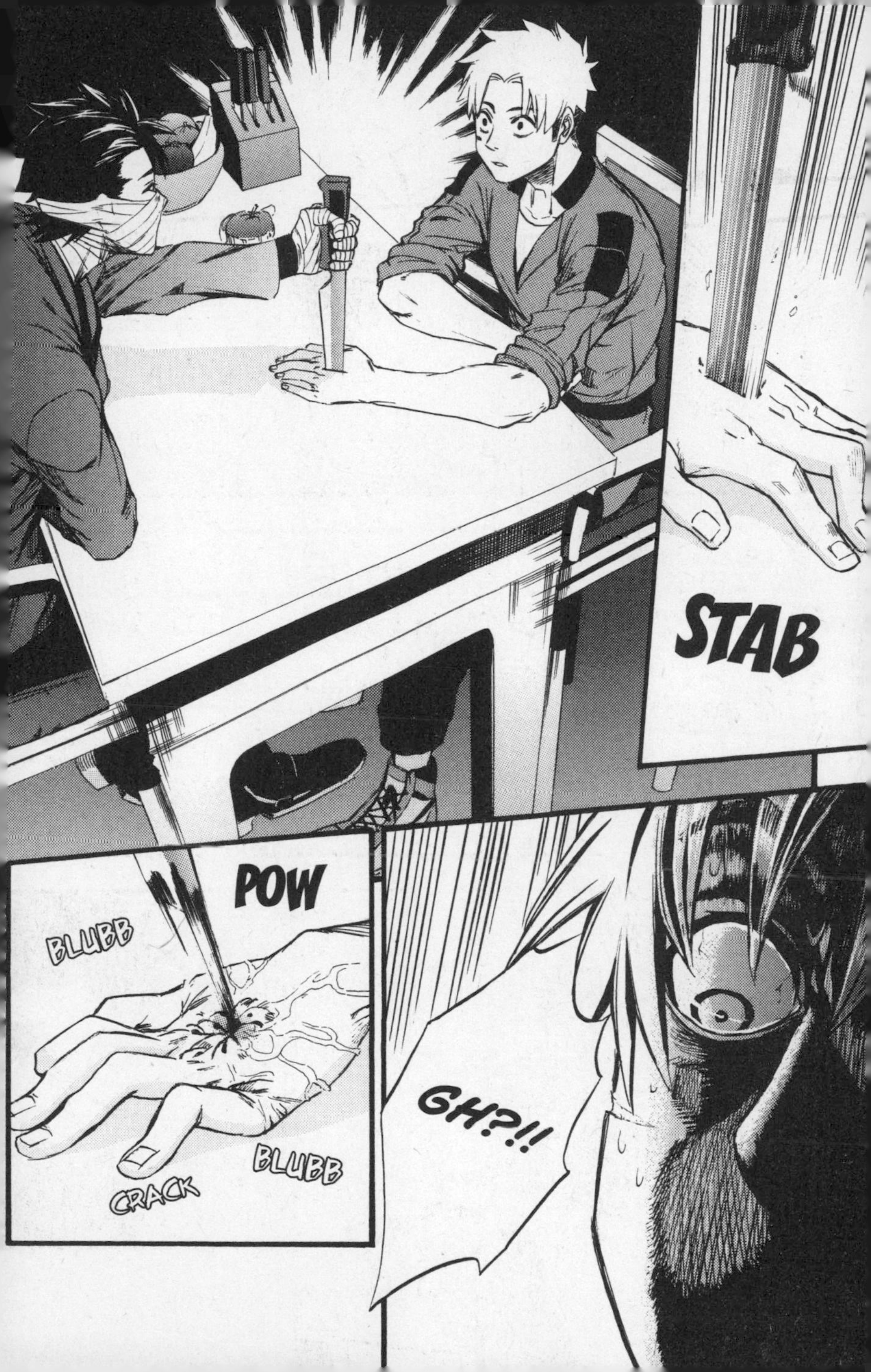
STAB
GH?!!
POW
BLUBB
BLUBB
CRACK

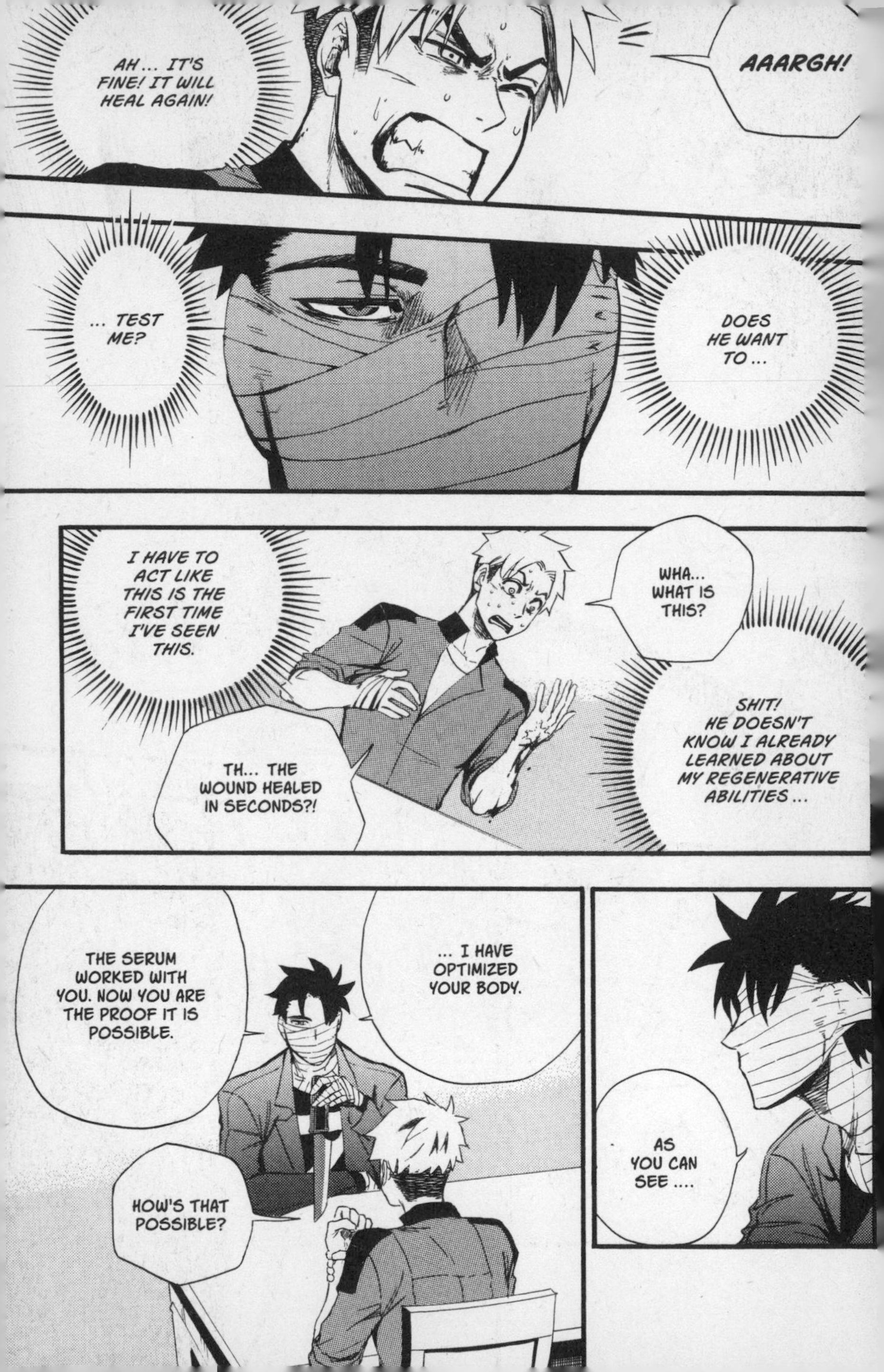
AAARGH!
AH ... IT'S FINE! IT WILL HEAL AGAIN!
DOES HE WANT TO ...
... TEST ME?
WHA... WHAT IS THIS?
SHIT! HE DOESN'T KNOW I ALREADY LEARNED ABOUT MY REGENERATIVE ABILITIES ...
I HAVE TO ACT LIKE THIS IS THE FIRST TIME I'VE SEEN THIS.
TH... THE WOUND HEALED IN SECONDS?!
AS YOU CAN SEE ....
... I HAVE OPTIMIZED YOUR BODY.
THE SERUM WORKED WITH YOU. NOW YOU ARE THE PROOF IT IS POSSIBLE.
HOW'S THAT POSSIBLE?

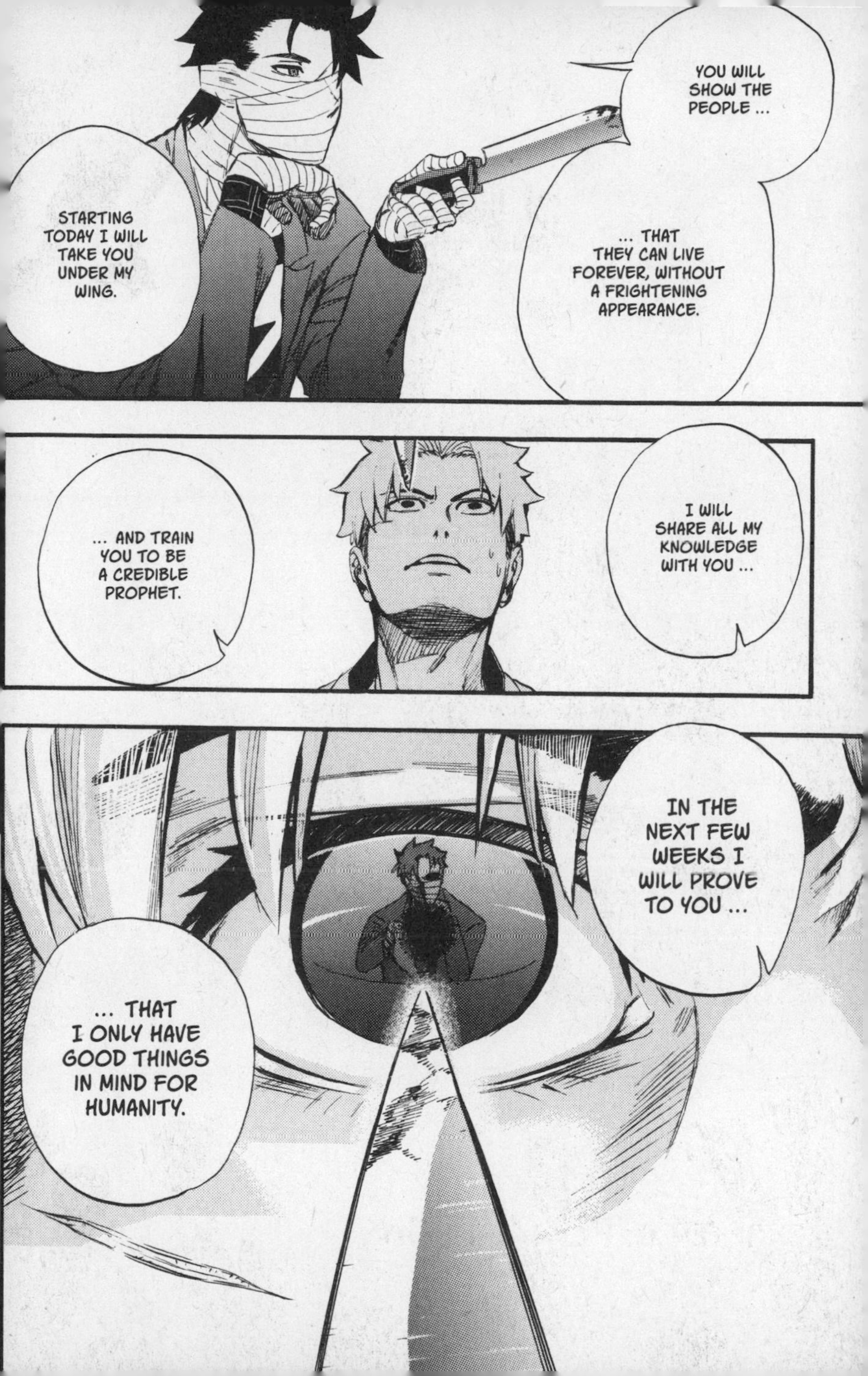
YOU WILL SHOW THE PEOPLE ...
... THAT THEY CAN LIVE FOREVER, WITHOUT A FRIGHTENING APPEARANCE.
STARTING TODAY I WILL TAKE YOU UNDER MY WING.
I WILL SHARE ALL MY KNOWLEDGE WITH YOU ...
... AND TRAIN YOU TO BE A CREDIBLE PROPHET.
IN THE NEXT FEW WEEKS I WILL PROVE TO YOU ...
... THAT I ONLY HAVE GOOD THINGS IN MIND FOR HUMANITY.

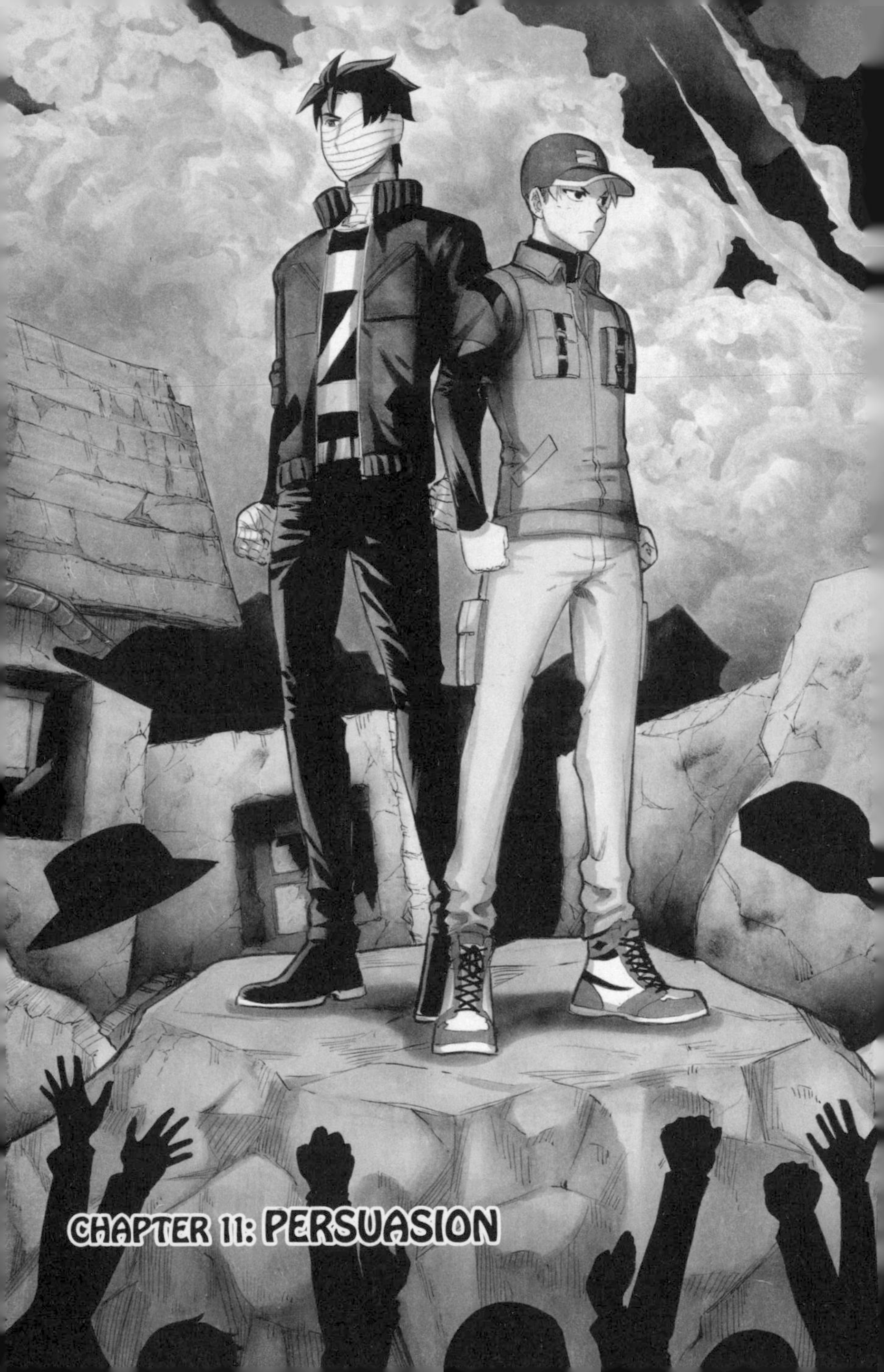
CHAPTER 11: PERSUASION

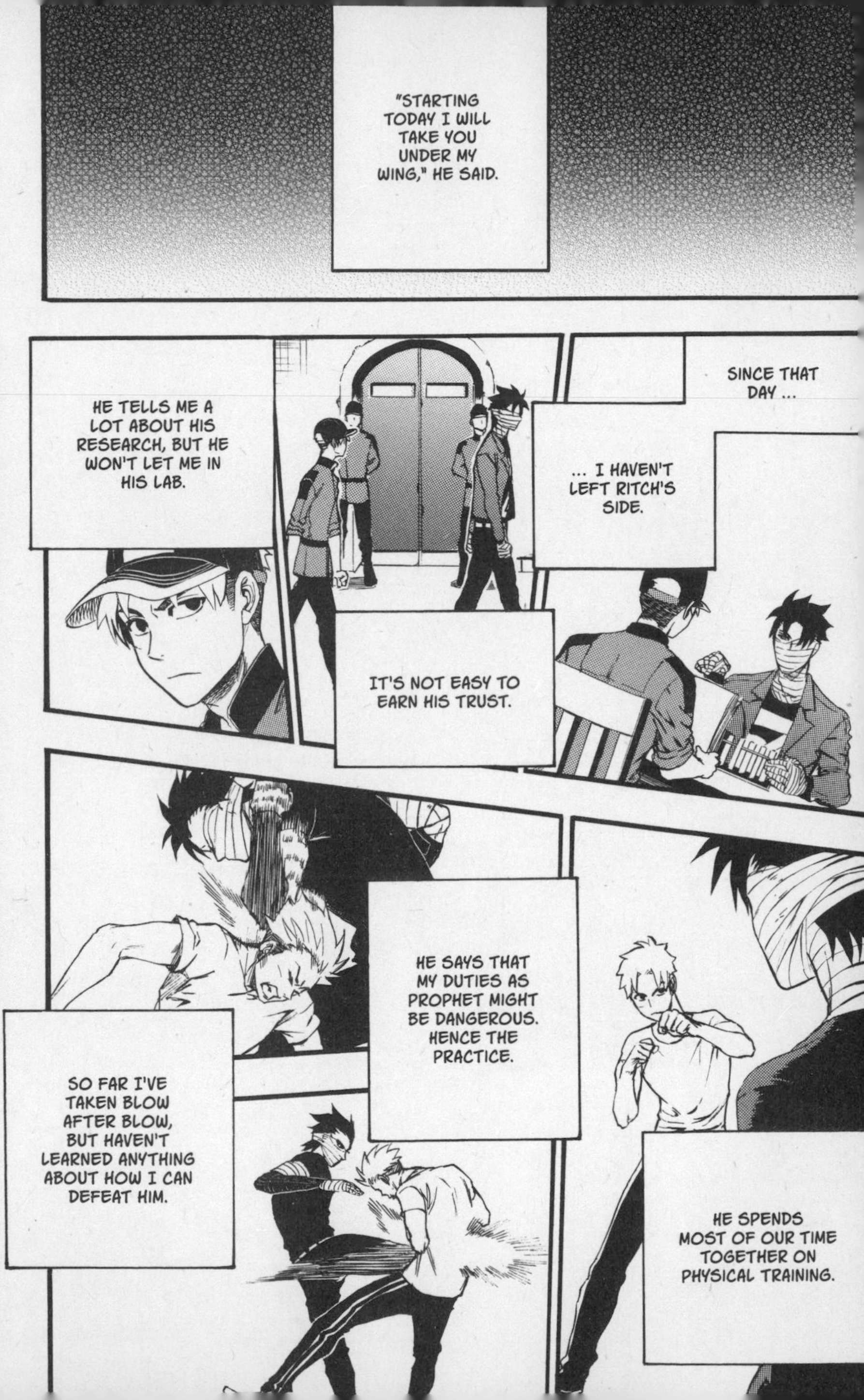
"STARTING TODAY I WILL TAKE YOU UNDER MY WING," HE SAID.
SINCE THAT DAY ...
... I HAVEN'T LEFT RITCH'S SIDE.
HE TELLS ME A LOT ABOUT HIS RESEARCH, BUT HE WON'T LET ME IN HIS LAB.
IT'S NOT EASY TO EARN HIS TRUST.
HE SPENDS MOST OF OUR TIME TOGETHER ON PHYSICAL TRAINING.
HE SAYS THAT MY DUTIES AS PROPHET MIGHT BE DANGEROUS. HENCE THE PRACTICE.
SO FAR I'VE TAKEN BLOW AFTER BLOW, BUT HAVEN'T LEARNED ANYTHING ABOUT HOW I CAN DEFEAT HIM.

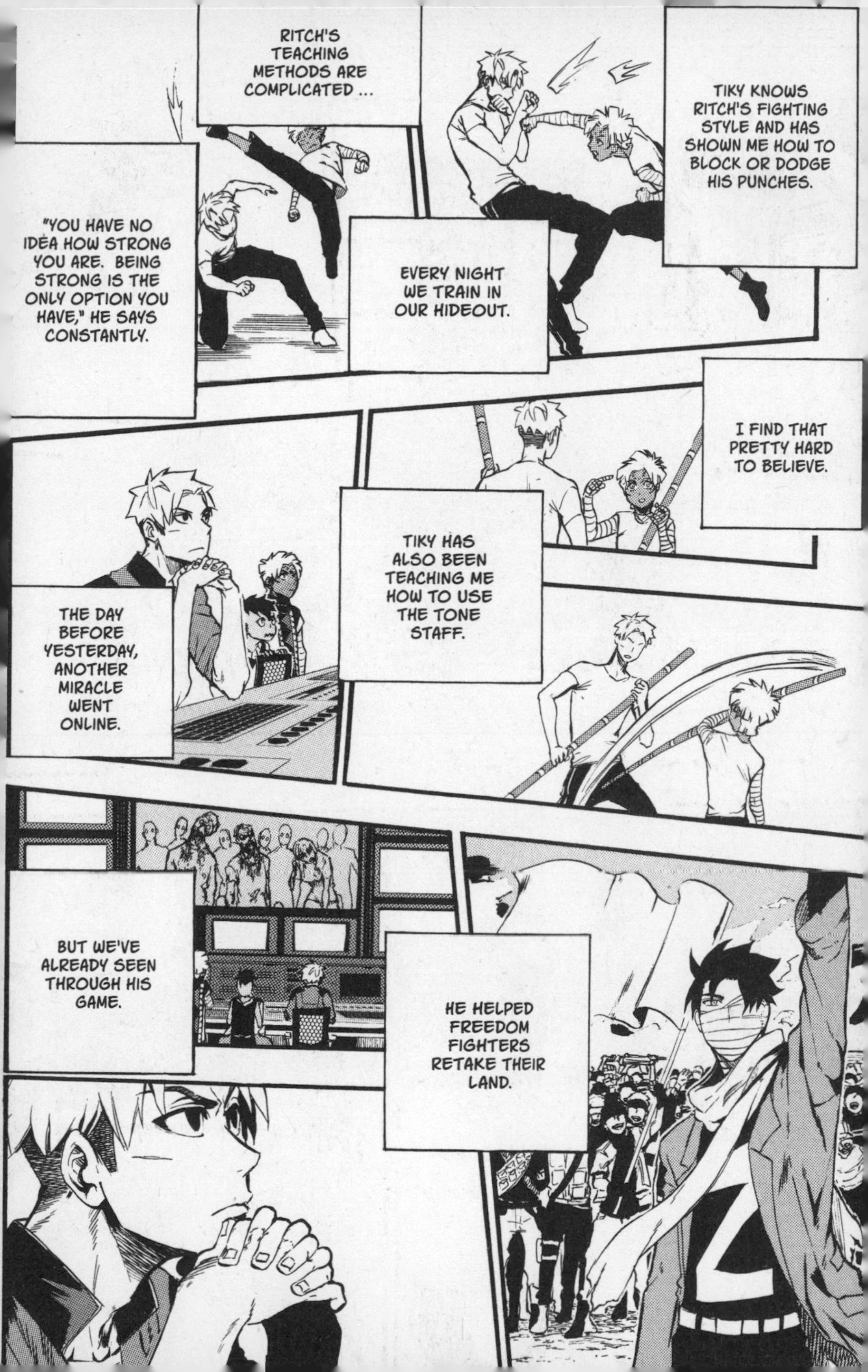
TIKY KNOWS RITCH'S FIGHTING STYLE AND HAS SHOWN ME HOW TO BLOCK OR DODGE HIS PUNCHES.
EVERY NIGHT WE TRAIN IN OUR HIDEOUT.
RITCH'S TEACHING METHODS ARE COMPLICATED ...
"YOU HAVE NO IDEA HOW STRONG YOU ARE. BEING STRONG IS THE ONLY OPTION YOU HAVE," HE SAYS CONSTANTLY.
I FIND THAT PRETTY HARD TO BELIEVE.
TIKY HAS ALSO BEEN TEACHING ME HOW TO USE THE TONE STAFF.
THE DAY BEFORE YESTERDAY, ANOTHER MIRACLE WENT ONLINE.
HE HELPED FREEDOM FIGHTERS RETAKE THEIR LAND.
BUT WE'VE ALREADY SEEN THROUGH HIS GAME.

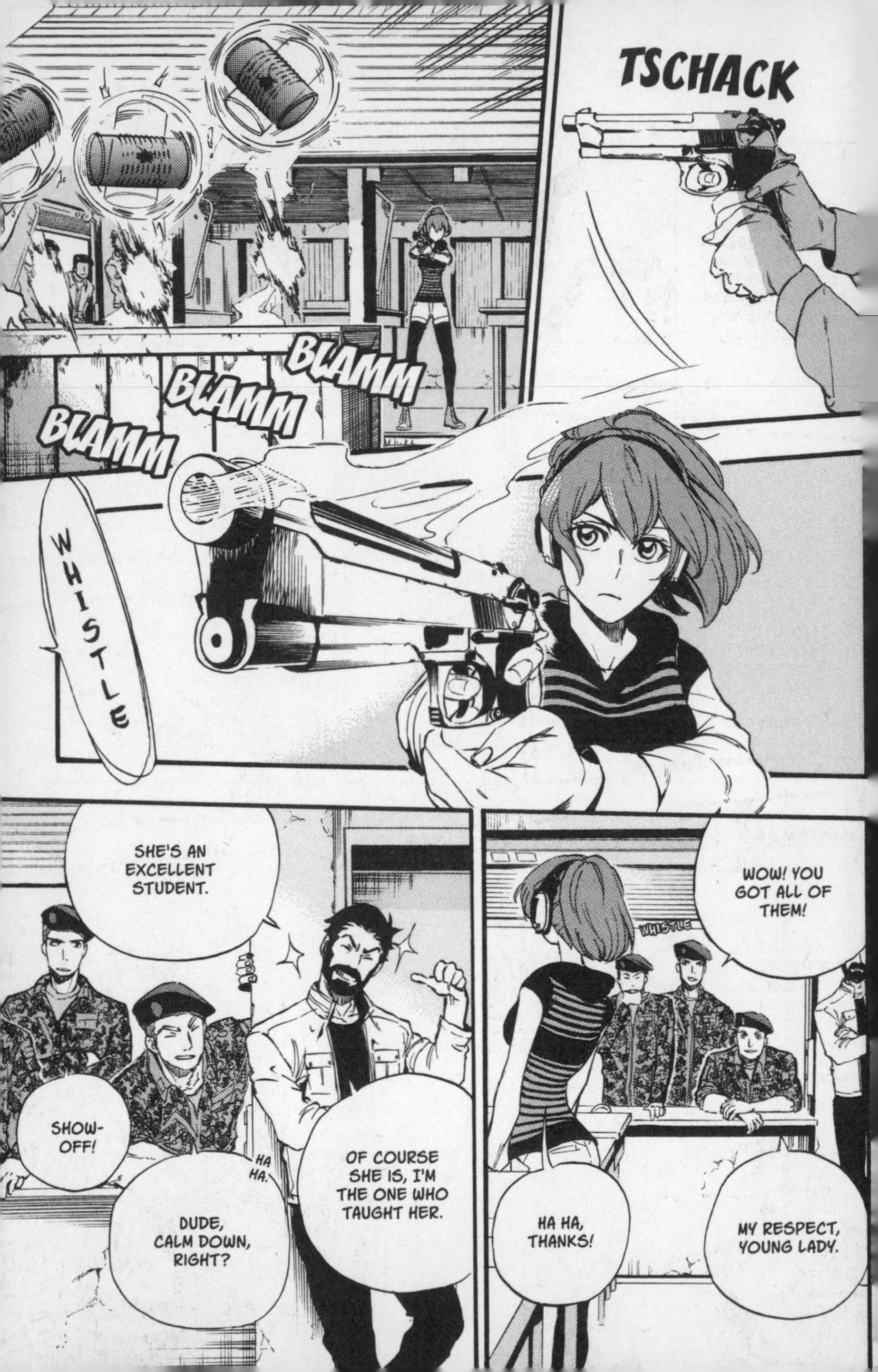
TSCHACK
BLAMM
BLAMM
BLAMM
WHISTLE
WOW! YOU GOT ALL OF THEM!
WHISTLE
MY RESPECT, YOUNG LADY.
HA HA, THANKS!
SHE'S AN EXCELLENT STUDENT.
OF COURSE SHE IS, I'M THE ONE WHO TAUGHT HER.
HA HA.
DUDE, CALM DOWN, RIGHT?
SHOW-OFF!

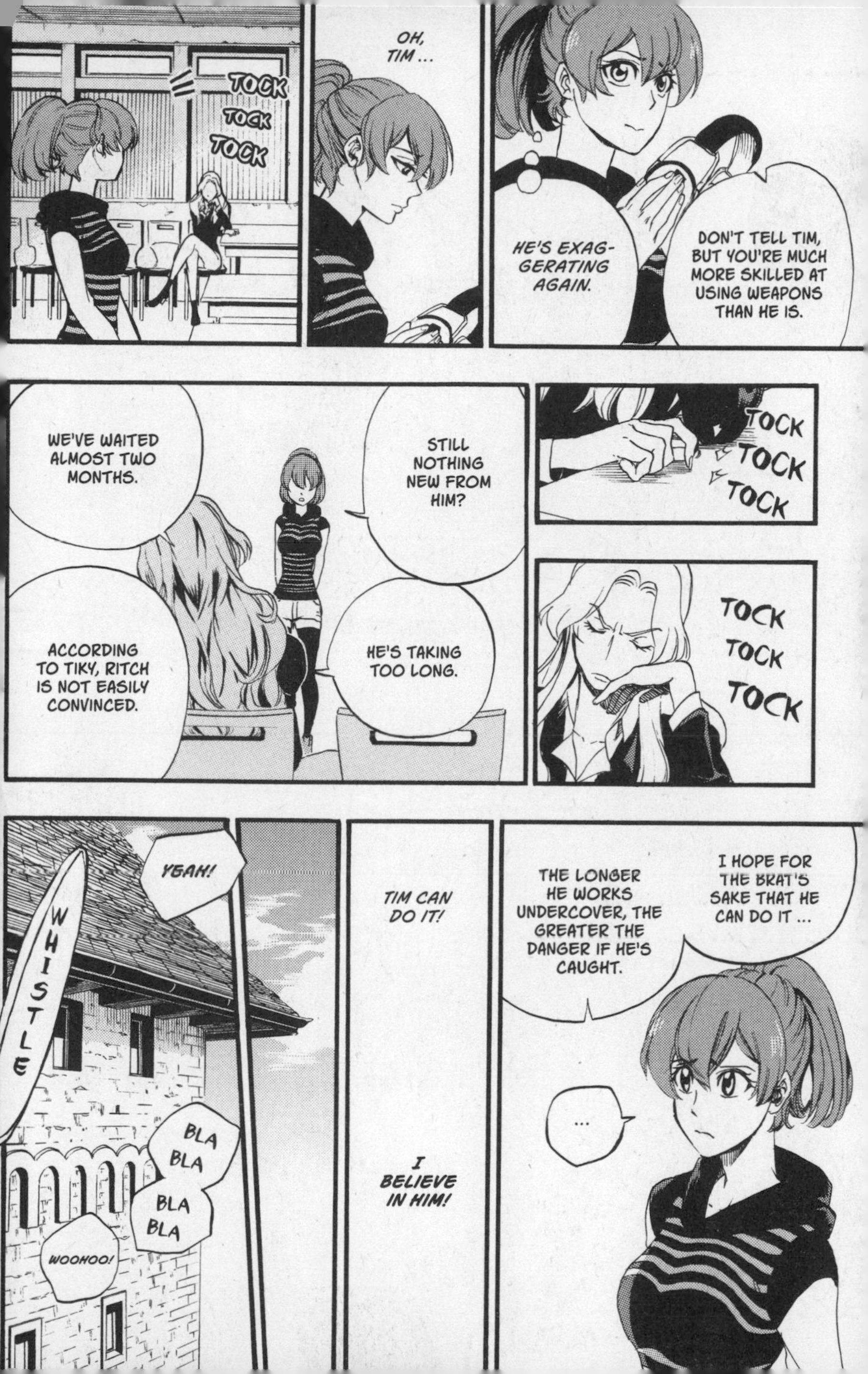
DON'T TELL TIM, BUT YOU'RE MUCH MORE SKILLED AT USING WEAPONS THAN HE IS.
HE'S EXAG-GERATING AGAIN.
OH, TIM ...
TOCK
TOCK
TOCK
TOCK
TOCK
TOCK
TOCK
TOCK
TOCK
STILL NOTHING NEW FROM HIM?
WE'VE WAITED ALMOST TWO MONTHS.
HE'S TAKING TOO LONG.
ACCORDING TO TIKY, RITCH IS NOT EASILY CONVINCED.
I HOPE FOR THE BRAT'S SAKE THAT HE CAN DO IT ...
THE LONGER HE WORKS UNDERCOVER, THE GREATER THE DANGER IF HE'S CAUGHT.
...
TIM CAN DO IT!
I BELIEVE IN HIM!
YEAH!
WHISTLE
BLA BLA
BLA BLA
WOOHOO!

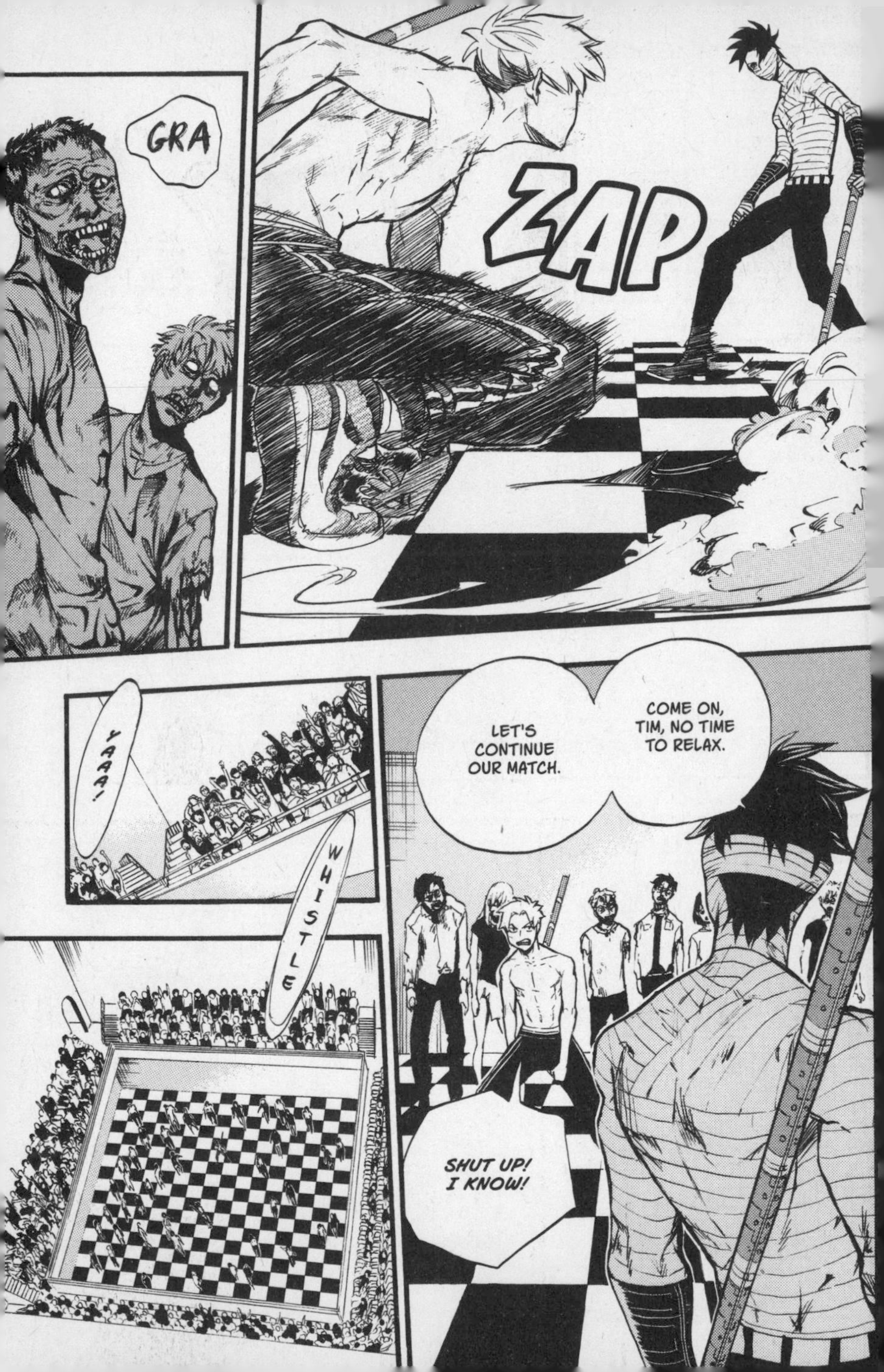
ZAP
GRA
COME ON, TIM, NO TIME TO RELAX.
LET'S CONTINUE OUR MATCH.
SHUT UP! I KNOW!
YAAAA!
WHISTLE

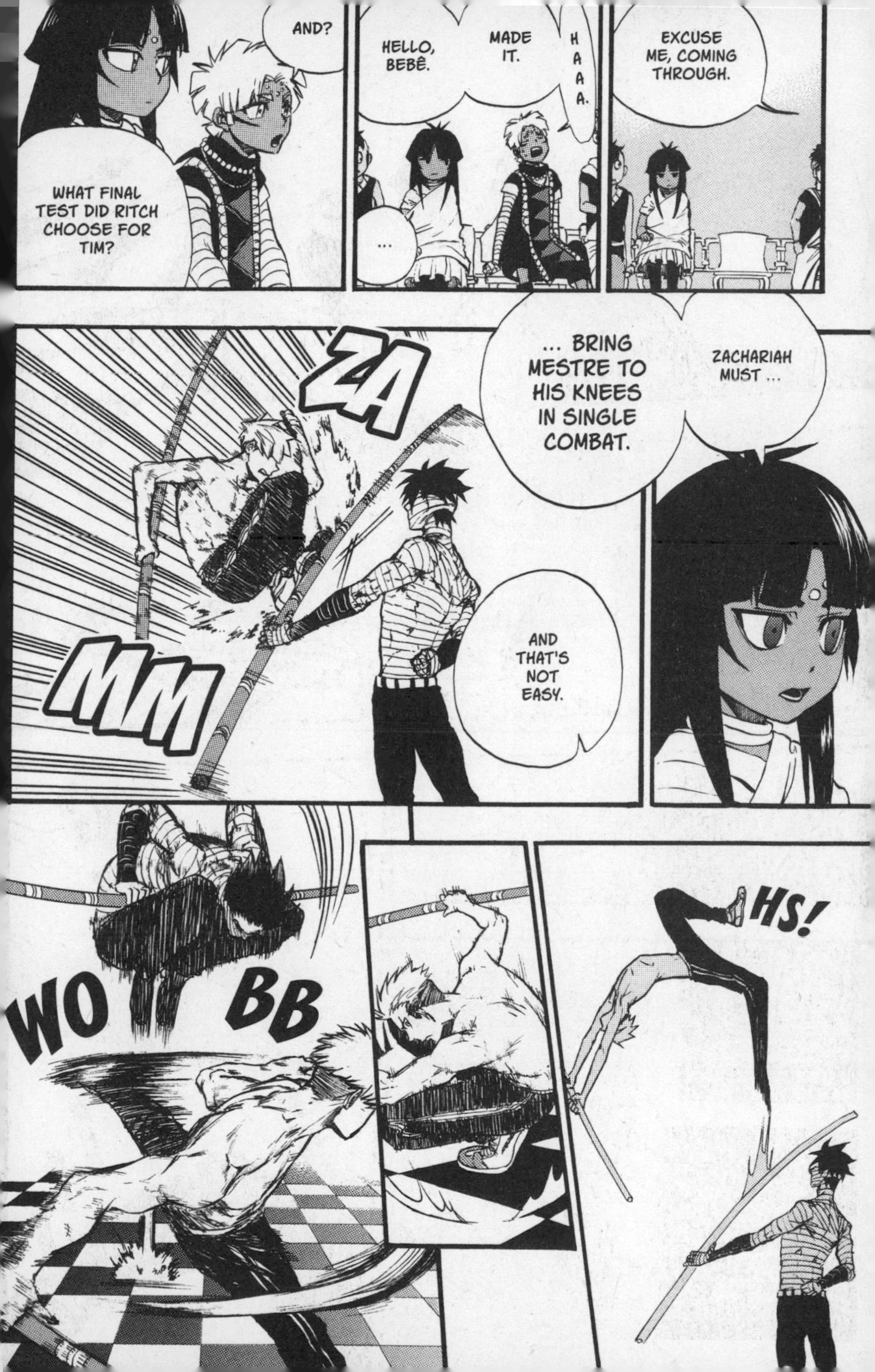
EXCUSE ME, COMING THROUGH.
HAAA.
MADE IT.
HELLO, BEBÊ.
...
AND?
WHAT FINAL TEST DID RITCH CHOOSE FOR TIM?
ZACHARIAH MUST ...
... BRING MESTRE TO HIS KNEES IN SINGLE COMBAT.
ZA
AND THAT'S NOT EASY.
MM
HS!
WO
BB

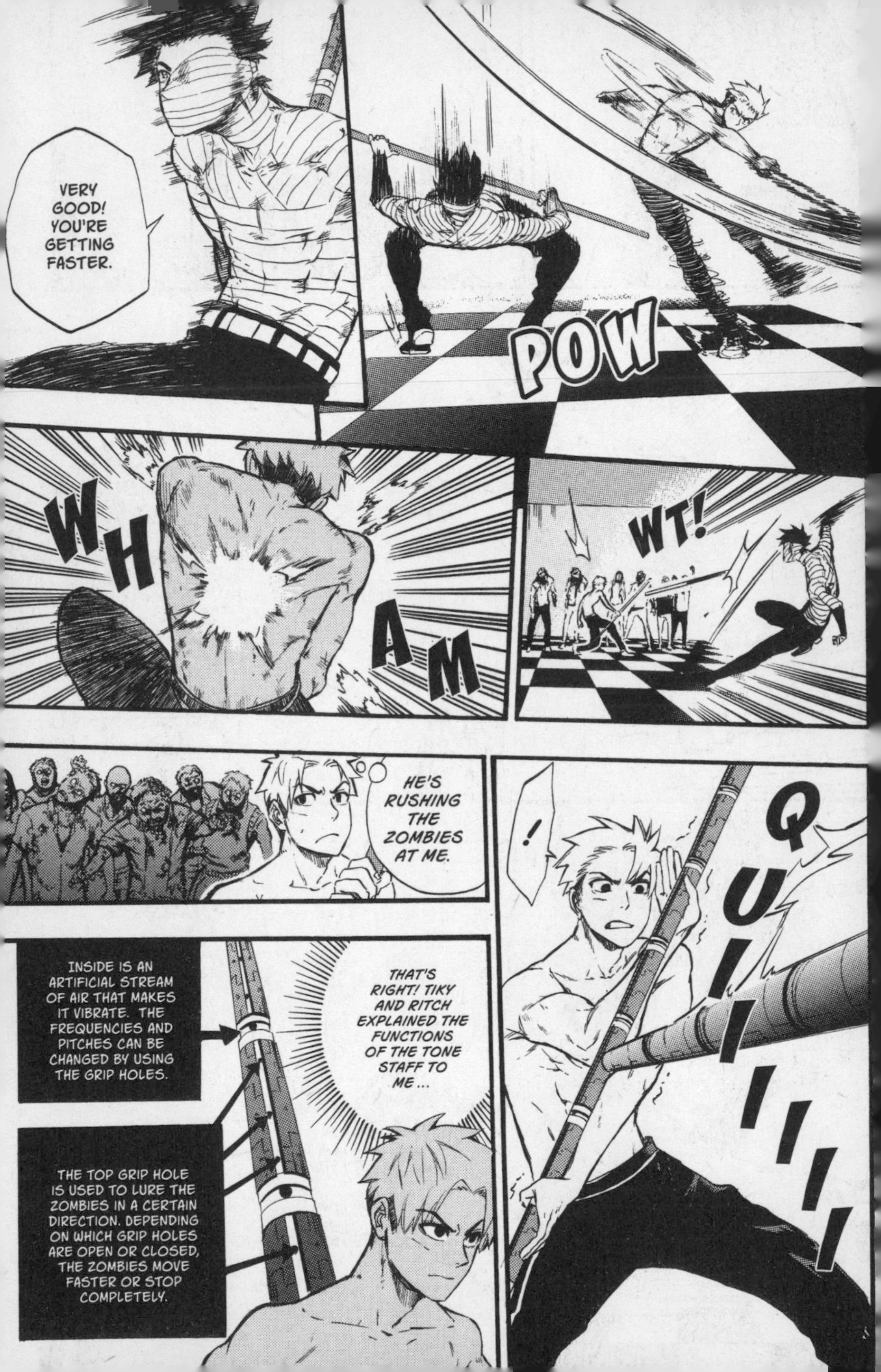
POW
VERY GOOD! YOU'RE GETTING FASTER.
WT!
WH
AM
!
QUIIIIII
HE'S RUSHING THE ZOMBIES AT ME.
THAT'S RIGHT! TIKY AND RITCH EXPLAINED THE FUNCTIONS OF THE TONE STAFF TO ME...
INSIDE IS AN ARTIFICIAL STREAM OF AIR THAT MAKES IT VIBRATE. THE FREQUENCIES AND PITCHES CAN BE CHANGED BY USING THE GRIP HOLES.
THE TOP GRIP HOLE IS USED TO LURE THE ZOMBIES IN A CERTAIN DIRECTION. DEPENDING ON WHICH GRIP HOLES ARE OPEN OR CLOSED, THE ZOMBIES MOVE FASTER OR STOP COMPLETELY.

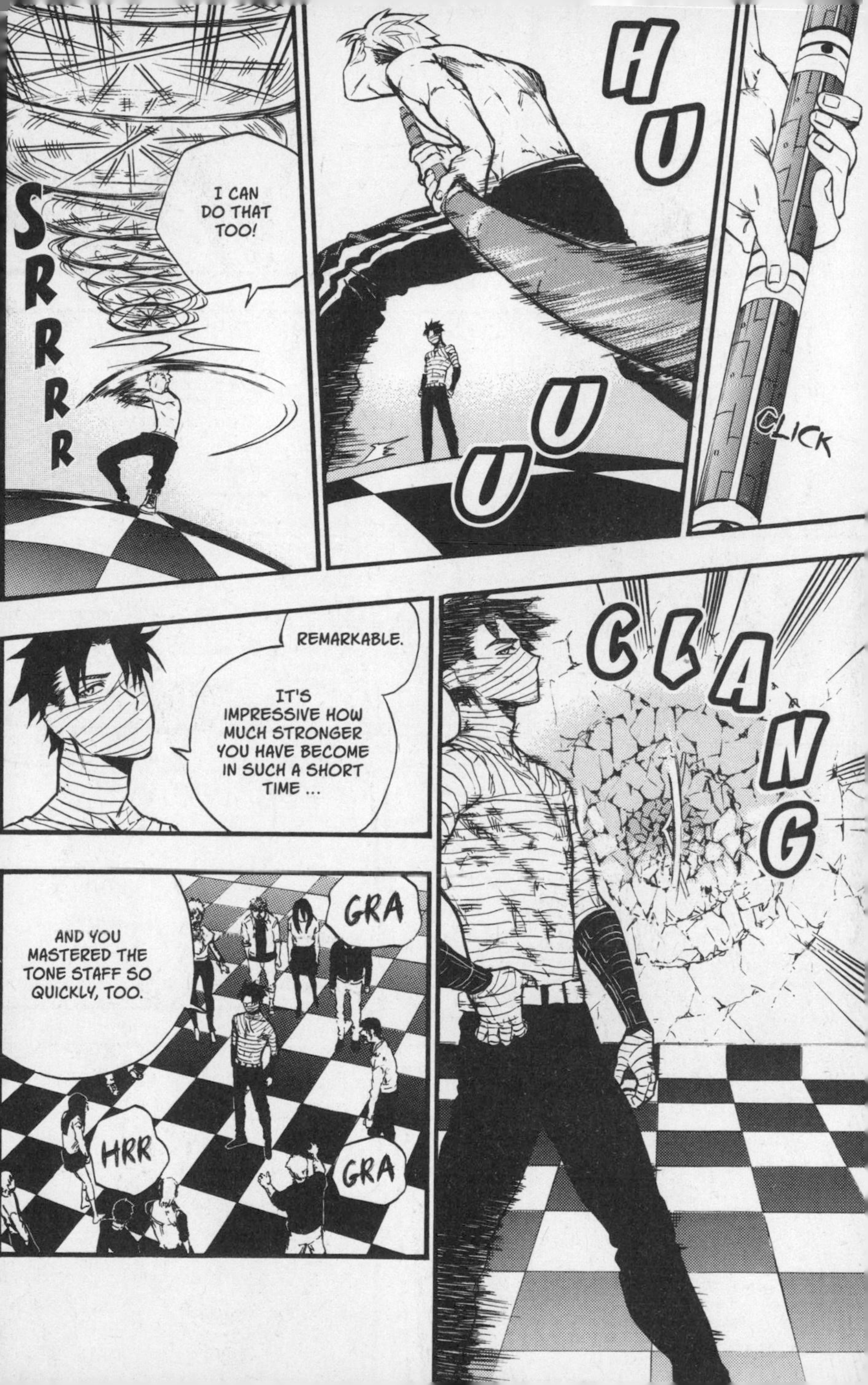
CLICK
HUUUU
SRRRR
I CAN DO THAT TOO!
CLANG
REMARKABLE.
IT'S IMPRESSIVE HOW MUCH STRONGER YOU HAVE BECOME IN SUCH A SHORT TIME ...
GRA
AND YOU MASTERED THE TONE STAFF SO QUICKLY, TOO.
HRR
GRA

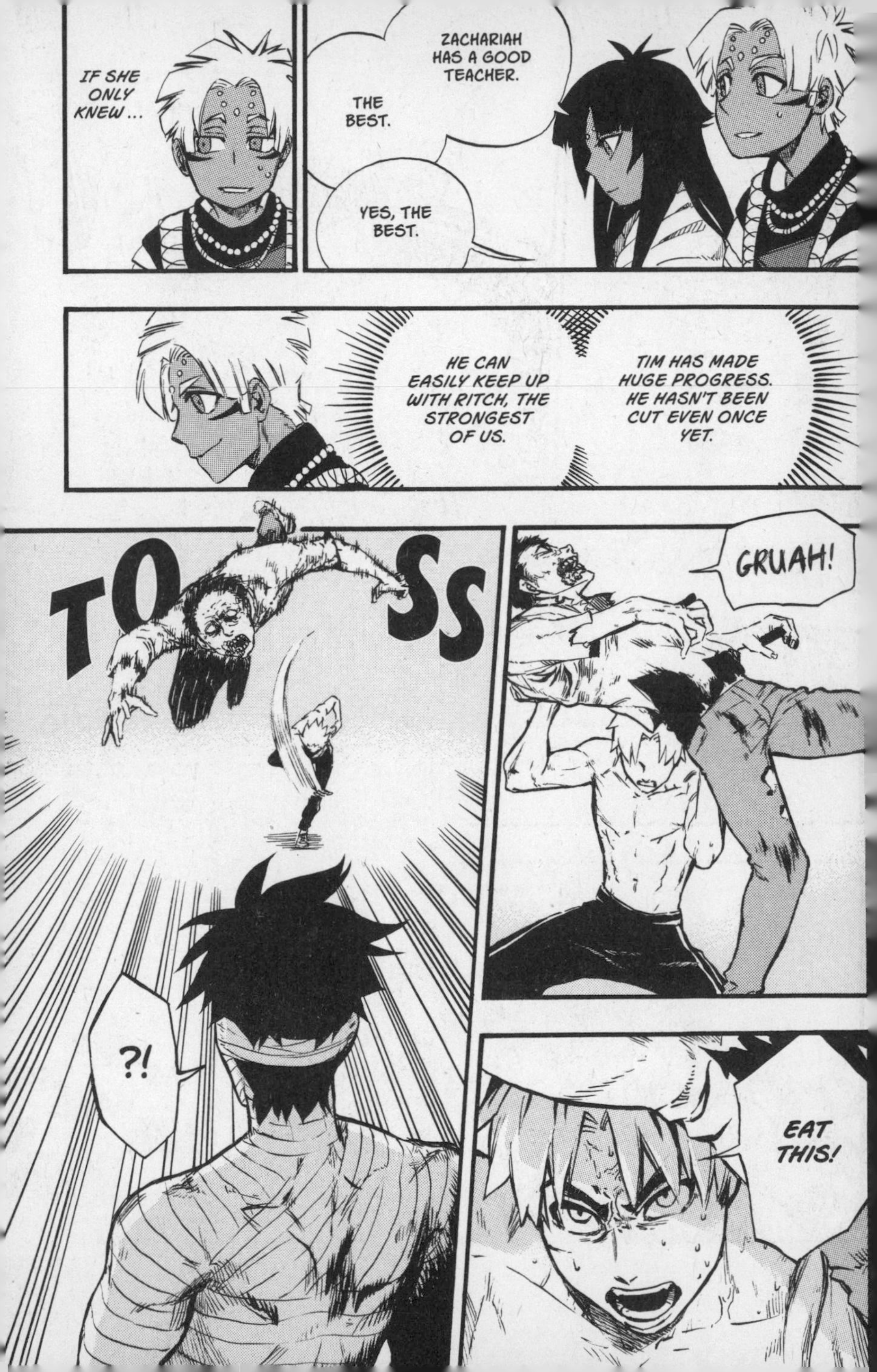

ZACHARIAH HAS A GOOD TEACHER.
THE BEST.
YES, THE BEST.
IF SHE ONLY KNEW...
TIM HAS MADE HUGE PROGRESS. HE HASN'T BEEN CUT EVEN ONCE YET.
HE CAN EASILY KEEP UP WITH RITCH, THE STRONGEST OF US.
GRUAH!
EAT THIS!
TOSS
?!

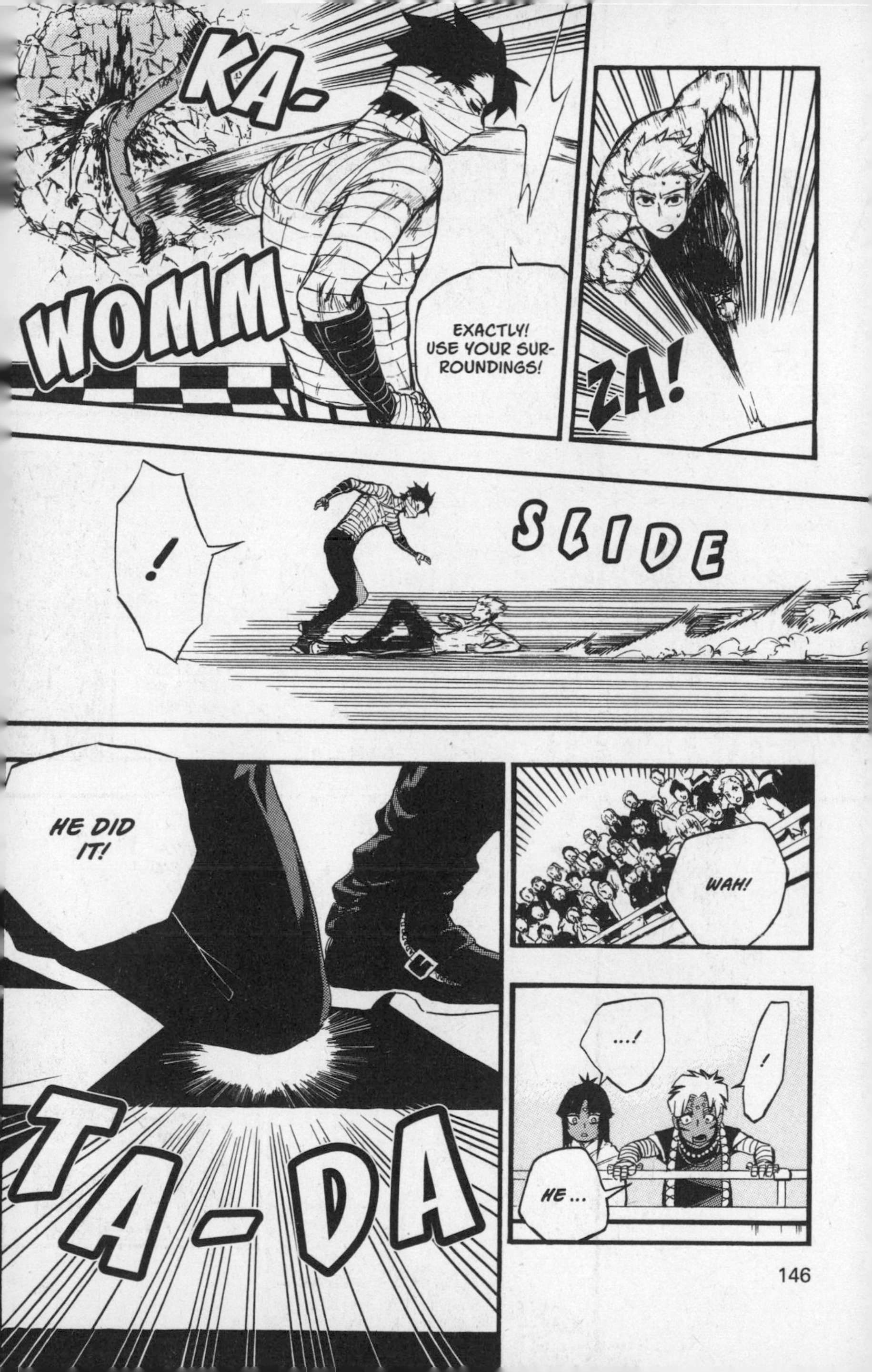
ZA!
KA-
WOMM
EXACTLY! USE YOUR SUR-ROUNDINGS!
SLIDE
!
WAH!
!
...!
HE ...
HE DID IT!
TA-DA

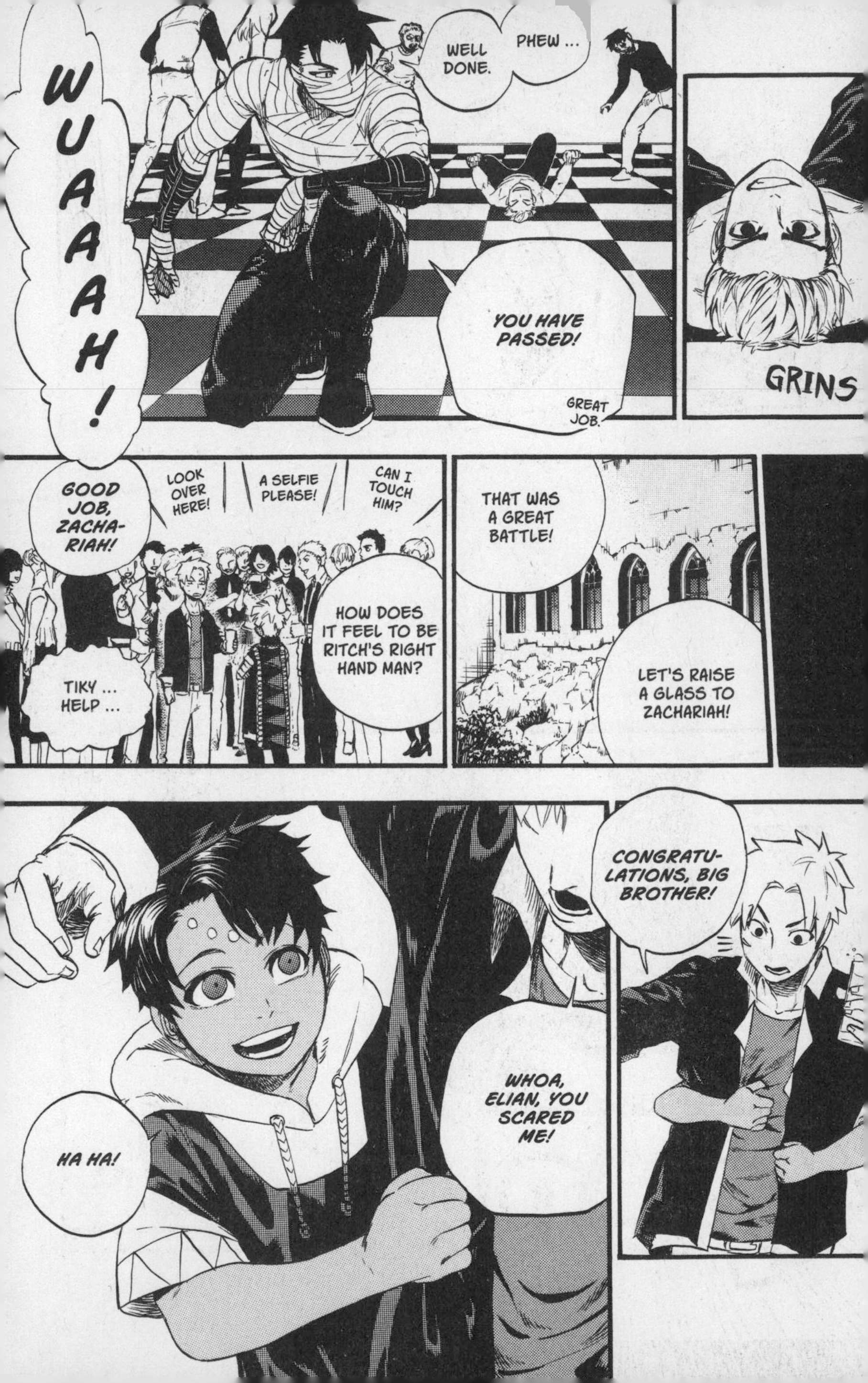
GRINS
PHEW ...
WELL DONE.
YOU HAVE PASSED!
GREAT JOB.
WUAAAH!
THAT WAS A GREAT BATTLE!
LET'S RAISE A GLASS TO ZACHARIAH!
CAN I TOUCH HIM?
A SELFIE PLEASE!
LOOK OVER HERE!
GOOD JOB, ZACHARIAH!
HOW DOES IT FEEL TO BE RITCH'S RIGHT HAND MAN?
TIKY ... HELP ...
CONGRATULATIONS, BIG BROTHER!
WHOA, ELIAN, YOU SCARED ME!
HA HA!

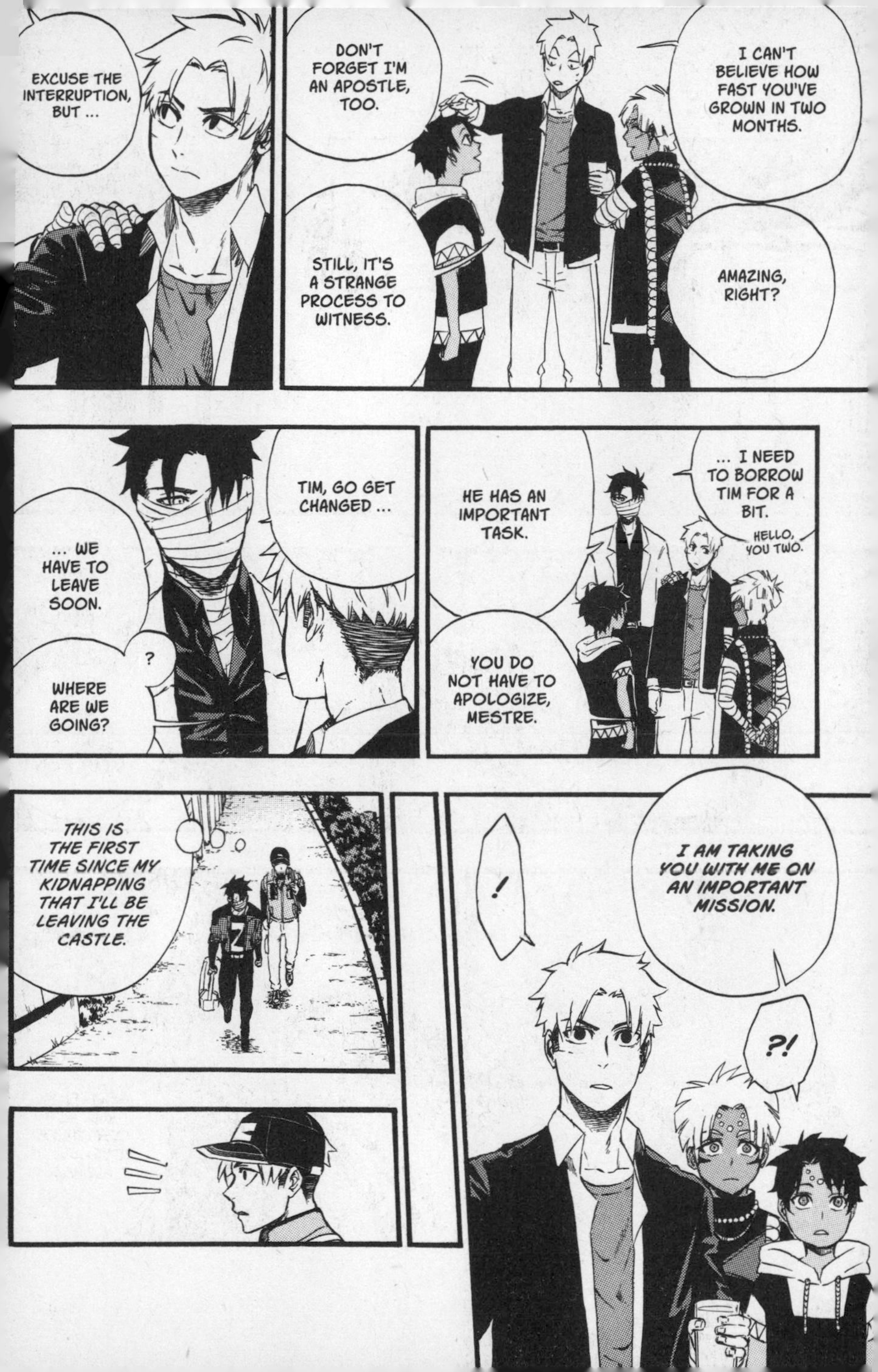
I CAN'T BELIEVE HOW FAST YOU'VE GROWN IN TWO MONTHS.
DON'T FORGET I'M AN APOSTLE, TOO.
AMAZING, RIGHT?
STILL, IT'S A STRANGE PROCESS TO WITNESS.
EXCUSE THE INTERRUPTION, BUT ...
... I NEED TO BORROW TIM FOR A BIT.
HE HAS AN IMPORTANT TASK.
HELLO, YOU TWO.
YOU DO NOT HAVE TO APOLOGIZE, MESTRE.
TIM, GO GET CHANGED ...
... WE HAVE TO LEAVE SOON.
?
WHERE ARE WE GOING?
I AM TAKING YOU WITH ME ON AN IMPORTANT MISSION.
!
?!
THIS IS THE FIRST TIME SINCE MY KIDNAPPING THAT I'LL BE LEAVING THE CASTLE.

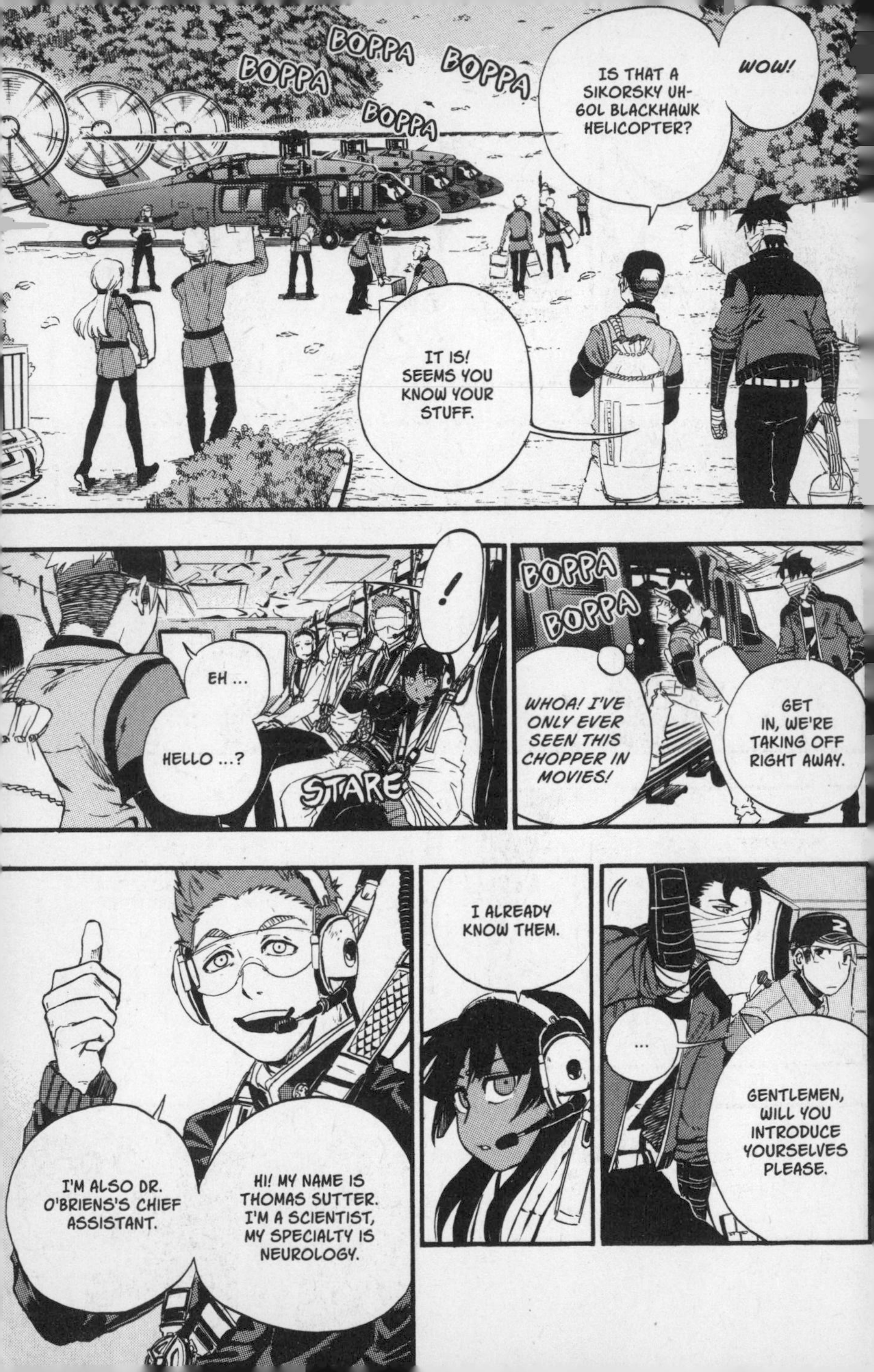
WOW!
IS THAT A SIKORSKY UH-60L BLACKHAWK HELICOPTER?
BOPPA BOPPA
BOPPA BOPPA
IT IS! SEEMS YOU KNOW YOUR STUFF.
BOPPA BOPPA
GET IN, WE'RE TAKING OFF RIGHT AWAY.
WHOA! I'VE ONLY EVER SEEN THIS CHOPPER IN MOVIES!
!
EH ...
HELLO ...?
STARE
GENTLEMEN, WILL YOU INTRODUCE YOURSELVES PLEASE.
...
I ALREADY KNOW THEM.
HI! MY NAME IS THOMAS SUTTER. I'M A SCIENTIST, MY SPECIALTY IS NEUROLOGY.
I'M ALSO DR. O'BRIENS'S CHIEF ASSISTANT.

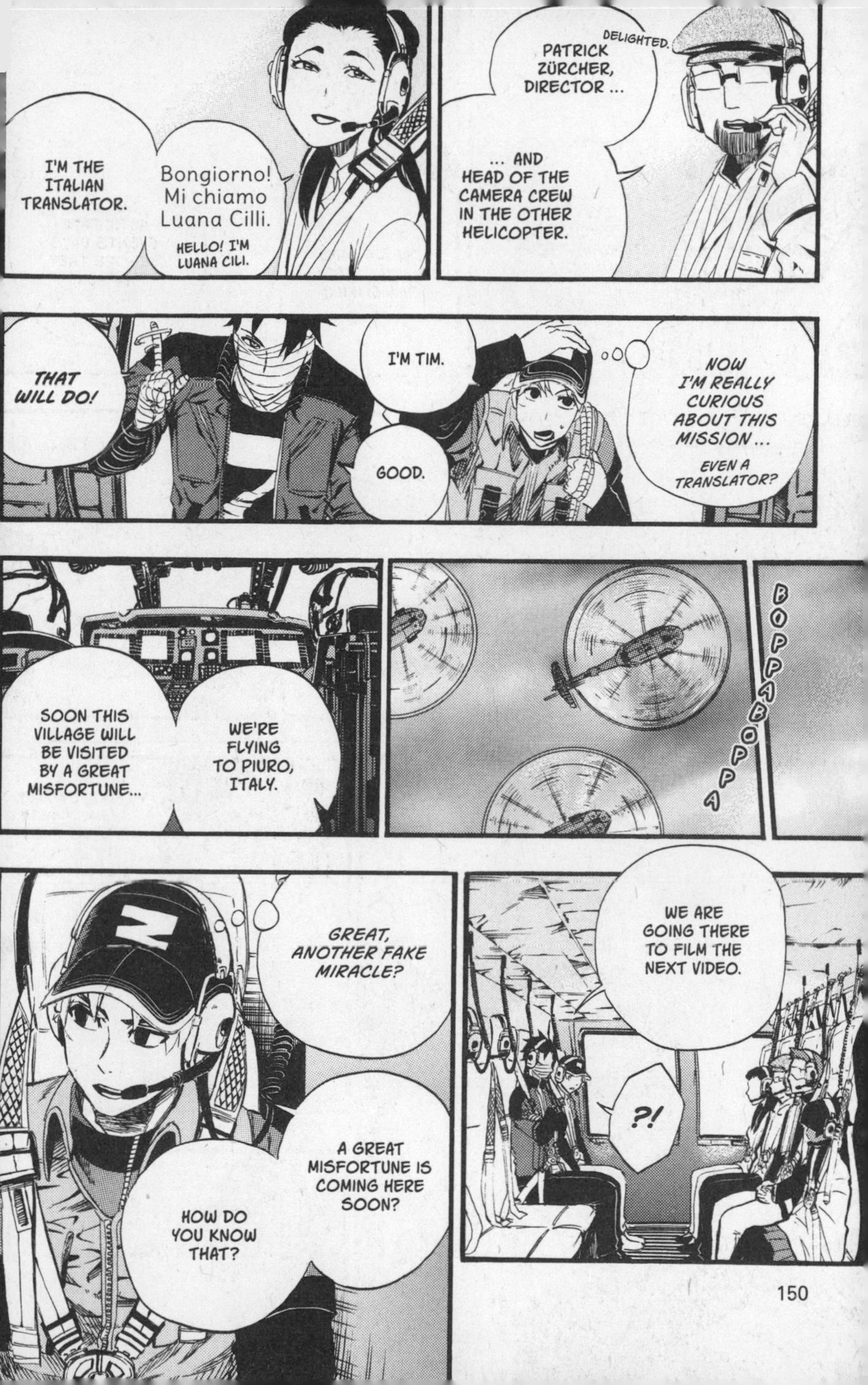
DELIGHTED.
PATRICK ZÜRCHER, DIRECTOR ...
... AND HEAD OF THE CAMERA CREW IN THE OTHER HELICOPTER.
Bongiorno! Mi chiamo Luana Cilli.
HELLO! I'M LUANA CILI.
I'M THE ITALIAN TRANSLATOR.
NOW I'M REALLY CURIOUS ABOUT THIS MISSION ...
EVEN A TRANSLATOR?
I'M TIM.
GOOD.
THAT WILL DO!
BOPPABOPPA
WE'RE FLYING TO PIURO, ITALY.
SOON THIS VILLAGE WILL BE VISITED BY A GREAT MISFORTUNE...
WE ARE GOING THERE TO FILM THE NEXT VIDEO.
?!
GREAT, ANOTHER FAKE MIRACLE?
A GREAT MISFORTUNE IS COMING HERE SOON?
HOW DO YOU KNOW THAT?

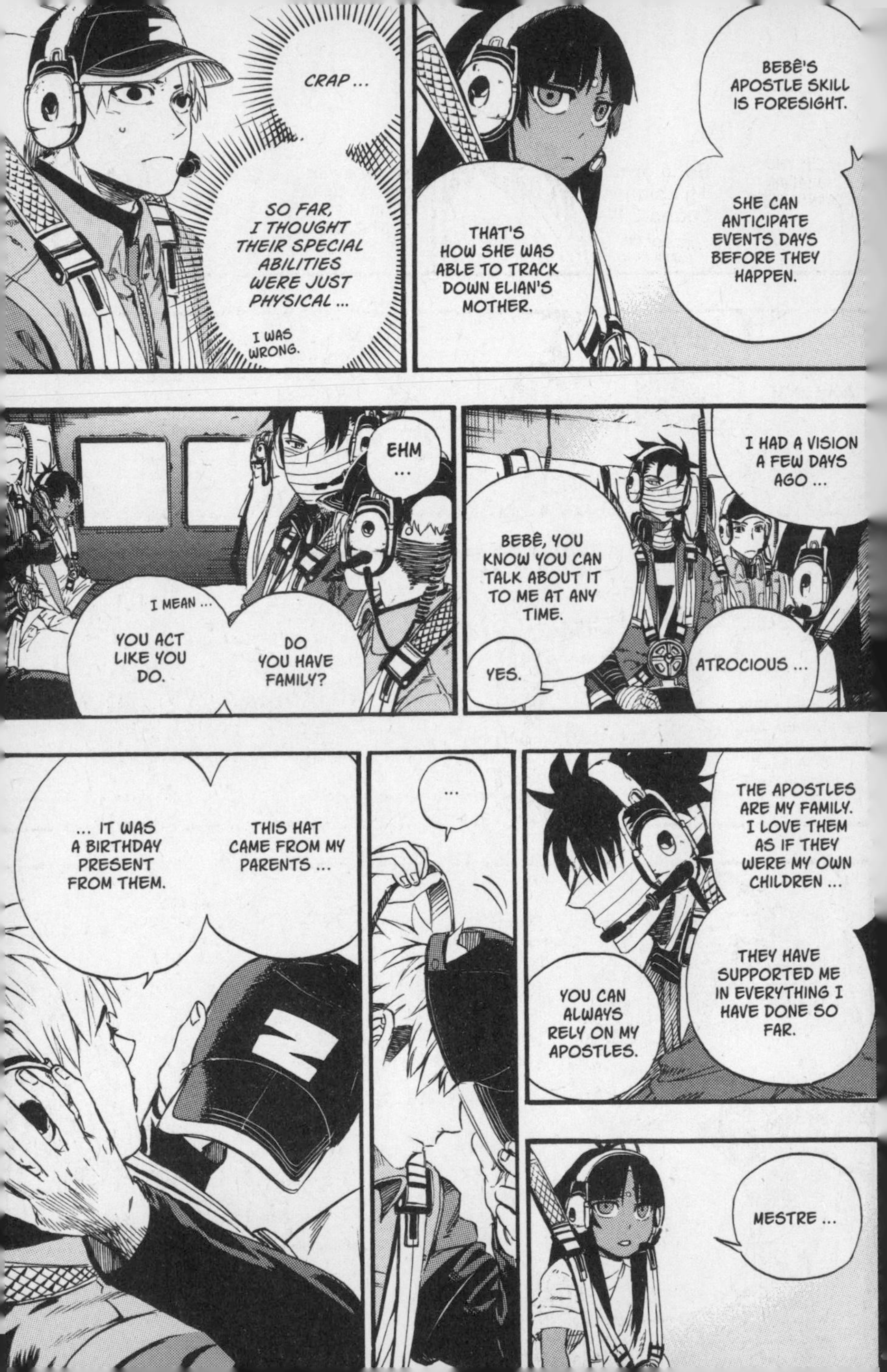
BEBÊ'S APOSTLE SKILL IS FORESIGHT.
SHE CAN ANTICIPATE EVENTS DAYS BEFORE THEY HAPPEN.
THAT'S HOW SHE WAS ABLE TO TRACK DOWN ELIAN'S MOTHER.
CRAP ...
SO FAR, I THOUGHT THEIR SPECIAL ABILITIES WERE JUST PHYSICAL ...
I WAS WRONG.
I HAD A VISION A FEW DAYS AGO ...
BEBÊ, YOU KNOW YOU CAN TALK ABOUT IT TO ME AT ANY TIME.
YES.
ATROCIOUS ...
EHM ...
DO YOU HAVE FAMILY?
I MEAN ...
YOU ACT LIKE YOU DO.
THE APOSTLES ARE MY FAMILY. I LOVE THEM AS IF THEY WERE MY OWN CHILDREN ...
THEY HAVE SUPPORTED ME IN EVERYTHING I HAVE DONE SO FAR.
YOU CAN ALWAYS RELY ON MY APOSTLES.
MESTRE ...
...
THIS HAT CAME FROM MY PARENTS ...
... IT WAS A BIRTHDAY PRESENT FROM THEM.

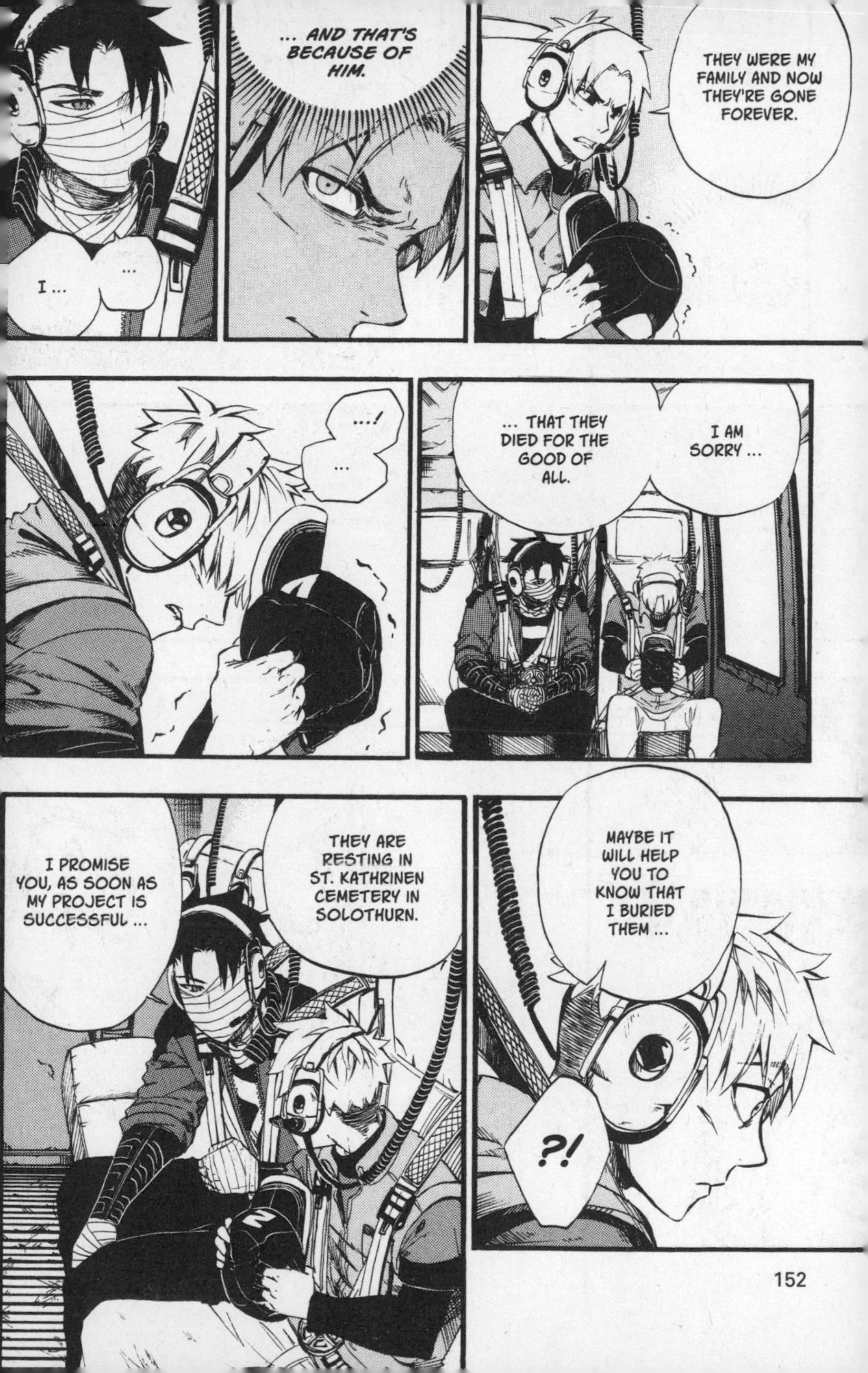
THEY WERE MY FAMILY AND NOW THEY'RE GONE FOREVER.
... AND THAT'S BECAUSE OF HIM.
...
I ...
I AM SORRY ...
... THAT THEY DIED FOR THE GOOD OF ALL.
...!
...
MAYBE IT WILL HELP YOU TO KNOW THAT I BURIED THEM ...
?!
THEY ARE RESTING IN ST. KATHRINEN CEMETERY IN SOLOTHURN.
I PROMISE YOU, AS SOON AS MY PROJECT IS SUCCESSFUL ...

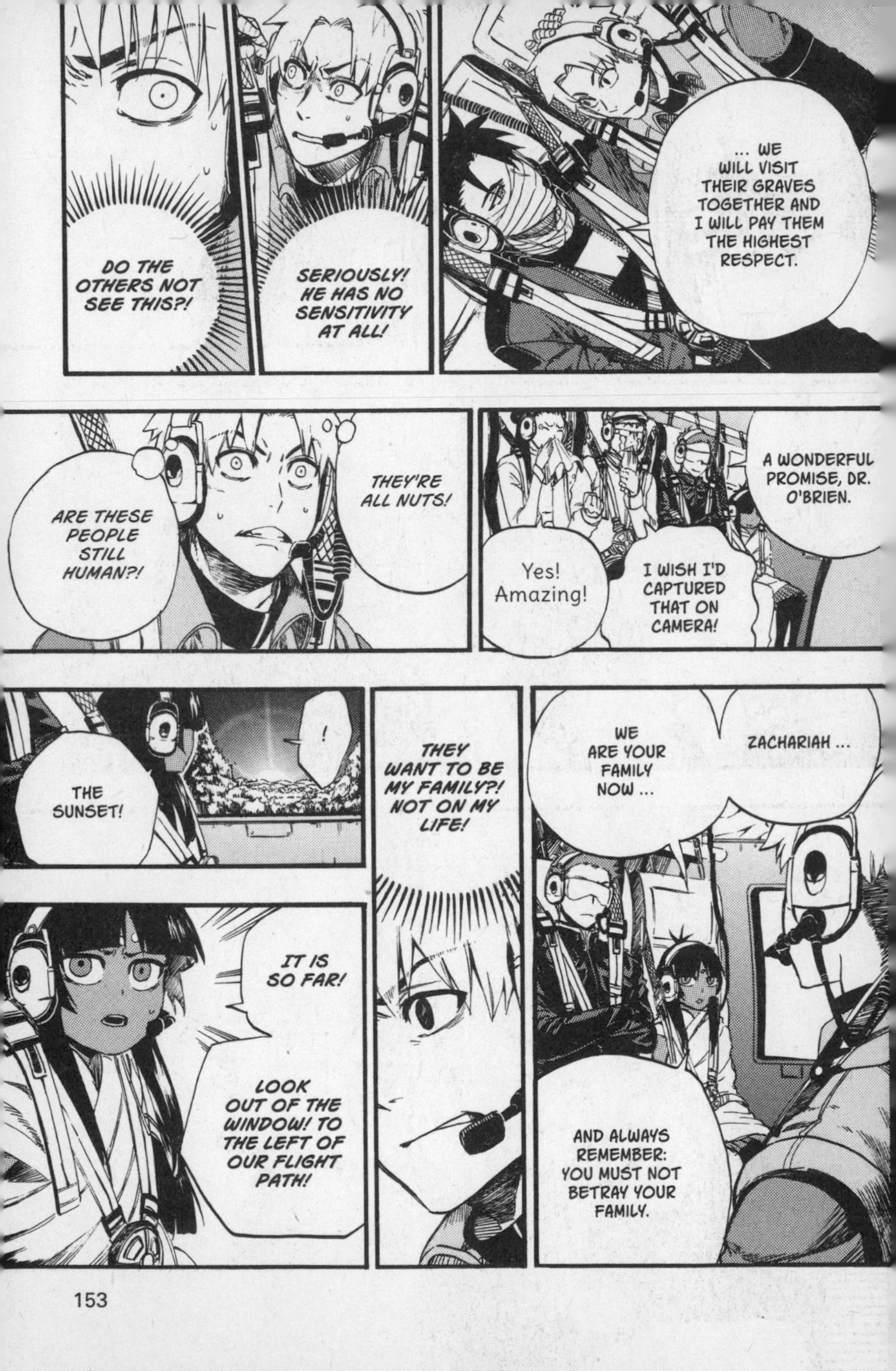
... WE WILL VISIT THEIR GRAVES TOGETHER AND I WILL PAY THEM THE HIGHEST RESPECT.
SERIOUSLY! HE HAS NO SENSITIVITY AT ALL!
DO THE OTHERS NOT SEE THIS?!
A WONDERFUL PROMISE, DR. O'BRIEN.
I WISH I'D CAPTURED THAT ON CAMERA!
Yes! Amazing!
THEY'RE ALL NUTS!
ARE THESE PEOPLE STILL HUMAN?!
ZACHARIAH ...
WE ARE YOUR FAMILY NOW ...
AND ALWAYS REMEMBER: YOU MUST NOT BETRAY YOUR FAMILY.
THEY WANT TO BE MY FAMILY?! NOT ON MY LIFE!
!
THE SUNSET!
IT IS SO FAR!
LOOK OUT OF THE WINDOW! TO THE LEFT OF OUR FLIGHT PATH!

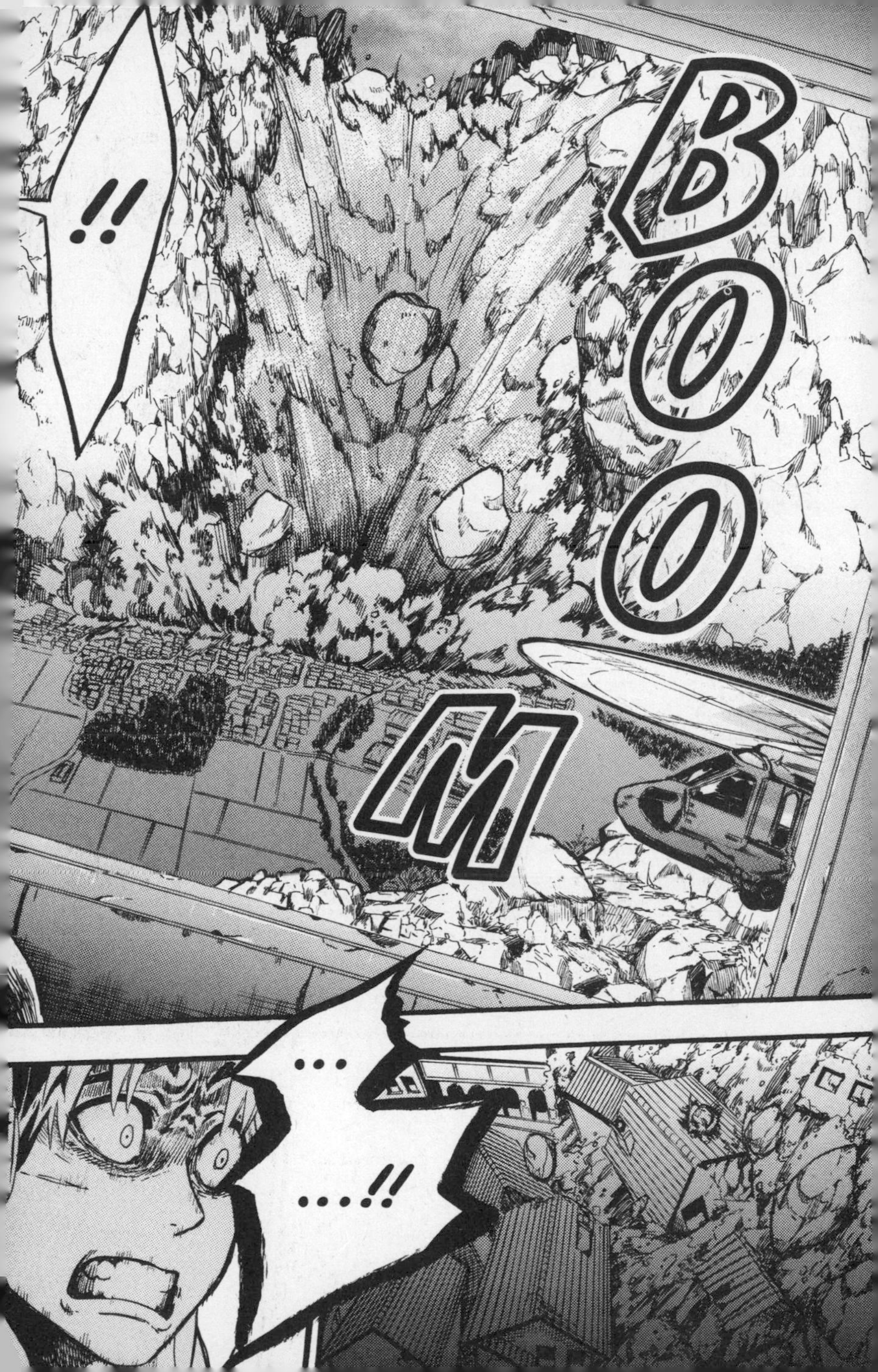
BOOM
!!
...
....!!

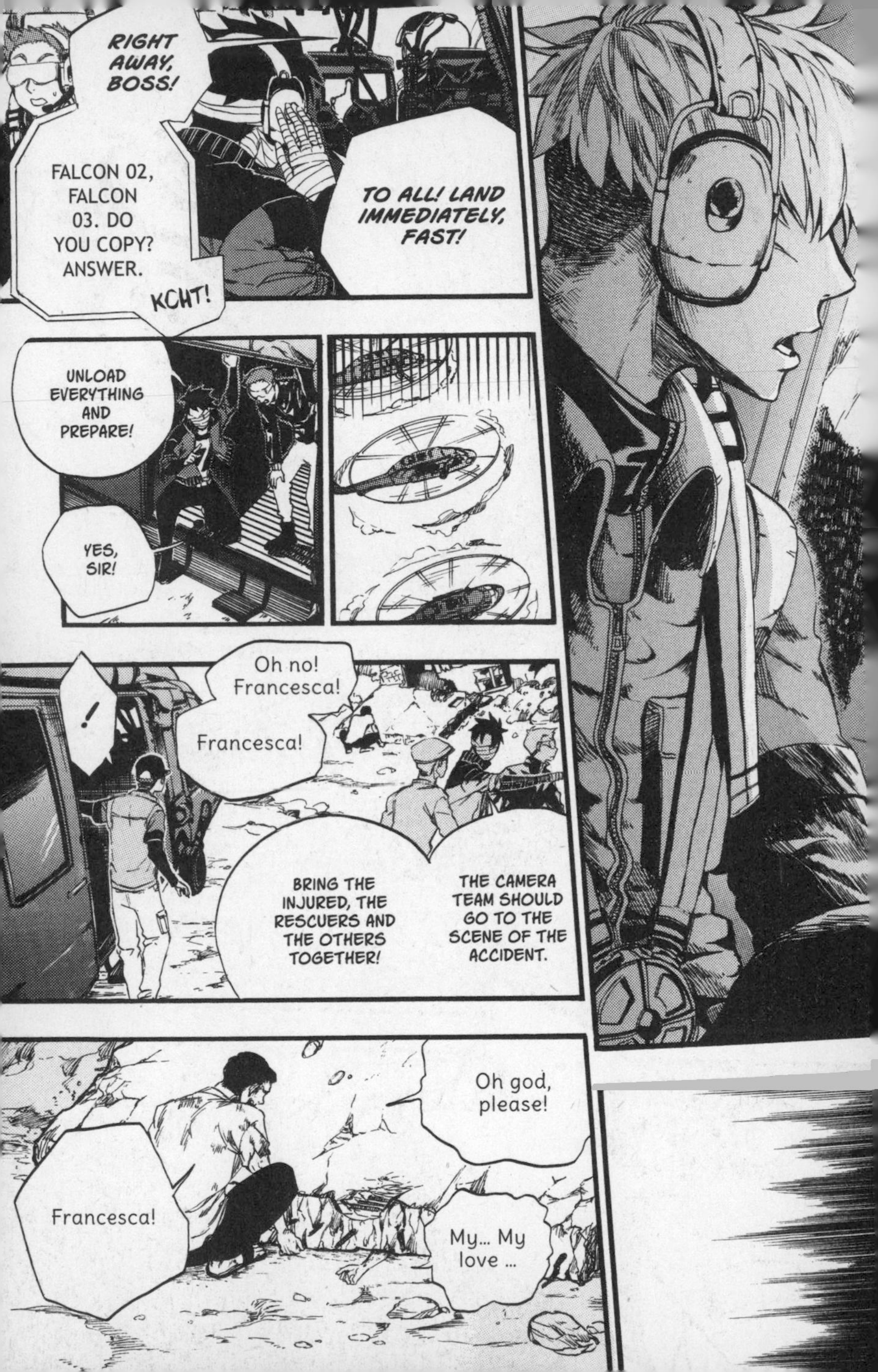

TO ALL! LAND IMMEDIATELY, FAST!
RIGHT AWAY, BOSS!
FALCON 02, FALCON 03. DO YOU COPY? ANSWER.
KCHT!
UNLOAD EVERYTHING AND PREPARE!
YES, SIR!
Oh no! Francesca!
Francesca!
!
THE CAMERA TEAM SHOULD GO TO THE SCENE OF THE ACCIDENT.
BRING THE INJURED, THE RESCUERS AND THE OTHERS TOGETHER!
Oh god, please!
My... My love ...
Francesca!

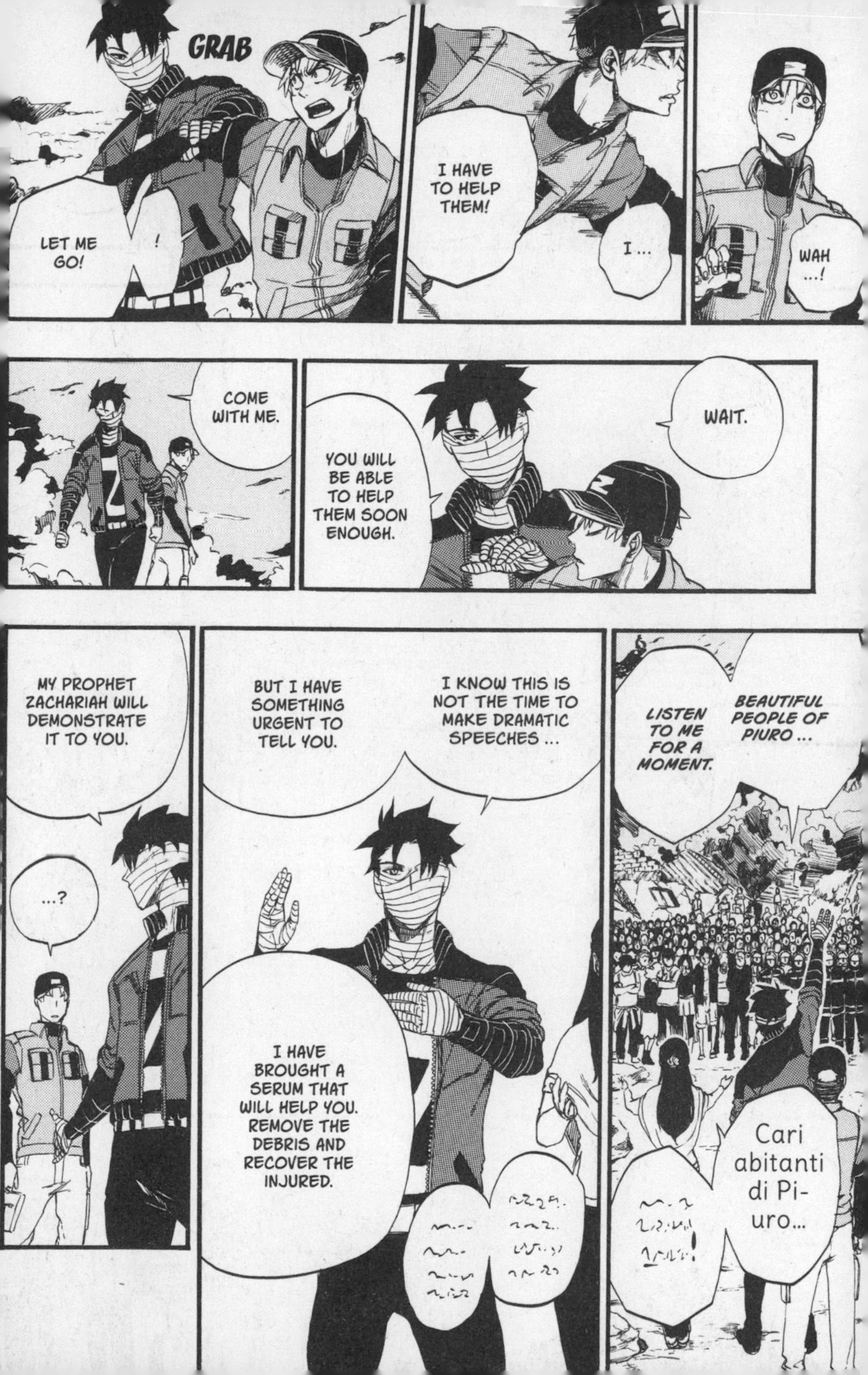
WAH ...!
I ...
I HAVE TO HELP THEM!
GRAB
!
LET ME GO!
WAIT.
YOU WILL BE ABLE TO HELP THEM SOON ENOUGH.
COME WITH ME.
BEAUTIFUL PEOPLE OF PIURO ...
LISTEN TO ME FOR A MOMENT.
Cari abitanti di Piuro...
I KNOW THIS IS NOT THE TIME TO MAKE DRAMATIC SPEECHES ...
BUT I HAVE SOMETHING URGENT TO TELL YOU.
I HAVE BROUGHT A SERUM THAT WILL HELP YOU. REMOVE THE DEBRIS AND RECOVER THE INJURED.
MY PROPHET ZACHARIAH WILL DEMONSTRATE IT TO YOU.
...?

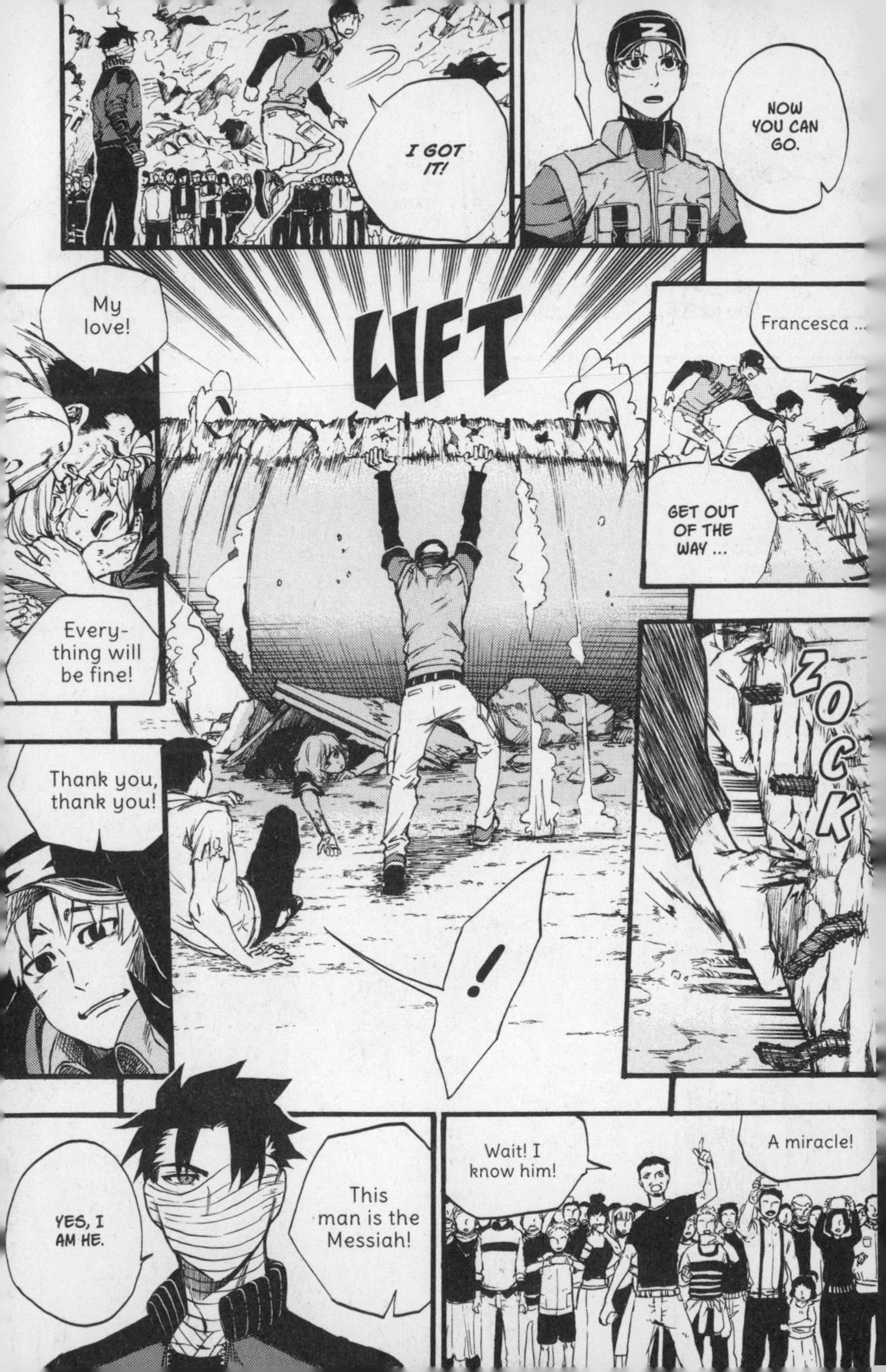
NOW YOU CAN GO.
I GOT IT!
Francesca ...
GET OUT OF THE WAY ...
ZOCK
LIFT
!
My love!
Every-thing will be fine!
Thank you, thank you!
A miracle!
Wait! I know him!
This man is the Messiah!
YES, I AM HE.

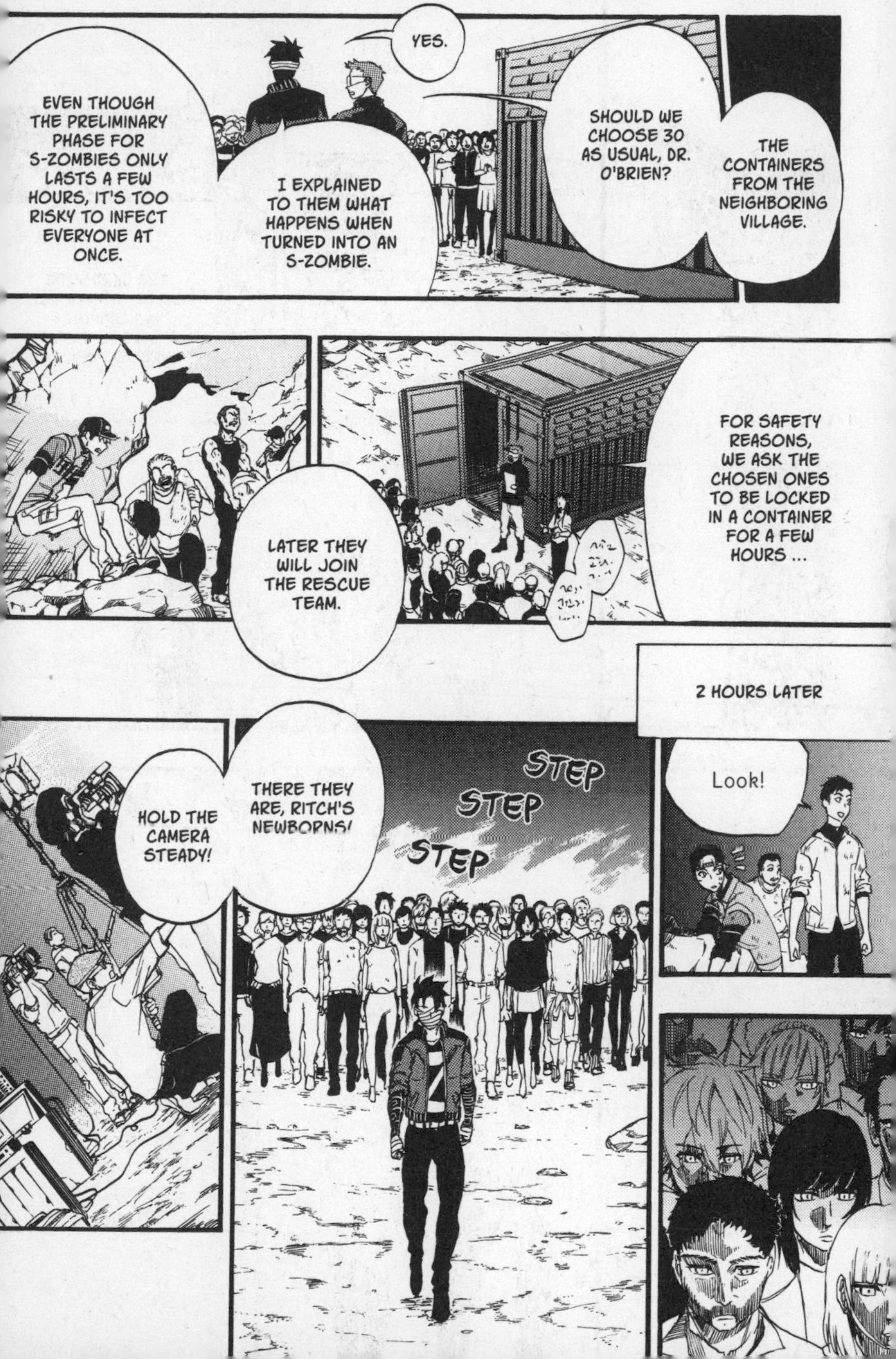
THE CONTAINERS FROM THE NEIGHBORING VILLAGE.
SHOULD WE CHOOSE 30 AS USUAL, DR. O'BRIEN?
YES.
I EXPLAINED TO THEM WHAT HAPPENS WHEN TURNED INTO AN S-ZOMBIE.
EVEN THOUGH THE PRELIMINARY PHASE FOR S-ZOMBIES ONLY LASTS A FEW HOURS, IT'S TOO RISKY TO INFECT EVERYONE AT ONCE.
FOR SAFETY REASONS, WE ASK THE CHOSEN ONES TO BE LOCKED IN A CONTAINER FOR A FEW HOURS ...
LATER THEY WILL JOIN THE RESCUE TEAM.
2 HOURS LATER
Look!
STEP
STEP
STEP
THERE THEY ARE, RITCH'S NEWBORNS!
HOLD THE CAMERA STEADY!

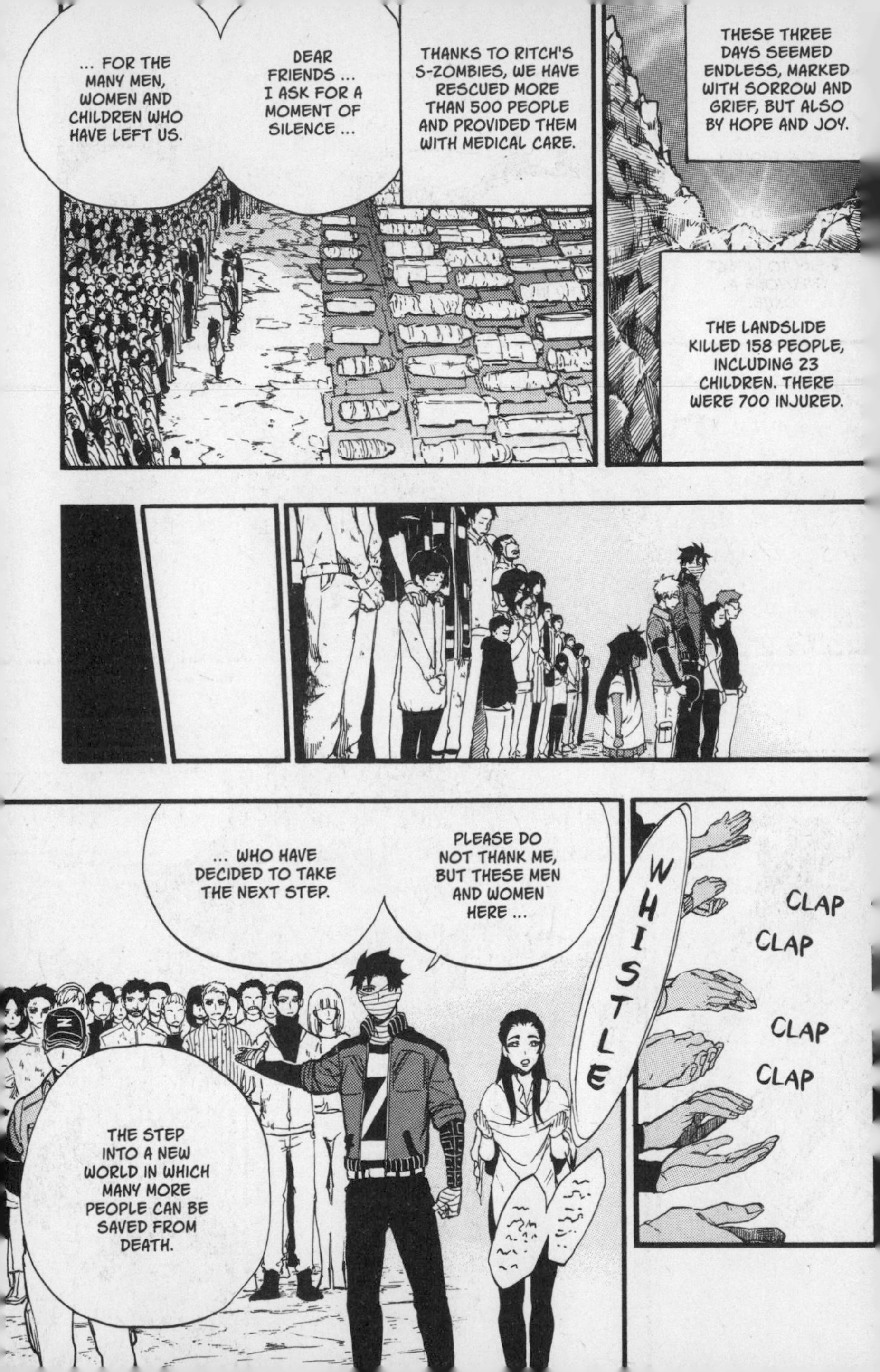
THESE THREE DAYS SEEMED ENDLESS, MARKED WITH SORROW AND GRIEF, BUT ALSO BY HOPE AND JOY.
THE LANDSLIDE KILLED 158 PEOPLE, INCLUDING 23 CHILDREN. THERE WERE 700 INJURED.
THANKS TO RITCH'S S-ZOMBIES, WE HAVE RESCUED MORE THAN 500 PEOPLE AND PROVIDED THEM WITH MEDICAL CARE.
DEAR FRIENDS ... I ASK FOR A MOMENT OF SILENCE ...
... FOR THE MANY MEN, WOMEN AND CHILDREN WHO HAVE LEFT US.
WHISTLE
CLAP
CLAP
CLAP
CLAP
PLEASE DO NOT THANK ME, BUT THESE MEN AND WOMEN HERE ...
... WHO HAVE DECIDED TO TAKE THE NEXT STEP.
THE STEP INTO A NEW WORLD IN WHICH MANY MORE PEOPLE CAN BE SAVED FROM DEATH.

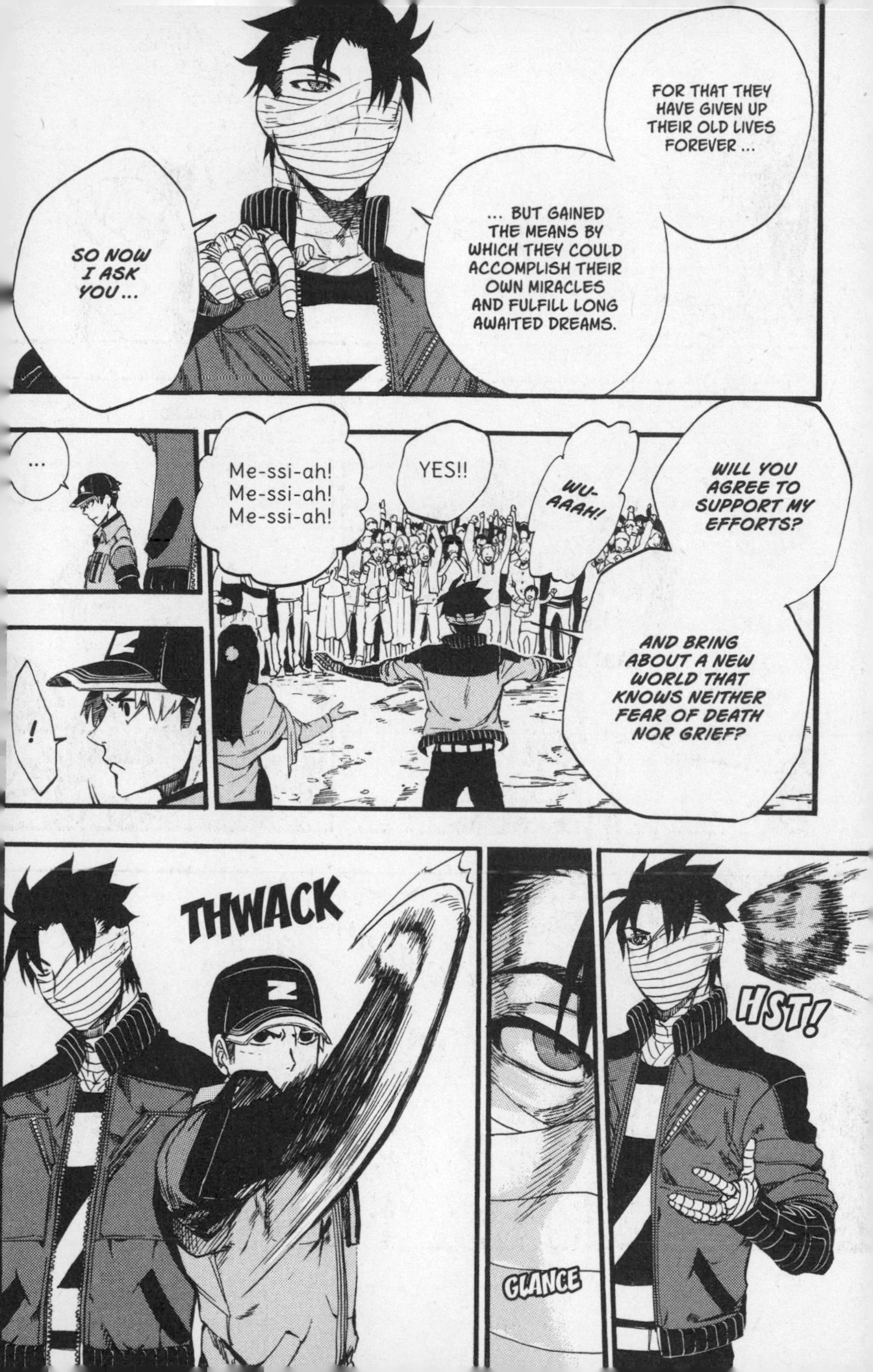
FOR THAT THEY HAVE GIVEN UP THEIR OLD LIVES FOREVER ...
... BUT GAINED THE MEANS BY WHICH THEY COULD ACCOMPLISH THEIR OWN MIRACLES AND FULFILL LONG AWAITED DREAMS.
SO NOW I ASK YOU ...
WILL YOU AGREE TO SUPPORT MY EFFORTS?
AND BRING ABOUT A NEW WORLD THAT KNOWS NEITHER FEAR OF DEATH NOR GRIEF?
WU-AAAH!
YES!!
Me-ssi-ah! Me-ssi-ah! Me-ssi-ah!
...
!
HST!
GLANCE
THWACK

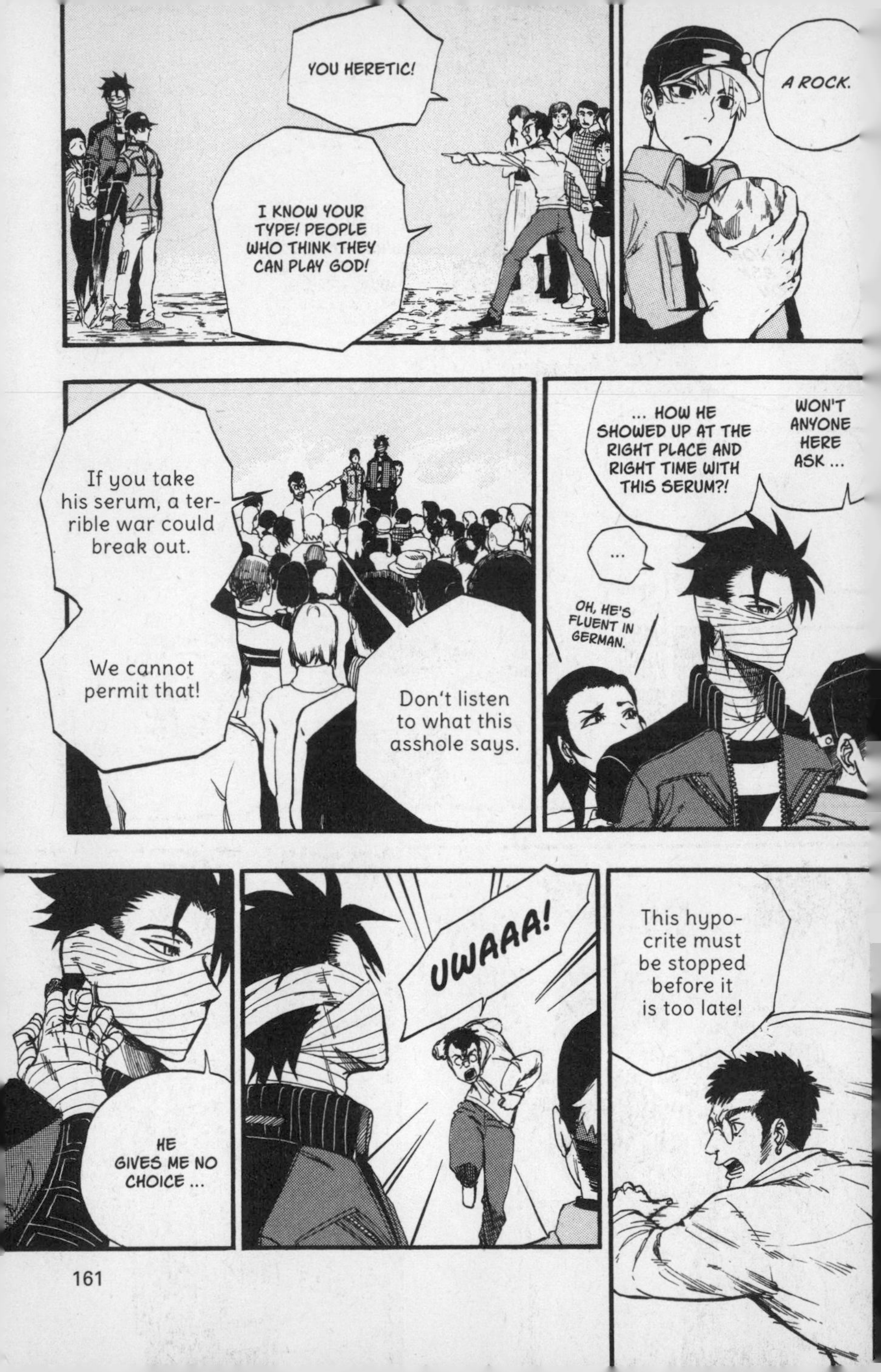
A ROCK.
YOU HERETIC!
I KNOW YOUR TYPE! PEOPLE WHO THINK THEY CAN PLAY GOD!
WON'T ANYONE HERE ASK ...
... HOW HE SHOWED UP AT THE RIGHT PLACE AND RIGHT TIME WITH THIS SERUM?!
...
OH, HE'S FLUENT IN GERMAN.
If you take his serum, a terrible war could break out.
We cannot permit that!
Don't listen to what this asshole says.
This hypocrite must be stopped before it is too late!
UWAAA!
HE GIVES ME NO CHOICE ...

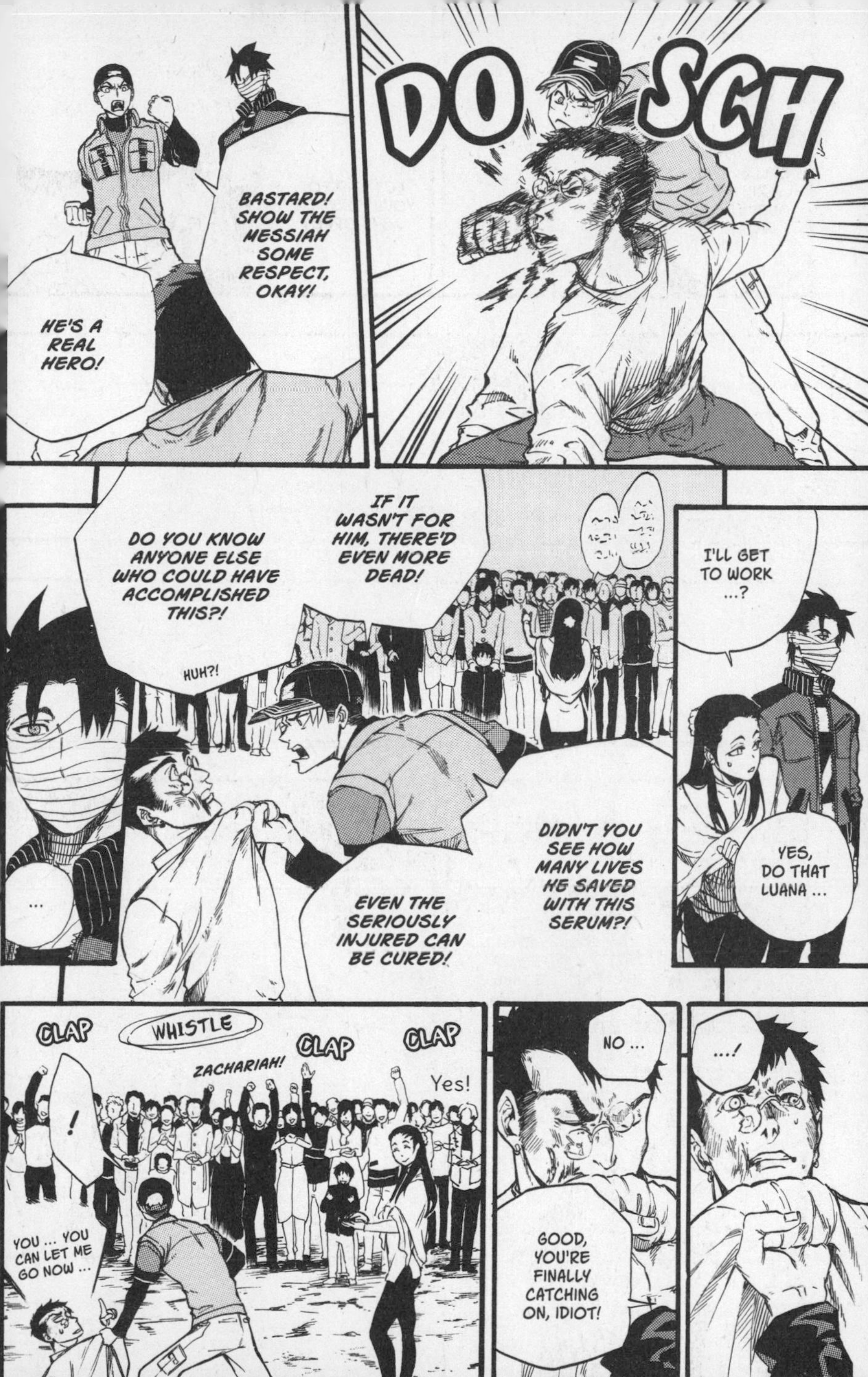
DO SCH
BASTARD! SHOW THE MESSIAH SOME RESPECT, OKAY!
HE'S A REAL HERO!
I'LL GET TO WORK ...?
YES, DO THAT LUANA ...
IF IT WASN'T FOR HIM, THERE'D EVEN MORE DEAD!
DO YOU KNOW ANYONE ELSE WHO COULD HAVE ACCOMPLISHED THIS?!
HUH?!
DIDN'T YOU SEE HOW MANY LIVES HE SAVED WITH THIS SERUM?!
EVEN THE SERIOUSLY INJURED CAN BE CURED!
...
...!
NO ...
GOOD, YOU'RE FINALLY CATCHING ON, IDIOT!
CLAP
CLAP
Yes!
ZACHARIAH!
WHISTLE
CLAP
!
YOU ... YOU CAN LET ME GO NOW ...

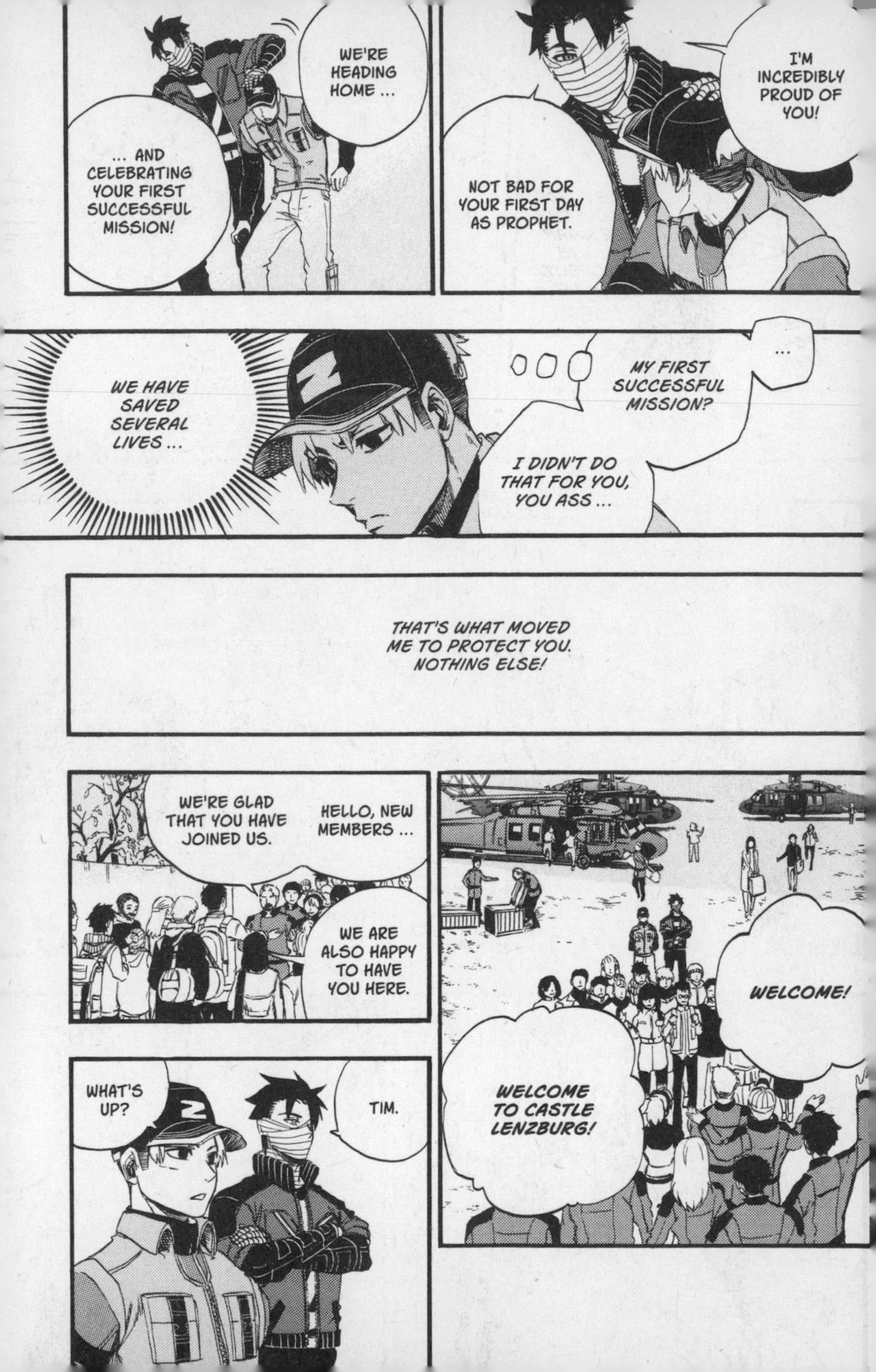
I'M INCREDIBLY PROUD OF YOU!
NOT BAD FOR YOUR FIRST DAY AS PROPHET.
WE'RE HEADING HOME ...
... AND CELEBRATING YOUR FIRST SUCCESSFUL MISSION!
...
MY FIRST SUCCESSFUL MISSION?
I DIDN'T DO THAT FOR YOU, YOU ASS ...
WE HAVE SAVED SEVERAL LIVES ...
THAT'S WHAT MOVED ME TO PROTECT YOU. NOTHING ELSE!
WELCOME!
WELCOME TO CASTLE LENZBURG!
HELLO, NEW MEMBERS ...
WE'RE GLAD THAT YOU HAVE JOINED US.
WE ARE ALSO HAPPY TO HAVE YOU HERE.
TIM.
WHAT'S UP?

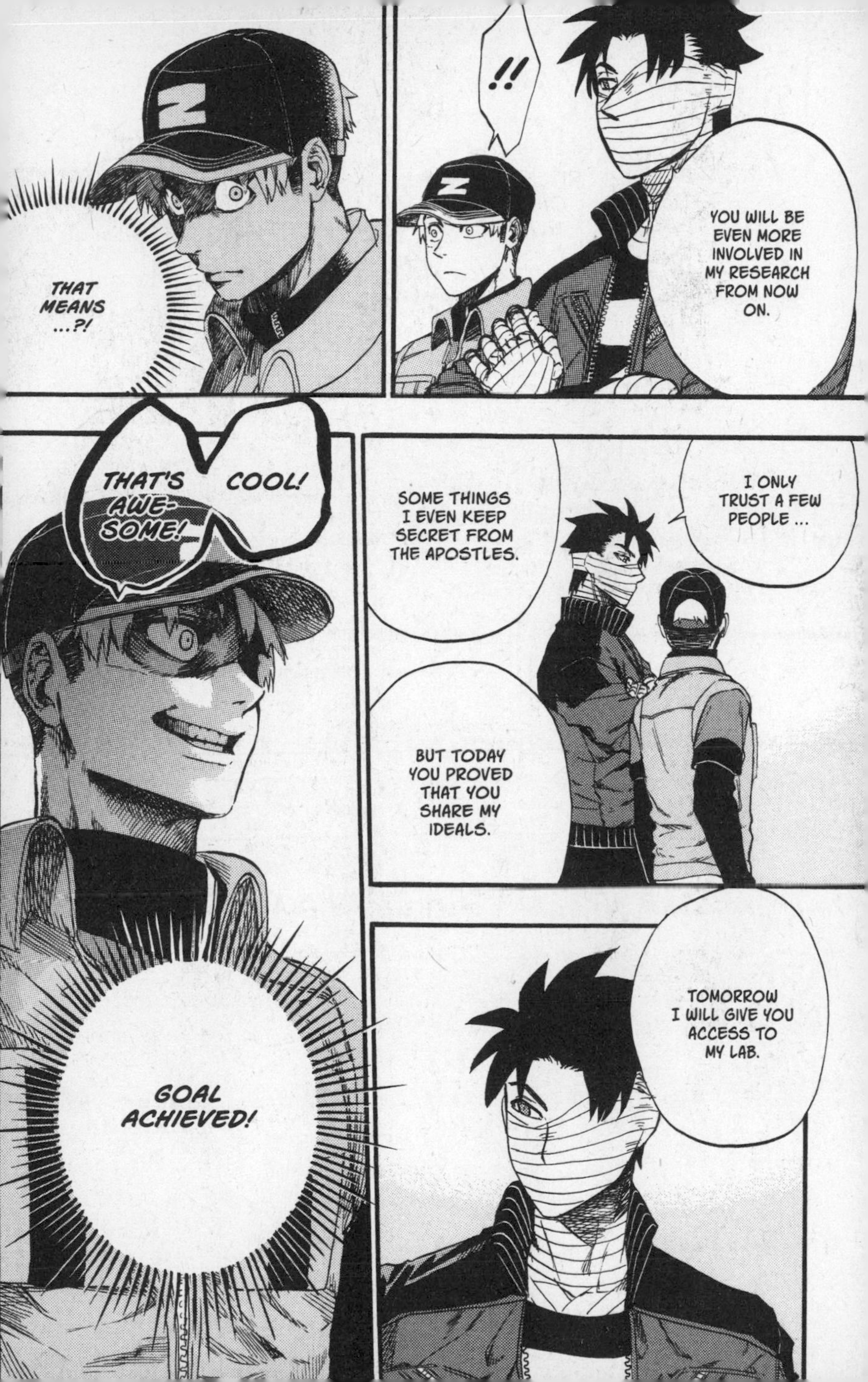
!!
YOU WILL BE EVEN MORE INVOLVED IN MY RESEARCH FROM NOW ON.
THAT MEANS ...?!
I ONLY TRUST A FEW PEOPLE ...
SOME THINGS I EVEN KEEP SECRET FROM THE APOSTLES.
BUT TODAY YOU PROVED THAT YOU SHARE MY IDEALS.
TOMORROW I WILL GIVE YOU ACCESS TO MY LAB.
THAT'S COOL! AWE-SOME!
GOAL ACHIEVED!

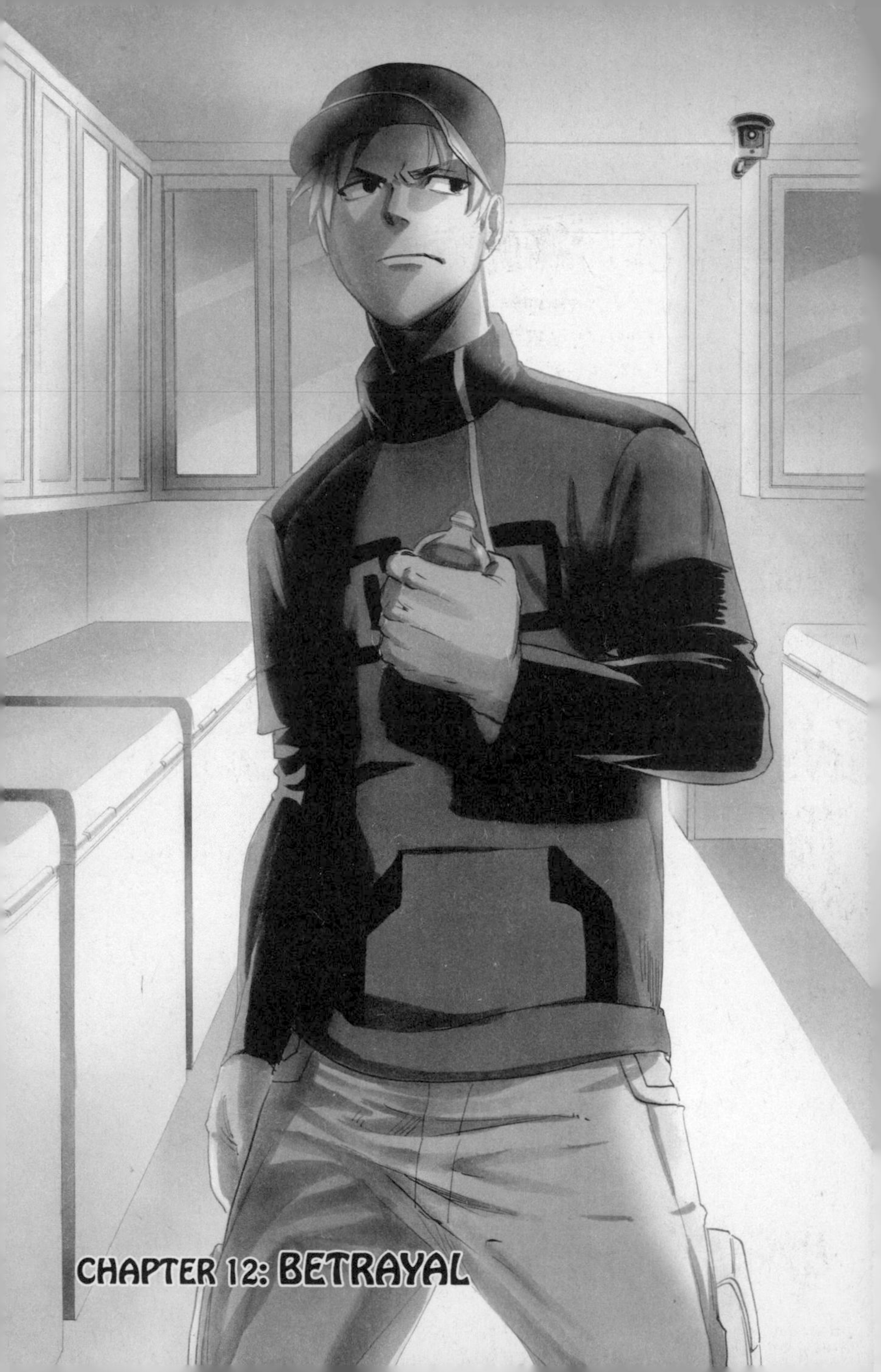
CHAPTER 12: BETRAYAL

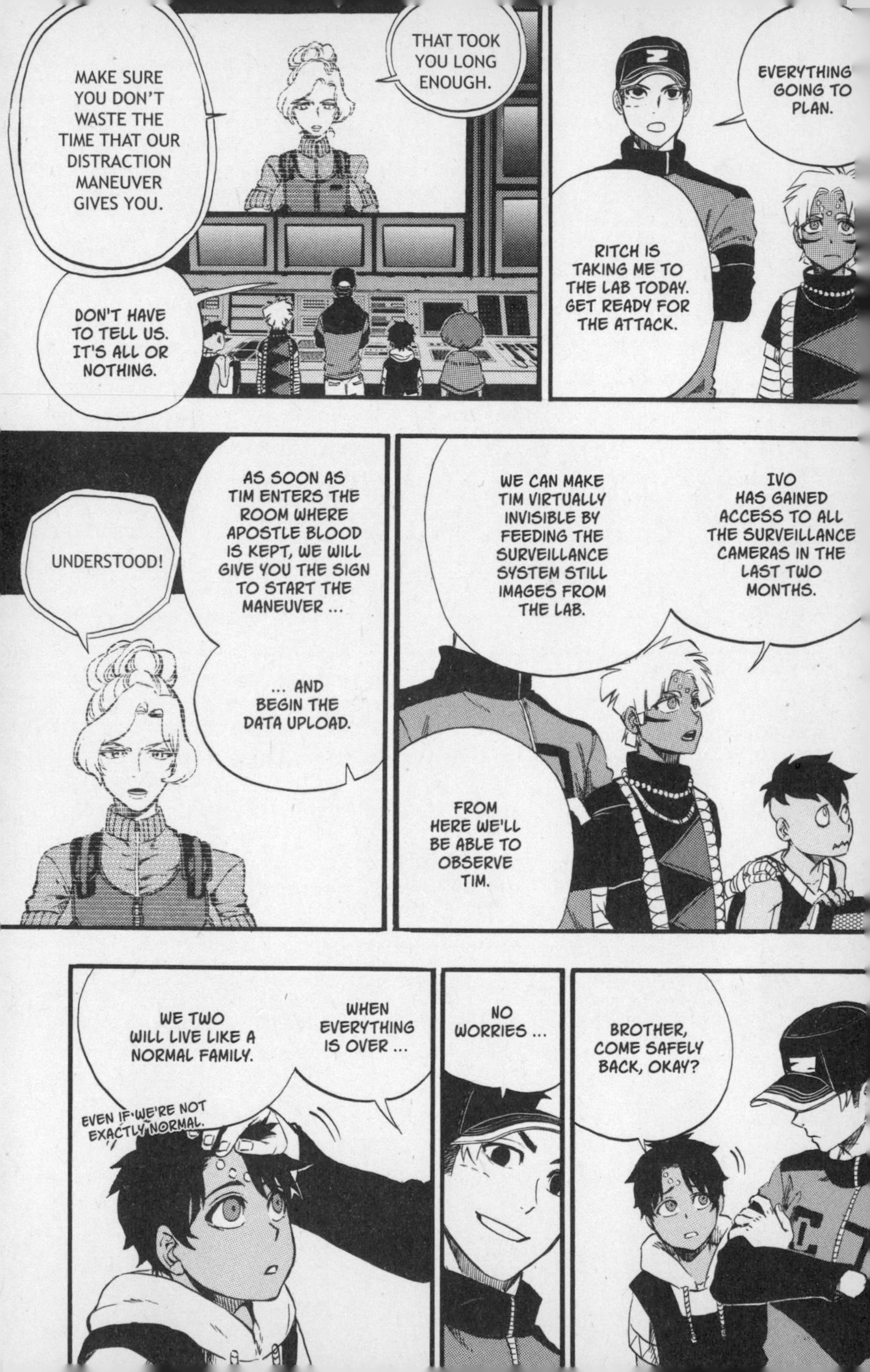
EVERYTHING GOING TO PLAN.
RITCH IS TAKING ME TO THE LAB TODAY. GET READY FOR THE ATTACK.
THAT TOOK YOU LONG ENOUGH.
MAKE SURE YOU DON'T WASTE THE TIME THAT OUR DISTRACTION MANEUVER GIVES YOU.
DON'T HAVE TO TELL US. IT'S ALL OR NOTHING.
IVO HAS GAINED ACCESS TO ALL THE SURVEILLANCE CAMERAS IN THE LAST TWO MONTHS.
WE CAN MAKE TIM VIRTUALLY INVISIBLE BY FEEDING THE SURVEILLANCE SYSTEM STILL IMAGES FROM THE LAB.
FROM HERE WE'LL BE ABLE TO OBSERVE TIM.
AS SOON AS TIM ENTERS THE ROOM WHERE APOSTLE BLOOD IS KEPT, WE WILL GIVE YOU THE SIGN TO START THE MANEUVER ...
UNDERSTOOD!
... AND BEGIN THE DATA UPLOAD.
BROTHER, COME SAFELY BACK, OKAY?
NO WORRIES ...
WHEN EVERYTHING IS OVER ...
WE TWO WILL LIVE LIKE A NORMAL FAMILY.
EVEN IF WE'RE NOT EXACTLY NORMAL.

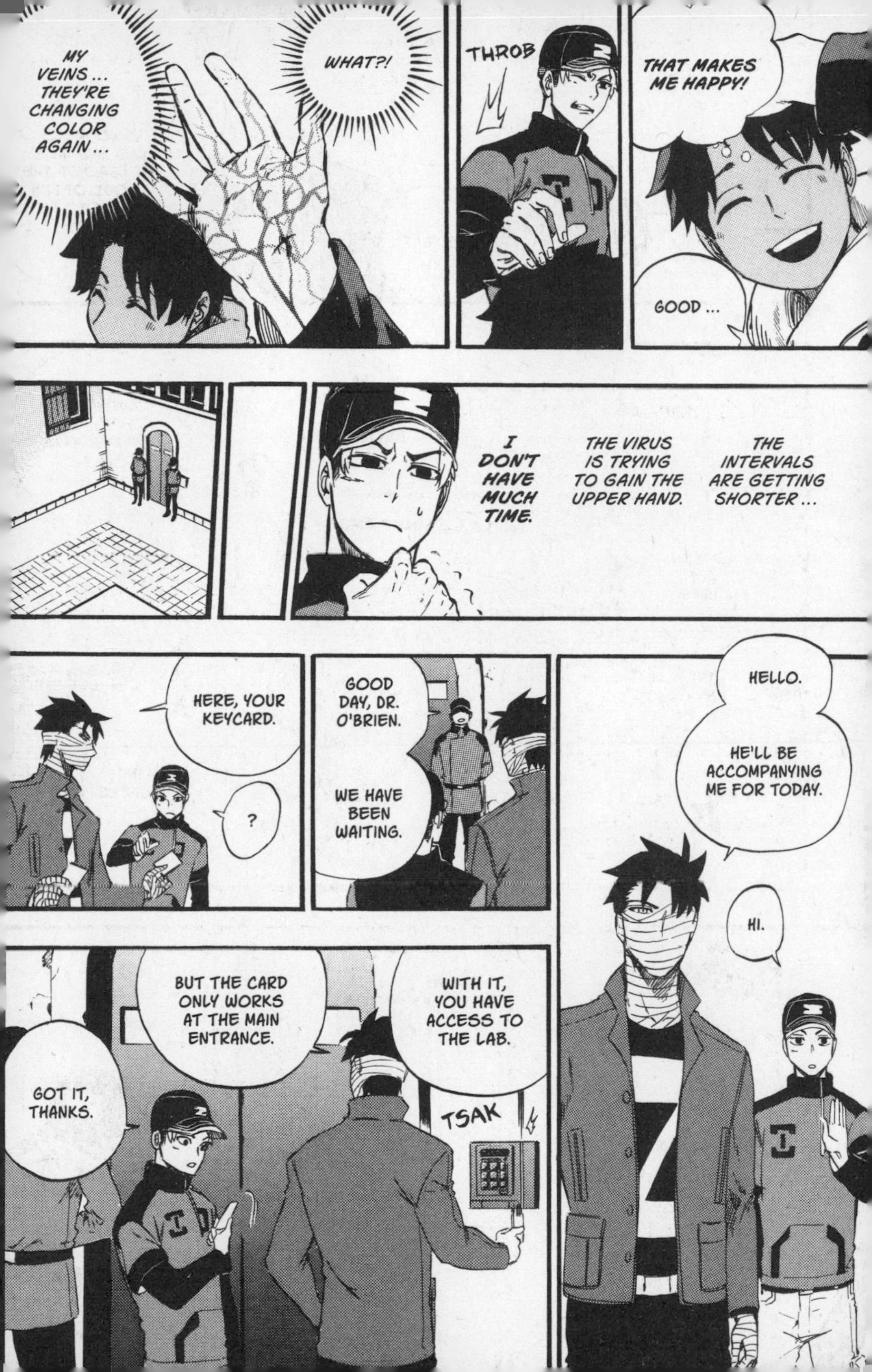
THAT MAKES ME HAPPY!
GOOD ...
THROB
WHAT?!
MY VEINS ... THEY'RE CHANGING COLOR AGAIN ...
THE INTERVALS ARE GETTING SHORTER ...
THE VIRUS IS TRYING TO GAIN THE UPPER HAND.
I DON'T HAVE MUCH TIME.
HELLO.
HE'LL BE ACCOMPANYING ME FOR TODAY.
HI.
GOOD DAY, DR. O'BRIEN.
WE HAVE BEEN WAITING.
HERE, YOUR KEYCARD.
?
WITH IT, YOU HAVE ACCESS TO THE LAB.
BUT THE CARD ONLY WORKS AT THE MAIN ENTRANCE.
TSAK
GOT IT, THANKS.

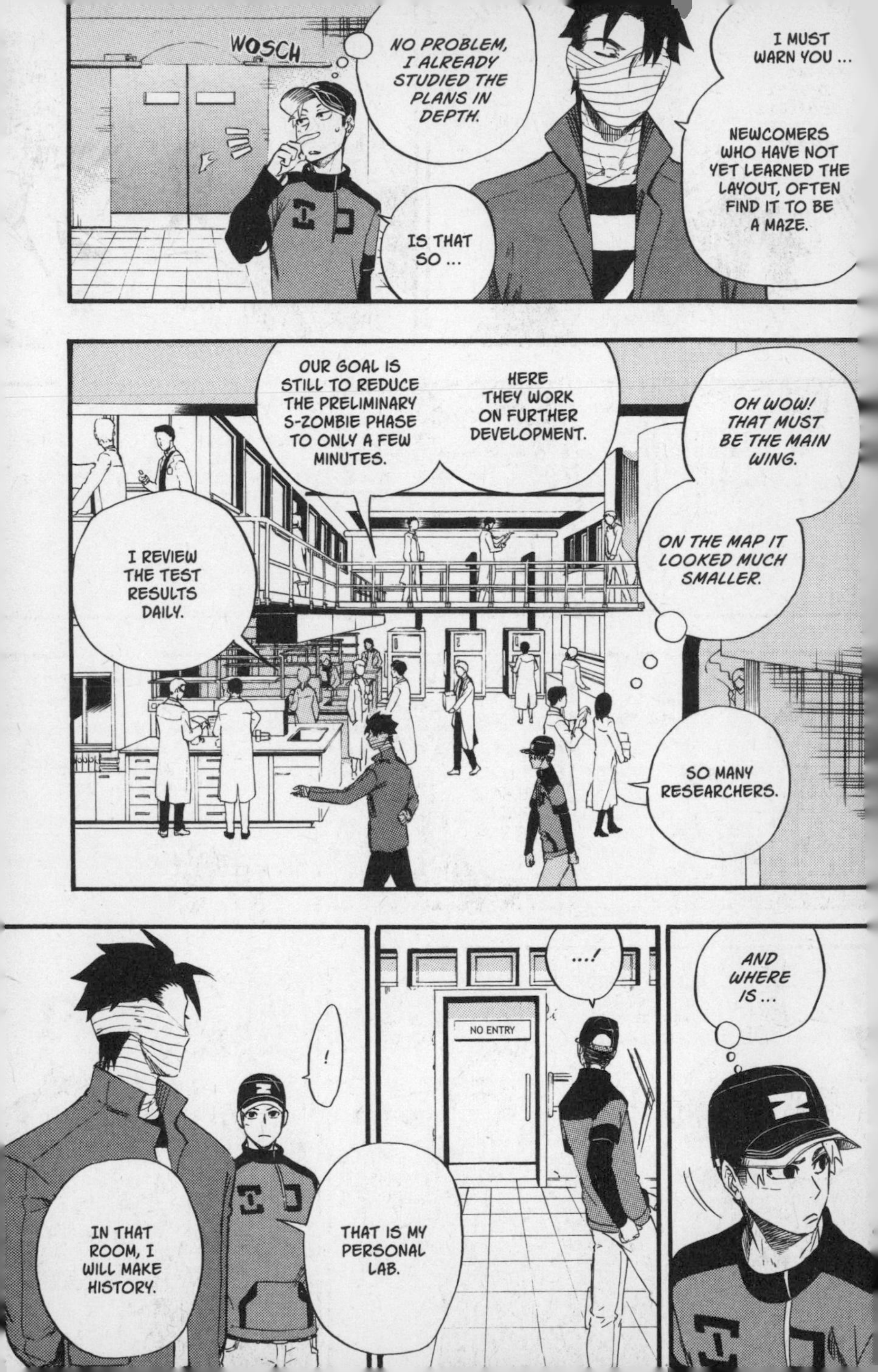
I MUST WARN YOU ...
NEWCOMERS WHO HAVE NOT YET LEARNED THE LAYOUT, OFTEN FIND IT TO BE A MAZE.
WOSCH
NO PROBLEM, I ALREADY STUDIED THE PLANS IN DEPTH.
IS THAT SO ...
OH WOW! THAT MUST BE THE MAIN WING.
ON THE MAP IT LOOKED MUCH SMALLER.
SO MANY RESEARCHERS.
HERE THEY WORK ON FURTHER DEVELOPMENT.
OUR GOAL IS STILL TO REDUCE THE PRELIMINARY S-ZOMBIE PHASE TO ONLY A FEW MINUTES.
I REVIEW THE TEST RESULTS DAILY.
AND WHERE IS ...
...!
NO ENTRY
!
THAT IS MY PERSONAL LAB.
IN THAT ROOM, I WILL MAKE HISTORY.

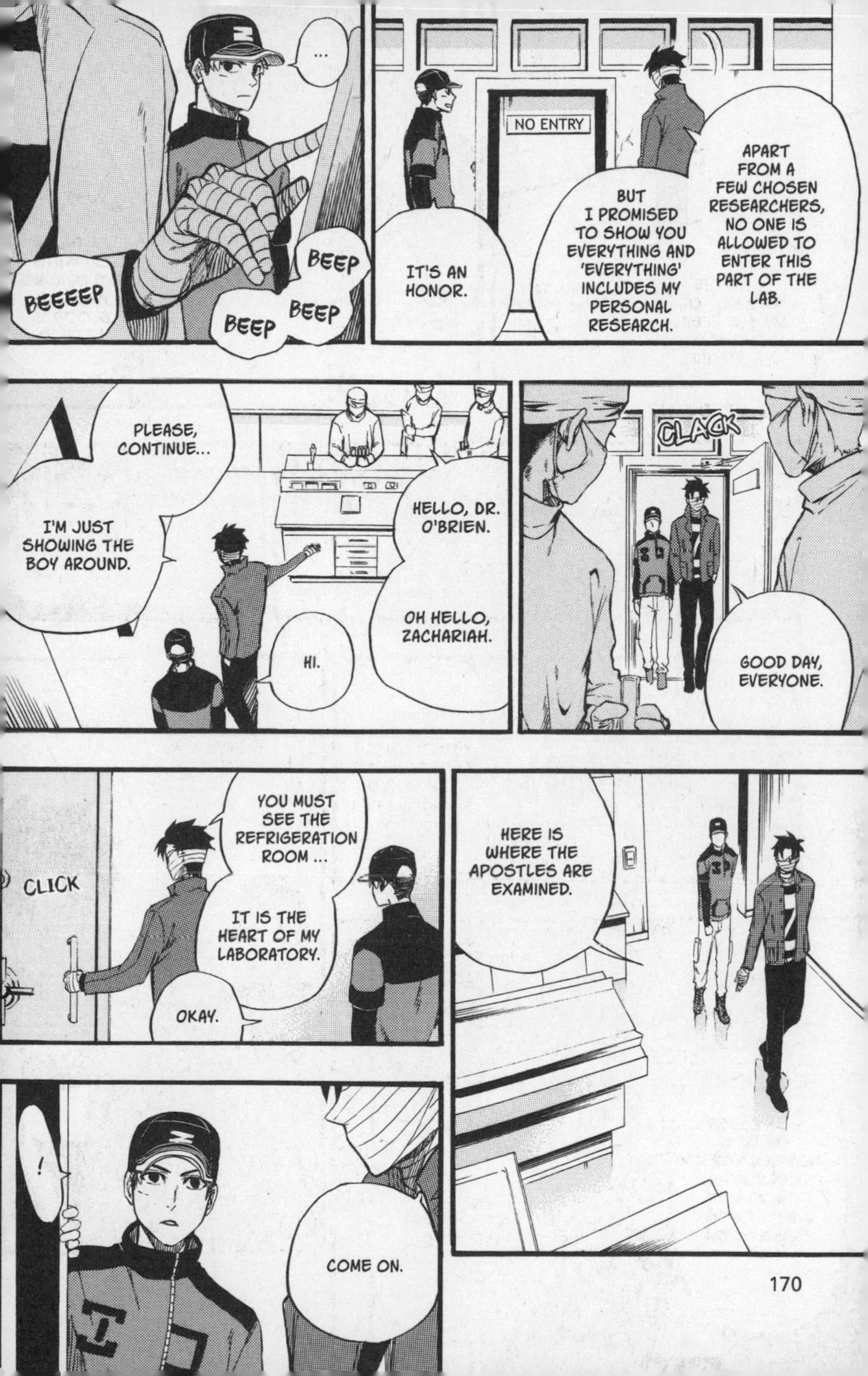
NO ENTRY
APART FROM A FEW CHOSEN RESEARCHERS, NO ONE IS ALLOWED TO ENTER THIS PART OF THE LAB.
BUT I PROMISED TO SHOW YOU EVERYTHING AND 'EVERYTHING' INCLUDES MY PERSONAL RESEARCH.
IT'S AN HONOR.
...
BEEP
BEEP
BEEP
BEEEEP
CLACK
GOOD DAY, EVERYONE.
HELLO, DR. O'BRIEN.
OH HELLO, ZACHARIAH.
HI.
PLEASE, CONTINUE...
I'M JUST SHOWING THE BOY AROUND.
HERE IS WHERE THE APOSTLES ARE EXAMINED.
YOU MUST SEE THE REFRIGERATION ROOM ...
IT IS THE HEART OF MY LABORATORY.
OKAY.
CLICK
COME ON.
!

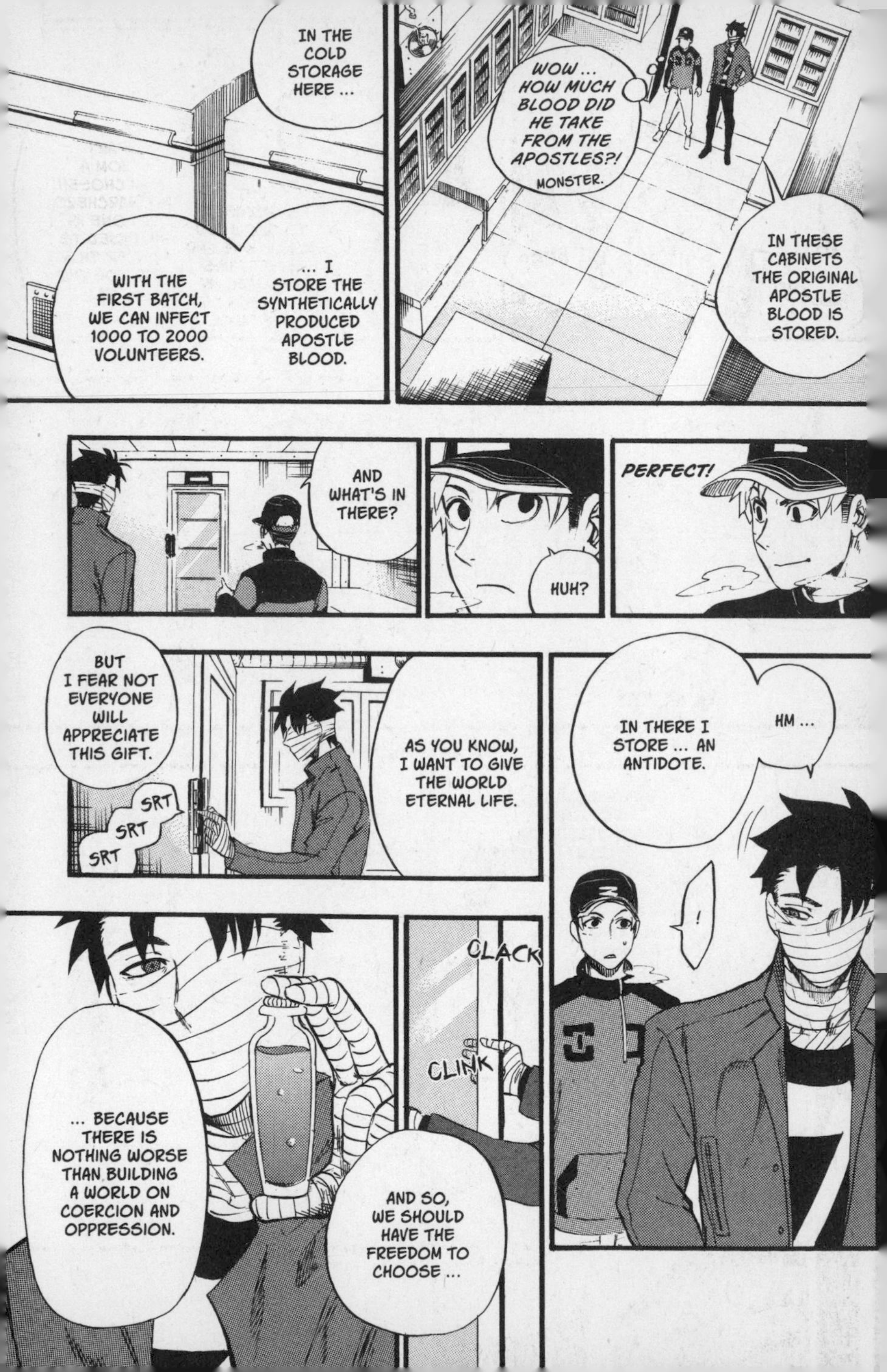
IN THESE CABINETS THE ORIGINAL APOSTLE BLOOD IS STORED.
WOW ... HOW MUCH BLOOD DID HE TAKE FROM THE APOSTLES?!
MONSTER.
IN THE COLD STORAGE HERE ...
... I STORE THE SYNTHETICALLY PRODUCED APOSTLE BLOOD.
WITH THE FIRST BATCH, WE CAN INFECT 1000 TO 2000 VOLUNTEERS.
PERFECT!
HUH?
AND WHAT'S IN THERE?
IN THERE I STORE ... AN ANTIDOTE.
HM ...
!
AS YOU KNOW, I WANT TO GIVE THE WORLD ETERNAL LIFE.
BUT I FEAR NOT EVERYONE WILL APPRECIATE THIS GIFT.
SRT
SRT
SRT
CLACK
CLINK
AND SO, WE SHOULD HAVE THE FREEDOM TO CHOOSE ...
... BECAUSE THERE IS NOTHING WORSE THAN BUILDING A WORLD ON COERCION AND OPPRESSION.

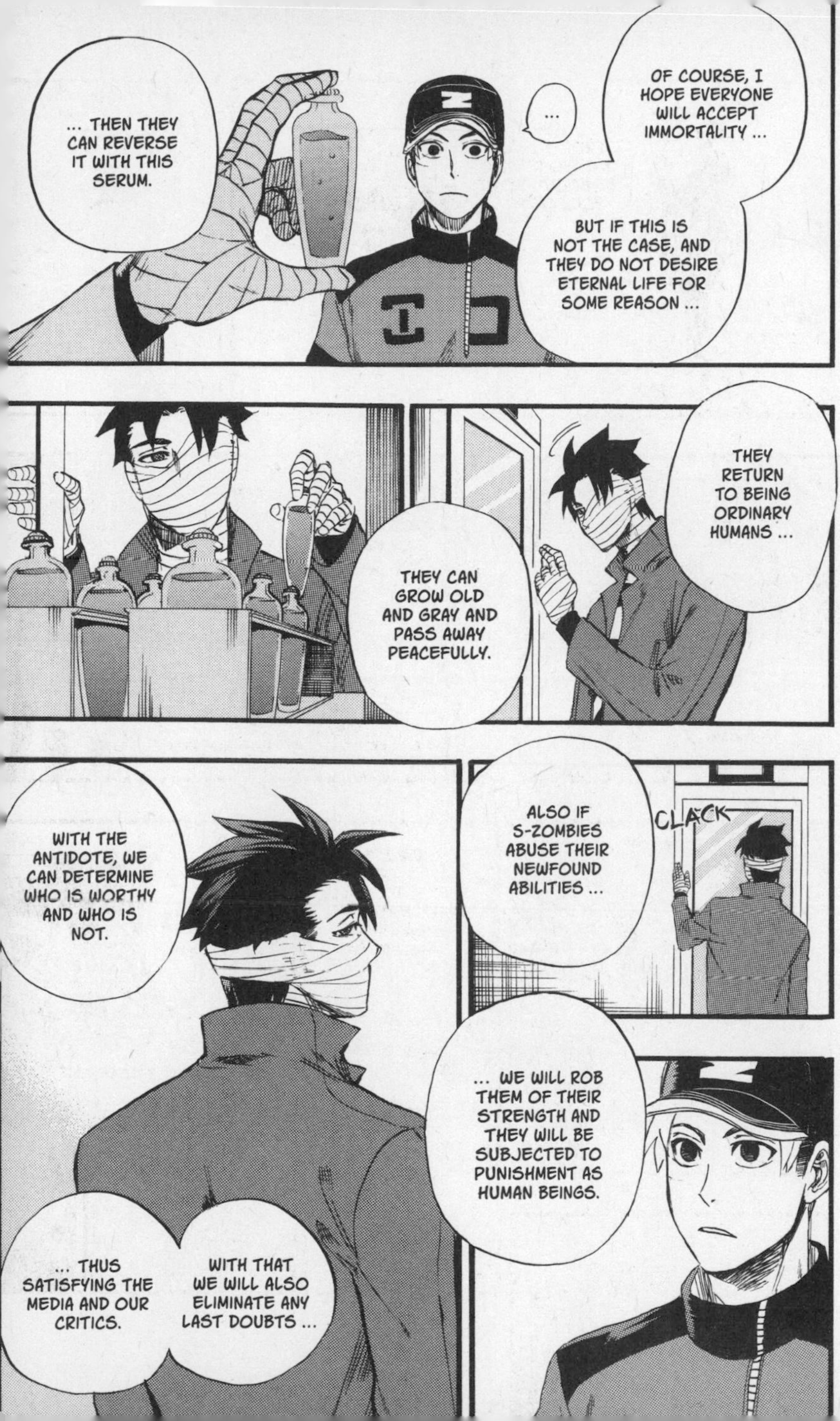

OF COURSE, I HOPE EVERYONE WILL ACCEPT IMMORTALITY ...
...
BUT IF THIS IS NOT THE CASE, AND THEY DO NOT DESIRE ETERNAL LIFE FOR SOME REASON ...
... THEN THEY CAN REVERSE IT WITH THIS SERUM.
THEY RETURN TO BEING ORDINARY HUMANS ...
THEY CAN GROW OLD AND GRAY AND PASS AWAY PEACEFULLY.
ALSO IF S-ZOMBIES ABUSE THEIR NEWFOUND ABILITIES ...
CLACK
... WE WILL ROB THEM OF THEIR STRENGTH AND THEY WILL BE SUBJECTED TO PUNISHMENT AS HUMAN BEINGS.
WITH THE ANTIDOTE, WE CAN DETERMINE WHO IS WORTHY AND WHO IS NOT.
WITH THAT WE WILL ALSO ELIMINATE ANY LAST DOUBTS ...
... THUS SATISFYING THE MEDIA AND OUR CRITICS.

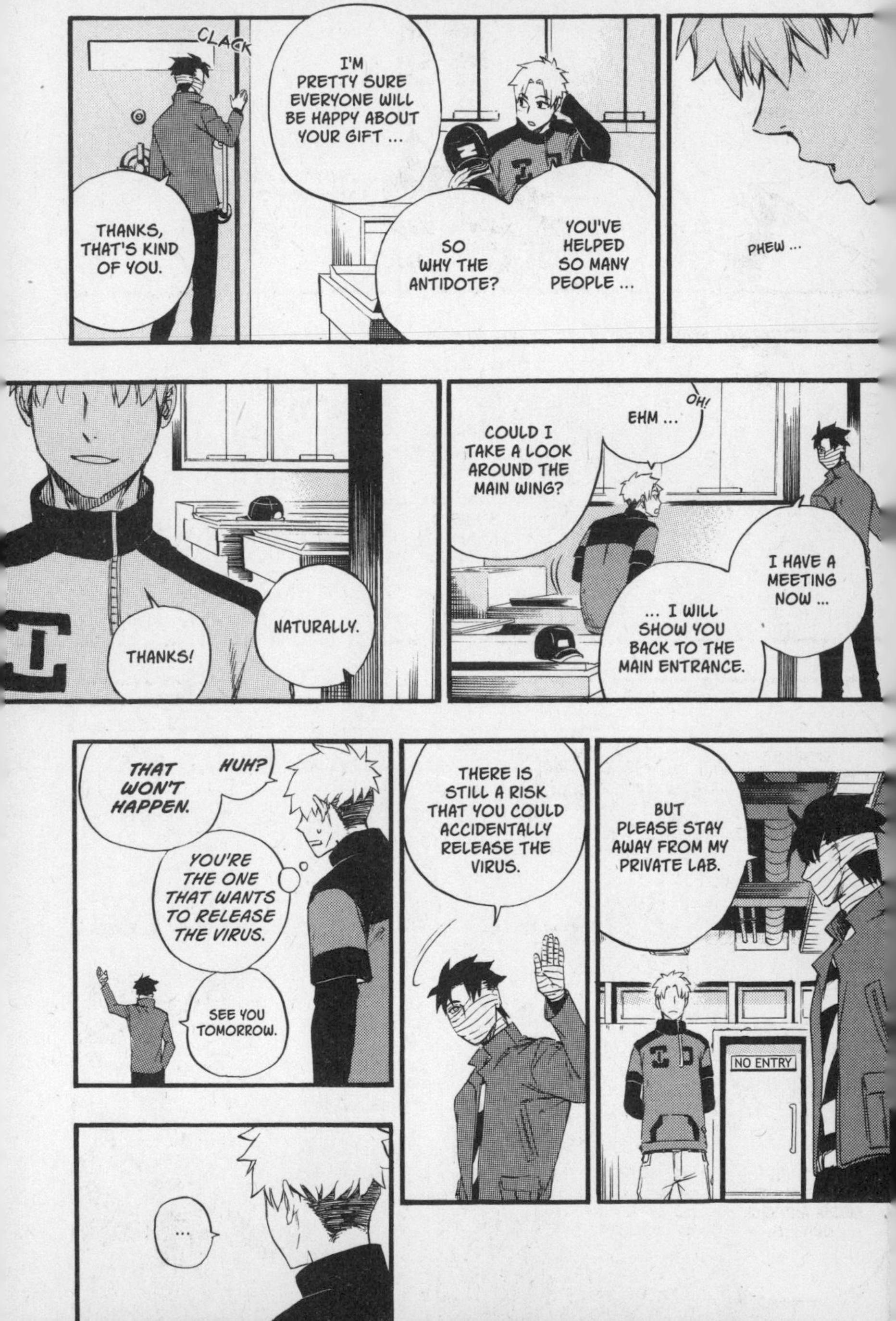
PHEW ...
I'M PRETTY SURE EVERYONE WILL BE HAPPY ABOUT YOUR GIFT ...
YOU'VE HELPED SO MANY PEOPLE ...
SO WHY THE ANTIDOTE?
CLACK
THANKS, THAT'S KIND OF YOU.
OH!
EHM ...
COULD I TAKE A LOOK AROUND THE MAIN WING?
I HAVE A MEETING NOW ...
... I WILL SHOW YOU BACK TO THE MAIN ENTRANCE.
NATURALLY.
THANKS!
BUT PLEASE STAY AWAY FROM MY PRIVATE LAB.
NO ENTRY
THERE IS STILL A RISK THAT YOU COULD ACCIDENTALLY RELEASE THE VIRUS.
HUH?
THAT WON'T HAPPEN.
YOU'RE THE ONE THAT WANTS TO RELEASE THE VIRUS.
SEE YOU TOMORROW.
...

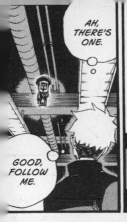

LET'S DO THIS!
WHERE ARE THE CAMERAS?
TIKY AND THE OTHERS MUST HAVE EYES ON ME.
AH, THERE'S ONE.
GOOD, FOLLOW ME.
...
...!
GULP
THE SHOW MUST GO ON.
ZOOM ...
HSS ...
HE HE HE.
I MEMORIZED RITCH'S PASSCODE EARLIER.
HI.
?!

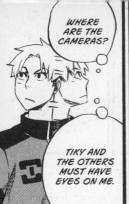

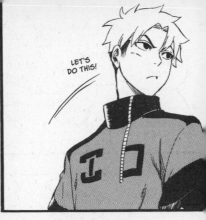

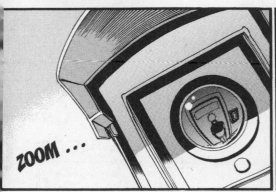

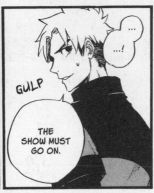

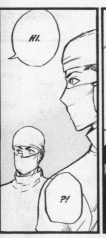

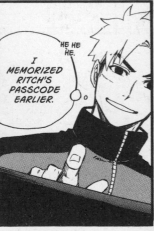

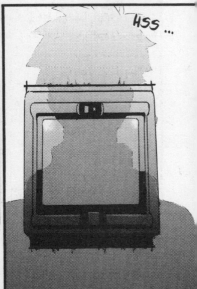

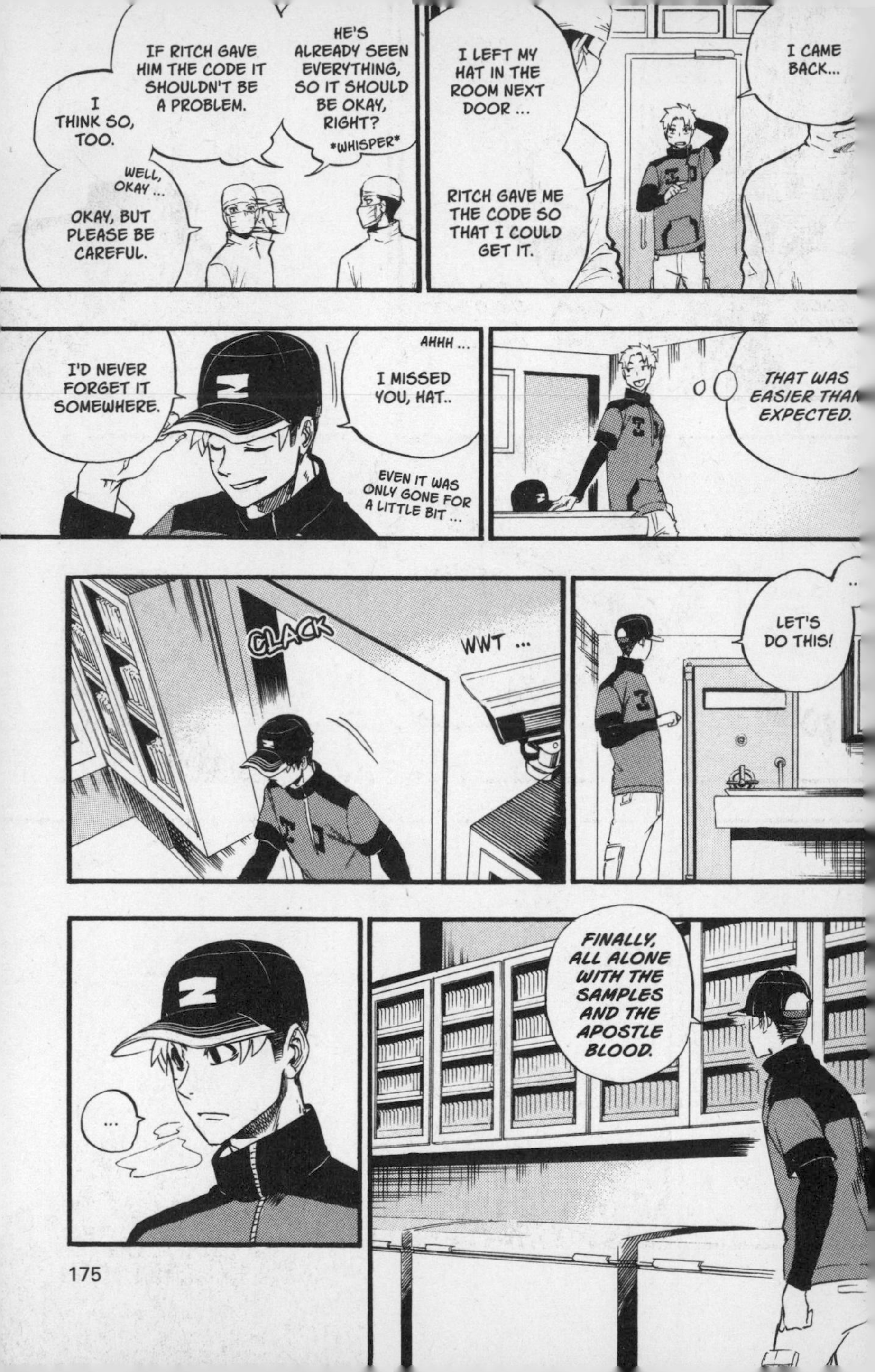

I CAME BACK...
I LEFT MY HAT IN THE ROOM NEXT DOOR ...
RITCH GAVE ME THE CODE SO THAT I COULD GET IT.
HE'S ALREADY SEEN EVERYTHING, SO IT SHOULD BE OKAY, RIGHT?
*WHISPER*
IF RITCH GAVE HIM THE CODE IT SHOULDN'T BE A PROBLEM.
I THINK SO, TOO.
WELL, OKAY ...
OKAY, BUT PLEASE BE CAREFUL.
THAT WAS EASIER THAN EXPECTED.
AHHH ...
I MISSED YOU, HAT..
EVEN IT WAS ONLY GONE FOR A LITTLE BIT ...
I'D NEVER FORGET IT SOMEWHERE.
..
LET'S DO THIS!
WWT ...
CLACK
FINALLY, ALL ALONE WITH THE SAMPLES AND THE APOSTLE BLOOD.
...

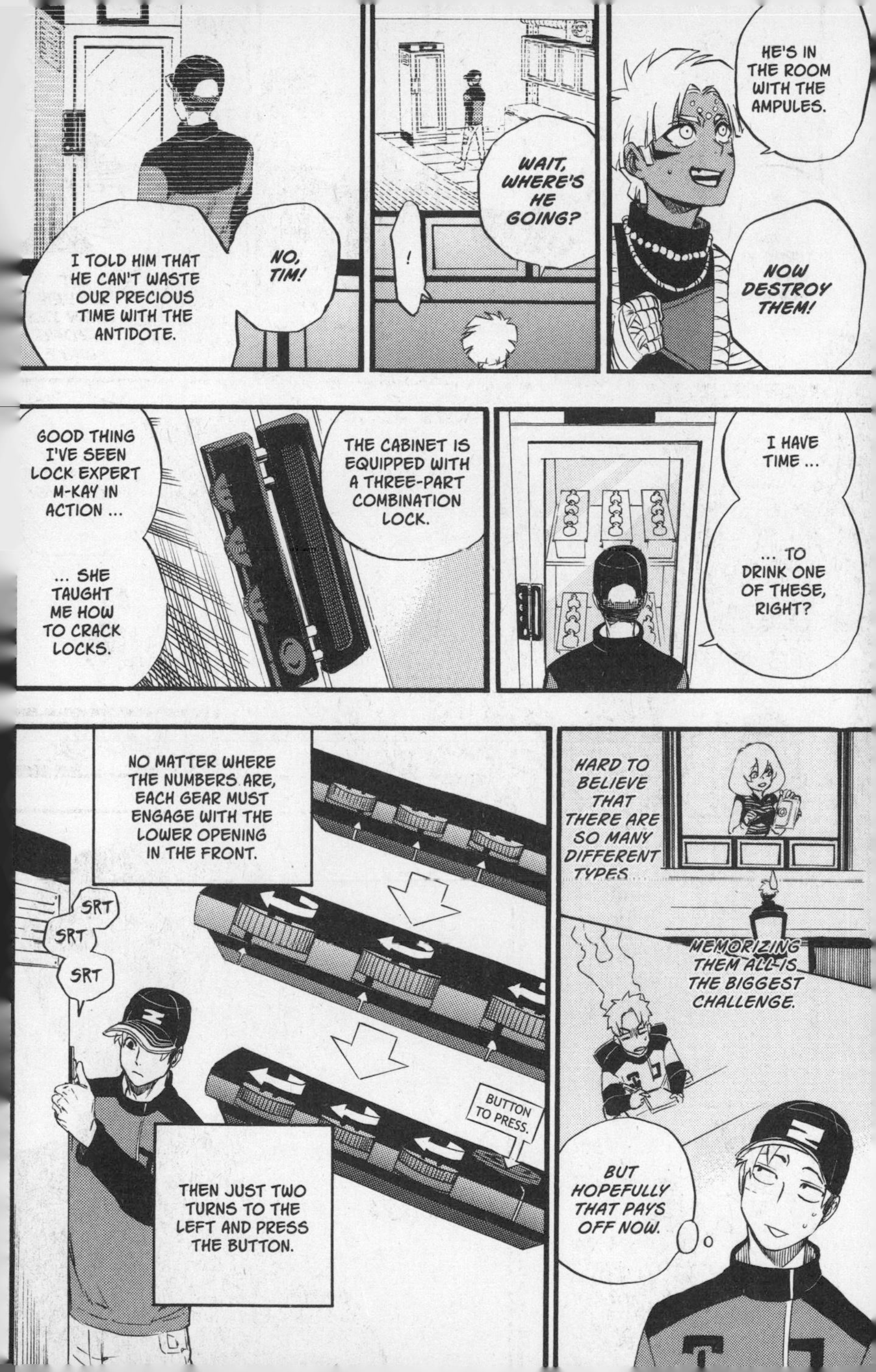
HE'S IN THE ROOM WITH THE AMPULES.
NOW DESTROY THEM!
WAIT, WHERE'S HE GOING?
!
NO, TIM!
I TOLD HIM THAT HE CAN'T WASTE OUR PRECIOUS TIME WITH THE ANTIDOTE.
I HAVE TIME ...
... TO DRINK ONE OF THESE, RIGHT?
THE CABINET IS EQUIPPED WITH A THREE-PART COMBINATION LOCK.
GOOD THING I'VE SEEN LOCK EXPERT M-KAY IN ACTION ...
... SHE TAUGHT ME HOW TO CRACK LOCKS.
HARD TO BELIEVE THAT THERE ARE SO MANY DIFFERENT TYPES.
MEMORIZING THEM ALL IS THE BIGGEST CHALLENGE.
BUT HOPEFULLY THAT PAYS OFF NOW.
NO MATTER WHERE THE NUMBERS ARE, EACH GEAR MUST ENGAGE WITH THE LOWER OPENING IN THE FRONT.
SRT
SRT
SRT
BUTTON TO PRESS.
THEN JUST TWO TURNS TO THE LEFT AND PRESS THE BUTTON.

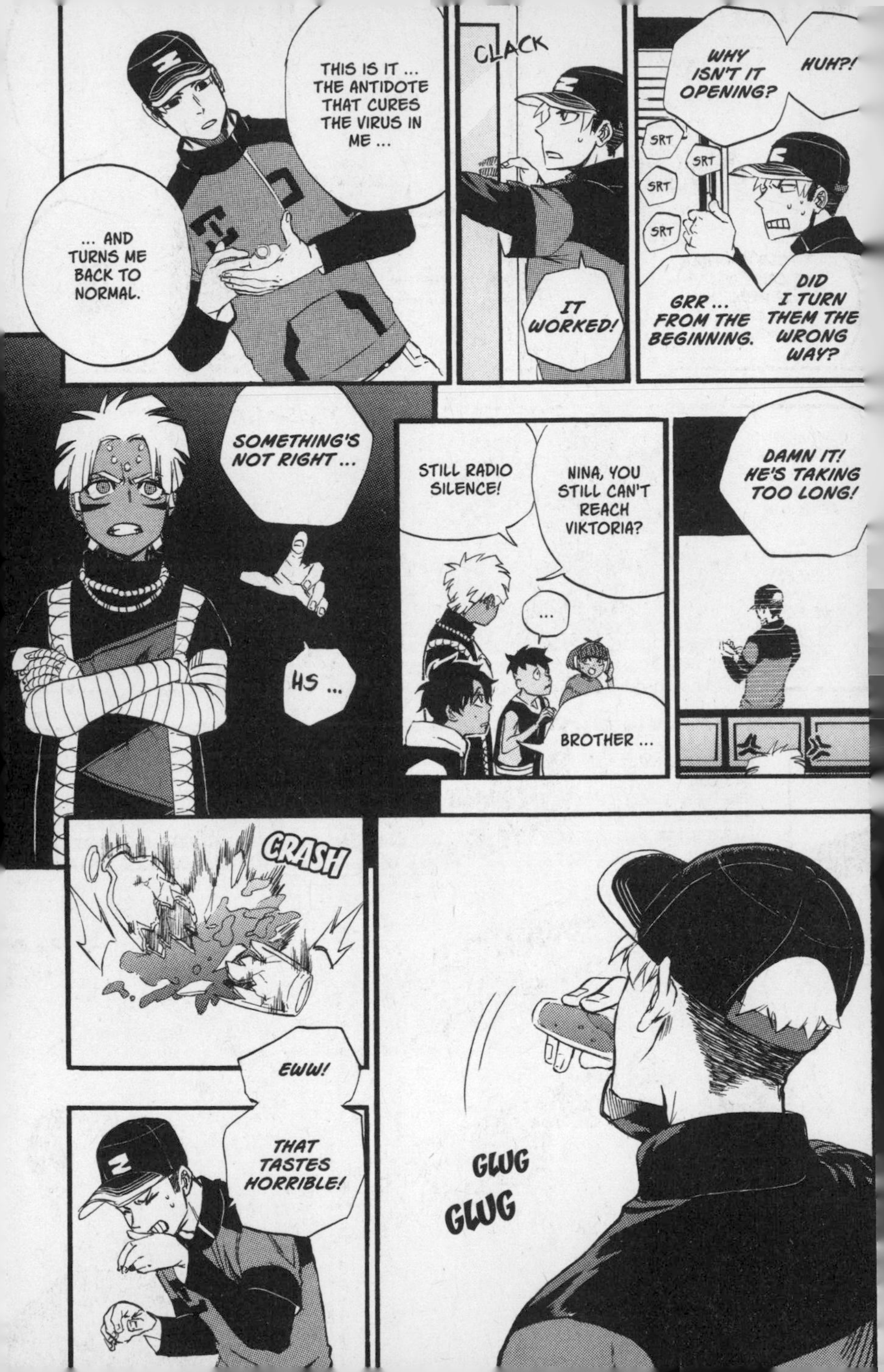
HUH?!
WHY ISN'T IT OPENING?
SRT
SRT
SRT
SRT
DID I TURN THEM THE WRONG WAY?
GRR ... FROM THE BEGINNING.
CLACK
IT WORKED!
THIS IS IT ... THE ANTIDOTE THAT CURES THE VIRUS IN ME ...
... AND TURNS ME BACK TO NORMAL.
DAMN IT! HE'S TAKING TOO LONG!
NINA, YOU STILL CAN'T REACH VIKTORIA?
STILL RADIO SILENCE!
...
BROTHER ...
SOMETHING'S NOT RIGHT ...
HS ...
GLUG
GLUG
CRASH
EWW!
THAT TASTES HORRIBLE!

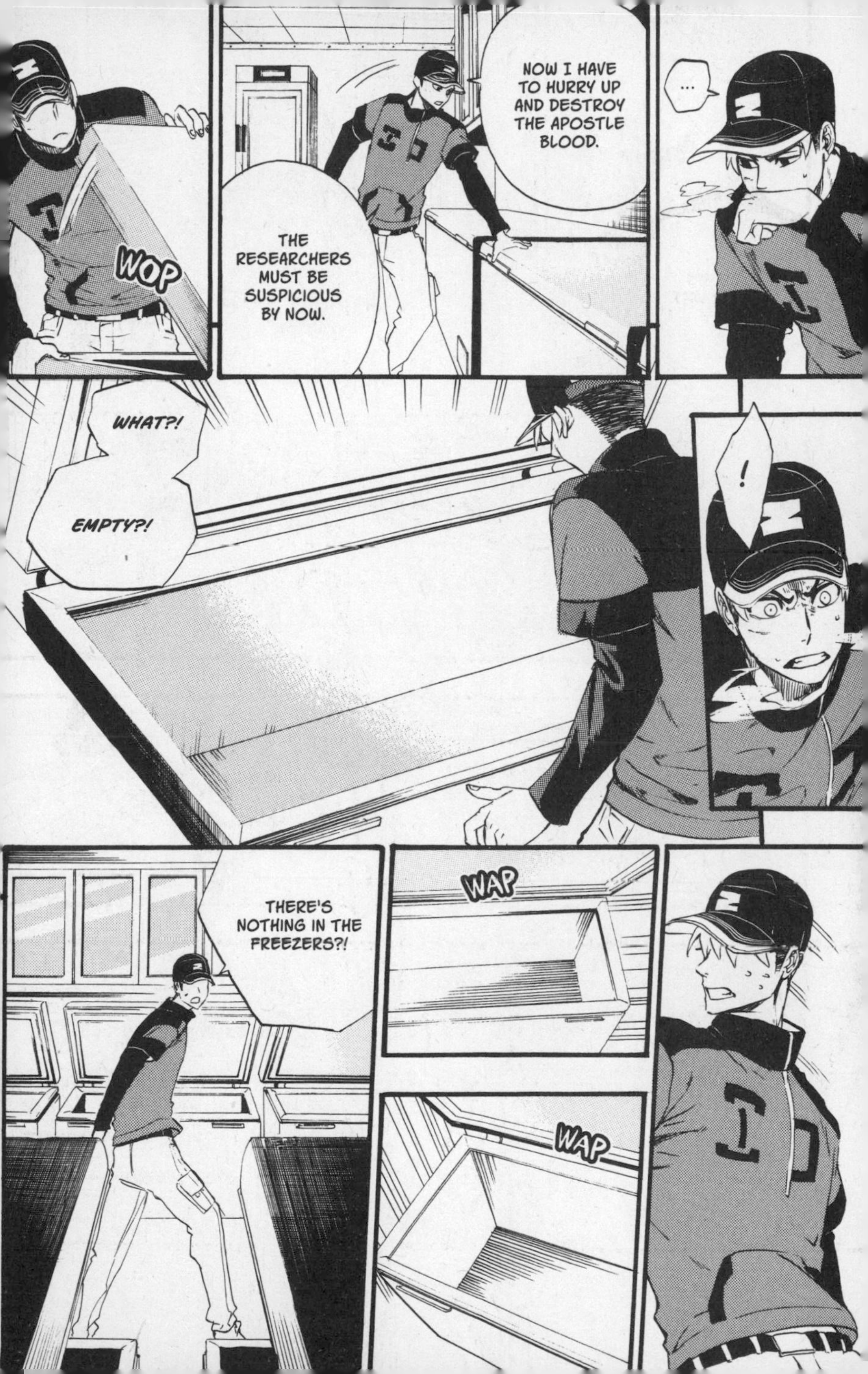
...
NOW I HAVE TO HURRY UP AND DESTROY THE APOSTLE BLOOD.
THE RESEARCHERS MUST BE SUSPICIOUS BY NOW.
WOP
!
WHAT?!
EMPTY?!
WAP
WAP
THERE'S NOTHING IN THE FREEZERS?!

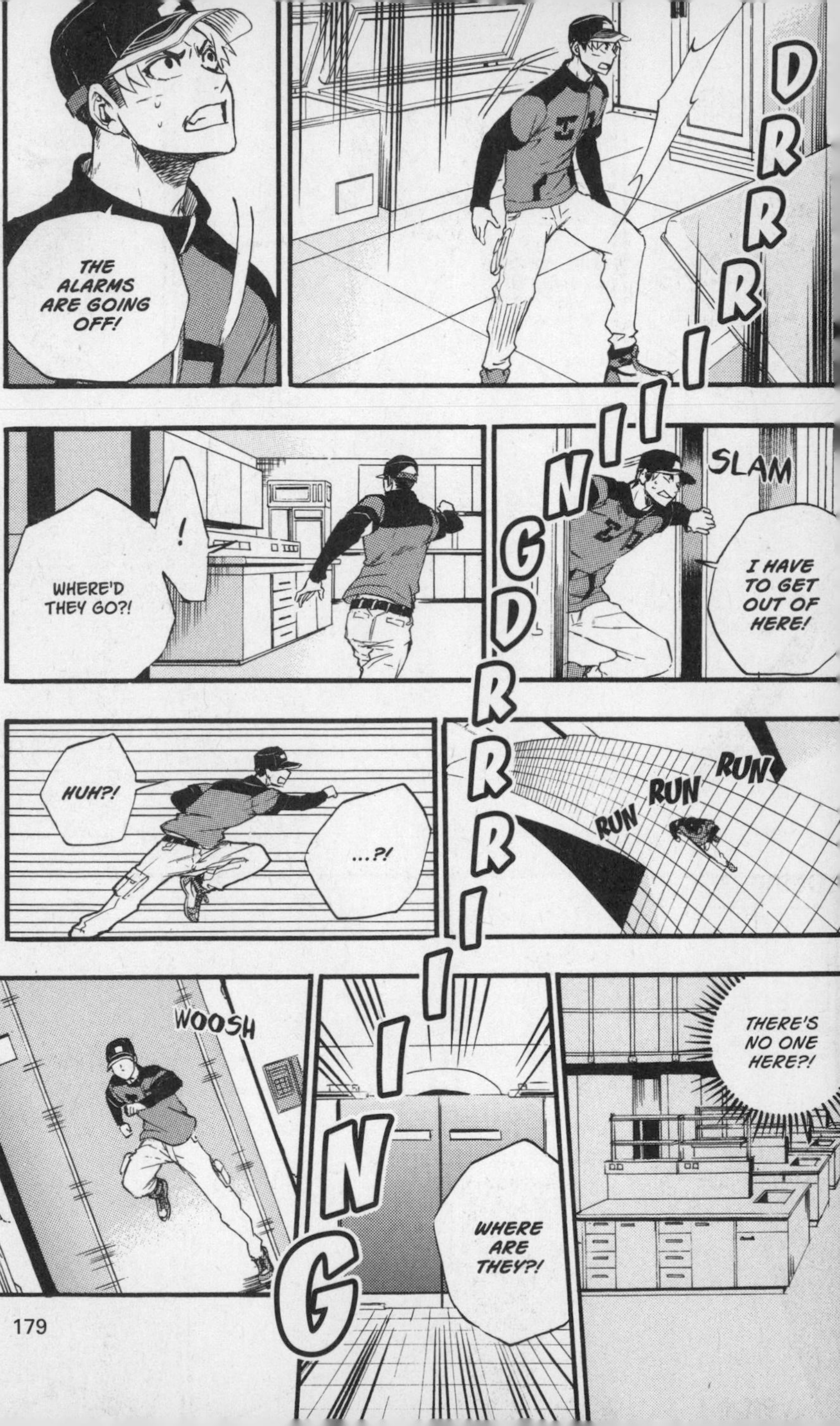
DRRRIIING
THE ALARMS ARE GOING OFF!
SLAM
I HAVE TO GET OUT OF HERE!
!
WHERE'D THEY GO?!
DRRRIIIING
RUN RUN RUN
HUH?!
...?!
THERE'S NO ONE HERE?!
WHERE ARE THEY?!
WOOSH

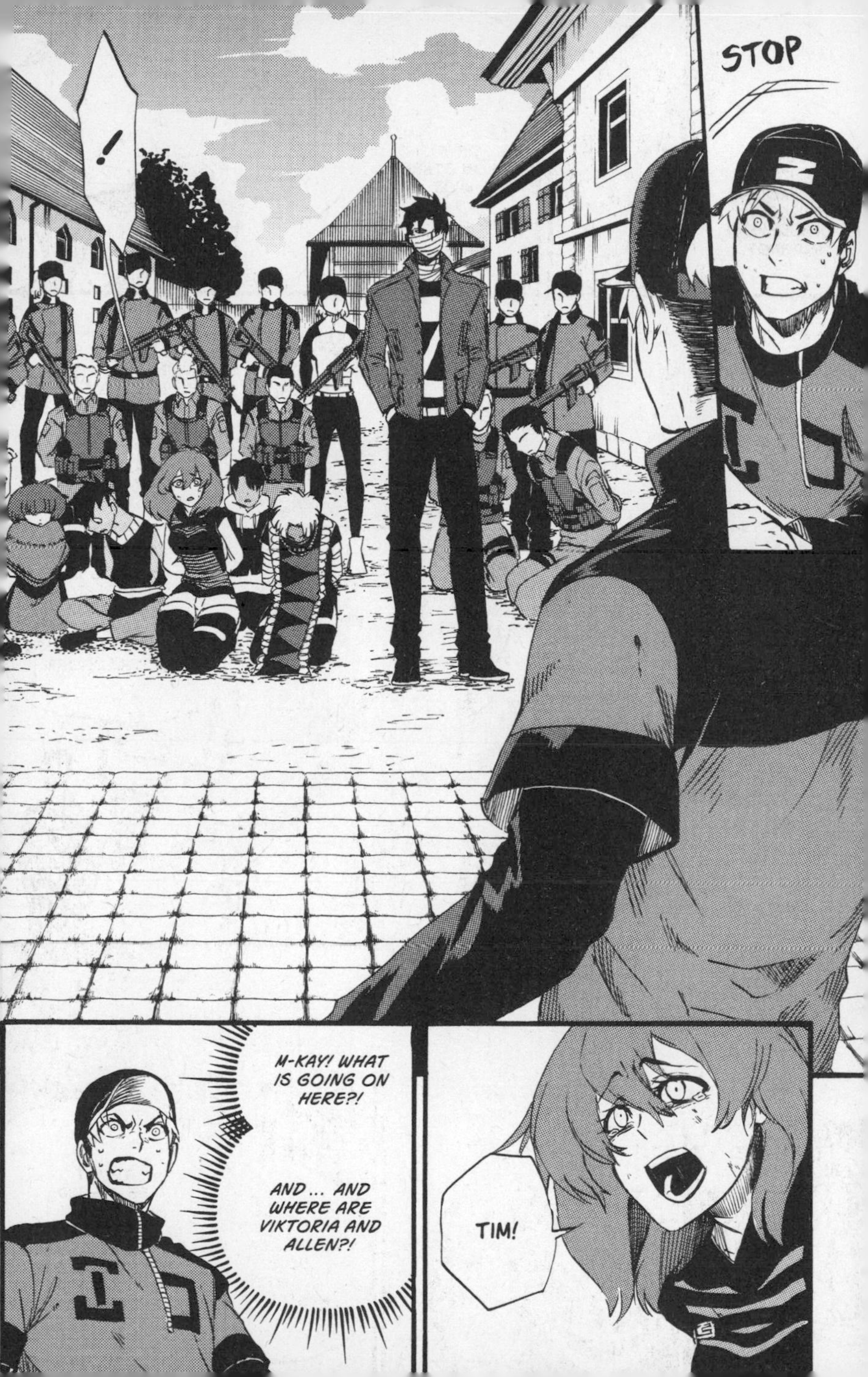
STOP
!
TIM!
M-KAY! WHAT IS GOING ON HERE?!
AND ... AND WHERE ARE VIKTORIA AND ALLEN?!

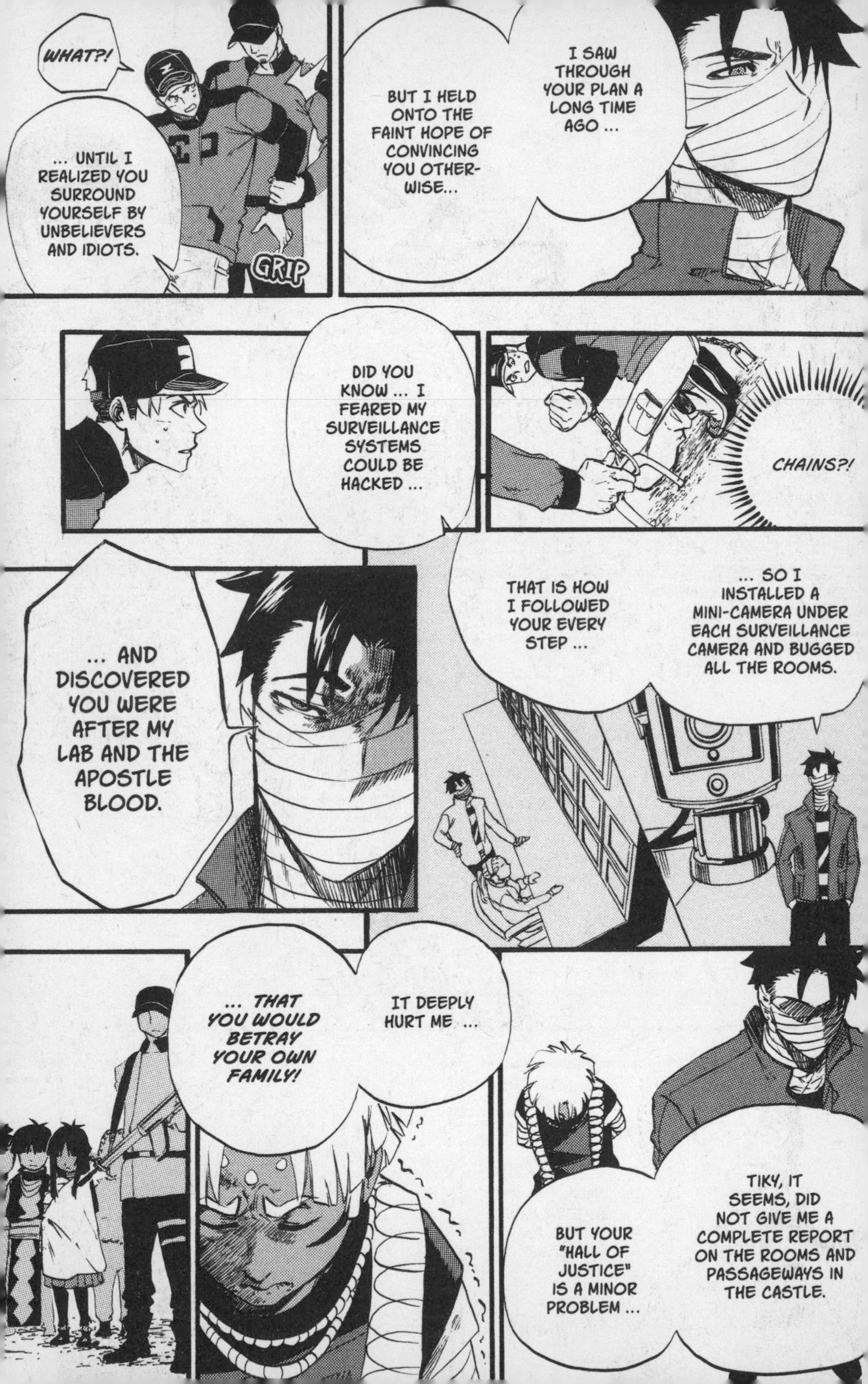
I SAW THROUGH YOUR PLAN A LONG TIME AGO ...
BUT I HELD ONTO THE FAINT HOPE OF CONVINCING YOU OTHER-WISE...
WHAT?!
... UNTIL I REALIZED YOU SURROUND YOURSELF BY UNBELIEVERS AND IDIOTS.
GRIP
CHAINS?!
DID YOU KNOW ... I FEARED MY SURVEILLANCE SYSTEMS COULD BE HACKED ...
... SO I INSTALLED A MINI-CAMERA UNDER EACH SURVEILLANCE CAMERA AND BUGGED ALL THE ROOMS.
THAT IS HOW I FOLLOWED YOUR EVERY STEP ...
... AND DISCOVERED YOU WERE AFTER MY LAB AND THE APOSTLE BLOOD.
TIKY, IT SEEMS, DID NOT GIVE ME A COMPLETE REPORT ON THE ROOMS AND PASSAGEWAYS IN THE CASTLE.
BUT YOUR "HALL OF JUSTICE" IS A MINOR PROBLEM ...
IT DEEPLY HURT ME ...
... THAT YOU WOULD BETRAY YOUR OWN FAMILY!

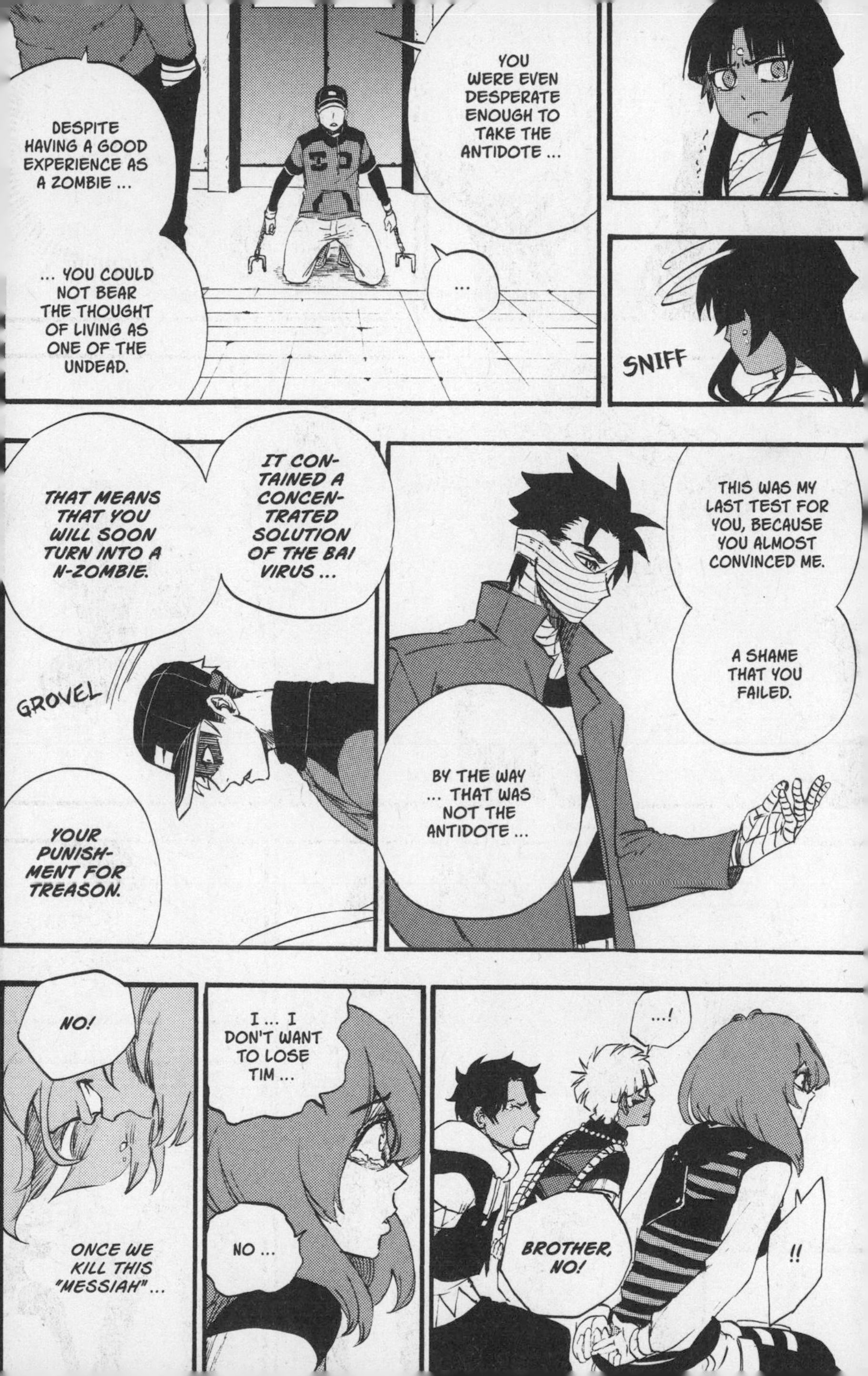
SNIFF
YOU WERE EVEN DESPERATE ENOUGH TO TAKE THE ANTIDOTE ...
...
DESPITE HAVING A GOOD EXPERIENCE AS A ZOMBIE ...
... YOU COULD NOT BEAR THE THOUGHT OF LIVING AS ONE OF THE UNDEAD.
THIS WAS MY LAST TEST FOR YOU, BECAUSE YOU ALMOST CONVINCED ME.
A SHAME THAT YOU FAILED.
BY THE WAY ... THAT WAS NOT THE ANTIDOTE ...
IT CONTAINED A CONCENTRATED SOLUTION OF THE BAI VIRUS ...
THAT MEANS THAT YOU WILL SOON TURN INTO A N-ZOMBIE.
GROVEL
YOUR PUNISHMENT FOR TREASON.
...!
!!
BROTHER, NO!
I ... I DON'T WANT TO LOSE TIM ...
NO ...
NO!
ONCE WE KILL THIS "MESSIAH" ...

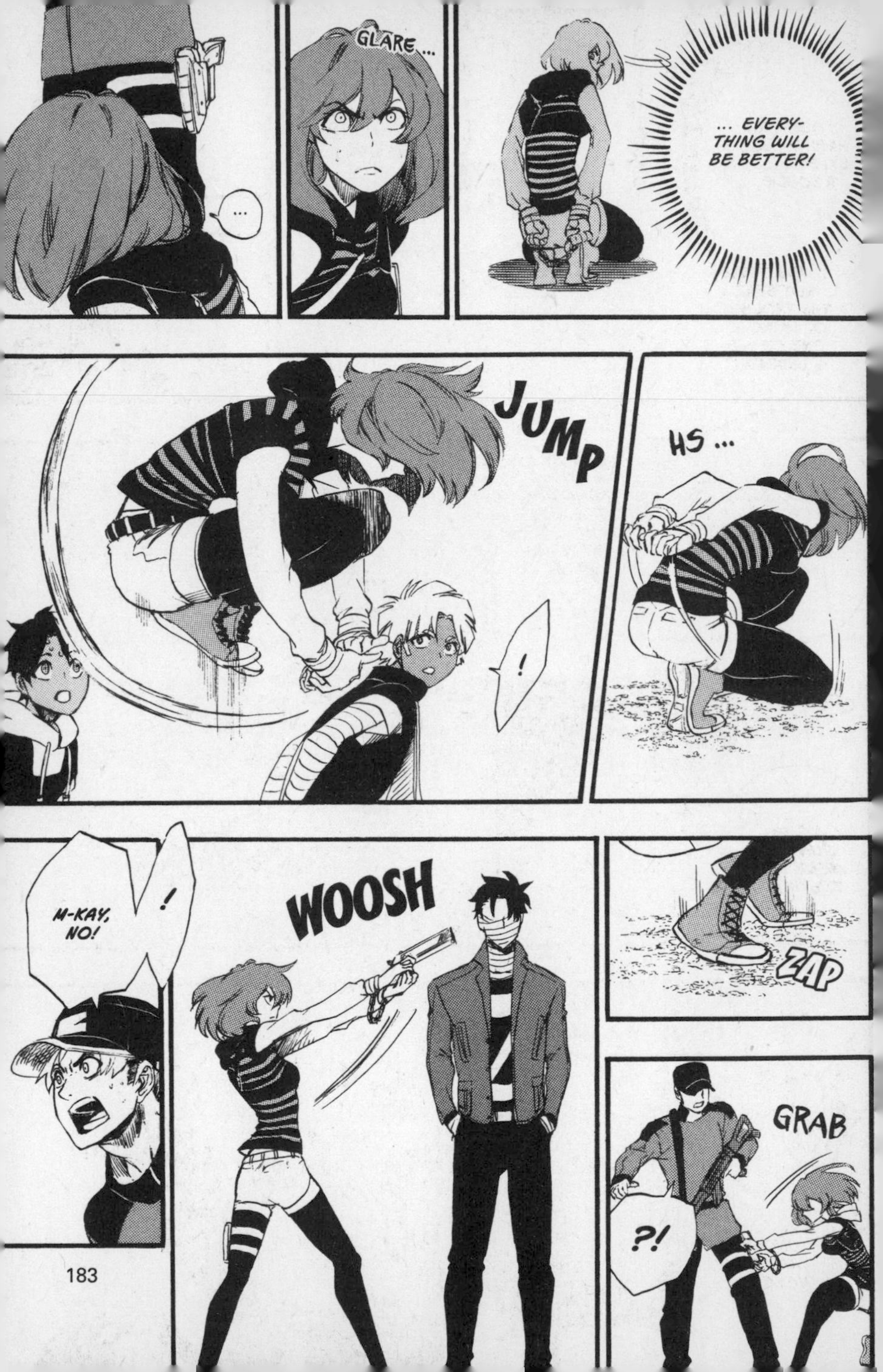
... EVERY-THING WILL BE BETTER!
GLARE ...
...
HS ...
JUMP
!
ZAP
GRAB
?!
WOOSH
!
M-KAY, NO!

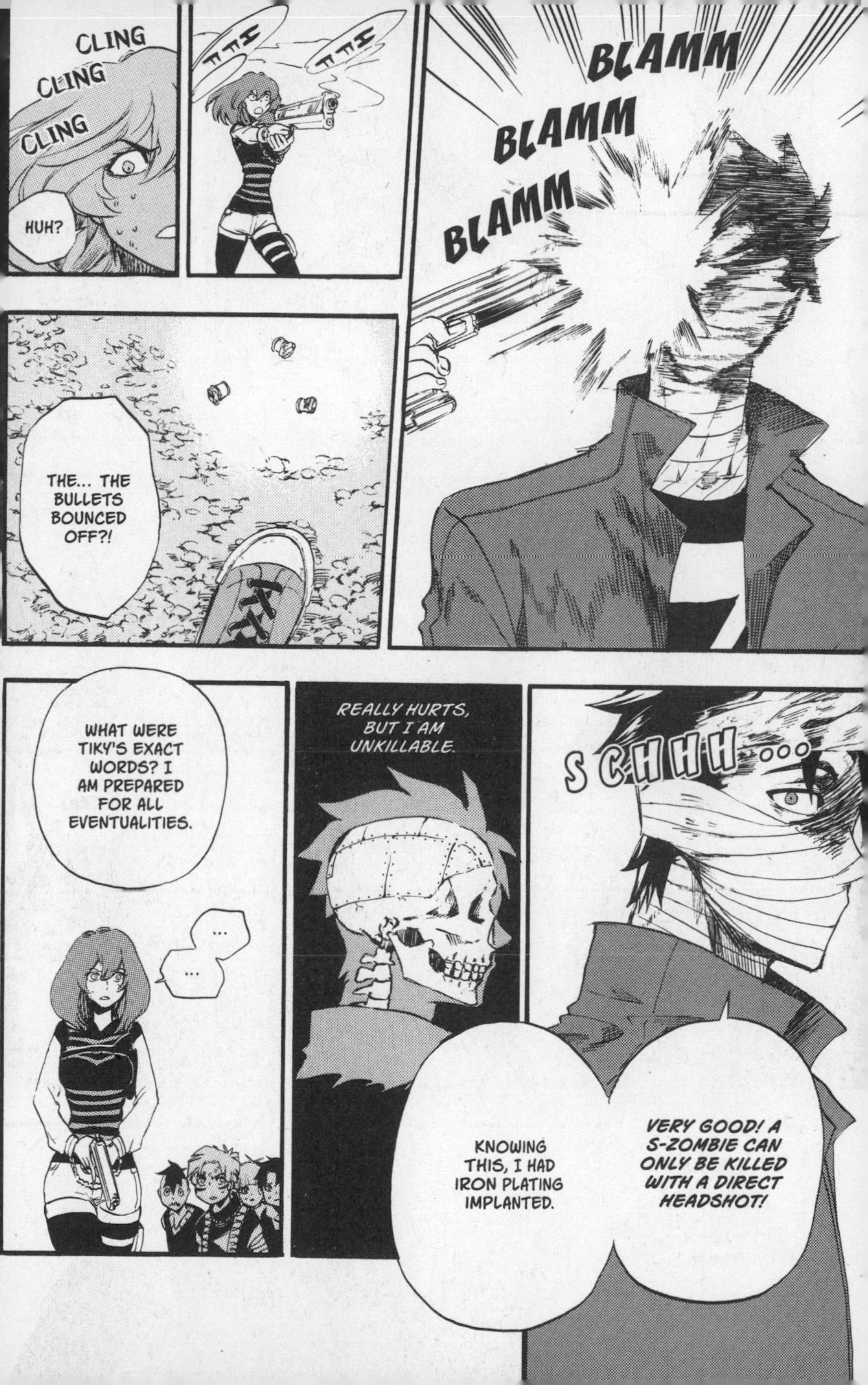
BLAMM
BLAMM
BLAMM
CLING
CLING
CLING
HUH?
THE... THE BULLETS BOUNCED OFF?!
SCHHH...
VERY GOOD! A S-ZOMBIE CAN ONLY BE KILLED WITH A DIRECT HEADSHOT!
KNOWING THIS, I HAD IRON PLATING IMPLANTED.
REALLY HURTS, BUT I AM UNKILLABLE.
WHAT WERE TIKY'S EXACT WORDS? I AM PREPARED FOR ALL EVENTUALITIES.
...
...

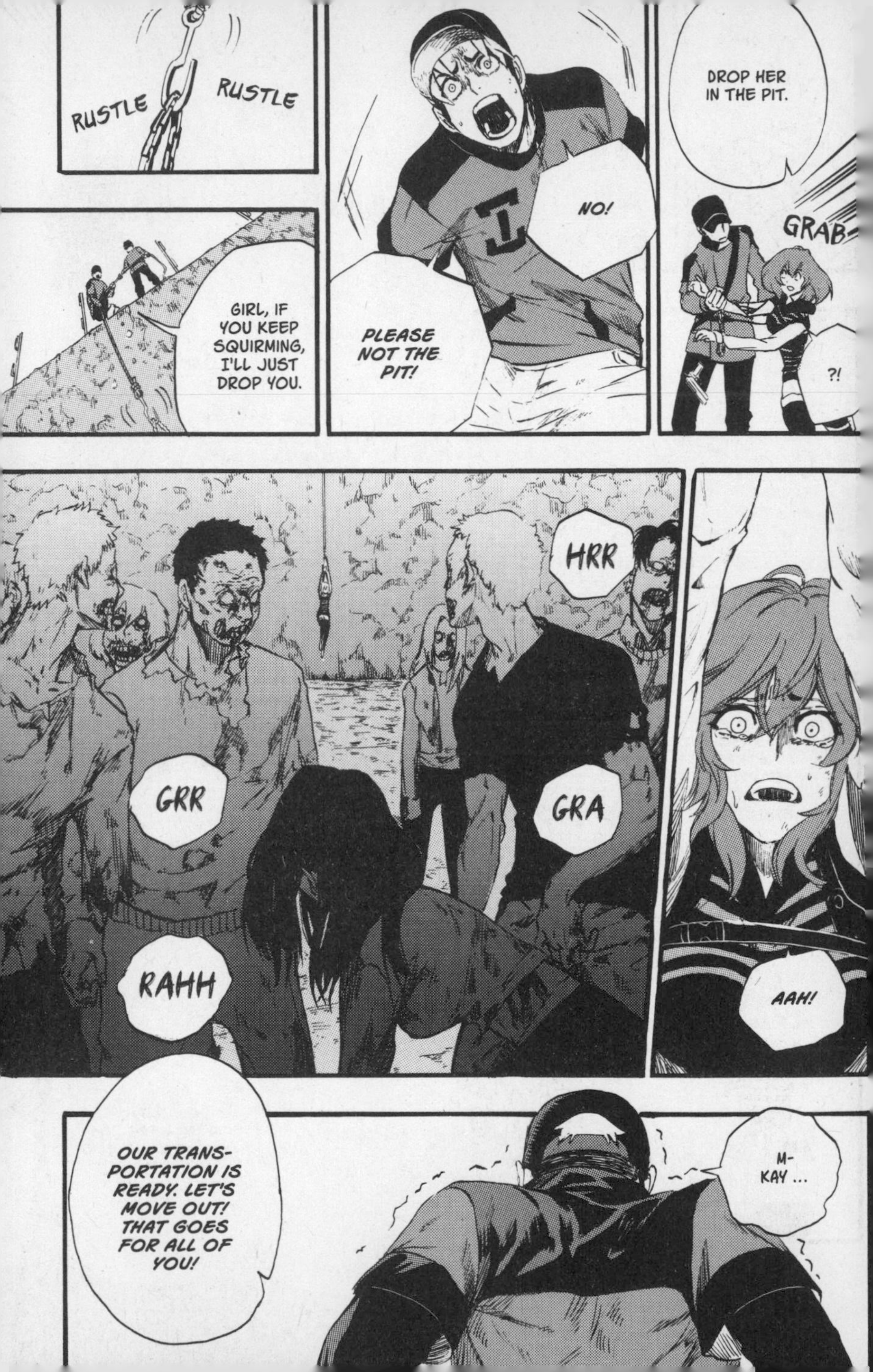

DROP HER IN THE PIT.
GRAB-
?!
NO!
PLEASE NOT THE PIT!
RUSTLE
RUSTLE
GIRL, IF YOU KEEP SQUIRMING, I'LL JUST DROP YOU.
AAH!
HRR
GRA
GRR
RAHH
M-KAY ...
OUR TRANS-PORTATION IS READY. LET'S MOVE OUT! THAT GOES FOR ALL OF YOU!

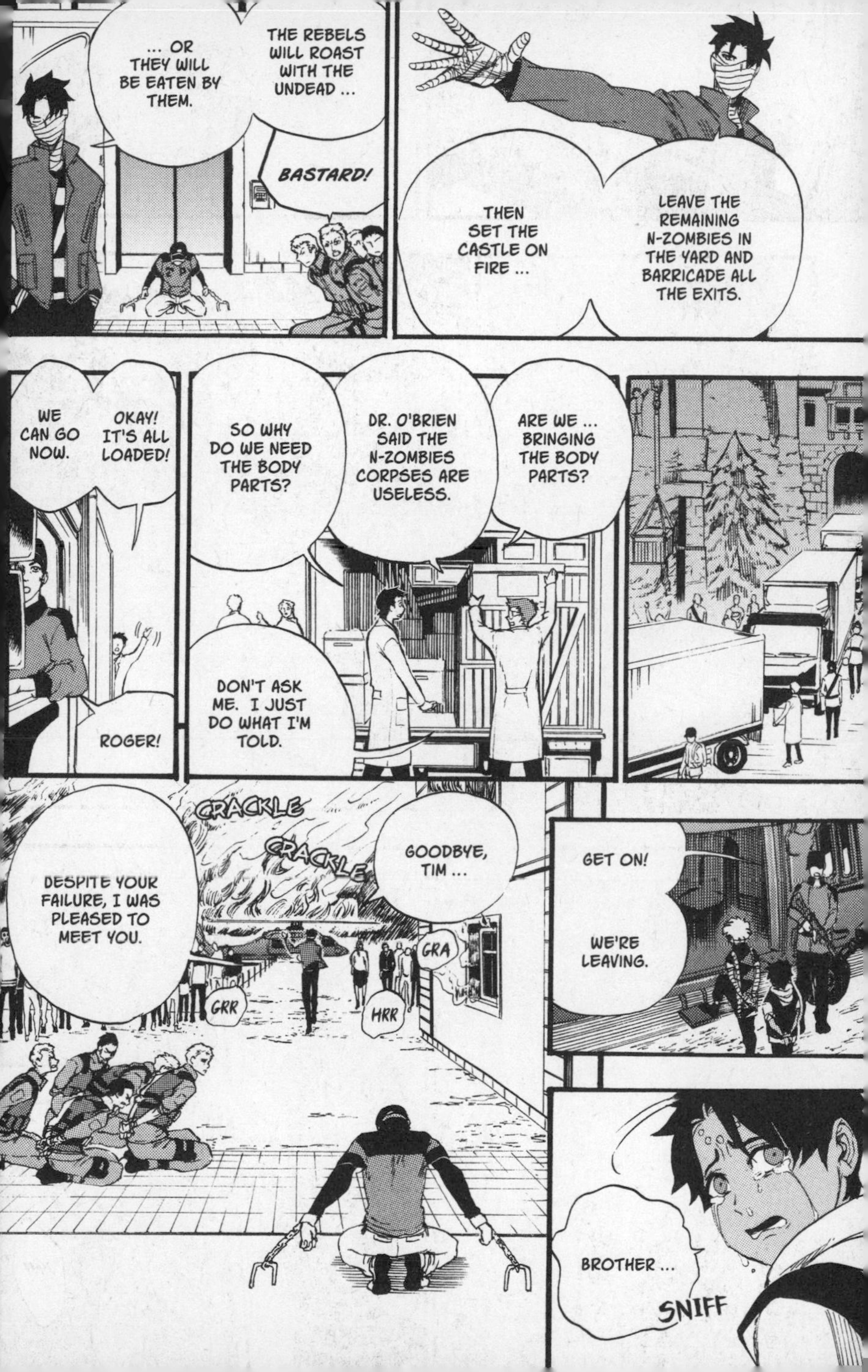
LEAVE THE REMAINING N-ZOMBIES IN THE YARD AND BARRICADE ALL THE EXITS.
THEN SET THE CASTLE ON FIRE ...
THE REBELS WILL ROAST WITH THE UNDEAD ...
... OR THEY WILL BE EATEN BY THEM.
BASTARD!
ARE WE ... BRINGING THE BODY PARTS?
DR. O'BRIEN SAID THE N-ZOMBIES CORPSES ARE USELESS.
SO WHY DO WE NEED THE BODY PARTS?
DON'T ASK ME. I JUST DO WHAT I'M TOLD.
OKAY! IT'S ALL LOADED!
WE CAN GO NOW.
ROGER!
GET ON!
WE'RE LEAVING.
BROTHER ...
SNIFF
GOODBYE, TIM ...
CRACKLE
CRACKLE
DESPITE YOUR FAILURE, I WAS PLEASED TO MEET YOU.
GRA
GRR
HRR

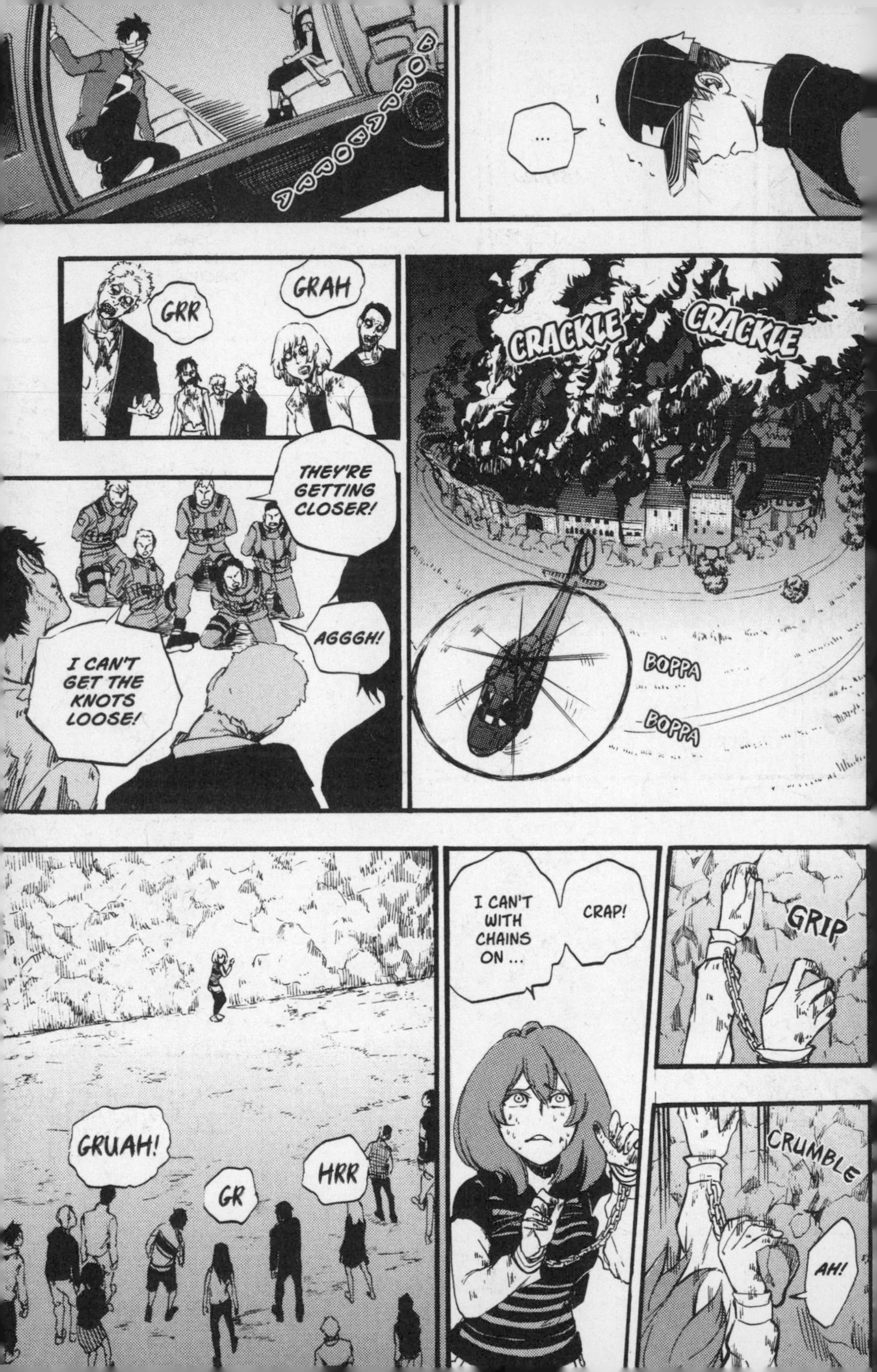
...
BOPPABOPPA
CRACKLE
CRACKLE
BOPPA
BOPPA
GRAH
GRR
THEY'RE GETTING CLOSER!
AGGGH!
I CAN'T GET THE KNOTS LOOSE!
GRIP
CRUMBLE
AH!
CRAP!
I CAN'T WITH CHAINS ON ...
HRR
GR
GRUAH!

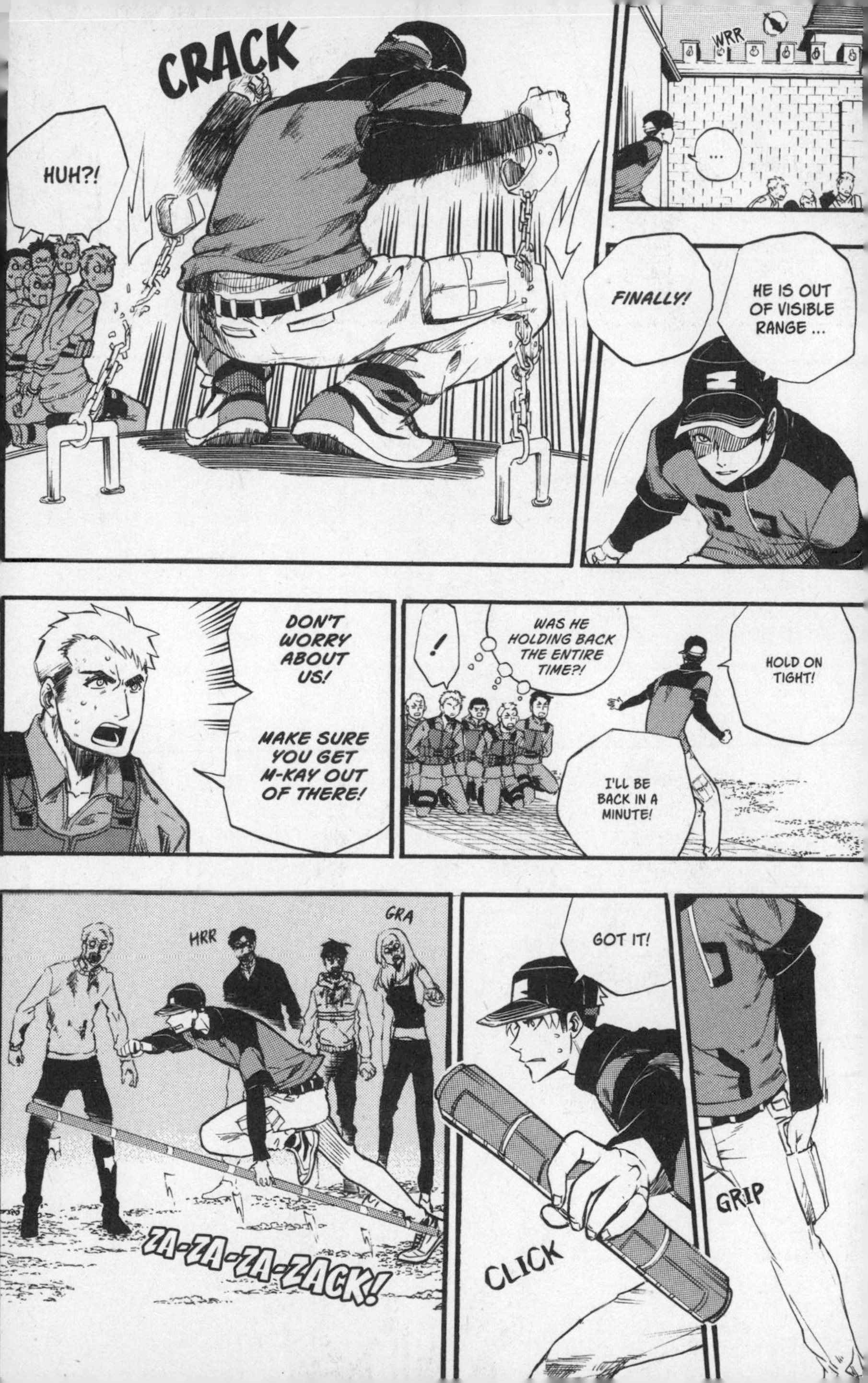
WRR
...
HE IS OUT OF VISIBLE RANGE ...
FINALLY!
CRACK
HUH?!
HOLD ON TIGHT!
WAS HE HOLDING BACK THE ENTIRE TIME?!
!
I'LL BE BACK IN A MINUTE!
DON'T WORRY ABOUT US!
MAKE SURE YOU GET M-KAY OUT OF THERE!
GOT IT!
GRIP
CLICK
GRA
HRR
ZA-ZA-ZA-ZACK!

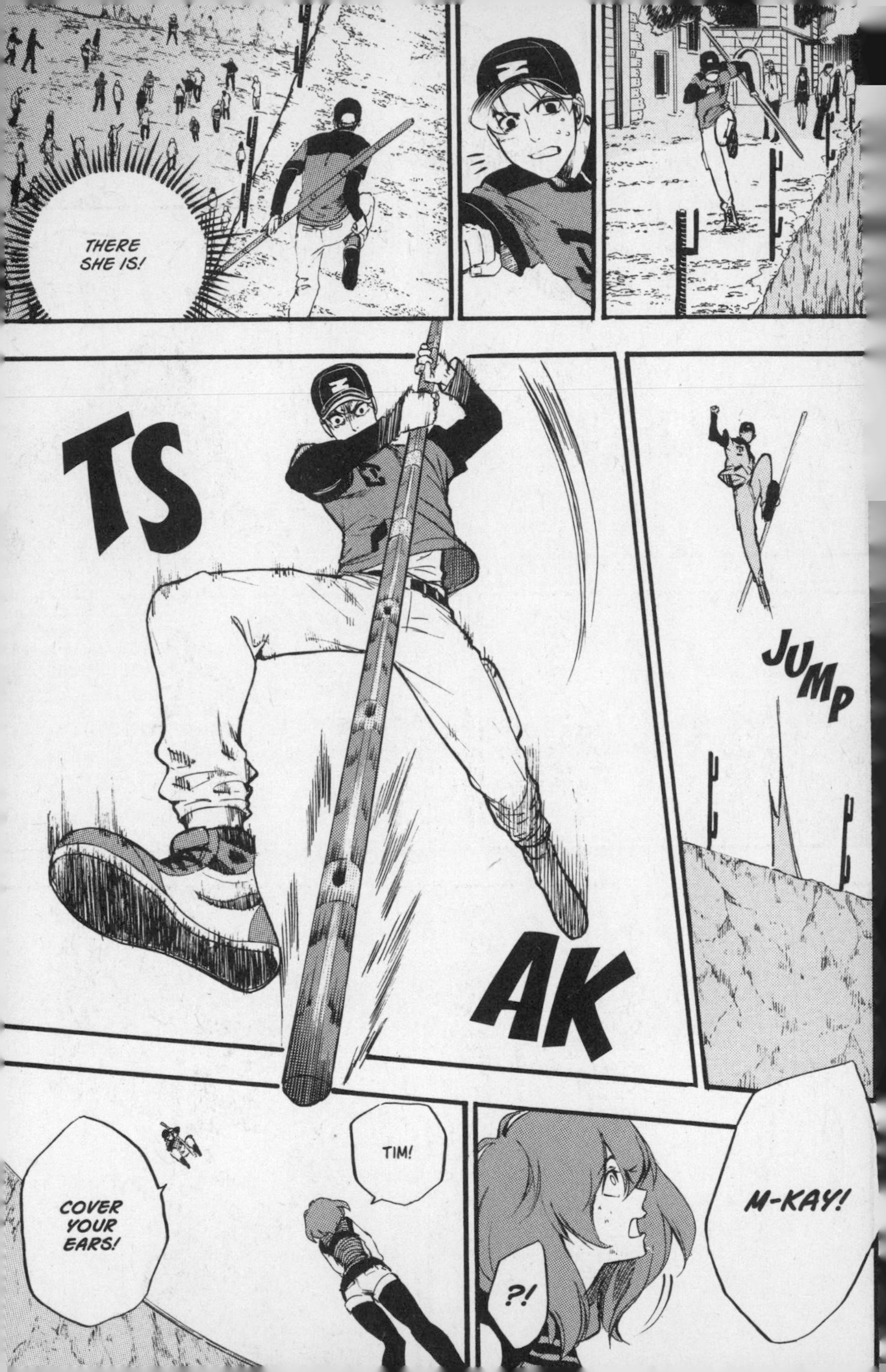
THERE SHE IS!
TS
AK
JUMP
COVER YOUR EARS!
TIM!
?!
M-KAY!

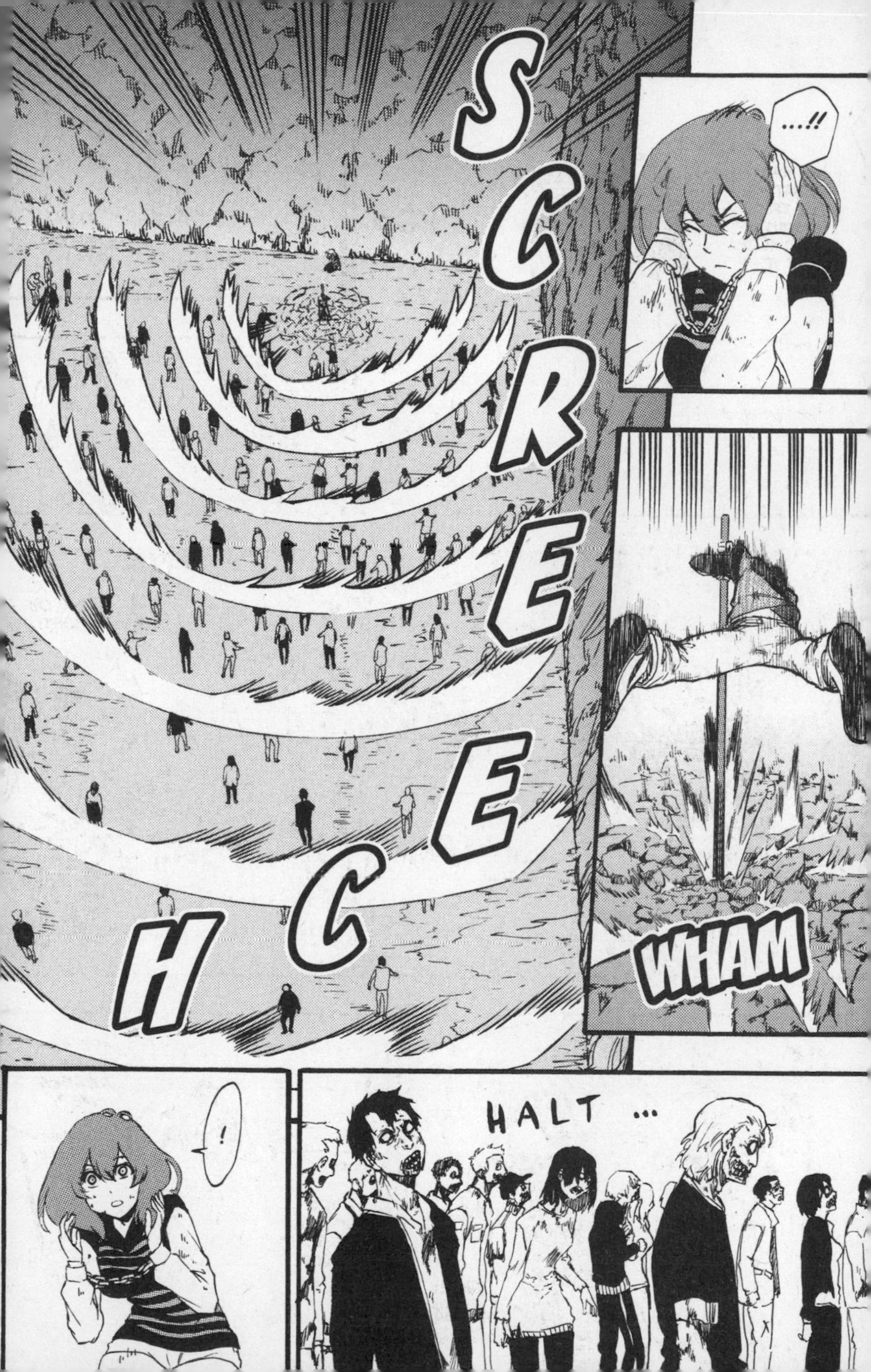
...!!
WHAM
SCREECH
HALT ...
!

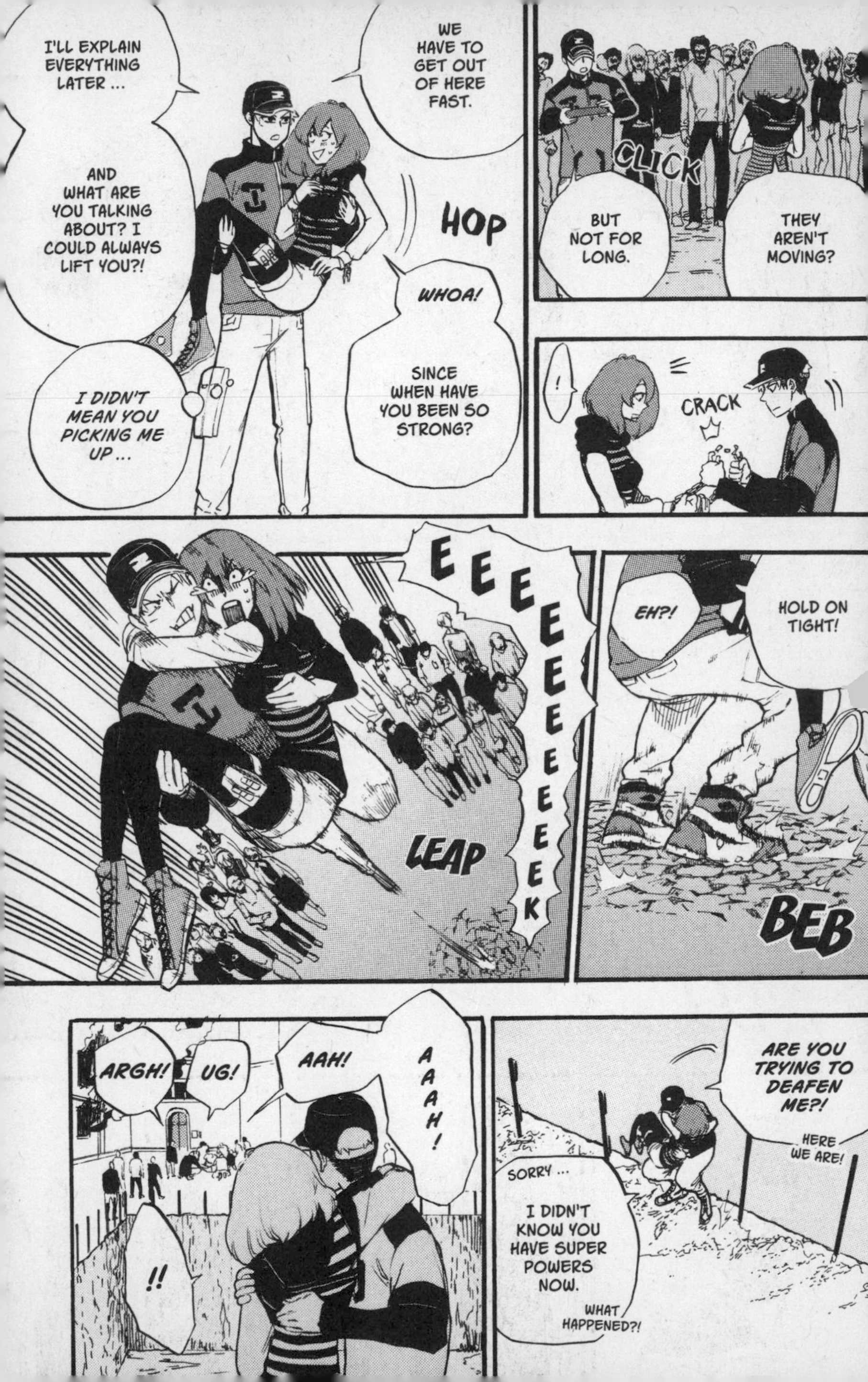
CLICK
THEY AREN'T MOVING?
BUT NOT FOR LONG.
!
CRACK
WE HAVE TO GET OUT OF HERE FAST.
I'LL EXPLAIN EVERYTHING LATER ...
HOP
WHOA!
SINCE WHEN HAVE YOU BEEN SO STRONG?
AND WHAT ARE YOU TALKING ABOUT? I COULD ALWAYS LIFT YOU?!
I DIDN'T MEAN YOU PICKING ME UP ...
HOLD ON TIGHT!
EH?!
BEB
EEEEEEEEEEEK
LEAP
ARE YOU TRYING TO DEAFEN ME?!
HERE WE ARE!
SORRY ...
I DIDN'T KNOW YOU HAVE SUPER POWERS NOW.
WHAT HAPPENED?!
AAAAH!
AAH!
UG!
ARGH!
!!

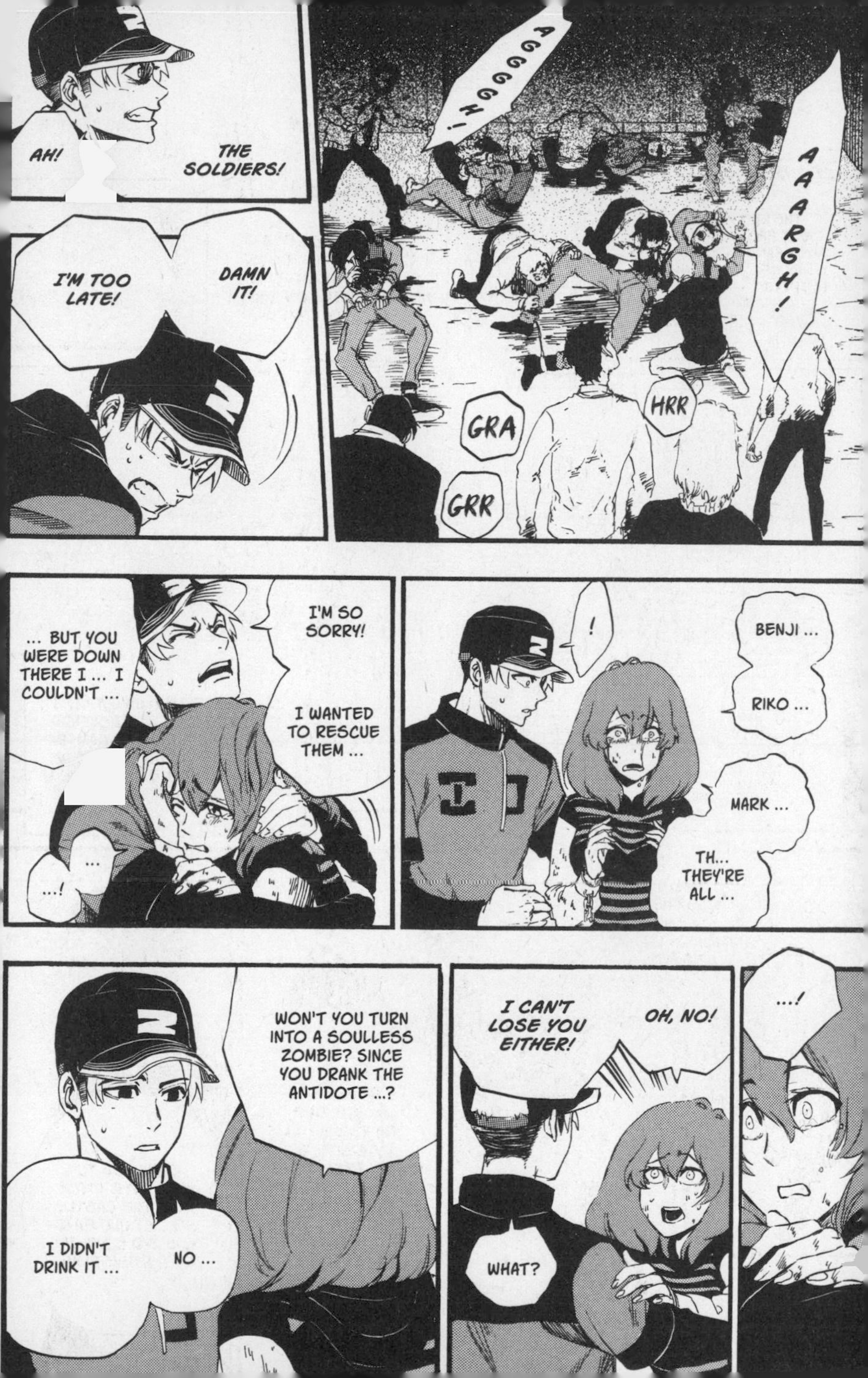
AGGGGH!
AAAARGH!
HRR
GRA
GRR
THE SOLDIERS!
AH!
DAMN IT!
I'M TOO LATE!
!
BENJI ...
RIKO ...
MARK ...
TH... THEY'RE ALL ...
I'M SO SORRY!
I WANTED TO RESCUE THEM ...
... BUT YOU WERE DOWN THERE I ... I COULDN'T ...
...
...!
...!
OH, NO!
I CAN'T LOSE YOU EITHER!
WHAT?
WON'T YOU TURN INTO A SOULLESS ZOMBIE? SINCE YOU DRANK THE ANTIDOTE ...?
NO ...
I DIDN'T DRINK IT ...

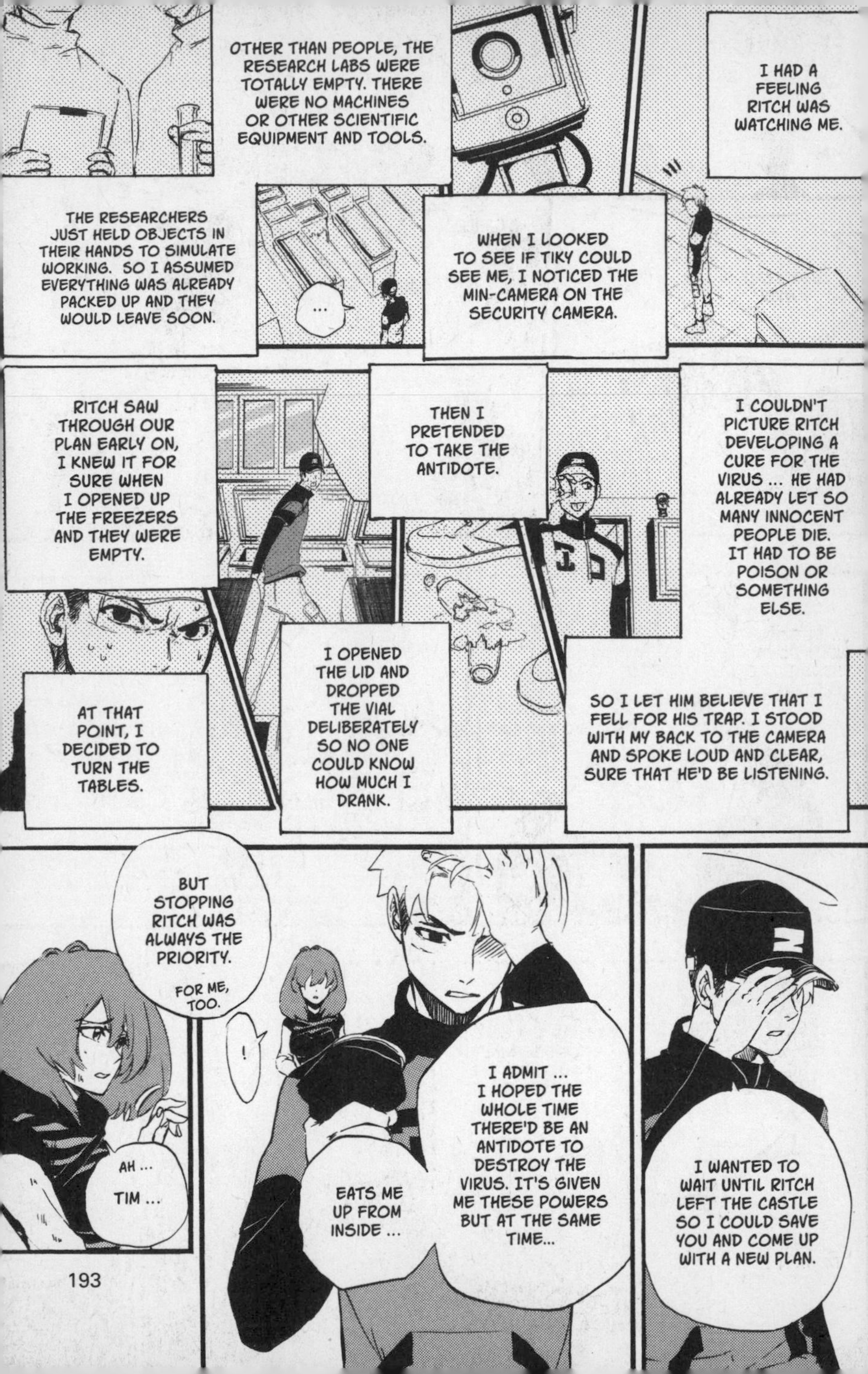

I HAD A FEELING RITCH WAS WATCHING ME.
WHEN I LOOKED TO SEE IF TIKY COULD SEE ME, I NOTICED THE MIN-CAMERA ON THE SECURITY CAMERA.
OTHER THAN PEOPLE, THE RESEARCH LABS WERE TOTALLY EMPTY. THERE WERE NO MACHINES OR OTHER SCIENTIFIC EQUIPMENT AND TOOLS.
THE RESEARCHERS JUST HELD OBJECTS IN THEIR HANDS TO SIMULATE WORKING. SO I ASSUMED EVERYTHING WAS ALREADY PACKED UP AND THEY WOULD LEAVE SOON.
...
I COULDN'T PICTURE RITCH DEVELOPING A CURE FOR THE VIRUS ... HE HAD ALREADY LET SO MANY INNOCENT PEOPLE DIE. IT HAD TO BE POISON OR SOMETHING ELSE.
SO I LET HIM BELIEVE THAT I FELL FOR HIS TRAP. I STOOD WITH MY BACK TO THE CAMERA AND SPOKE LOUD AND CLEAR, SURE THAT HE'D BE LISTENING.
THEN I PRETENDED TO TAKE THE ANTIDOTE.
I OPENED THE LID AND DROPPED THE VIAL DELIBERATELY SO NO ONE COULD KNOW HOW MUCH I DRANK.
RITCH SAW THROUGH OUR PLAN EARLY ON, I KNEW IT FOR SURE WHEN I OPENED UP THE FREEZERS AND THEY WERE EMPTY.
AT THAT POINT, I DECIDED TO TURN THE TABLES.
I WANTED TO WAIT UNTIL RITCH LEFT THE CASTLE SO I COULD SAVE YOU AND COME UP WITH A NEW PLAN.
I ADMIT ... I HOPED THE WHOLE TIME THERE'D BE AN ANTIDOTE TO DESTROY THE VIRUS. IT'S GIVEN ME THESE POWERS BUT AT THE SAME TIME...
!
EATS ME UP FROM INSIDE ...
BUT STOPPING RITCH WAS ALWAYS THE PRIORITY.
FOR ME, TOO.
AH ... TIM ...

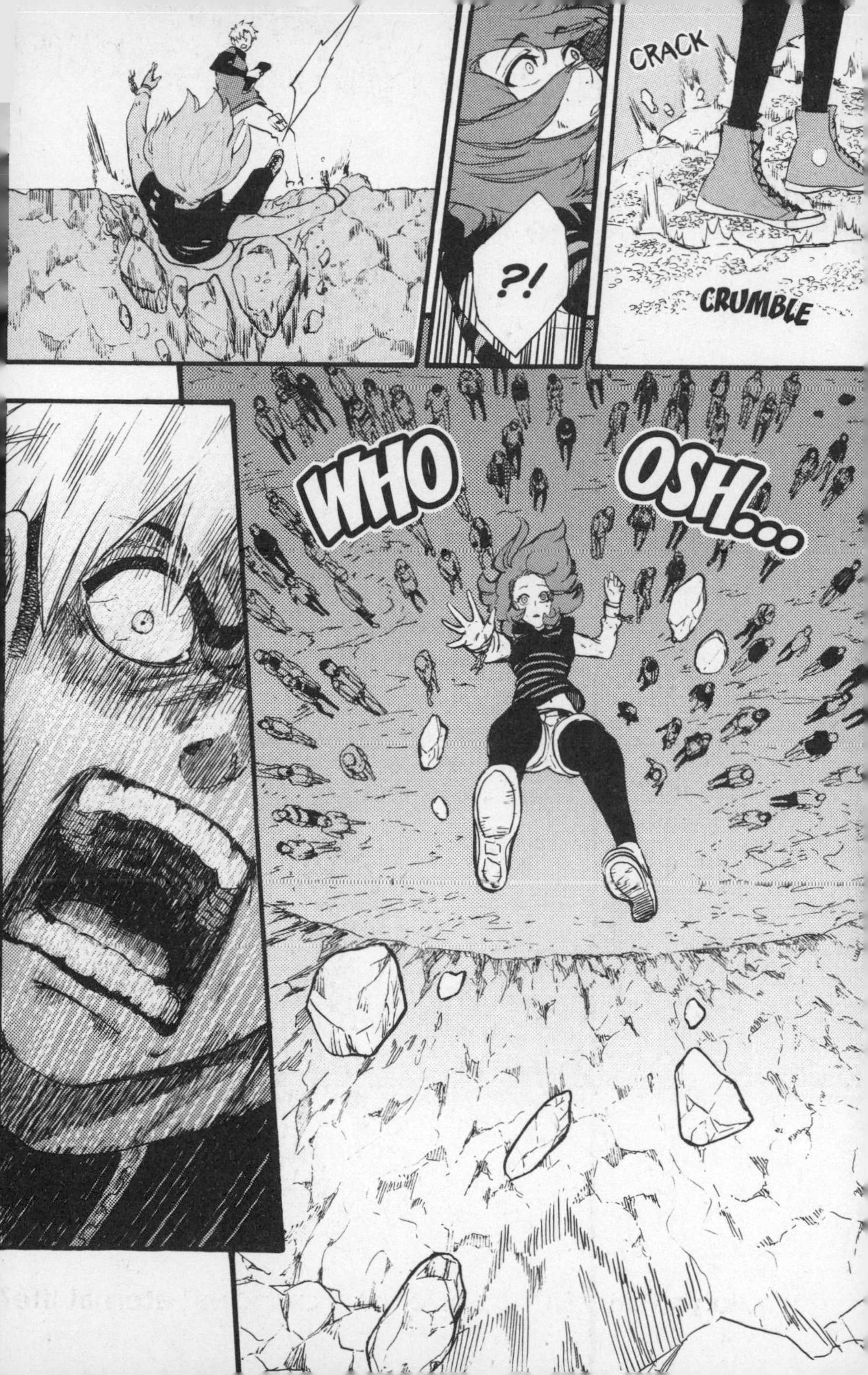
CRACK
CRUMBLE
?!
WHOOSH...

## In the next volume of

# UNDEAD MESSIAH

Tim's attempts to infiltrate Ritch's organization and bring him down from the inside have failed, and now he must formulate a new plan — and quickly. But Ritch's narcissistic machinations show no signs of slowing, and his carefully planned global appearances have only made the world fall in love with him as their potential savior.

The fate of humanity rests with the answer to one, simple question:

**Would *you* take Ritch's offer of a chance at eternal life?**

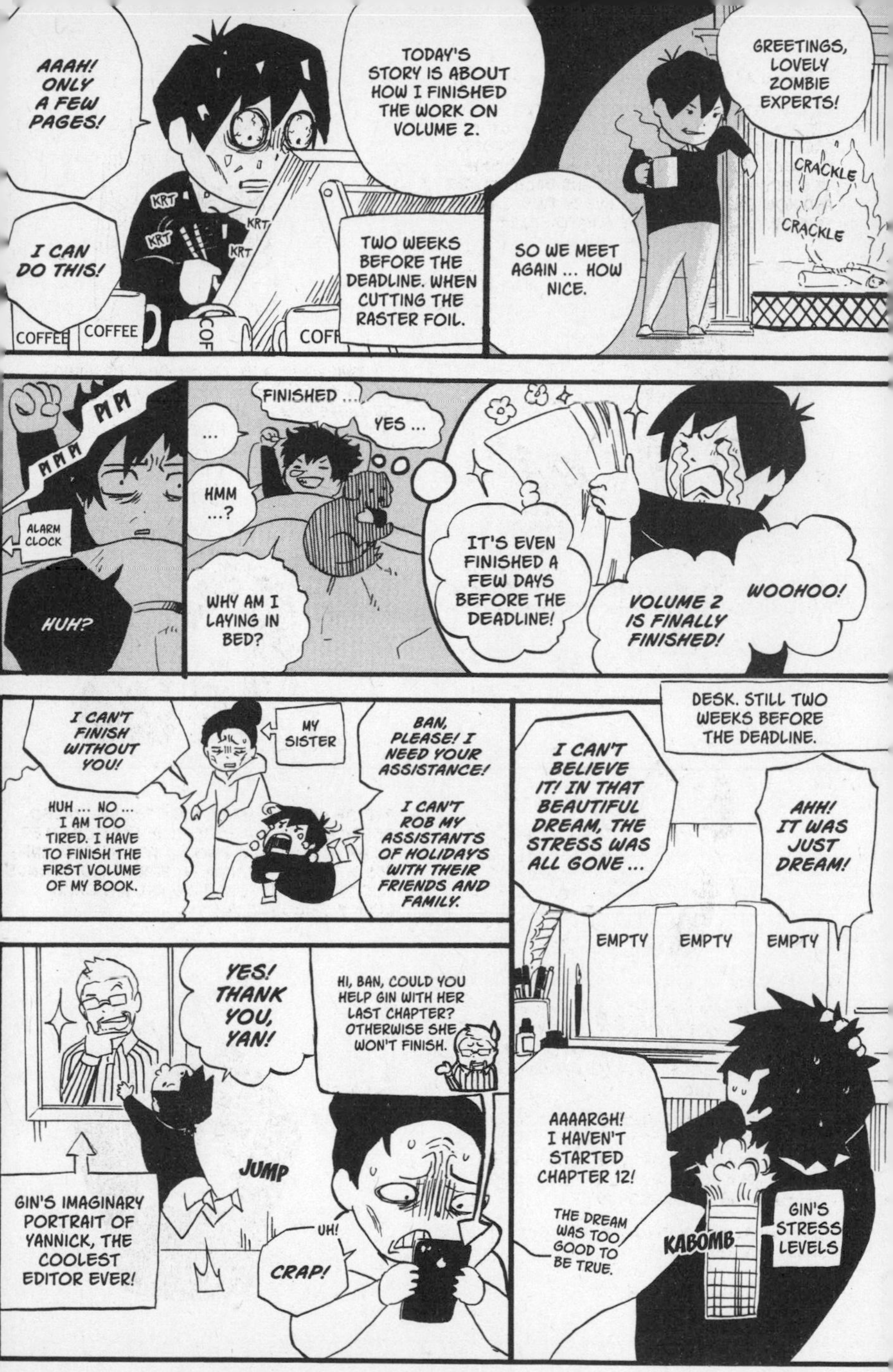
GREETINGS, LOVELY ZOMBIE EXPERTS!
CRACKLE
CRACKLE
SO WE MEET AGAIN ... HOW NICE.
TODAY'S STORY IS ABOUT HOW I FINISHED THE WORK ON VOLUME 2.
AAAH! ONLY A FEW PAGES!
TWO WEEKS BEFORE THE DEADLINE. WHEN CUTTING THE RASTER FOIL.
KRT
KRT
KRT
KRT
I CAN DO THIS!
COFF
COF
COFFEE
COFFEE
WOOHOO!
VOLUME 2 IS FINALLY FINISHED!
IT'S EVEN FINISHED A FEW DAYS BEFORE THE DEADLINE!
FINISHED ...
YES ...
...
HMM ...?
WHY AM I LAYING IN BED?
PI PI
PI PI PI
ALARM CLOCK
HUH?
DESK. STILL TWO WEEKS BEFORE THE DEADLINE.
AHH! IT WAS JUST DREAM!
I CAN'T BELIEVE IT! IN THAT BEAUTIFUL DREAM, THE STRESS WAS ALL GONE ...
EMPTY
EMPTY
EMPTY
AAAARGH! I HAVEN'T STARTED CHAPTER 12!
THE DREAM WAS TOO GOOD TO BE TRUE.
GIN'S STRESS LEVELS
KABOMB
BAN, PLEASE! I NEED YOUR ASSISTANCE!
I CAN'T ROB MY ASSISTANTS OF HOLIDAYS WITH THEIR FRIENDS AND FAMILY.
MY SISTER
I CAN'T FINISH WITHOUT YOU!
HUH ... NO ... I AM TOO TIRED. I HAVE TO FINISH THE FIRST VOLUME OF MY BOOK.
HI, BAN, COULD YOU HELP GIN WITH HER LAST CHAPTER? OTHERWISE SHE WON'T FINISH.
UH!
CRAP!
YES! THANK YOU, YAN!
JUMP
GIN'S IMAGINARY PORTRAIT OF YANNICK, THE COOLEST EDITOR EVER!

## *EPILOGUE*

AT THIS POINT, I WOULD LIKE TO ONCE AGAIN THANK YAN, MY EDITOR AND CO-AUTHOR. OUR HARMONIOUS COLLABORATION IS (HOPEFULLY) REFLECTED IN VOLUME 2 OF UNDEAD MESSIAH. IT'S GREAT HOW WE UNDERSTAND EACH OTHER AND HOW OUR IDEAS UNITE EVERY TIME. I HOPE THIS TEAM-UP LASTS FOREVER! *GIGGLE*

GIN
YAN

DILARA
CHANTAL

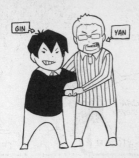

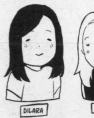

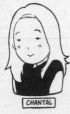

A THANK YOU TO MY TRADITIONAL DRAWING ASSISTANTS, DILARA AND CHANTAL, WHO I GOT TO KNOW IN ONE OF MY SINGING CLASSES IN SWITZERLAND. THEY HAVE WORKED ON THE SPOT BLACKS AND RASTERING. WITHOUT THEIR HELP, I WOULD NEVER HAVE FINISHED.

ALSO MY FAVORITE ASSISTANTS FOR THE DIGITAL PROCESSING, THE TWO VANESSAS, MANY THANKS!

I'M STILL ALIVE ...

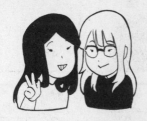

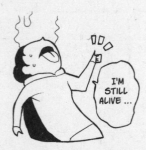

AND OF COURSE MY TWIN SISTER BAN ZARBO, ESPECIALLY DEALING WITH THE LAST CHAPTER. THANK YOU FOR HELPING ME TO THE END! AND ALSO I WANT TO THANK MY FAMILY AND FRIENDS FOR THEIR UNDERSTANDING AND PATIENCE DURING THIS HARD TIME.

MY BIGGEST THANKS GOES AGAIN TO MY READERS, SO YOU! I'M HAPPY THAT YOU DECIDED TO FOLLOW THE STORY OF TIM AND BUY THE SECOND VOLUME OF UNDEAD MESSIAH.

OF COURSE YOU ARE INVITED TO WRITE TO ME ABOUT HOW YOU FELT ABOUT THIS VOLUME. YOUR FEEDBACK ON VOLUME ONE HELPED ME A LOT AND I'M SURE IT WILL BE THE SAME THIS TIME AROUND.

SEND ME A MESSAGE TO THE FOLLOWING EMAIL ADDRESS:

GIN.ZARBO@HOTMAIL.COM

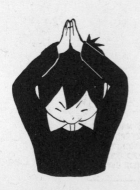

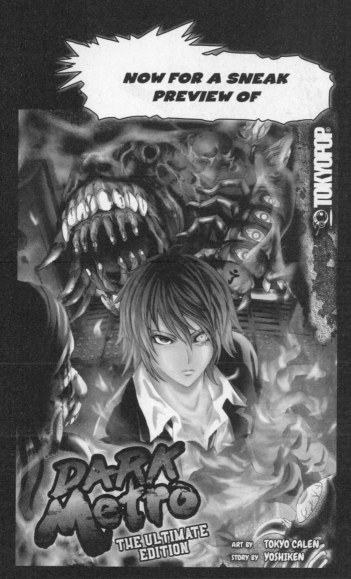

**NOW FOR A SNEAK PREVIEW OF**

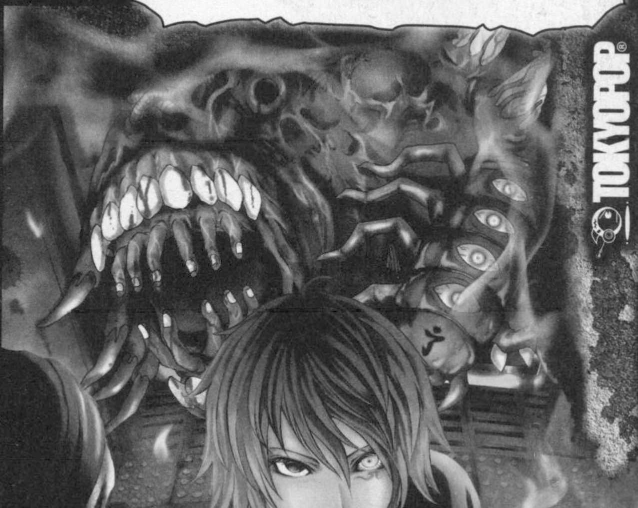
TOKYOPOP
DARK METRO
THE ULTIMATE EDITION
ART BY TOKYO CALEN
STORY BY YOSHIKEN

WHAT LIES BELOW TOKYO'S SUBWAY SYSTEM IS MORE FRIGHTENING THAN YOU COULD HAVE EVER IMAGINED... DEEP BENEATH TOKYO THERE EXISTS A BOUNDARY BETWEEN THIS WORLD AND THE NEXT: THE LAND OF THE DEAD -- AND THIS MYSTERIOUS YOUNG MAN SEIYA IS ITS GUIDE. IN THIS COLLECTION OF BONE-CHILLING STORIES, FOLLOW THE TWISTED TALES OF DEAD AND HAUNTINGS THAT INHIBIT THIS HORRIFYING UNDERWORLD, WHERE INNOCENT YOUTH FALL VICTIM TO THE GHOSTS WHO LURK IN TOKYO'S UNDERGROUND. NOW THE THIRD AND FINAL VOLUME IN THIS CHILLING SERIES WILL BE AVAILABLE IN ENGLISH FOR THE FIRST TIME.

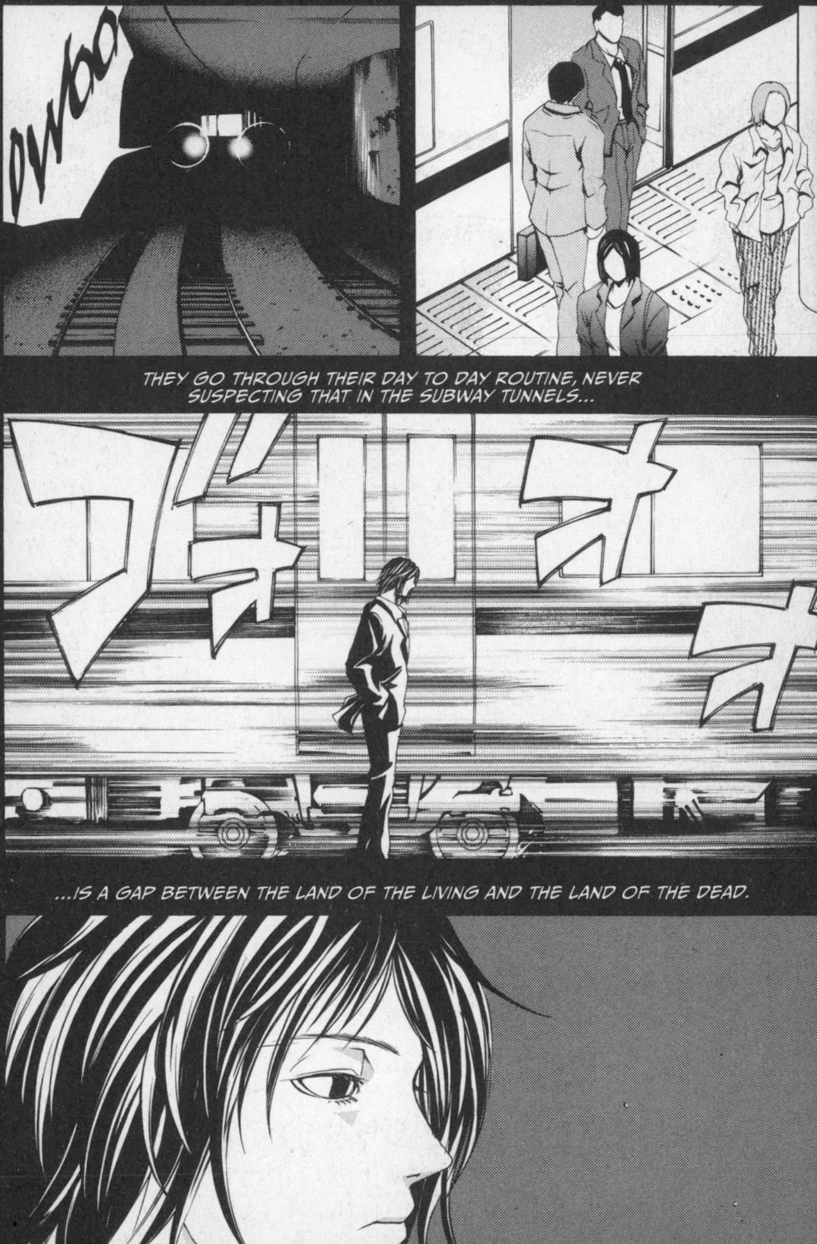
DWOO
THEY GO THROUGH THEIR DAY TO DAY ROUTINE, NEVER SUSPECTING THAT IN THE SUBWAY TUNNELS...
ブォーオオ
...IS A GAP BETWEEN THE LAND OF THE LIVING AND THE LAND OF THE DEAD.

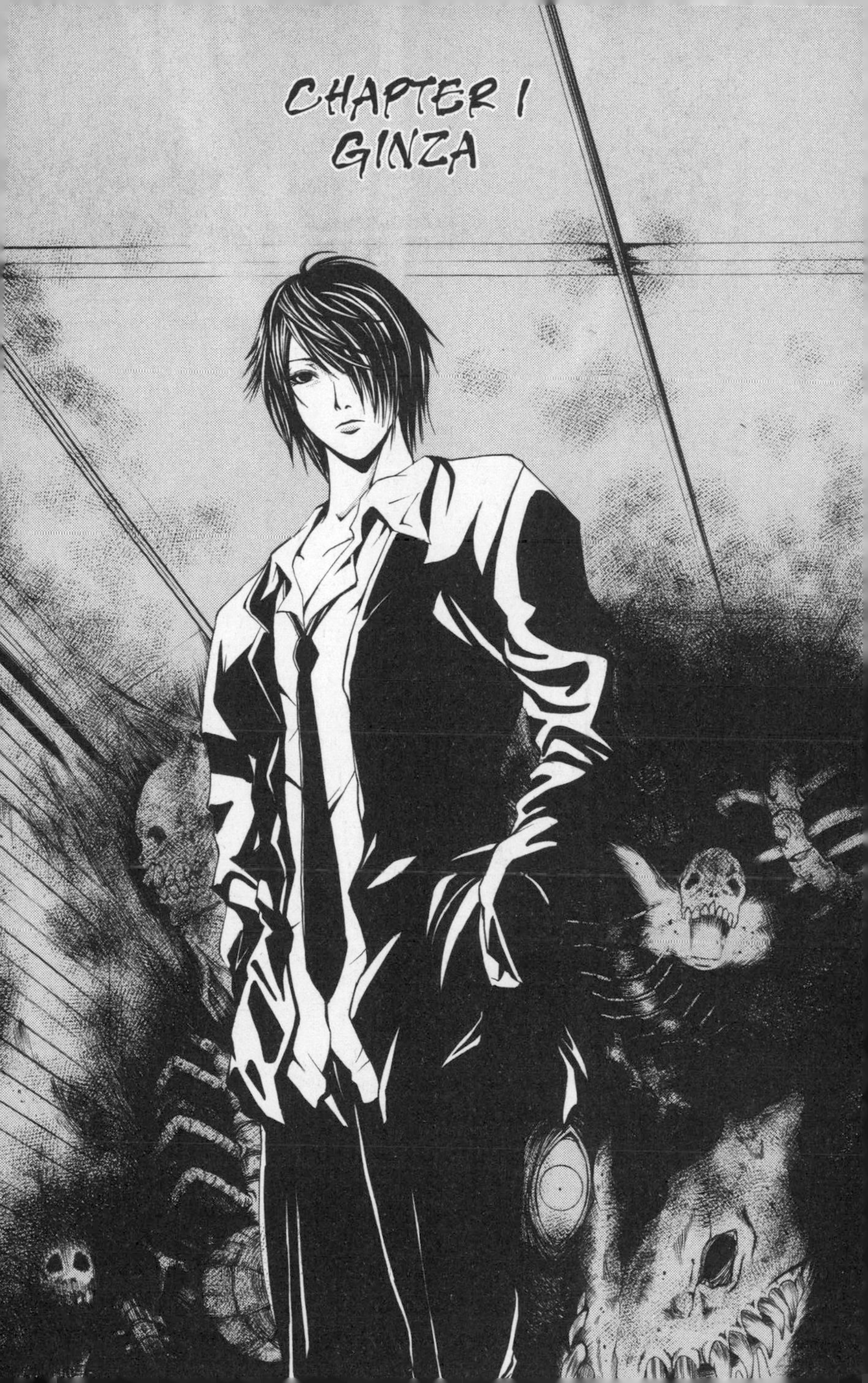
CHAPTER 1
GINZA

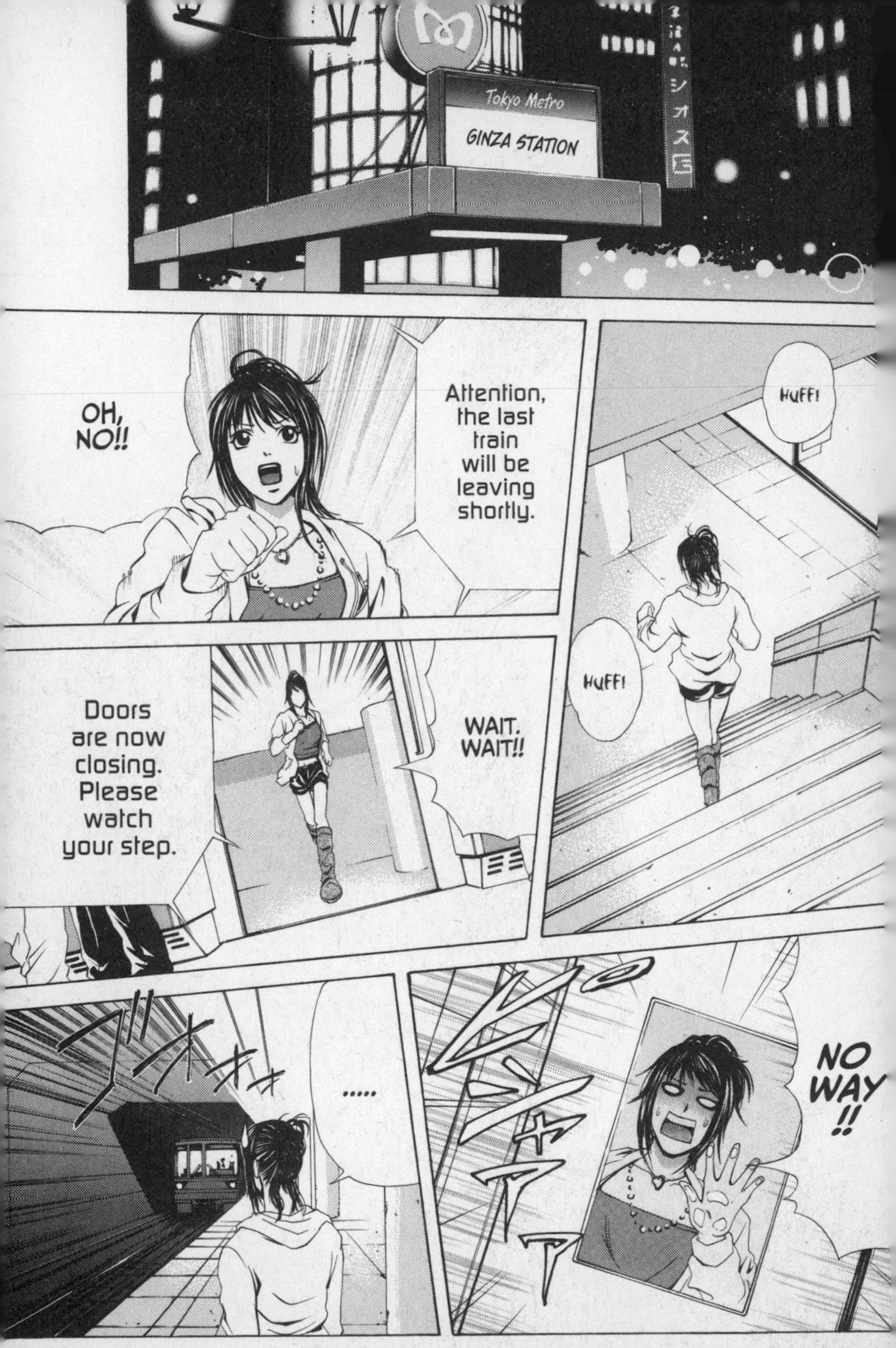
Tokyo Metro
GINZA STATION
HUFF!
HUFF!
Attention, the last train will be leaving shortly.
OH, NO!!
WAIT. WAIT!!
Doors are now closing. Please watch your step.
NO WAY!!
.....

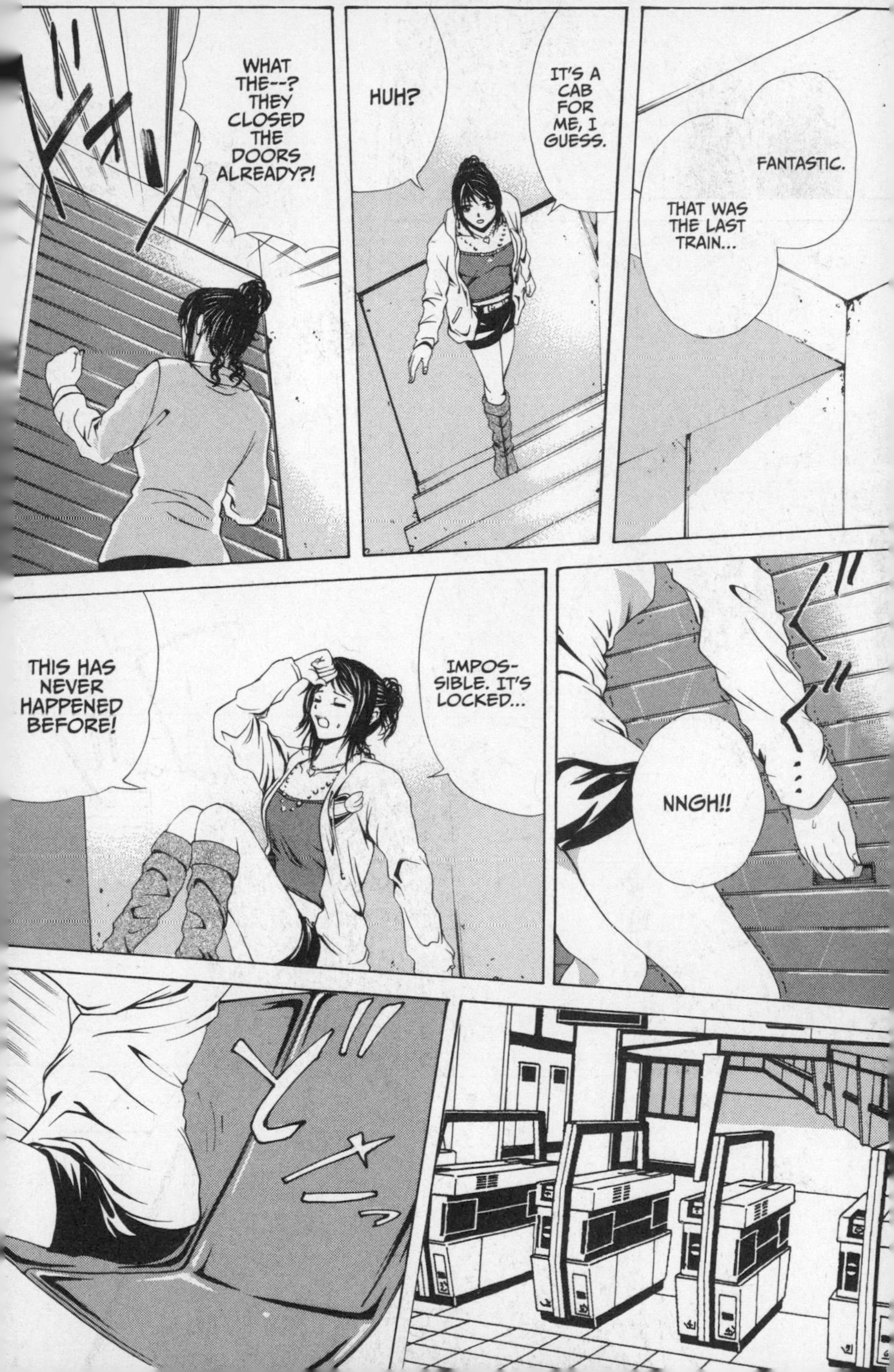
FANTASTIC.
THAT WAS THE LAST TRAIN...
IT'S A CAB FOR ME, I GUESS.
HUH?
WHAT THE--? THEY CLOSED THE DOORS ALREADY?!
NNGH!!
IMPOS-SIBLE. IT'S LOCKED...
THIS HAS NEVER HAPPENED BEFORE!

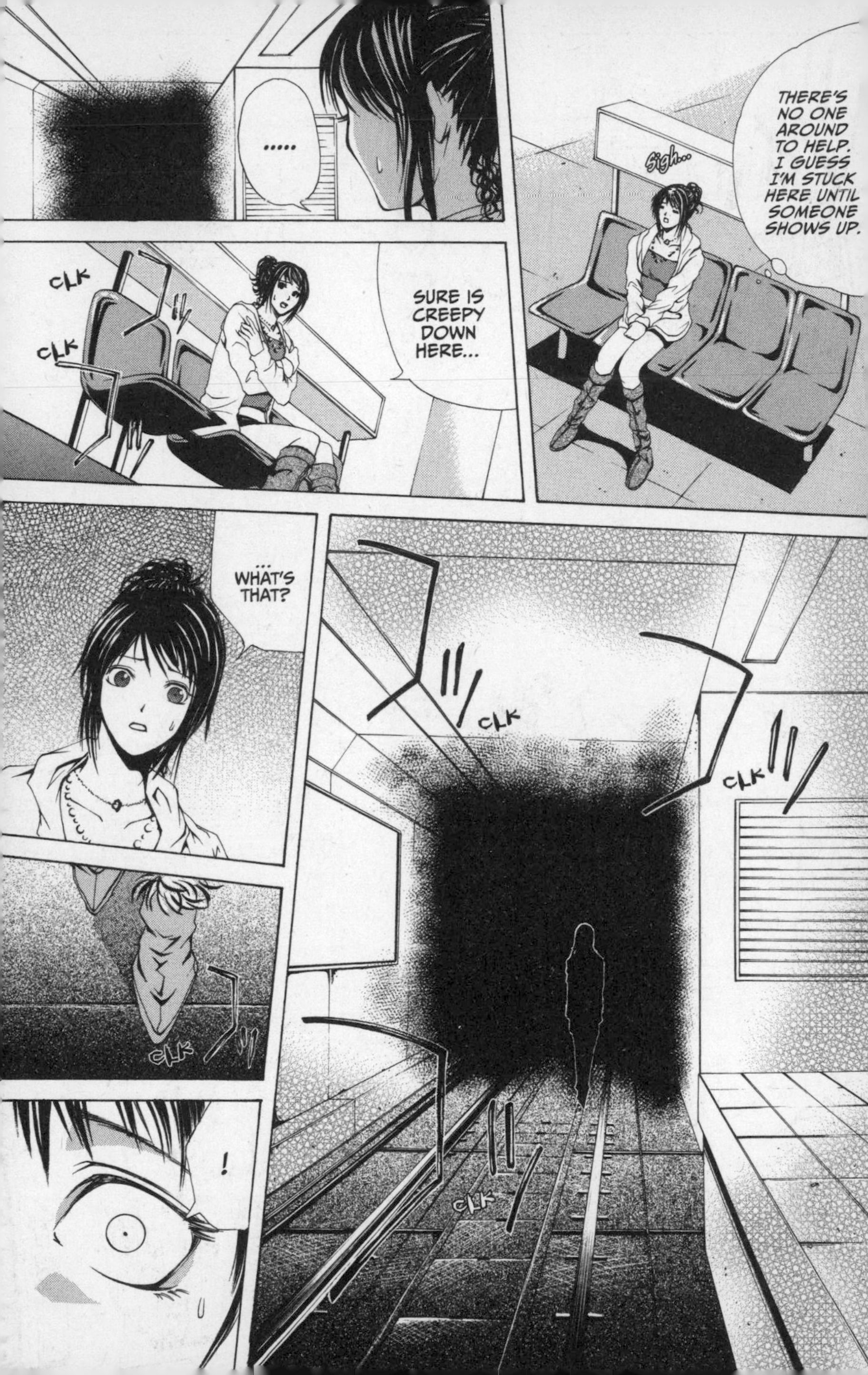
THERE'S NO ONE AROUND TO HELP. I GUESS I'M STUCK HERE UNTIL SOMEONE SHOWS UP.
Sigh...
.....
SURE IS CREEPY DOWN HERE...
CLK
CLK
CLK
CLK
CLK
CLK
... WHAT'S THAT?
CLK
!

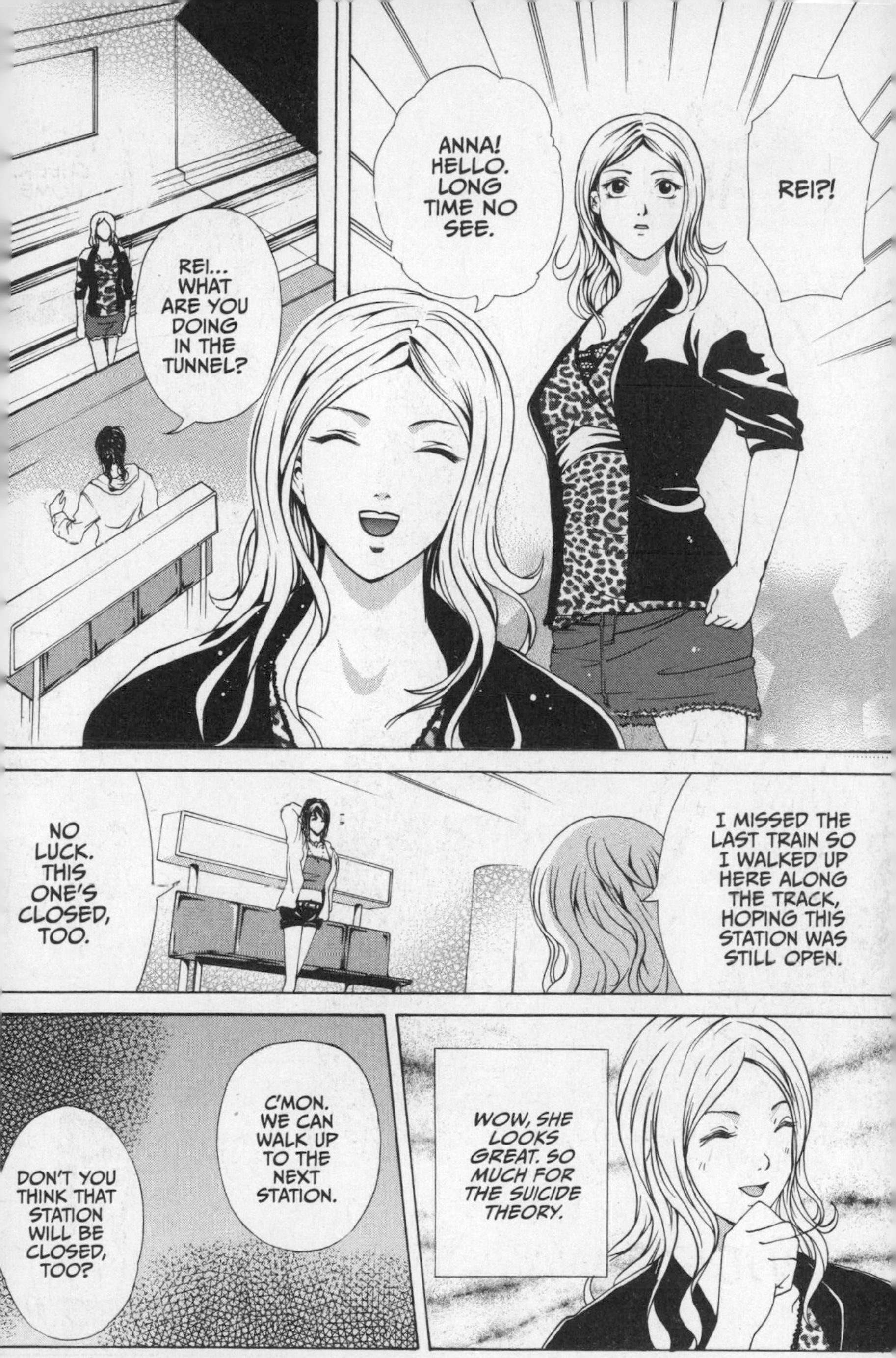
REI?!
ANNA! HELLO. LONG TIME NO SEE.
REI... WHAT ARE YOU DOING IN THE TUNNEL?
I MISSED THE LAST TRAIN SO I WALKED UP HERE ALONG THE TRACK, HOPING THIS STATION WAS STILL OPEN.
NO LUCK. THIS ONE'S CLOSED, TOO.
*WOW, SHE LOOKS GREAT. SO MUCH FOR THE SUICIDE THEORY.*
C'MON. WE CAN WALK UP TO THE NEXT STATION.
DON'T YOU THINK THAT STATION WILL BE CLOSED, TOO?

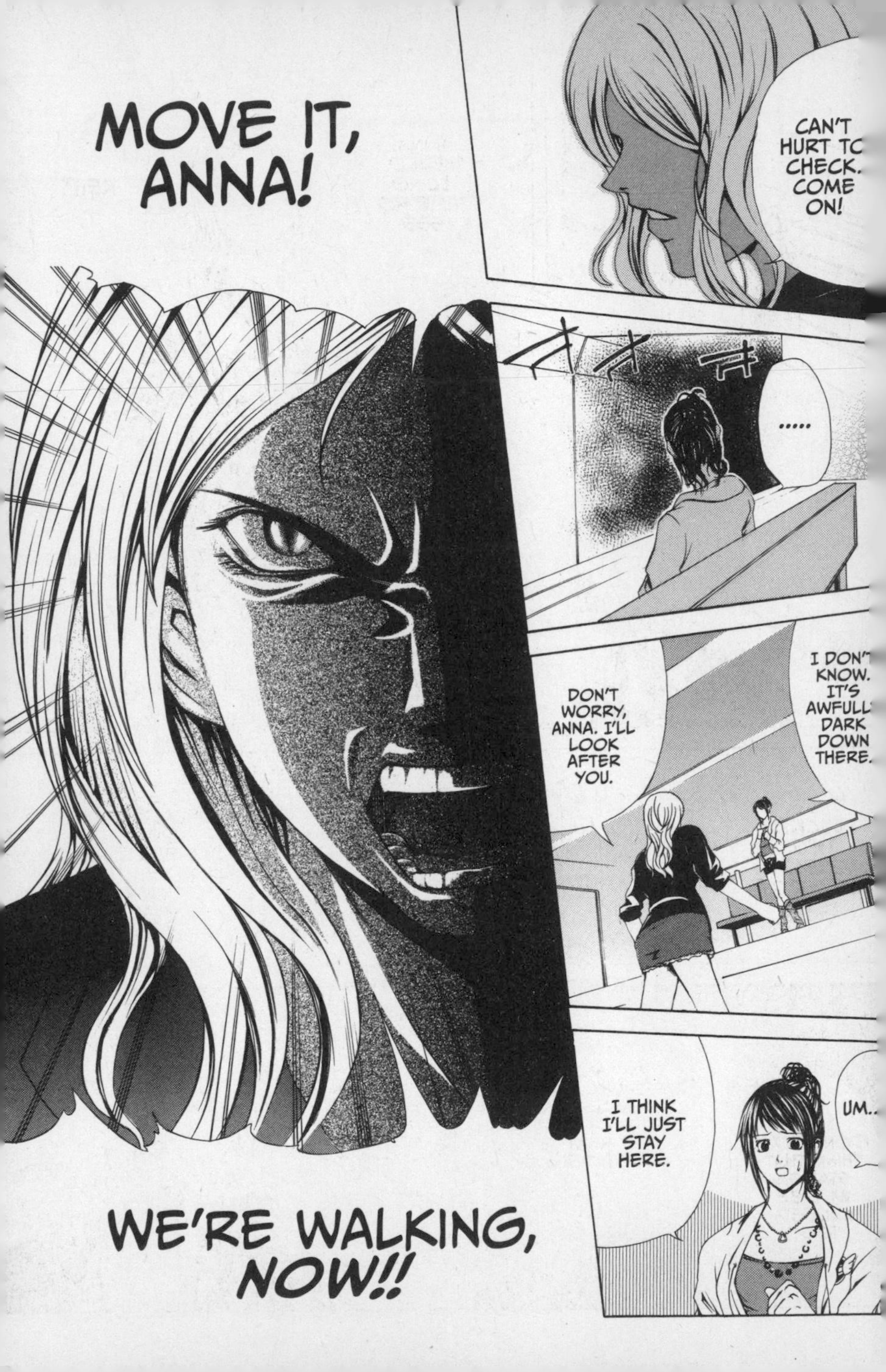
CAN'T HURT TO CHECK. COME ON!
.....
I DON'T KNOW. IT'S AWFULL DARK DOWN THERE.
DON'T WORRY, ANNA. I'LL LOOK AFTER YOU.
UM..
I THINK I'LL JUST STAY HERE.
MOVE IT, ANNA!
WE'RE WALKING, NOW!!

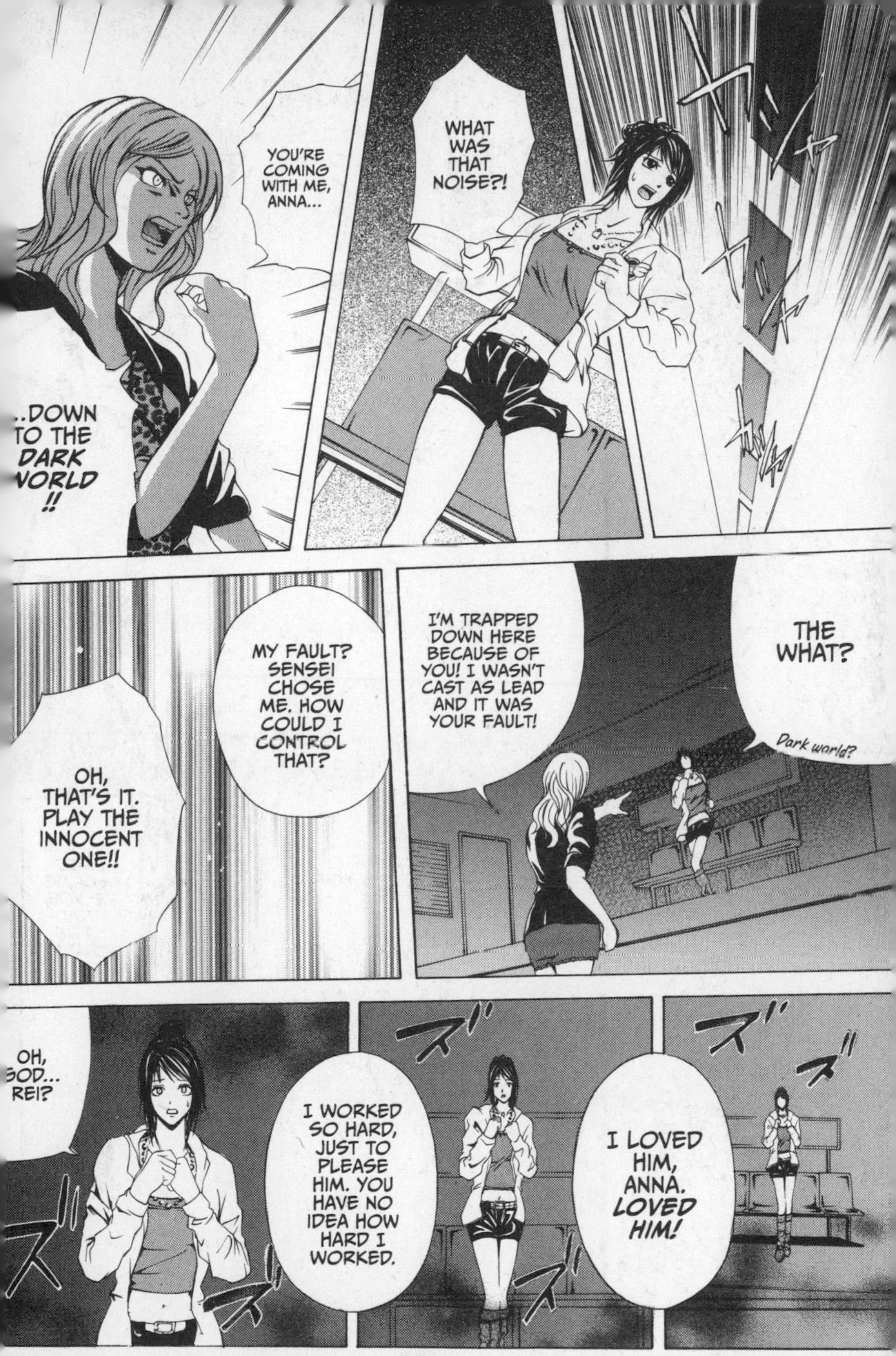
WHAT WAS THAT NOISE?!
YOU'RE COMING WITH ME, ANNA...
..DOWN TO THE DARK WORLD!!
THE WHAT?
Dark world?
I'M TRAPPED DOWN HERE BECAUSE OF YOU! I WASN'T CAST AS LEAD AND IT WAS YOUR FAULT!
MY FAULT? SENSEI CHOSE ME. HOW COULD I CONTROL THAT?
OH, THAT'S IT. PLAY THE INNOCENT ONE!!
I LOVED HIM, ANNA. LOVED HIM!
I WORKED SO HARD, JUST TO PLEASE HIM. YOU HAVE NO IDEA HOW HARD I WORKED.
OH, GOD... REI?

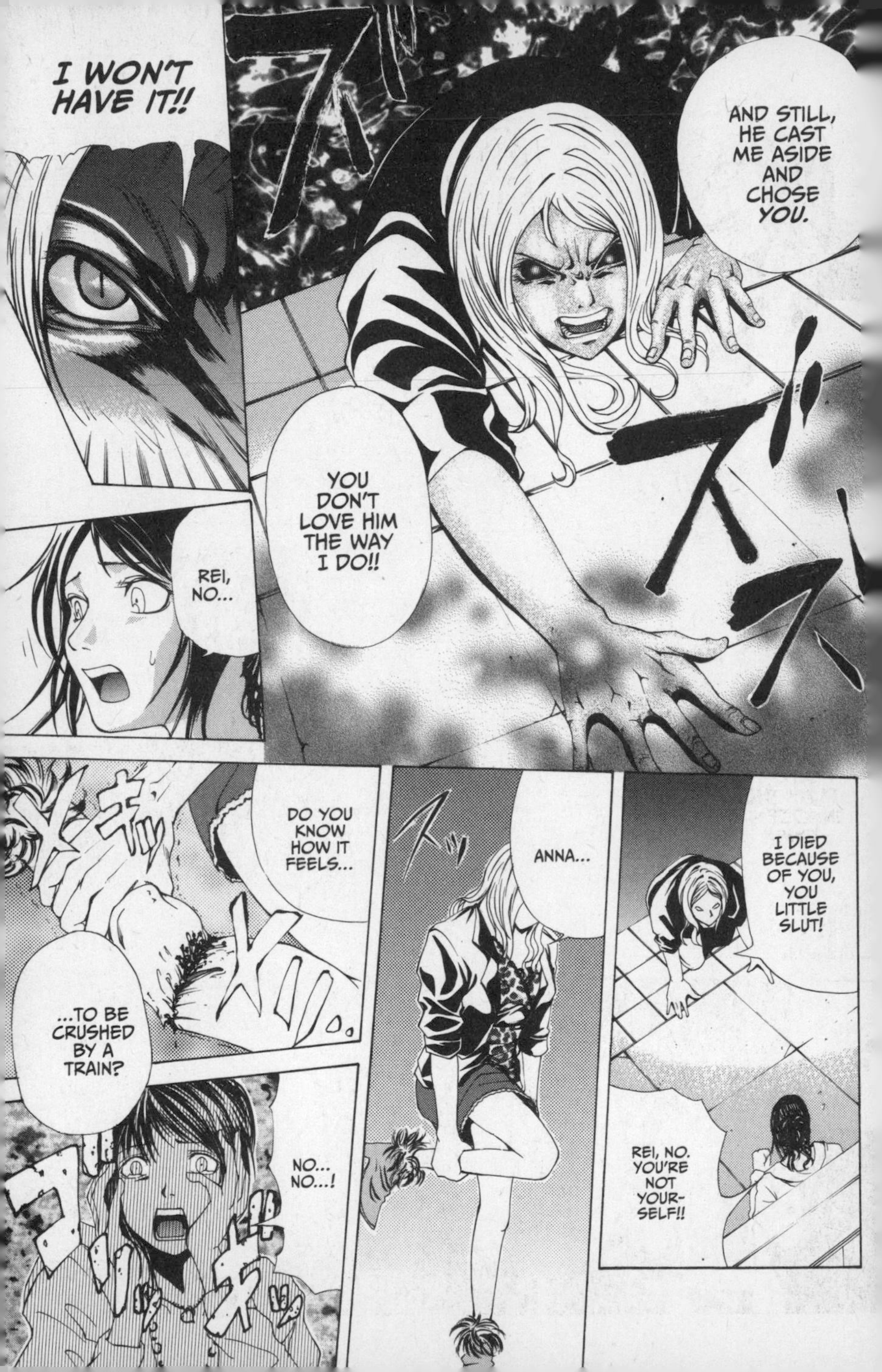
AND STILL, HE CAST ME ASIDE AND CHOSE YOU.
YOU DON'T LOVE HIM THE WAY I DO!!
I WON'T HAVE IT!!
REI, NO...
I DIED BECAUSE OF YOU, YOU LITTLE SLUT!
REI, NO. YOU'RE NOT YOUR-SELF!!
ANNA...
DO YOU KNOW HOW IT FEELS...
...TO BE CRUSHED BY A TRAIN?
NO... NO...!

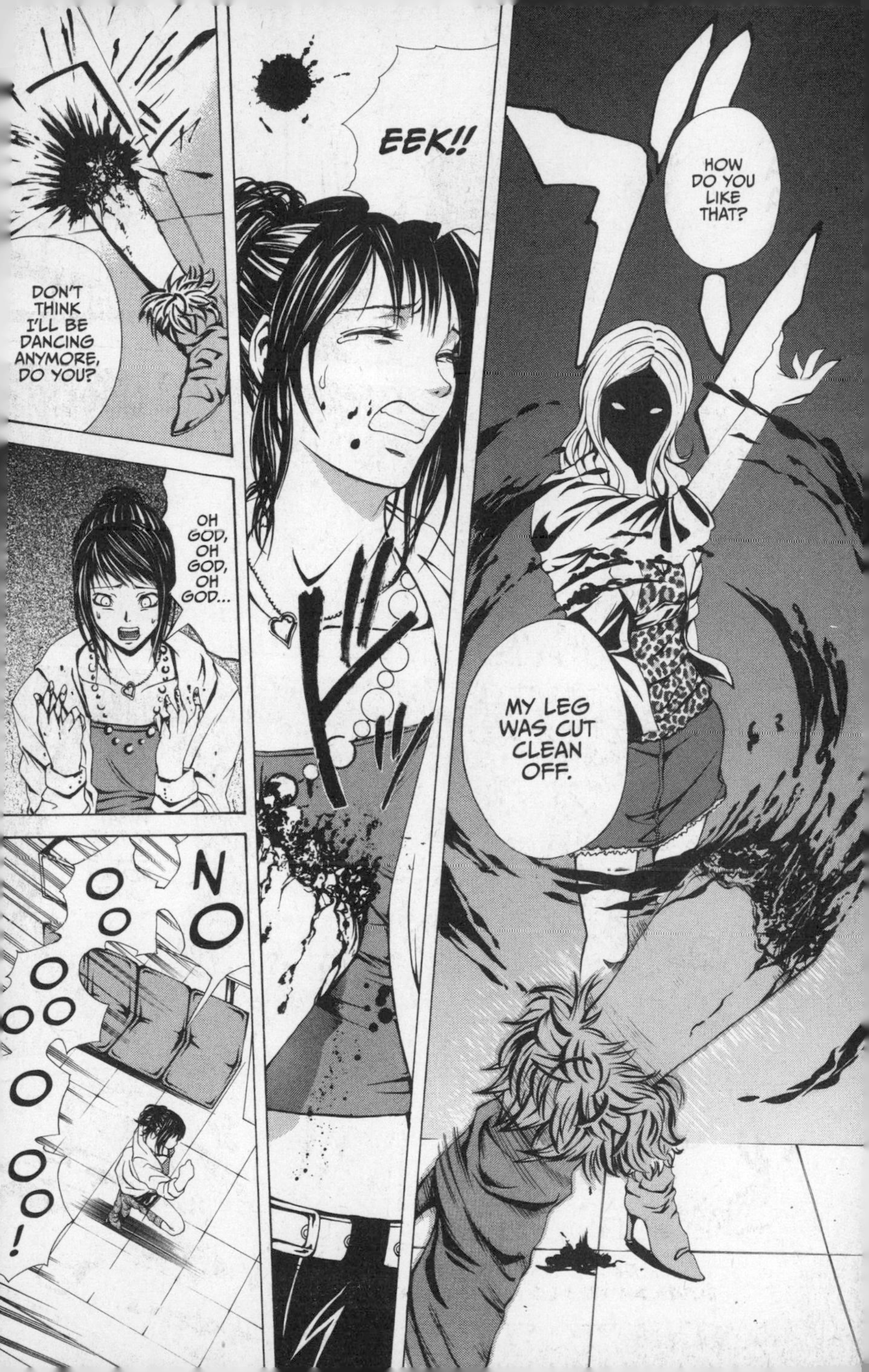
HOW DO YOU LIKE THAT?
MY LEG WAS CUT CLEAN OFF.
EEK!!
DON'T THINK I'LL BE DANCING ANYMORE, DO YOU?
OH GOD, OH GOD, OH GOD...
NOOOOOOOOOO!

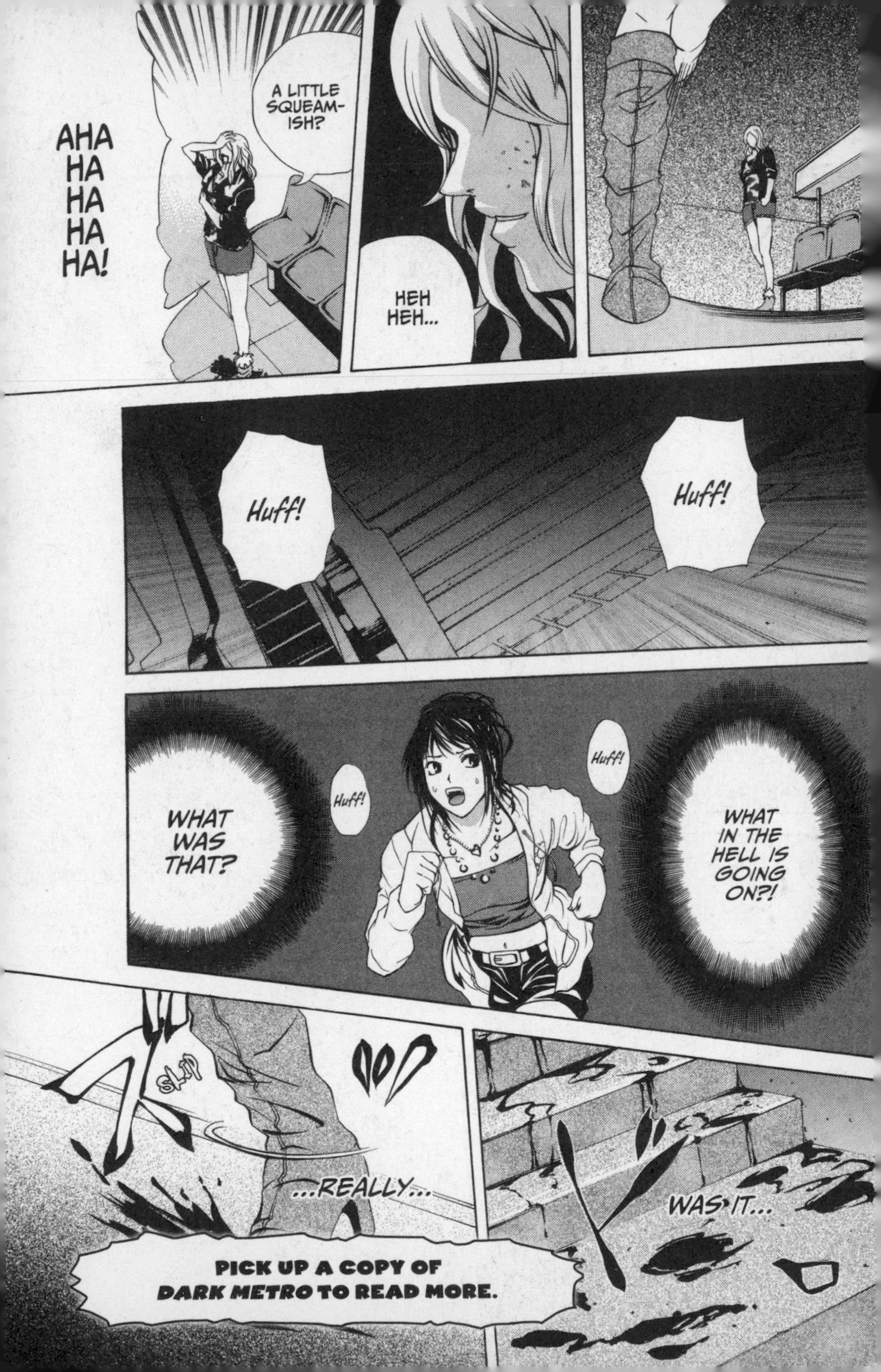
HEH HEH...
A LITTLE SQUEAMISH?
AHA HA HA HA HA!
Huff!
Huff!
WHAT IN THE HELL IS GOING ON?!
Huff!
Huff!
WHAT WAS THAT?
WAS IT...
SLIP
...REALLY...
PICK UP A COPY OF DARK METRO TO READ MORE.

# The Author

"WHERE IS THERE IS A WILL THERE IS A WAY!"
IS GIN ZARBO'S CREDO, AND SINCE BEING BORN
IN 1993 IN SWITZERLAND THIS MANGA ARTIST ALWAYS
FOUND A WAY TO REALIZE HER DREAMS: SHE DREW HER
FIRST MANGA AT THE AGE OF 13 AND HER FIRST DOUJINSHI
COPE SOUL BROUGHT HER TO SELF-PUBLISHING.
2017 FOLLOWED WITH UNDEAD MESSIAH, HER FIRST
PUBLICATION WITH A PUBLISHER. GIN HAS COMMITTED TO
THE SHONEN GENRE AND LIKES TO READ SERIES SUCH
AS BLEACH (TITE KUBO) AND TOKYO GHOUL (SUI ISHIDA),
BUT ALSO BOYS' LOVE MANGA LIKE TEN COUNT (RIHITO
TAKARAI) OR LOVE STAGE!! (EIKI EIKI). THE IMPRESSIVE
MANGA COLLECTION IN HER STUDIO IS SHARED WITH
HER TWIN SISTER BAN, WHO HAS ALSO BEEN PUBLISHED
BY TOKYOPOP.  GIN'S FATHER IS FROM ITALY AND HER
MOTHER COMES FROM THE DOMINICAN REPUBLIC.
CULTURAL DIVERSITY IS ESPECIALLY IMPORTANT
TO GIN AND IS REFLECTED IN HER STORIES.

FACEBOOK: GINZARBO
TWITTER: GIN_ZARBO
INSTAGRAM: GIN.ZARBO

## *Undead Messiah Volume 2*
## Manga by: Gin Zarbo

Publishing Associate - Janae Young
Marketing Associate - Kae Winters
Technology and Digital Media Assistant - Phillip Hong
Digital Media Coordinator - Rico Brenner-Quiñonez
Licensing Specialist - Arika Yanaka
Translator - Kenneth Shinabery
Copy-editor - M. Cara Carper
Graphic Designer - Phillip Hong
Retouching and Lettering - Vibrraant Publishing Studio
Editor-in-Chief & Publisher - Stu Levy

A  Manga

TOKYOPOP and 🐸 are trademarks or registered trademarks of TOKYOPOP Inc.

TOKYOPOP inc.
5200 W Century Blvd
Suite 705
Los Angeles, CA 90045 USA

E-mail: info@TOKYOPOP.com
Come visit us online at www.TOKYOPOP.com

f www.facebook.com/TOKYOPOP
🐦 www.twitter.com/TOKYOPOP
▶ www.youtube.com/TOKYOPOPTV
P www.pinterest.com/TOKYOPOP
📷 www.instagram.com/TOKYOPOP

ISBN: 978-1-4278-5942-6
First TOKYOPOP Printing: October 2018
10 9 8 7 6 5 4 3 2 1
Printed in CANADA

# STOP

## THIS IS THE BACK OF THE BOOK!

**How do you read manga-style? It's simple! Let's practice -- just start in the top right panel and follow the numbers below!**

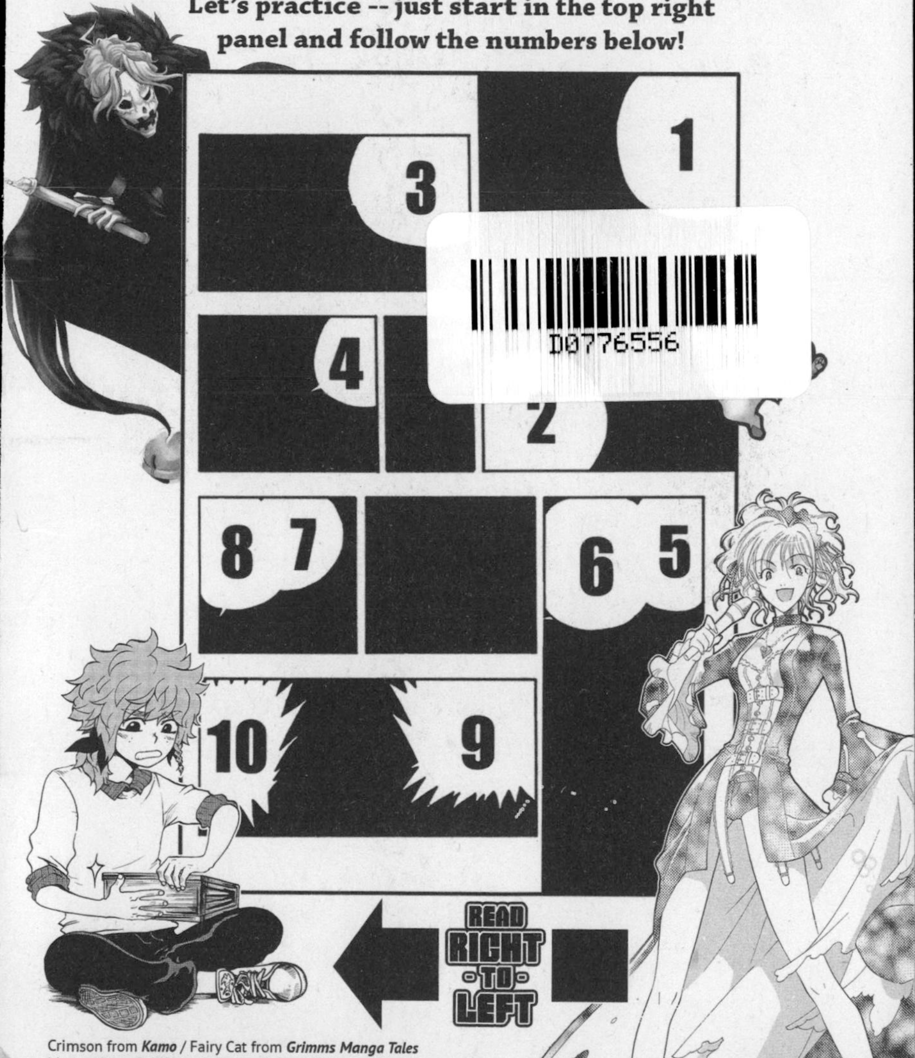
1
2
3
4
5
6
7
8
9
10
READ RIGHT-TO-LEFT



Crimson from *Kamo* / Fairy Cat from *Grimms Manga Tales*
Morrey from *Goldfisch* / Princess Ai from *Princess Ai*